A HISTORY OF SAUDI ARABIA

This updated edition analyses the challenges, both internal and external, facing Saudi Arabia in the twenty-first century. Two new chapters discuss the political, economic and social developments in the aftermath of 9/11, painting a vivid picture of a country shocked by terrorism and condemned by the international community. Madawi Al-Rasheed reveals that fragmentation of royal politics, a failing economy and fermenting Islamist dissent posed serious threats to state and society in 2001. She assesses the consequent state reforms introduced under pressure of terrorism, international scrutiny and a social mobilisation of men, women and minorities struggling to shape their future against the background of repression and authoritarian rule. While Saudi Arabia is still far from establishing a fourth state, there are signs that the people are ready for a serious change that will lead them to a state of institutions rather than princes.

MADAWI AL-RASHEED is Professor of Anthropology of Religion at King's College, London. She specialises in Saudi history, politics, religion and society. Her recent publications include *Contesting the Saudi State* (2007) and *Kingdom without Borders* (2008).

A HISTORY OF SAUDI ARABIA

Second Edition

MADAWI AL-RASHEED

King's College, London

CAMBRIDGE
UNIVERSITY PRESS

CAMBRIDGE
UNIVERSITY PRESS

University Printing House, Cambridge CB2 8BS, United Kingdom

Cambridge University Press is part of the University of Cambridge.

It furthers the University's mission by disseminating knowledge in the pursuit of education, learning and research at the highest international levels of excellence.

www.cambridge.org
Information on this title: www.cambridge.org/9780521747547

First edition published 2002
Reprinted 2002, 2003, 2005, 2006, 2007
Second edition 2010
3rd printing 2014

A catalogue record for this publication is available from the British Library

Library of Congress Cataloguing in Publication data
Al-Rasheed, Madawi.
A history of Saudi Arabia / Madawi al-Rasheed. – 2nd ed.
p. cm.
Includes bibliographical references and index.
ISBN 978-0-521-76128-4 (hardback)
1. Saudi Arabia – History – 20th century. 2. Saudi Arabia – History – 21st century. I. Title.
DS224.52.A43 2010
953.805 – dc22 2009043212

ISBN 978-0-521-76128-4 Hardback
ISBN 978-0-521-74754-7 Paperback

In memory of ʿAbṭa and
her daughters Juwahir and Waṭfa

Contents

List of illustrations — *page* x
List of tables — xi
Preface — xii
Chronology — xvi
Glossary — xx
Map 1 Saudi Arabia, main regions and cities — xxiii
Map 2 Saudi Arabia, main tribes — xxiv

Introduction — 1

1 Society and politics, 1744–1818 and 1824–1891 — 13
The origins of Al Saʿud (1744–1818) — 14
A fragile Saʿudi revival (1824–1891) — 22
The Rashidi emirate in Haʾil (1836–1921) — 25
The Sharifian emirate in Hijaz — 29
Hasa in the nineteenth century — 33
Emirate formation in Arabia — 35

2 The emerging state, 1902–1932 — 37
The capture of Riyadh (1902) — 37
The First World War and Ibn Saʿud (1914–1918) — 39
The capture of Haʾil (1921) — 41
The capture of Hijaz (1925) — 42
The *muṭawwaʿa* of Najd — 46
The *ikhwan* — 56
An alliance not so holy: Ibn Saʿud, the *muṭawwaʿa* and the *ikhwan* — 59
The collapse of the *ikhwan* rebellion — 66

3 Control and loyalty, 1932–1953 — 69
Marginalising Saʿudi collateral branches — 69
Consolidating Ibn Saʿud's line of descent — 71
Power and pomp in the pre-oil era: the *majlis* — 77
State affairs — 83

The oil concession (1933) 87
Oil in commercial quantities 89
Oil and society in the 1940s and 1950s 92
Saudi Arabia and Britain 97
The end of an era 101

4 The politics of dissent, 1953–1973 102
The reign of King Saʿud (1953–1964) 102
Saudi Arabia and the Arab world in the 1950s 110
Saudi Arabia and the United States in the 1950s and early 1960s 113
The reign of King Faysal (1964–1975) 116
Faysal and the Arab world 124

5 From affluence to austerity, 1973–1990 130
Affluence: the oil embargo (1973) 131
Vulnerabilities: Saʿudi–American relations in the 1970s 135
The reign of King Khalid (1975–1982) 138
Austerity: the reign of King Fahd (1982–2005) 143
Saudi Arabia and the Gulf context in the 1980s 150
Saʿudi–American relations in the 1980s 154

6 The Gulf War and its aftermath, 1990–2000 158
Saʿudi responses to the Gulf War 163
State responses: the reforms of March 1992 166
The Islamist opposition 171
Succession 180

7 Narratives of the state, narratives of the people 182
Official historiography 183
Political speech 190
The historical narrative challenged 192
The centennial celebrations: the capture of Riyadh revisited 197
The centennial celebrations challenged 208

8 The challenges of a new era 211
Internal challenges 212
External pressures 233

9 Modernising authoritarian rule 242
The state reformist agenda 242
A new king 253
Society's reformist agenda 261

Conclusion 275

Appendix I: Al Saʿud rulers in Dirʿiyyah (1744–1818) 278

Appendix II: Al Saʿud rulers in Riyadh (1824–1891) 279
Appendix III: Ibn Saʿud's sons (1900–1953) 280
Notes 281
Bibliography 291
Index 306

Illustrations

1 Street scene, Riyadh, circa 1940. © Popperfoto *page* 99
2 King Faysal in the Regents Park mosque, 1967. © Popperfoto 125
3 The Kaʿba, Mecca. © Popperfoto 140
4 US army tanks deployed in the Gulf War, 1990. © AFP/Popperfoto 159
5 Women shopping in downtown Jeddah. © AFP/Popperfoto 162
6 Invitation to the centennial celebrations, 1999. 198
7 Advertising Ibn Saʿud's biography on CD-ROM. 200
8 Publicity literature from the centennial celebrations, 1999. 203

Tables

1 Government revenues 1946–1952 *page* 90
2 Volume of petroleum export and GDP 1965–1975 116
3 Volume of petroleum export and GDP in billion SA riyals 1982–1997 144
4 Saʿudi oil production 218
5 Oil prices 2000–2008 218
6 The Saʿudi budget 219
7 Unemployment 220

Preface

The impact of 9/11 on Saudi Arabia was immense. It focused the attention of the international community on a regime regarded as an important economic, religious and political force in the Arab world. Throughout the twentieth century Saudi Arabia had enjoyed a friendly alliance with the USA and other European countries, in addition to amicable relations with the Muslim world. Its economic wealth and oil reserves protected it from international scrutiny and the calls for democratisation that swept the world after the end of the Cold War. The regime was able to conduct its internal affairs freely, knowing that there would be no international pressure to change its political, religious or social policies. The international community was content to accept Saudi Arabia as it was, provided that the flow of oil, investment opportunities and arms contracts were not disrupted. International calls for democratisation, the emancipation of women, religious freedom and respect for minority rights were often heard, but no serious attempts to pressurise Saudi Arabia in those directions were on the agenda of those who supported the Saʿudi regime and guaranteed its security – mainly the USA and its major European partners. Saudi Arabia invoked Islam and tradition to block any serious political change. The Saʿudi leadership used oil wealth and development projects to protect itself from internal criticism. Saʿudis were brought up to appreciate security, prosperity, employment and welfare services, which they accepted as a substitute for political participation and democratisation. In return for loyalty and acquiescence, they received handouts, economic opportunities, education, shelter and other services. On a few occasions dissent, such as that of the Islamists in the 1980s and 1990s, erupted over the ideological orientation of the state and its foreign policies. Dissidents demanded greater Islamisation of the state and criticised the leadership for its intimate relations with the West. Such dissent was expressed violently in the case of the seizure of the Mecca mosque by Juhayman al-ʿUtaybi in 1979, and in two major terrorist attacks in the 1990s, mainly targeting the American presence. The state contained the dissents by deploying two strategies: first, it responded to calls for Islamisation in the public sphere; and second, it increased its security and surveillance measures. None of the dissenters, with the exception of Juhayman's movement, questioned the foundation of the Saʿudi state or the legitimacy of its leadership, or threatened its continuity.

The confrontation between the regime and a violent jihadi Islamist trend began early in the twenty-first century. It proved different from previous instances of Islamist dissent, as it questioned both the legitimacy of the house of Saʿud and its right to rule. Although the dissidents' slogans called for the removal of infidels from the Arabian Peninsula, clear statements from Usama Bin Laden and the leaders of al-Qaʿidah in the Arabian Peninsula directly attacked the leadership, and dubbed it blasphemous. This was followed by a wave of terror in Saʿudi cities that killed hundreds of Saʿudis, Westerners and Arabs. This coincided with serious economic problems, political stagnation and social unrest. The last years of the reign of the ailing King Fahd brought to the surface the changing nature of the Saʿudi state, which thenceforth began to consist of multiple actors, each competing to carve out a political space on the map of Saudi Arabia. National debt and economic slowdown plagued the country and slowed its ability to absorb the growing population. The educational infrastructure and the welfare services deteriorated, and failed to respond to the new demographic realities of the country. Oil revenues were either plundered or channelled into unproductive but prestigious construction projects. Saʿudis were desperately awaiting serious improvement of their economic situation when they came face to face with terrorism.

The participation of fifteen Saʿudis in the attack on the World Trade Center in New York forced the international community to see Saudi Arabia through a new lens. The previous silence over its internal political affairs, religious tradition and social norms was lifted, subjecting its leadership and society to outside scrutiny. The Saʿudi leadership felt compelled to address international scrutiny and respond to an unprecedented internal mobilisation. It had no choice but to appropriate the rhetoric of reform before it was either imposed from outside or hijacked by active Saʿudi constituencies. Serious political reform remained unattainable, while the leadership engaged in economic liberalisation and timid social and religious change. Opening up the economy proved easier than anticipated, as the country started benefiting from the rise in oil prices that began in 2003. Taming the religious sphere and curbing the influence of radical preachers and texts also proved easier than formulating a political reform agenda. The state remained resistant to civil society's calls for greater political participation in anticipation of the establishment of a constitutional monarchy.

The leadership was active on two fronts. First, it increased its security measures to contain terrorism, and launched a campaign to restrict the propagation of radical religious ideas, believed to be the mobilising ideological weapon of al-Qaʿidah. Second, it set a social and religious reform agenda, promising to increase consultation and respond to the demands of the constituency. In most cases, however, these demands were contradictory: Saʿudi society was polarised along ideological lines, with Islamists and liberals imagining reform in different ways. Islamists envisaged greater respect for the country's Islamic heritage and tradition. They remained resistant to the idea of social liberalisation and moderation. Liberals identified the causes of terrorism as emanating from strict religious interpretations and restrictions on freedoms. Their reform agenda envisaged less religious indoctrination and preaching. The task of the leadership was to reconcile the two opposed views and extract loyalty from both. By 2008 the state had managed to contain terrorism and project itself as the champion of reform.

This second edition captures in two additional chapters the challenges, both internal and external, facing Saudi Arabia in the twenty-first century. Chapter 8 deals with the political, economic, security and international pressures that coincided with 9/11. This was a time when neither the leadership nor society was prepared for the outcomes of global terrorism, which turned into a serious local problem. The Saʿudi leadership suddenly found itself in an advantageous position after its oil revenues more than doubled as a result of the dramatic increase in oil prices. Part of this new wealth, dubbed 'the second period of affluence', was invested in projects designed to improve the Saʿudi economy, increase employment opportunities and contain dissent.

Chapter 9 discusses how modernising authoritarian rule became a substitute for serious political reforms. This modernisation involved reforming the royal house, establishing National Dialogue Forums, instituting municipal elections in Saʿudi cities and engaging with human rights. The chapter also highlights the internal social and political mobilisation of Saʿudis themselves, whose voices, petitions, literary productions and activism reached new frontiers and stretched the boundaries of official tolerance. A newly formed political trend calling for constitutional monarchy drew on the participation of academics, intellectuals and professionals from both sides of the ideological divide, both Islamists and liberals. Minorities aspired towards greater inclusion under new slogans calling for respect of religious freedom, human rights and greater political participation in government and civil society. Slogans promoting the idea of of *wataniyya* (citizenship) replaced ambiguous global solidarities such as the Muslim *umma*. Women began to be more visible and articulate in pressing for equality and recognition. Novelists, writers and bloggers benefited from globalisation and new communication technologies, using them to open up Saʿudi society and challenge its political, religious and social authoritarian tradition and history of secrecy. Reform and repression progressed hand in hand. The rhetoric of reform succeeded in enlisting society in formulating a vision of its future, under the patronage of the state. Repression deterred those who aspired towards real political change. With the advent of the twenty-first century, Saʿudis seem to be heading towards a fourth state, as authoritarianism undergoes serious cosmetic changes. It remains to be seen whether this change will eventually lead to a new polity, founded on solid representative institutions. Such drastic change is unlikely to materialise in the short term, yet it cannot be ruled out in the future.

Chronology

1517	Ottoman authority established in Hijaz
1550	Ottoman authority established in Hasa
1670	Banu Khalid rebel against the Ottomans in Hasa
1744	Muhammad ibn ʿAbd al-Wahhab arrives in Dirʿiyyah
1780	The Saʿudi–Wahhabi emirate expands in Qasim
1792	The Saʿudi–Wahhabi emirate expands in southern Najd
1797	Qatar and Bahrain acknowledge Saʿudi authority
1801	Saʿudi–Wahhabi forces raid Karbalaʾ in Iraq
1802	Saʿudi–Wahhabi emirate expands in Hijaz
1804	Madina acknowledges Saʿudi authority
1811	Egyptian troops land in Yanbuʿ
1818	Egyptian troops sack Dirʿiyyah
1824	Turki ibn ʿAbdullah re-establishes Saʿudi authority in Riyadh
1830	Saʿudi rule expands into Hasa
1834	Turki ibn ʿAbdullah assassinated by his cousin, Mishari
	Turki's son Faysal becomes amir in Riyadh
1836	The Rashidis establish their rule in Haʾil
1837	Saʿudi ruler Faysal captured by Egyptian troops and sent to Cairo
1843	Faysal returns to Riyadh
1865	Faysal dies
	Faysal's son ʿAbdullah rules in Riyadh
1871	The Ottomans occupy Hasa
	The Ottomans occupy ʿAsir
1891	Saʿudi rule in Riyadh terminated by the Rashidis
1893	The Saʿudis take refuge in Kuwait
1902	Ibn Saʿud captures Riyadh
	Riyadh ʿ*ulama* swear allegiance to Ibn Saʿud
1903	Ibn Saʿud adopts the title 'Sultan of Najd'

1904	Abha in ʿAsir falls under Ibn Saʿud's authority
1906	Ibn Saʿud conquers Qasim
1908	Ibn Saʿud challenged by his cousins, the ʿAraʾif
	The Ottomans appoint Ḥusayn ibn ʿAli Sharif of Mecca
1912	Ibn Saʿud establishes the first *ikhwan* settlement, ʿArṭawiyyah, for the Muṭayr tribe
1913	Ibn Saʿud establishes the *ikhwan* settlement al-Ghaṭghaṭ for the ʿUtayba tribe
	Ibn Saʿud conquers Hasa
1915	Britain acknowledges Ibn Saʿud as ruler of Najd and Hasa
1916	Sharif Ḥusayn declares himself King of the Arabs
1924	Taʾif in Hijaz falls under Ibn Saʿud's authority
	Sharif ʿAli replaces his father, Sharif Ḥusayn, in Hijaz
1925	Jeddah surrenders to Ibn Saʿud
1926	Ibn Saʿud declares himself 'King of Hijaz and Sultan of Najd'
1927	The *ikhwan* rebel against Ibn Saʿud
1928	Ibn Saʿud meets the Riyadh *ʿulama* to solve the *ikhwan* crisis
1930	Ibn Saʿud defeats the *ikhwan* rebels
1932	Ibn Saʿud declares his realm the Kingdom of Saudi Arabia
1933	Ibn Saʿud signs the oil concession
1939	The first oil tanker with Saʿudi oil leaves Raʾs Tannura
1945	Ibn Saʿud meets American President Franklin D. Roosevelt
	Ibn Saʿud meets British Prime Minister Winston Churchill
1946	Ibn Saʿud visits Cairo
1953	The Council of Ministers established
	Ibn Saʿud dies; his son Saʿud becomes King
	Saʿudi ARAMCO workers organise the first demonstration
1955	A plot for a coup by Saʿudi army officers discovered
1956	Saʿudi ARAMCO workers riot in the eastern province
1961	The movement of the Free Princes established by Prince Ṭalal ibn ʿAbd al-ʿAziz
1964	King Saʿud abdicates
	Faysal becomes King
1969	Saʿud dies in Greece
1973	As a result of the oil embargo, oil prices increase
1975	King Faysal assassinated by his nephew, Prince Faysal ibn Musaʿid
	Khalid becomes King

1979	The siege of Mecca mosque
1980	The Shiʿa riot in the eastern province
1981	The Gulf Cooperation Council established
1982	King Khalid dies; Fahd becomes King
1986	Oil prices decrease to their lowest level since the 1970s King Fahd adopts the title 'Custodian of the Two Holy Mosques'
1990	Saddam Husayn invades Kuwait Saʿudi women defy the ban on women driving in Riyadh
1991	The Gulf War starts The liberal petition sent to King Fahd The Islamist petition sent to King Fahd
1992	A sixty-member Consultative Council established Saʿudi Islamists publish the Memorandum of Advice King Fahd announces a series of reforms
1993	The Committee for the Defence of Legitimate Rights in Saudi Arabia (CDLR) established in Riyadh
1996	Terrorist explosions at Khobar Towers Terrorist explosions at al-ʿUlaiyya American military mission, Riyadh The number of members appointed to the Consultative Council increased to ninety
1999	Saudi Arabia starts the centennial celebrations
2000	Oil prices rise above $30 per barrel Two Saʿudis hijack Saudi Arabian Airline flight from Jeddah to London; they surrender in Baghdad
2001	Fifteen Saʿudis participate in the attack on the World Trade Center in New York and the Pentagon in Washington
2003	Saʿudi Foreign Minister Saʿud al-Faysal says his country will not take part in the invasion of Iraq Saddam's regime is toppled by the US-led invasion of Iraq Saʿudi suicide bombers kill thirty-five people at an expatriate housing compound in Riyadh First National Dialogue Forum is held in Riyadh Saʿudi intellectuals and professionals sign the first petition calling for political reform A small demonstration in Riyadh calls for respect for human rights and the release of political prisoners Another major suicide attack on a residential housing compound kills seventeen people

2004 Suicide bombers kill four members of the security forces at their headquarters in Riyadh
Several constitutional reformers are arrested
Suicide bombers kill five foreign workers at Yanbuʿ
BBC security correspondent Frank Gardner is seriously injured and his cameraman killed in Riyadh
Security forces kill ʿAbd al-ʿAziz al-Muqrin, leader of al-Qaʿidah in the Arabian Peninsula
The American consulate in Jeddah is attacked; five members of staff and security personnel are killed
2005 Suicide bombers kill more than twenty people at an oil company compound in al-Khobar
Crown Prince ʿAbdullah visits the USA
Municipal elections held in Saʿudi cities
King Fahd dies and ʿAbdullah becomes King
Three security officers killed in clashes with jihadis
Saudi Arabia officially joins the World Trade Organisation
2006 Saʿudi security forces kill six al-Qaʿidah activists
2007 Ministry of the Interior spokesman announces the arrest of 172 suspected terrorists
Terrorists kill four French nationals
King ʿAbdullah announces the establishment of the Committee of Allegiance, consisting of thirty-five princes
Intelligence services arrest fifteen intellectuals and professionals in Jeddah
Saudi Arabia announces the biggest budget in its history
King ʿAbdullah visits the Vatican
2008 Ministry of the Interior spokesman announces the arrest of more than 500 suspected terrorists
Oil prices reach $143 per barrel
First interfaith dialogue is held in Mecca

Glossary

ahl al-bayt	the Prophet's household
ahl al-ḥal wa al-ʿaqd	Saʿudi society ('the people who tie and loose')
ʿalmaniyyun	secularists
amin sir	clerk
amir	ruler, prince
ʿamm	public
al-ʿammiyya	vernacular Arabic
ʿarḍa	sword dance
ʿaṣabiyya madhhabiyya	sectarian solidarity
ʿaṣabiyya najdiyya	Najdi solidarity
ʿaṣabiyya qabaliyya	tribal solidarity
ʿashura	anniversary of al-Ḥusayn's death
badu	bedouins
baghi	usurper
bayʿa	oath of allegiance
bidʿa	innovation, heresy
daʿwa	religious call, mission
dira	tribal territory
diwan	royal court
duʿat al-islah al-dusturi	advocates of constitutional reform
fatwa (pl. *fatawa*)	religious opinion issued by *shariʿa* experts
fiqh	Islamic jurisprudence
fitna	strife, dissent
ghulat	religious extremists
ḥaḍar	sedentary population
ḥajj	pilgrimage to Mecca
ḥizb siyasi	political party
hujjar	village settlements
ḥuquq	rights
husayniyat	Shiʿi mourning houses

ʿibada	Islamic rituals
ʿid al-aḍḥa	festival marking the pilgrimage season
ʿid al-fiṭr	festival marking the end of Ramaḍan
iḥtilal	occupation
ikhwan (sing. *khawi*)	Muslim brothers/companions, tribal force
ʿilm	knowledge
imam	prayer leader/leader of Muslim community
imara	emirate
infitaḥ	openness
iṣlaḥ	reform
al-jahiliyya	the age of ignorance
al-jazira al-ʿarabiyya	the Arabian Peninsula
jihad	holy war
kafir	blasphemous
khaḍiri	non-tribal people
khilwa	intimate encounter between an unrelated man and woman, unaccompanied by a chaperon
al-khuluq	morality
khuṣuṣiya	the uniqueness of the Islamic tradition of Saudi Arabia
khuwwa	tribute
kufr	unbelief
mahdi	one who guides
majlis (pl. *majalis*)	council
majlis ʿamm	public council
majlis al-dars	study session
majlis al-shura	consultative council
multazim	young Muslim fighters
muṭawwaʿa (sing. *muṭawwaʿ*)	Najdi religious specialist/volunteer
nahḍa	renaissance, awakening
al-naksa	the June 1967 humiliation
naṣiḥa	advice
al-nawaṣib	pejorative Shiʿi name for hostile Sunnis
niʿma	divine abundance
qaḍi	judge
rafiḍa	rejectionists, those who distort Islam

ramaḍan	Ramaḍan, the fasting month
shariʿa	Islamic legal code and rules
shaykh	tribal leader/religious scholar
shirk	polytheism, associationism
shura	consultation
sura	Qurʾanic verse
al-shuʿba al-siyasiyya	political committee
taʿaṣub	fanaticism
taghrib	Westernisation
takfir	the labelling of non-Wahhabi Muslims as unbelievers
tawḥid	doctrine of the oneness of God/ unification
thaqafat al-hiwar	public dialogue
thaqafat al-irhab	the ideology of terrorism
ʿulama (sing. *ʿalim*)	religious scholars
umma	Muslim community
wali	Ottoman governor
waqf (pl. *awqaf*)	religious endowment
al-waṣatiyya	the middle path of Islam
waṭan	country, fatherland
waṭaniyya	citizenship
zakat	Islamic tax

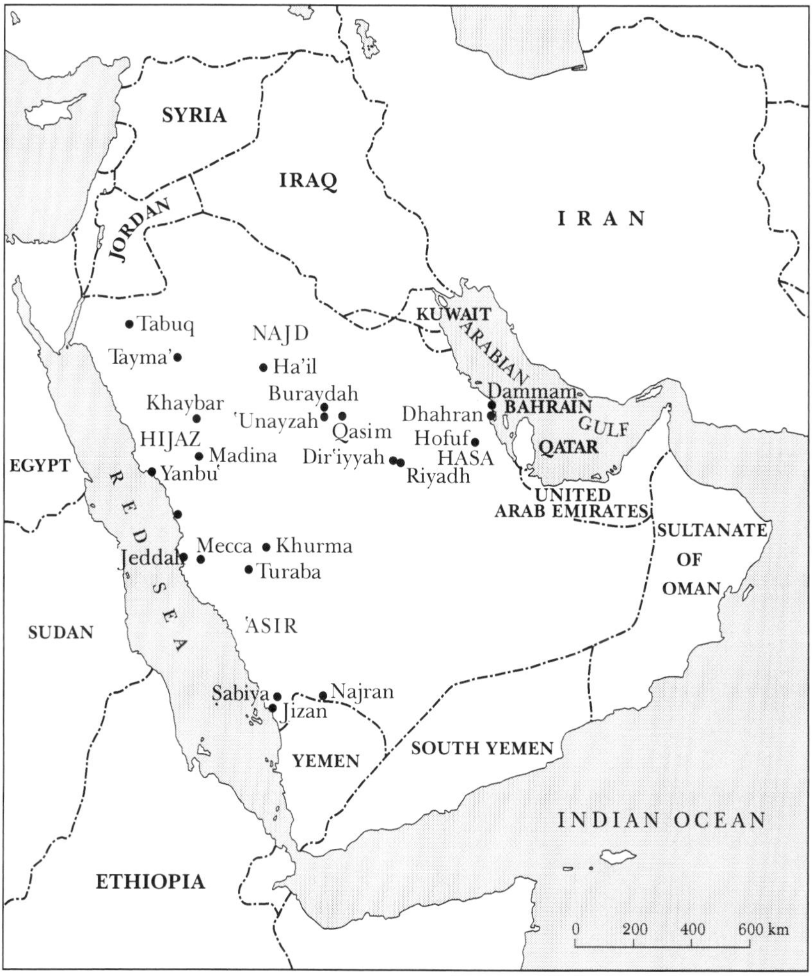

Map 1 Saudi Arabia, main regions and cities. *Source:* F. Clements, *Saudi Arabia, World Bibliographical Series* (Oxford: Clio Press, 1979; reprinted 1988). Courtesy of Clio Press.

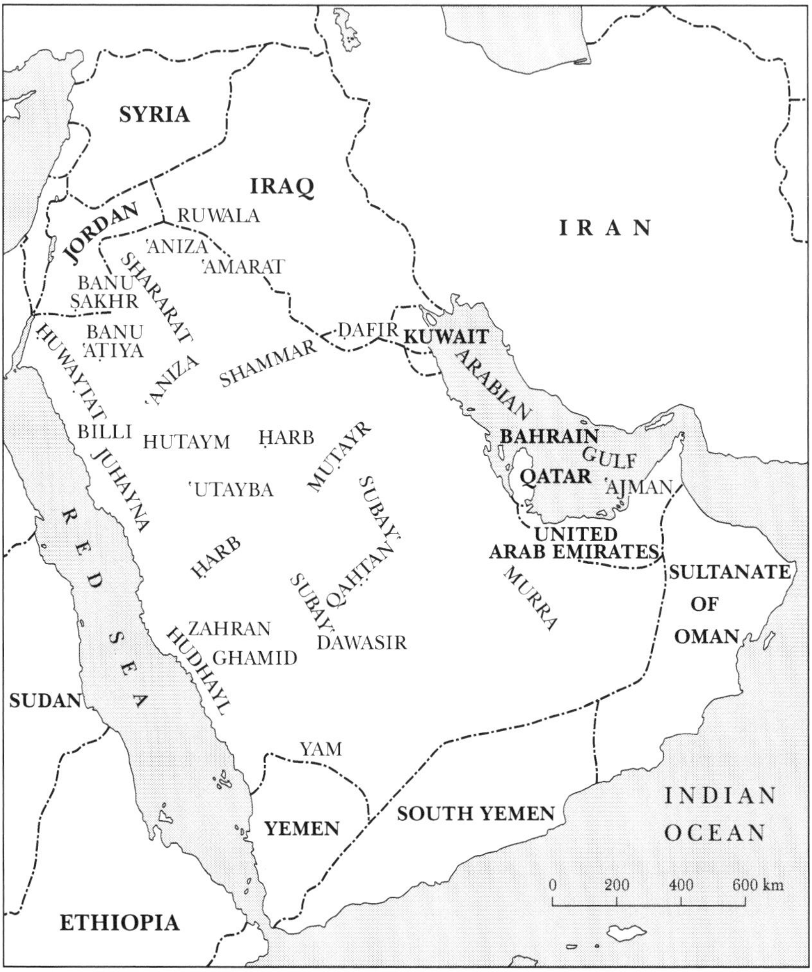

Map 2 Saudi Arabia, main tribes. *Source:* D. Schofield and R. Kemp, *The Kingdom of Saudi Arabia* (London: Stacey International, 1990). Courtesy of Stacey International.

Introduction

The dominant narrative in the history of Saudi Arabia in the twentieth century is that of state formation, a process that started in the interior of Arabia under the leadership of the Al Saʿud. While this leadership was not new (it was visible in the history of Arabia in the eighteenth and nineteenth centuries), the modern state of 1932 distinguished itself by creating a stable and durable realm that successfully incorporated Hijaz, ʿAsir and Hasa, in addition to the central province of Najd. The state brought diverse people and vast territories under its authority as a result of a long campaign of conquest.

In its early days the course taken by the new state resembles a cycle familiar in the region. Since the eighteenth century, several ambitious local rulers (from the Al Saʿud and others) had tried to expand their authority over adjacent territories, but their attempts failed for a variety of reasons. The Al Saʿud and other local rulers founded polities which were, however, destroyed shortly after they reached a substantial level of expansion. Given this historical background, the state of 1932 is often seen as a success story. In this story the legendary figure of ʿAbd al-ʿAziz ibn ʿAbd al-Raḥman Al Saʿud (thereafter Ibn Saʿud), the founder of the Kingdom of Saudi Arabia, is dominant. The fact that his state has not vanished as so many earlier emirates did adds to the credibility of the story. This book is an attempt to explore the continuities and discontinuities in Saʿudi social and political history.

In the nineteenth century, there were several attempts to bring more of Arabia under direct Ottoman rule. The Ottoman–Egyptian invasion of Arabia in 1818 and the Ottoman occupation of Hasa and ʿAsir in 1871 were meant to establish direct Ottoman authority in the peninsula. However, vast territories remained without an Ottoman governor. Several local amirs in the interior were recognised as 'ruling on behalf of the Sultan' and occasionally they were sent subsidies and gifts to cement alliance and ensure obedience. The Ottomans expected local rulers to restrain their followers from attacking pilgrimage caravans and Ottoman garrisons stationed in more vital regions, for example in Hijaz and Hasa.

This situation was maintained until the defeat of the Ottoman Empire during the First World War. While Sharif Ḥusayn of Hijaz actively supported Britain against the Ottomans, other influential rulers distanced themselves from a war that did not closely influence their domains. Ibn Rashid in Haʾil declared his allegiance to the Ottoman Sultan without offering any serious military support, while Ibn Saʿud in Riyadh sided with the British without being directly involved in the war against the Ottomans.

What was to become of Arabia following the collapse of the Ottoman Empire after the First World War? When France and Britain partitioned Ottoman territories under the mandate system, Arabia fell within Britain's sphere of influence. Arabia, however, was not to become a colony similar to other colonies in the British Empire. During the war, Britain cultivated intimate relationships with two main local powers, Sharif Ḥusayn and Ibn Saʿud, but failed to reconcile their claims to rule Arabia after the war. Britain's conflicting policies and promises together with its financial support strengthened both rulers. The idea that Arabia could be unified became more realistic, now that there were only two strong rivals, one in Hijaz and one in Najd. The throne of Sharif Ḥusayn was sacrificed in favour of Ibn Saʿud, who took over Hijaz in 1925, ousting the Sharifian family in the process. In 1932, Ibn Saʿud declared himself king and his realm the Kingdom of Saudi Arabia.

Najd's nominal incorporation in the Ottoman Empire and the fact that it did not become a colony similar to other Arab countries in the twentieth century led many scholars to comment on its unique history. Its modern state is often considered as an indigenous formation assisted by the unique efforts of its founder, Ibn Saʿud. While Saudi Arabia did not inherit a colonial administration or a nationalist elite similar to that developed elsewhere in the Arab world, one must not exaggerate its so-called unique history. Britain did not turn Saudi Arabia into a colony, but British influence during the first three decades of the twentieth century was paramount. It is difficult to imagine Ibn Saʿud successfully conquering one region after another without British subsidies. The weakened Ottoman Empire accepted his conquest of Hasa in 1913. Unable to reverse the situation, the Ottomans recognised Ibn Saʿud as the *de facto* ruler of Najd. Britain later sanctioned this in 1915 when she recognised that 'Najd, Hasa, Qatif, and Jubayl and their dependencies are the territories of Ibn Saʿud'. Similarly, his conquest of the Rashidi emirate in 1921 was only possible with British weapons and generous subsidies. His expansion into Hijaz in 1925 took place at a time when Britain was growing tired of Sharif Ḥusayn's demands, perceived as a threat to British interests. Britain was more than happy to see Sharif Ḥusayn removed from Hijaz, leaving his sons, Faysal and ʿAbdullah, on the thrones of two newly created monarchies in Trans-Jordan and Iraq. Throughout the 1920s and 1930s, Britain remained the main external player behind the formation of the Saʿudi state. While Saudi Arabia escaped some of the ruptures of direct colonial rule, state formation and the unification of Arabia under Saʿudi leadership must be understood in the context of British intervention in the Middle East. Britain's influence weakened only after the Second World War, when the USA began to assume a greater role.

To argue, however, that the Saʿudi state of 1932 was a British 'invention' misses an important aspect of the internal dynamics that shaped the state and led to its consolidation. While Britain may have been a key force behind state formation, the rise and consolidation of the Saʿudi state resulted from a complex process that cannot be traced to any single external factor.

The twentieth century witnessed the emergence of a state imposed on people without a historical memory of unity or national heritage which would justify their inclusion in a single entity. With the exception of a substantial Shiʿa minority in Hasa, the majority of Saʿudis are Sunni Muslims. The population, however, had been divided by regional and tribal differences that militated against national unity or unification. Saudi Arabia shared this important characteristic with several Arab countries that came into being during the period between the two great wars. While the borders of many Arab states were drawn in accordance with French and British policies, the four regions that comprised Saudi Arabia (Najd, Hasa, Hijaz and ʿAsir) were 'unified' as a result of their conquest by an indigenous leadership, sanctioned by a colonial power.

The unification of Arabia under the leadership of Ibn Saʿud was a process that lasted some thirty years. Between 1902 and 1932, Ibn Saʿud defeated several rivals until his realm reached the limits acceptable to Britain. Where France had been the colonial power, republics emerged. But in Saudi Arabia a kingdom was founded, as in parts of the Arab world where Britain had been influential, namely Trans-Jordan and Iraq.

Saudi Arabia is, however, different from other Arab countries. The conquests of Ibn Saʿud did not proceed under nationalistic rhetoric or the discourse of independence and self-rule. With the exception of Hijaz, where such rhetoric emerged during the Arab revolt (1916) associated with Sharif Ḥusayn who aspired to become 'King of the Arabs', the rest of Saudi

Arabia had no experience of such aspirations. Moreover, Britain did not distinguish herself by great efforts to generate discourses on independence and autonomy.

The conquest of Arabia by an indigenous ruler took place with a very different symbolic vocabulary. Ibn Saʿud relied on ancestral claims to rule over a region that 'once belonged to his ancestors'. When he returned to Riyadh from his exile in Kuwait in 1902, he was merely restoring or extending the Al Saʿud claim over the town. Similarly, further expansion in Qasim, Hasa, northern Najd, Hijaz and ʿAsir was undertaken with the intention of restoring his family's authority over territories that had been once incorporated under Saʿudi leadership. This was a reference to the short-lived experience of the eighteenth century when the first Saʿudi–Wahhabi emirate (1744–1818) succeeded briefly in stretching the limits of Saʿudi rule beyond their small provincial capital, Dirʿiyyah. This historical precedent proved to be a justification for expansion in the early decades of the twentieth century.

Alone, however, this justification fell short of convincing Ibn Saʿud's local rivals to accept his rule. Force was mightier than vague ancestral claims. Most regions were incorporated in Ibn Saʿud's realm only after he had overcome the resistance of local leadership. Coercion proceeded in tandem with the revival of Wahhabism, the reformist movement that once inspired the people of southern Najd to expand beyond the interior of Arabia. As early as 1902, Ibn Saʿud enlisted the *muṭawwaʿa* (religious ritual specialists) of Najd, in the process of expansion. The *muṭawwaʿa* were behind the formation of the *ikhwan*, a tribal military force that was dedicated to fight in the name of *jihad* (holy war) against the 'infidels', a loosely defined category that at times included people who were not easily persuaded to accept Saʿudi leadership.

The project of unifying Arabia was a gradual process assisted by several factors that were beyond the control of Ibn Saʿud. The defeat of the Ottoman Empire in the First World War and the encouragement of Britain allowed Ibn Saʿud to fill a power vacuum in Arabia. The unification of vast territories under his rule after he had secured Riyadh in 1902 could not easily have been anticipated. The popular historiography of this period tends to paint a picture of Ibn Saʿud as a 'desert warrior' who had the genius and foresight from the very beginning. It took thirty years of warfare and more than fifty-two battles between 1902 and 1932 before the project materialised. The idea of a Saʿudi state was a late development, certainly not associated with Ibn Saʿud's early conquests.

While it is difficult to imagine a kingdom of Saudi Arabia without Ibn Saʿud, one must go beyond miracles and personal genius. Personalities and agents are important, but they operate within a historical context that shapes their success and failure. I intend to move away from the historiography that glorifies the role of single actors and concentrate on the interaction between historical events and society that led to the consolidation of the Saʿudi state of 1932. Readers will find that this book does not have an obvious chronology listing battle after battle to document the successful stages of the unification of Arabia. Nor does it have a chronology of the reigns of the kings who have ruled since 1932. Instead, a thematic approach that highlights the importance of social, political and economic variables has been adopted to explore a possible interpretation of the rise of the Saʿudi state and its later consolidation.

Crucial to any understanding of modern Saʿudi history is the observation that this history shows a striking accommodation between the old and the new. Saudi Arabia's position as the location of the holiest shrines of Islam is at the heart of this accommodation. This has meant that Saʿudi internal politics and society are not only the concern of its own rather small population, but also the concern of millions of Muslims in the world. The symbolic significance of Saudi Arabia for Islam and Muslims cannot be overestimated. It has become a prerogative for its people and state to preserve its Islamic heritage. It is also a prerogative to cherish the responsibilities of geographical accident which have made it the destination not only of Muslim pilgrims but also the direction for their five daily prayers. The country's transformation in the twentieth century is shaped by this important fact that required a careful and reluctant immersion in modernity. The preservation of the 'old', the 'authentic' tradition progressed with an eye on the 'new', the 'modern' and the 'alien'. Saudi Arabia's specific Islamic tradition, namely Wahhabi teachings, did not encourage an easy immersion in modernity in the twentieth century. From the very beginning, the ruling group stumbled across several obstacles when they introduced the most simple of technologies (for example cars, the telegraph and television, among other innovations). Objections from conservative religious circles were overcome as a result of a combination of force and negotiations. Social and political change proved more problematic and could not be easily implemented without generating debates that threatened the internal stability of the country and alienated important and influential sections of society.

In addition to its specific religious heritage, modern Saudi Arabia emerged against the social, economic and political diversity of its population. The cosmopolitan Hijaz and Hasa with their long history of contact with the outside world were incorporated into the interior, a region that assumed hegemony with the consolidation of the modern state in spite of its relative isolation throughout the previous two hundred years. The social values and political tradition of Najd were generalised to the whole country after 1932. Resistance to rapid social and political change had always been generated in Najd, where the most conservative elements in society continue to be found even at the beginning of the twenty-first century. A combination of a strong tribal tradition in the interior, together with a strict interpretation of Islam in the major towns and oases, made this region most resistant to *bidʿa*, 'innovations or heresy'. Given that the Al Saʿud's leadership had always been based on the allegiance of the sedentary communities of Najd, the *ḥaḍar*, their rule was dependent on accommodating this region's interests, aspirations and political tradition.

The accommodation between the old and the new became more urgent with the discovery of huge quantities of oil under Saudi Arabia's desert territories. With oil, the Saʿudi state began to have unprecedented wealth at its disposal to build its economic and material infrastructure and transform its landscape beyond recognition. In the process, both state and society faced an urgent challenge. Can the 'old' Najdi tradition be preserved? Can it coexist with a juxtaposition of the 'new'? These questions proved to be especially difficult in a society that has undergone rapid modernisation. How to benefit from oil wealth while remaining faithful to Islam and tradition has generated unresolved tensions that have accompanied state and nation building since the early 1930s. Colonialism or its absence is irrelevant because Saudi Arabia has been drawn into the international context and world power politics since the early decades of the twentieth century. With the discovery of oil in the 1930s, Saudi Arabia's incorporation in the world economy became an important aspect of its historical development.

Chapter 1 sets out the historical background to the formation of the present Saʿudi state. It examines the Al Saʿud's rule in the eighteenth and nineteenth centuries with the intention of setting the scene for the revival of their leadership with the capture of Riyadh in 1902. It also identifies the main power centres in Najd, Hijaz and Hasa that previously challenged their authority. This chapter identifies the 'emirate' as a polity dominant in Arabian history. The emirate (*imara*) is a genre of political centralisation often referred to in the literature as a dynasty (Al-Rasheed 1991) or chiefdom (Kostiner 1993; 2000) to distinguish it from the 'state', believed to be a later development.

Earlier emirates in central Arabia often shared a number of characteristics:

(a) the dominance of prominent ruling lineages based in oases or towns;
(b) fierce power struggles within ruling lineages and fluctuating boundaries;
(c) expansion by conquest and raids;
(d) the imposition of Islamic tax or tribute on conquered territories;
(e) the confirmation of local rulers or their occasional replacement by representatives/governors;
(f) the maintenance of law and order;
(g) a mixed economy of trade, agriculture and pastoral nomadism;
(h) the flow of economic surplus from the periphery of the emirate to the centre where it was redistributed to gain loyalty and allegiance; and
(i) the maintenance of contacts with external powers, mainly the Ottoman Empire in the nineteenth century and later Britain, both a source of new resources outside the indigenous economy.

While previous emirates had failed to unify Arabia, some succeeded in establishing spheres of influence over territories away from the core of the emirate. In the nineteenth century, the Sharifs in Hijaz, and the Saʿudis and Rashidis in central Arabia, all strove to consolidate emirates that exhibited the above-mentioned features. These emirates remained fragile and continued to compete with each other in an attempt to control parts of Arabia. While the Sharifs had no ambition to control central Arabia, their attention was drawn into Yemen. The Rashidis and Saʿudis competed in central Arabia. Sometimes external forces (for example the Ottomans and Britain) fuelled their rivalry. This often led to the intensification of warfare between emirates that aspired to expand beyond their core territories.

The allegations of 'chaos' and 'fragmentation' of Arabia's politics prior to the formation of the modern state in 1932 are misrepresentations that fail to explain the modern history of the region. Arabia had the experience of political centralisation manifested in the emergence of local emirates based in the main oases of the interior and Hijaz. While these emirates cannot be defined as fully fledged states, they exhibited regular and generally acceptable attempts to bring people and territories under the authority of urban-based leadership. The fact that all such emirates failed to create durable polities should not diminish their importance for understanding previous political structures and the present configuration – the state of 1932.

In the case of the first and second Saʿudi–Wahhabi emirates (1744–1818 and 1824–91), a coalition of tribal confederations assisted in expansion.

However, the main impetus behind the consolidation of Saʿudi rule came from the *ḥaḍar* communities of Najd, the inhabitants of the towns and oases. It was among the *ḥaḍar* that Wahhabism emerged, thus providing an ideological rationale for expansion and the establishment of an Islamic moral and political order. While bedouins played a prominent role in conquest, they remained peripheral at the level of leadership. This was also true of the Rashidi and Sharifian emirates where leadership was drawn mainly from a sedentarised tribal lineage in the case of the former and a holy lineage in the case of the latter.

The Saʿudi–Wahhabi emirates were the precursors of the modern state. In its early days, the Saʿudi state of 1932 was similar to those that had preceded it. With the discovery of oil in Saudi Arabia, the state was able to break away from the emirate pattern.

Chapter 2 follows the story of Ibn Saʿud's conquest of Arabia between 1902 and 1932 without exploring the details of the various battles that resulted in the unification of the country under Saʿudi leadership. Instead, it examines the important role of religion in politics and highlights the crucial contribution of a force not given enough attention in the literature on Saudi Arabia, namely the *muṭawwaʿa* of Najd. While most accounts of the consolidation of the Saʿudi state privilege the *ikhwan* tribal force deployed by Ibn Saʿud against his rivals (Habib 1978; Kishk 1981; Kostiner 1993), this chapter will argue that a particular version of that ritualistic Islam developed by the sedentarised religious scholars of Najd equally contributed to the expansion of Ibn Saʿud's domain. Wahhabism is often considered as legitimising Saʿudi rule, but this legitimacy needed to be visualised and represented. The *muṭawwaʿa* were active agents in this process. They domesticated the population in the name of Islam, but also enforced Saʿudi authority under the guise of a vigorous programme to 'Islamise' the people of Arabia. Both the Saʿudi leadership and the *muṭawwaʿa* represented the interests of the Najdi *ḥaḍar* communities at the expense of those of the bedouin tribal population. Although the tribal population was an important military instrument in the expansion of Saʿudi rule after 1912, it was marginalised as soon as the major conquests were completed in the late 1920s. The idea of a Saʿudi state was definitely a product of the efforts of the *muṭawwaʿa*, a sedentary community that regarded both tribal and bedouin elements as the antithesis of an Islamic moral order.

This interpretation of the origin of the Saʿudi state will correct popular descriptions of the state as 'tribal' or 'bedouin'. While tribal social organisation was dominant among substantial sections of society, political tribalism played a minor role in shaping the emerging state. The durability of the Saʿudi state of 1932 is a function of the fact that it does not represent the interests of a single tribal/bedouin group, since its leadership was drawn from outside the major tribal groups of Arabia. Hence this leadership was able to play the role of mediator between the various tribes, the sedentary communities and the more cosmopolitan regions of Hijaz and Hasa.

After the state was declared in 1932, there remained the task of maintaining loyalty and control. The continuity of kingship was dependent on creating a royal lineage capable of providing future kings. Between 1932 and 1953, Ibn Saʿud marginalised collateral branches of the Al Saʿud and consolidated his line of descent (chapter 3). During this period, several marriages with Arabian nobility and religious families led to the birth of over forty sons, providing future kings, princes and governors. While the literature on Ibn Saʿud's marital unions highlights their potential for building alliances with important sections of society, marriages created a long-lasting dependence on the Saʿudi ruling group. This was a time when state infrastructure, bureaucracy and resources were invisible to the majority of Saʿudis. In the absence of important economic resources to consolidate authority over the conquered territories, the Saʿudi state was consolidated by marriage.

Moreover, the meagre resources of the state in the pre-oil era manifested themselves in elaborate feasts and handouts in cash and kind. Power was visualised in the context of the royal court that was the Saʿudi state. Understanding royal pomp casts a new perspective on the consolidation of this state and shows its continuity with the emirate pattern. In a manner reminiscent of tribal shaykhs and amirs, Ibn Saʿud consolidated his authority by turning the royal court into a centre for the redistribution and reallocation of resources. He appropriated surplus produce from certain sections of society and redistributed it among others in the pursuit of allegiance and loyalty. The consolidation of the Saʿudi state during this early period was not dependent on 'institutions', 'bureaucracies' and 'administration' (as there were none), but was a function of informal social and cultural mechanisms, specific to the Arabian Peninsula.

While Ibn Saʿud did not live long enough to see the transformation of the Saʿudi state and society, the discovery of oil in the late 1930s allowed him to consolidate his position as the main source of wealth and affluence. The King became the source of all largesse, now having at his disposal resources unknown to previous rulers in Arabia. Substantial funds were dedicated to the construction of imposing palaces hosting the ruling group, foreign guests and the royal court. During Ibn Saʿud's reign, however, state bureaucracy and institutions remained underdeveloped. The King was an absolute monarch, while delegating some responsibilities to his senior sons. The modest development of the country's infrastructure during this period was undertaken by ARAMCO, the American oil company that won the oil concession in 1933.

Ibn Saʿud died in 1953 and, as anticipated, his son Saʿud succeeded him (chapter 4). The reign of King Saʿud witnessed a fierce struggle among the royal family. Saʿud was challenged by his brother Crown Prince Faysal, resulting in his abdication in 1964. The struggle resulted from Saʿud's mismanagement of state finances but, more importantly, the conflict unveiled a political crisis following the death of Ibn Saʿud. How to divide Ibn Saʿud's patrimony among his senior descendants became an urgent issue that threatened the continuity of the state. This was aggravated by Saʿud's desire to promote his own sons in government at the expense of his senior half-brothers. The conflict led to the emergence of separate competing blocs within the royal family, whose interests could only be reconciled by removing Saʿud from the throne. Faysal emerged from this conflict with increasing powers that allowed him to rule as king and first prime minister, while placing recruited supporters from among his loyal brothers in key government ministries.

Ibn Saʿud's successors faced major challenges associated with rapid modernisation, transformation of the landscape and the emergence of new discourses rooted in modernity. Modernisation within an Islamic framework, the motto of King Faysal, became increasingly problematic towards the end of his reign. In the 1960s Arab nationalism in its Nasserite and Baʿthist versions was seen as a threat to the stability of Saʿudi rule. Faysal found in Islam a counter-ideology to defend the integrity and legitimacy of the Saʿudi state amidst attacks from opponents and rivals in the Arab world. Promoting the Islamic credentials of the Saʿudi state was, however, problematic.

Faysal was able to bring Saudi Arabia to the attention of the world when he declared an oil embargo on the United States and the West in 1973 (chapter 5). Saudi Arabia moved from the margin to the centre of Arab and world politics. In the 1970s its new wealth increased its vulnerability and prompted its leadership to search for an external power for protection. The Saʿudi–American liaison became problematic as it exposed the tension between Faysal's Islamic world-view and his close ties with the United States.

Faysal's successors, Khalid and Fahd, saw the unfolding of new forces and challenges. The siege of the Mecca mosque in 1979 was the first major challenge to the legitimacy of the ruling group since the *ikhwan* rebellion of 1927. The mosque siege unveiled the tension between the state and its own religion. It was vital to devise a formula for reconciling the state's immense wealth with the austerity of Wahhabi Islam. The incompatibility between religious dogma and royal pomp and the vulnerability of the royal family to attacks from within the ranks of their most loyal supporters (the religious establishment) shocked inside and outside observers who considered Saudi Arabia one of the most stable states in the Middle East. The constant search of the Saʿudi state for ways to accommodate the 'old' and the 'new' crumbled with the siege of the mosque.

The most outstanding social and political tensions appeared during the Gulf War of 1990 (chapter 6). The last decade of the twentieth century will be remembered as a turbulent time for the Saʿudi ruling group. Dissidents from within the rank and file of those who had previously been supporters of the Al Saʿud, namely the *ʿulama* (religious scholars), began to question their right to rule, political wisdom, economic policies and relations with the West. The government responded by introducing major reforms that had been promised before but were never delivered. The consolidation of an Islamist opposition surprised observers in a state that claims to rule according to the principles of the *shariʿa* (Islamic legal code). Chapter 6 assesses the origins of the Islamist opposition and attempts to explore the discourse and rhetoric of its most outspoken members.

While the state has relied heavily on projecting an image of itself as the guardian of Islam in its quest for legitimacy, it has also relied on historical narratives that highlight its role in the modernisation of the country. The final chapter examines state narratives, embedded in official historiography. The Saʿudi state invests heavily in shaping the historical imagination of its own people. The country's renaissance, *al-nahḍa*, under Saʿudi rule has become the basis for a new legitimacy. While the state dominates the material infrastructure and resources, it has become increasingly important to extend this domination to the symbolic realm of ideas and visions of the past, present and future. An examination of the content of Saʿudi history textbooks is important for understanding state legitimacy and nation building. In such textbooks the state highlights its effort to accommodate the country's Islamic heritage with its commitment to modernisation.

The centennial celebrations in 1999, marking one hundred years of Saʿudi rule, demonstrated how the state shares with its population a preoccupation with genealogy. State narratives invite people to abandon their own descent in favour of a universal *umma* (Muslim community), while celebrating its own genealogy, a line that starts with Ibn Saʿud, the first ancestor and founder of state and nation. With the centennial celebrations the Saʿudi state sealed the cult of personality around this historical figure. Narratives of the Saʿudi state, however, are also countered by other accounts that challenge official historiography. A society that is increasingly educated and literate is able to engage in debates about its own identity and history. Saʿudis who have benefited from the expansion of education since the 1960s are taking part in the debate about authenticity, heritage, tradition and the future of the country. They produce counter-narratives, undermining state monopoly over the historical imagination.

I have tried to present an interpretation of Saʿudi history that does not endorse the dominant official wisdom. This book does not dwell on the achievements of the last hundred years, a theme dominant in some of the literature, especially that produced under the auspices of the state. In such literature the historical process is submerged with propaganda for obvious political reasons. I present an interpretation of the historical data that privileges stories never told before in the context of a critical interpretation of Saʿudi history, state and society.

Measured in terms of material affluence, technology, modern health facilities and education, the achievements of the state are abundant and visible to people inside and outside Saudi Arabia. The state glorifies its efforts in these fields. To celebrate the Saʿudi National Day (usually on 23 September), the Ministry of Information places advertisements in local and international newspapers informing readers about the number of schools, hospitals, airports, factories and ports built under the auspices of the Al Saʿud. Similarly, the relative political stability of the regime has impressed outside observers in a region that has experienced turmoil, civil wars, coups and revolutions. In recent years, several volumes explained the stability and survival of monarchical rule not only in Saudi Arabia but also in neighbouring Gulf states (Gause 1994; 2000a; Herb 1999; Kostiner 2000).

However, the writing of the twentieth-century history of Saudi Arabia should explore the internal social dynamics that have shaped the character of this country, political system and adaptation to rapid change. To understand the last hundred years, one needs to engage in an 'unending dialogue between the present and the past' (Carr 1961: 30). This dialogue cannot be muted by the obvious material transformation, but should explore its progression, tensions and contradictions.

CHAPTER I

Society and politics, 1744–1818 and 1824–1891

The Ottoman Empire maintained a nominal suzerainty over the territory which is today part of the Kingdom of Saudi Arabia after its major expansion eastward in the first quarter of the sixteenth century. When Salim I occupied Egypt in 1517, he inherited the guardianship of Hijaz as the last Mamluks gave him the keys of Mecca. The Ottoman Sultan issued a firman confirming the amir of Mecca, Sharif Barakat, in his position. The Sultans later appointed governors in Jeddah and Madina (al-Sibaʿi 1984: 344), and ruled in Hijaz for four hundred years in cooperation with the Sharifian family.

While the incorporation of Hijaz in the Ottoman Empire was an extension of their rule in Egypt, their authority in eastern Arabia was an extension of their occupation of the Euphrates valley that began in 1534 when Sulayman the Magnificent conquered Baghdad. Hasa submitted voluntarily to the Ottomans in 1550 (Anscombe 1997: 12). This first phase of Ottoman occupation ended with the rebellion of the Banu Khalid in 1670 (ibid.). The Ottomans did not return to eastern Arabia until the time of Midhat Pasha in the 1870s.

The Ottomans, however, failed to extend their control into the interior of Arabia, known as Najd. Without a formal Ottoman presence, Najdi towns and oases were ruled by their own amirs, while tribal confederations maintained their independence and autonomy. In the eighteenth century, leadership in Najd, namely the first Saʿudi–Wahhabi emirate (1744–1818), challenged the authority of the Ottoman Empire in Hijaz, Iraq and Syria. This challenge resulted in the occupation of central Arabia by Muhammad ʿAli's forces, on behalf of the Ottoman Empire, in 1818. By 1841, Egyptian troops had retreated into Hijaz, leaving Najd in the hands of its local rulers. A second unsuccessful attempt to penetrate the interior followed the more definitive Ottoman occupation of Hasa in 1871. Once again, Najd remained autonomous. Local politics in this central part of Arabia came to play a major role in shaping the modern history of the country.

THE ORIGINS OF AL SAʿUD (1744–1818)

Local Najdi amirs enjoyed relative freedom to rule in the small settlements of Najd. Both the Sharifs of Mecca and the Banu Khalid rulers of Hasa tried to extend their control over Najd with the hope of extracting the meagre surplus produced by its agricultural communities (Fattah 1997: 47). However, neither the Hijazi Sharifs nor the Banu Khalid chiefs were able to integrate Najd into their sphere of influence. Najd itself was not an attractive region as it produced little surplus in dates and livestock. Its own population had always looked towards the coast of Hasa and beyond to survive. Its small merchants travelled as far as Basra and India, to supplement their limited resources.

In the eighteenth century Dirʿiyyah was a small settlement in Najd with a mixed population of farmers, merchants, artisans, minor *ʿulama* and slaves.[1] According to one source, the settlement did not have more than seventy households (Abu Ḥakima 1967: 30). Since 1727, a member of the Al Saʿud clan, Muhammad ibn Saʿud, had been the local ruler. The descent of Al Saʿud is often attributed to the Maṣalikh of Banu Waʾil, a tribal section of the north Arabian camel-herding ʿAniza tribe (Lorimer 1908: 1053). The Al Saʿud's association with the ʿAniza, however, remains suspicious since no historical source suggests that this tribal section played a role in their later expansion in Arabia.

Most probably the Al Saʿud were a sedentary group that founded the settlement of Dirʿiyyah. The settlement recognised the authority of the Saʿudi amir as a result of a combination of factors: his residence in the oasis and his ownership of cultivated land and wells around the settlement. It seems that the Al Saʿud were originally of the landholding merchant class of Najd. Muhammad ibn Saʿud (died 1765) was a landowner and a broker, financing the journeys of long-distance merchants (Fattah 1997: 47). Political skills of mediation and the ability to defend the settlement against raids by other oasis amirs and tribal confederations were important complementary attributes. In return for tribute from members of the settlement, the oasis amir became the defender of the inhabitants who served as his military force, enhanced by his own slaves. Collection of this tribute strengthened political leadership; it distinguished the amir and his lineage from that of other residents in the settlement.

Saʿudi leadership in Dirʿiyyah is best described as a traditional form of rule common in many settlements in Arabia at that time.[2] In the

1740s, the amir of Dirʿiyyah enjoyed limited authority beyond his own settlement. With the exception of his ability to collect tribute, the executive authority of an oasis ruler was fairly weak (al-Juhany 1983: 179).

It seems that the Saʿudi leadership was lacking in two respects: first, it lacked an identifiable tribal origin that would have guaranteed a strong association with a tribal confederation, similar, for example, to that of their contemporaries, Banu Khalid of Hasa. Second, the Saʿudi leadership lacked any great surplus of wealth. The Al Saʿud may have had some due to the collection of tribute from the settlement and involvement in trade, but this does not seem to have been a distinguishing characteristic. Their commercial interests at that time were not developed enough to ensure an income sufficiently substantial to enable them to expand their authority over other settlements or control a large network of caravan routes.

Given these limitations, it is not surprising that their authority remained confined to the small settlement of Dirʿiyyah. The fortunes of the Al Saʿud began to change with their adoption of the Wahhabi movement, associated with the reformer Muhammad ibn ʿAbd al-Wahhab (1703–92).[3]

Muhammad ibn ʿAbd al-Wahhab belonged to Banu Tamim, a Najdi sedentary tribe whose members were inhabitants of several oases in Najd (Abu Ḥakima 1967: 24). His family produced several religious scholars, but was not distinguished by wealth. According to one source, Muhammad ibn ʿAbd al-Wahhab lived 'in poverty with his three wives. He owned a *bustan*, date garden and ten or twenty cows' (ibid.: 26). Following the path of his ancestors, Muhammad ibn ʿAbd al-Wahhab travelled to Madina, Basra and Hasa to pursue religious education and probably wealth (al-ʿUthaymin 1997: 61–5). He returned to ʿUyaynah, where his father was a judge, to preach a new message.

The reformer distinguished himself by insisting on the importance of monotheism, the denunciation of all forms of mediation between God and believers, the obligation to pay *zakat* (Islamic tax to the leader of the Muslim community), and the obligation to respond to his call for holy war against those who did not follow these principles. Muhammad ibn ʿAbd al-Wahhab was concerned with purifying Islam from what he described as innovations and applying a strict interpretation of the *shariʿa*, both of which needed the support of a political authority. He considered cults of saints, the visiting of holy men's tombs and sacrifice to holy men, prevalent not only among the oases dwellers and the nomads of Arabia but also among Muslims encountered during his travels in Hijaz, Iraq and Syria, as manifestations of *bidʿa*. He formulated religious opinions regarding several practical matters. Among other things, he encouraged people to perform communal prayers and abstain from smoking tobacco. Most important, Muhammad ibn ʿAbd al-Wahhab insisted on the payment of *zakat*. He ruled that it should be paid on apparent wealth (such as agricultural produce) and concealed wealth, stored in gold and silver (Abu Ḥakima 1967: 195). The reformer declared that the veneration of saints, trees and other objects led to *kufr* (unbelief), blasphemy and polytheism and that the doctrine of the oneness of God, *tawḥid*, should be strictly respected.

Initially, the amir of ʿUyaynah, ʿUthman ibn Muʿammar, endorsed the reforms proposed by Muhammad ibn ʿAbd al-Wahhab, but later expelled him from the oasis under pressure from the Banu Khalid chiefs of Hasa. The reformer's severe punishment of those who were reluctant to perform communal prayers, his personal involvement in enforcing a rigid interpretation of the *shariʿa* and his stoning in public of a local woman accused of fornication antagonised the inhabitants of ʿUyaynah and their chief. It seems that the Banu Khalid chiefs of Hasa and overlords of Najd at the time also resented the reformer and feared the spread of his message. They ordered ʿUthman ibn Muʿammar to kill Muhammad ibn ʿAbd al-Wahhab, but ʿUthman decided to expel him rather than risk *fitna* (dissent) among the people who came under his authority. Muhammad ibn ʿAbd al-Wahhab and his family were asked to leave ʿUyaynah. The reformer arrived in Dirʿiyyah, forty miles away from ʿUyaynah, with the hope of convincing its Saʿudi amir to adopt his message.

Muhammad ibn ʿAbd al-Wahhab's reputation had already reached this small oasis. Muhammad ibn Saʿud received the reformer and granted him protection. Descriptions of the encounter between the ruler of Dirʿiyyah and Muhammad ibn ʿAbd al-Wahhab indicate that a pact was sealed between the two men in 1744. According to one source:

> Muhammad ibn Saʿud greeted Muhammad ibn ʿAbd al-Wahhab and said, 'This oasis is yours, do not fear your enemies. By the name of God, if all Najd was summoned to throw you out, we will never agree to expel you.' Muhammad ibn ʿAbd al-Wahhab replied, 'You are the settlement's chief and wise man. I want you to grant me an oath that you will perform *jihad* (holy war) against the unbelievers. In return you will be *imam*, leader of the Muslim community and I will be leader in religious matters.' (Abu Ḥakima 1967: 30)

According to this narrative, the Saʿudi ruler agreed to support the reformer's demand for *jihad*, a war against non-Muslims and those Muslims whose Islam did not conform to the reformer's teachings. In return the Saʿudi amir was acknowledged as political leader of the Muslim community.

Muhammad ibn ʿAbd al-Wahhab was guaranteed control over religious interpretation. The reformer started teaching his religious message in a mosque, specially built for him. He insisted on the attendance of men and children. Men who did not attend his special *dars* (teaching sessions) were required to pay a fine or shave their beards (ibid.: 32).

It is difficult to assess why the reformer had success in Dirʿiyyah, although the Wahhabi reform movement certainly provided an alternative source of legitimacy for the Al Saʿud. Muhammad ibn Saʿud adopted a religious message that promised an opportunity to compensate for the limitations of his rule. More specifically, Muhammad ibn ʿAbd al-Wahhab promised him wealth, in the form of *zakat* and expansion under his religious guidance. It is also probable that rivalry between the amirs of ʿUyaynah and Dirʿiyyah contributed to the success of a small settlement without particular political or economic significance. ʿUyaynah enjoyed far more prestige and importance than Dirʿiyyah at that time.

The historical alliance between the Wahhabi religious reformer and the ruler of Dirʿiyyah that was sealed in 1744 set the scene for the emergence of a religious emirate in central Arabia. Without Wahhabism, it is highly unlikely that Dirʿiyyah and its leadership would have assumed much political significance. There was no tribal confederation to support any expansion beyond the settlement, and there was also no surplus wealth that would have allowed Muhammad ibn Saʿud to assemble a fighting force with which to conquer other settlements. The settlement itself did not have sufficient manpower to initiate conquest of other oases or tribal territories.

From the early days of Saʿudi–Wahhabi expansion, the crucial element was to gain submission to the tenets of Wahhabi Islam among the population, both sedentary and nomadic. This submission led to the creation of a quasi-tribal confederation with which to conquer further territories in the absence of an identifiable 'Saʿudi tribal confederation'.

Wahhabism provided a novel impetus for political centralisation. Expansion by conquest was the only mechanism that would permit the emirate to rise above the limited confines of a specific settlement. With the importance of *jihad* in Wahhabi teachings, conquests of new territories became possible. The spread of the Wahhabi *daʿwa* (call), the purification of Arabia of unorthodox forms of religiosity and the enforcement of the *shariʿa* among Arabian society were fundamental demands of the Wahhabi movement. The amir of Dirʿiyyah took the Wahhabi reformer, recently expelled from ʿUyaynah, under his wing, and accepted these demands. Wahhabism impregnated the Saʿudi leadership with a new force, which proved to be crucial for the consolidation and expansion of Saʿudi rule.

Wahhabism promised this leadership clear benefits in the form of political and religious authority and material rewards, without which the conquest of Arabia would not have been possible. The resultant consolidation enabled the Saʿudi leadership to rise to prominence in the region.

The expansion of the Saʿudi–Wahhabi realm beyond Dirʿiyyah was dependent on the recruitment of a fighting force ready to spread the religious message of the reformist movement and Saʿudi political hegemony. The populations of the oases in southern Najd were the first to endorse Wahhabism and respond to its call for *jihad* against 'unbelievers'. Settled Najdis between the ages of eighteen and sixty were its first conscripts, the backbone of the Saʿudi–Wahhabi force. Some accepted Wahhabism out of conviction; others succumbed to it out of fear. It seems that the Saʿudi–Wahhabi emirate was based from the very beginning on the allegiance of the sedentary communities of Najd. Those who willingly accepted Wahhabism were expected to swear allegiance to its religio-political leadership and demonstrate their loyalty by agreeing to fight for its cause and pay *zakat* to its representatives. Those who resisted were subjected to raids that threatened their livelihood.

The same method of recruitment was used among the tribal confederations. Preaching and raids progressed simultaneously. While it was easy to maintain control over the oases, it proved more difficult to maintain the allegiance of the various Arabian tribes. The tribes generally managed to evade central authority due to their mobility and tradition of autonomy. However, once they had been subjugated, they proved to be an important fighting force, spreading the message of Wahhabism. They provided manpower with which to further the expansion of the Saʿudi–Wahhabi emirate. Participation in Saʿudi–Wahhabi expansion greatly appealed to the tribal confederations as it promised a share of the booty that resulted from raiding disobedient oasis dwellers and other tribes.

Coercion alone would not have guaranteed the level of expansion achieved by the Saʿudis by the end of the eighteenth century. Wahhabism promised salvation, not only in this world, but also in the next: submission to the teachings of Wahhabi Islam meant evasion of Wahhabi raids and promised spiritual rewards. Most accounts of the success of the Saʿudi–Wahhabi polity highlight the fact that raids were congruent with tribal practice, and as such they encouraged tribal confederations to take part in the expansion of the Saʿudi–Wahhabi realm with the promise of material rewards. However, this emphasis completely overlooks the spiritual dimension, a strong motivating force behind the eager submission of some sections of the population who had already been timidly but persistently trying to develop a spirituality deriving from the simple and austere message of Wahhabism. The Najdi population exhibited an attraction to its teachings that were in line with the orientation of some of its religious scholars. Before the rise of the Wahhabi movement, and as in other parts of the Islamic world which were some distance from the traditional centres of learning, the Najdi *ʿulama* travelled to Syria and Egypt to train with their intellectual mentors (al-Juhany 1983). Upon their return, these *ʿulama* developed into 'ritual specialists', whose main concern was *fiqh*, Islamic jurisprudence, a tradition which continues among the Saʿudi *ʿulama* of today, although for different reasons.

The specialisation of the Najdi *ʿulama* in *fiqh* reflects the concerns of the inhabitants of the Najdi towns and villages, which centred on pragmatic issues relating to marriage, divorce, inheritance, religious endowments, Islamic rituals and the Islamic legal codes. Najdi settlements had already aspired towards finding solutions for their practical problems and showed a religious awareness that predated the call of Muhammad ibn ʿAbd al-Wahhab (al-Juhany 1983: 252). While the reformer was still concerned with these practical issues, he distinguished himself from other Najdi *ʿulama* of the time by developing his ideas on *tawḥid*. Religious awareness in the Najdi settlements should not be overlooked as a factor facilitating the adoption of Wahhabism and the success of Saʿudi expansion.

The regular payment of *zakat* to the Saʿudi–Wahhabi leadership was a token of political submission, but also of religious duty. While this religious duty might not have been felt particularly strongly among the tribal confederations, it was definitely apparent among the oasis population of southern Najd whose allegiance to the Saʿudi leadership had rested on more solid ground.

We can also point to the appeal of the doctrine of the oneness of God to the tribal confederations, especially the nomadic sections. Such groups might not have had the same fascination as the sedentary population with Islamic rituals or jurisprudence (as they had their own tribal customs to deal with conflict and transgression), but it is certain that the doctrine of *tawḥid* did strike a nerve amongst them. The message of Muhammad ibn ʿAbd al-Wahhab certainly did not fall on deaf ears. Even those tribal confederations that fought against the Saʿudi–Wahhabi political agenda could not resist the temptation of a simple Islam free of excessive rituals and mediation. For instance, in spite of its ferocious resistance to political Wahhabism, the Shammar tribe accepted the doctrine of *tawḥid* in the eighteenth century. A prominent Shammar shaykh declared that his Islam remained faithful to the tenets of Wahhabism although his ancestors had fought battles with the Saʿudis since the middle of the eighteenth century. It seems that Wahhabism achieved the ultimate religious symbiosis between the nomads and the sedentary population by combining an uncompromising unitarian and puritanical Islam with an obsession with ritual specialisation and *fiqh*, thus responding to the needs of both the tribal confederations of the desert and the population of the oases of central Arabia.

Under the military leadership of Muhammad ibn Saʿud's son, ʿAbd al-ʿAziz (1765–1803), the Saʿudi leadership expanded into Riyadh, Kharj and Qasim by 1792.[4] Towns in central Najd received Wahhabi judges as representatives of the new religio-political order. Under the guise of spreading the Wahhabi message, the Saʿudi leadership subjugated most of the amirs in Najd. Those amirs were allowed to remain in their settlements as long as they paid *zakat* to the Saʿudi leader, a token of their submission to his authority.

After the completion of the campaigns in central Arabia, Saʿudi forces moved eastward into Hasa and succeeded in terminating the rule of Banu Khalid. A substantial proportion of the population of Hasa consisted of Shiʿis, representing in the eyes of the Wahhabis an extreme case of *ahl al-bidaʿ* (innovators). The subjugation of Qatif in 1780 opened the road to the coast of the Persian Gulf and Oman. Qatar acknowledged the authority of the Saʿudis in 1797. Bahrain followed suit and paid *zakat* to Dirʿiyyah.

The expansion of the Saʿudi forces to the west and in particular into Hijaz brought them into conflict with another religious authority, that of the Sharif of Mecca. In spite of the strong resistance of the Hijazis, Saʿud ibn ʿAbd al-ʿAziz (1803–14) established temporary Saʿudi hegemony over Taʾif in 1802, Mecca in 1803 and Madina in 1804. Sharif Ghalib of Mecca became a mere representative of the Saʿudis. The Wahhabi *ʿulama* ordered the destruction of the domed tombs of the Prophet and the caliphs in Madina in accordance with Wahhabi doctrine which forbade the construction of monuments on graves. According to Wahhabi teachings, graves should remain unmarked to discourage later visits and veneration by Muslims.

Saʿudi success in Hijaz encouraged southward expansion into ʿAsir, where local leaders adopted Wahhabism and for a while joined forces to march on Yemen. The strong resistance of the Yemenis, coupled with the unfamiliar geography of their mountainous country, prevented its incorporation into the Saʿudi–Wahhabi realm.

To the north-east Saʿudi expansion reached the fertile regions of Mesopotamia, threatening vital parts of the Ottoman Empire. In 1801 the holy city of Karbalaʾ was raided and plundered. Raids on the cities of Mesopotamia continued between 1801 and 1812 without resulting in the establishment of a strong Saʿudi–Wahhabi presence there due to the distance from their power base in Arabia. Wahhabi preoccupations in Mesopotamia revolved around gaining booty from these rich provinces. A similar pattern was maintained in Syria. Saʿudi forces raided cities and pilgrimage caravans without being able to establish a permanent base. Expansion by raid reached its limits in the north as it did in Yemen. The sacking of Shiʿa cities in Iraq angered its communities and resulted in the assassination of the Saʿudi leader ʿAbd al-ʿAziz in 1803 by a Shiʿa in the mosque of Dirʿiyyah in revenge for the plundering of Karbalaʾ.

Four factors facilitated the process of expansion. First, disunity and rivalry among local oasis amirs in Najd meant that the Saʿudis could gradually defeat them one by one. Second, internal disputes among members of the oases' ruling groups weakened their resistance and enabled the invaders to use dissidents for their purposes. Third, the migration of some Arabian Peninsula tribes to more fertile regions in Iraq and Syria aided the conquest. Under Saʿudi–Wahhabi pressure, several tribal confederations fled to Mesopotamia. Finally, the peaceful adoption of Wahhabism by the sedentary population of Najd provided grassroots support for the expansion even before it took place (ʿAbd al-Rahim 1976: 73).

The expansion of the first Saʿudi–Wahhabi emirate resulted in the creation of a political realm with fluctuating boundaries. The descendants of the Al Saʿud, legitimised by the Wahhabi leadership, provided a permanent political leadership in accordance with the oath of 1744. However, there were no mechanisms other than raids to ensure the durability of either the polity or its boundaries, and tribal confederations retained their ability to challenge Saʿudi–Wahhabi authority. Withdrawing the payment of *zakat* and organising counter-attacks on groups and territories within the Saʿudi–Wahhabi sphere of influence were recurrent challenges. Although there were rudimentary attempts at formalising political, economic and religious relations within the emirate, these were generally insufficient to hold the constituency together. There was a vague recognition of belonging to a Muslim community, but this did not preclude attachment to more specific tribal/regional identities.

Raids were rituals of rejuvenation, injecting fresh blood into the realm, especially when it was on the verge of disintegration. While these raids initially guaranteed expansion, they later proved detrimental to political continuity as the population began to resent the devastation they caused. When the Ottoman Empire responded to the Saʿudi–Wahhabi challenge by sending the troops of Muhammad ʿAli into Arabia in 1811, tribal confederations that had already suffered the punitive raids of the Saʿudis responded by switching allegiance to the foreign troops. Saʿud ibn ʿAbd al-ʿAziz died in 1814, leaving his son ʿAbdullah to face the challenge of the Egyptian troops. Muhammad ʿAli's son Ibrahim Pasha led the invasion of Najd after Egyptian troops established a strong base in Hijaz. Ibrahim Pasha arrived at the gates of Dirʿiyyah with '2,000 cavalrymen, 4,300 Albanian and Turkish soldiers, 1,300 Maghrebi cavalrymen, 150 gunners with around 15 guns, 20 weapons technicians and 11 sappers' (Vassiliev 1998: 154). The Saʿudis surrendered on 11 September 1818 after the total destruction of their capital and its fortifications. Ibrahim Pasha's troops plundered Dirʿiyyah and massacred several Wahhabi *ʿulama*. Those who survived were taken to Cairo together with ʿAbdullah (1814–18). He was later sent to Istanbul where he was beheaded. The sacking of Dirʿiyyah marked the end of the first Saʿudi–Wahhabi emirate.

A FRAGILE SAʿUDI REVIVAL (1824–1891)

After the withdrawal of Egyptian forces there was an attempt to re-establish Saʿudi–Wahhabi authority in 1824 when Turki ibn ʿAbdullah, the son of the beheaded Saʿudi ruler, returned to Riyadh, south of Dirʿiyyah.[5] Turki (1824–34) benefited from the partial retreat of the Egyptian troops from Najd under pressure from its local inhabitants. He was able to capture Riyadh with a small force gathered from among the inhabitants of several oases. After settling in Riyadh, Turki extended his control over ʿAriḍ, Kharj, Ḥoṭah, Maḥmal, Sudayr and Aflaj (Vassiliev 1998: 163). His authority in Ha'il and Qasim remained minimal, but he was able to reinforce recognition of Saʿudi authority in the Hasa region in 1830 (Winder 1965).

Although Turki was a strict Wahhabi *imam*, he was careful not to antagonise the Ottoman–Egyptian troops who were still in Hijaz, guarding the security of the pilgrimage caravans. However, the greatest challenge to Turki's authority came from internal dissension within his own family. In 1831 Turki faced the challenge of Mishari, a cousin whom he had appointed governor of Manfuhah. In 1834, Mishari successfully plotted the assassination of Turki while the Saʿudi forces were occupied in a war with Qatif and Bahrain. Turki was killed while coming out of the mosque after the Friday prayers (Vassiliev 1998: 167). His son Faysal immediately returned to

Riyadh from Hasa to restore his claim over the town. Faysal (1834–8) was assisted by the amir of Ha'il, ʿAbdullah ibn Rashid (1836–48), who 'killed Mishari with his own sword' (Lorimer 1908: 1097). Faysal defeated Mishari in 1834 and became the *imam* of the second Saʿudi–Wahhabi emirate.

Faysal's rule was disrupted again in 1837 when he refused to pay tribute to the Egyptian forces in Hijaz. The Egyptians sent an expedition to Riyadh. Faysal was captured and sent to Cairo. The Egyptians appointed a member of the Al Saʿud by the name of Khalid ruler in southern Najd. The situation was maintained until a member of a collateral branch of the Al Saʿud, ʿAbdullah ibn Thunayan, rebelled against Khalid, who fled from Riyadh to Jeddah. ʿAbdullah ibn Thunayan ruled in Riyadh until Faysal managed to escape from his captivity in Cairo and return to Riyadh in 1843. Faysal killed ʿAbdullah and started his second chieftainship, which lasted until his death in 1865.

After Faysal's death, his son ʿAbdullah (1865–71) became ruler in Riyadh. His half-brothers Saʿud, Muhammad and ʿAbd al-Raḥman competed with him for the leadership, which proved to be detrimental for the Saʿudis. When ʿAbdullah, the eldest son, became amir, his half-brother Saʿud resented his exclusion from power and began a military campaign to undermine his authority. Saʿud started a series of contacts with the rulers of ʿAsir and ʿAriḍ in the hope of gaining their loyalty against his brother. He also negotiated an alliance with the Murra, ʿAjman and Dawasir confederations, which were trying to maintain their autonomy by allying themselves with ʿAbdullah's rival brother. The internal struggle between the Saʿudi brothers was fuelled by the desire of the various confederations to free themselves from Saʿudi domination (Abu ʿAliya 1969: 156–97). Between 1870 and 1875 the Saʿudi brothers were not able to reach an agreement and continued to challenge each other.

Saʿud died in 1875, leaving his brothers ʿAbdullah and ʿAbd al-Raḥman in fierce competition for the leadership. Immediately after Saʿud's death, ʿAbd al-Raḥman became ruler in Riyadh while his brother ʿAbdullah and his nephews (Saʿud's sons) continued to challenge his authority. In 1887 ʿAbdullah appealed to the ruler of Ha'il, Muhammad ibn Rashid, to help him against his nephews. The ruler of Ha'il seized the opportunity to march on Riyadh. Saʿud's sons fled to Kharj, leaving their uncle in jail. The amir of Ha'il freed ʿAbdullah but took him as a hostage to his capital, leaving Salim al-Sibhan, one of his most loyal commanders, as the new governor of Riyadh (Vassiliev 1998: 201).

The new Rashidi governor of Riyadh pursued ʿAbdullah's nephews and eliminated most of them in Kharj. ʿAbdullah and his brother ʿAbd al-Raḥman were allowed to return to Riyadh as ʿAbdullah was both ill and old. ʿAbdullah died in 1889, and ʿAbd al-Raḥman ruled as a vassal of Ibn Rashid under the general governorship of Salim al-Sibhan.

In an attempt to restore his family's hegemony in southern Najd, ʿAbd al-Raḥman cooperated with the people of Qasim and sections of the Muṭayr tribal confederation, as both resented the rising power of the Rashidis. A Saʿudi alliance against the Rashidis was being formed. Muhammad ibn Rashid gathered all his forces, consisting of the Shammar, Muntafiq and Ḥarb confederations and marched into Qasim. The Rashidis and Qasimis met in Mulayda in 1891, and Muhammad ibn Rashid was victorious. With the defeat of his Qasimi allies, ʿAbd al-Raḥman fled Riyadh after an unsuccessful attempt to regain his power. He took refuge first among the Murra tribe of the Empty Quarter and later settled in Kuwait in 1893 under the patronage of the Al Sabah and with a stipend from the Ottoman government. The Ottoman government granted him a modest pension of 60 gold liras (Vassiliev 1998: 204). His capital, Riyadh, was taken by ibn Rashid's representative, ʿAjlan. It was the exile of the Al Saʿud to Kuwait that allowed a friendship to develop with the Al Sabah rulers of this port. This friendship proved crucial for the return of the Al Saʿud to Riyadh in the twentieth century.

While the disintegration of the first Saʿudi realm was partially due to the intervention of the Egyptians acting on behalf of the Ottoman Empire, the second realm collapsed for two reasons. First, the fragile Saʿudi leadership of the second half of the nineteenth century was further weakened by internal strife among members of the Saʿudi family. Second, the increasing power of a rival central Arabian emirate to the north of the Saʿudi base was able to undermine Saʿudi hegemony during the crucial period when the Saʿudis were struggling amongst themselves for political leadership.

With the flight of ʿAbd al-Raḥman, the Saʿudi capital, Riyadh, fell under the authority of the Rashidis. The remaining members of the Al Saʿud were taken as hostages to the Rashidi capital, Haʾil.

Riyadh remained under the authority of the Haʾil amirs until 1902 when ʿAbd al-Raḥman's son ʿAbd al-ʿAziz, known as Ibn Saʿud, returned from his exile in Kuwait, killed the Rashidi governor and declared himself amir of Riyadh: a third and final revival of Saʿudi rule began to take shape. This revival marked the beginning of the third Saʿudi state in the twentieth century.

THE RASHIDI EMIRATE IN HA'IL (1836–1921)

The fragile second Saʿudi–Wahhabi emirate (1824–91) coexisted with a new regional power to the north of Riyadh. The Rashidi emirate of Ha'il rose to eminence during the second half of the nineteenth century at the time when Saʿudi hegemony in central Arabia was declining.[6]

The Rashidi emirate was a polity deriving its legitimacy and power from one of Arabia's large tribal confederations, the Shammar. The impetus for centralisation came from an oasis-based leadership, that of the Rashidis, a tribal section already settled in Ha'il, an oasis in northern Najd (Al-Rasheed 1991). The Rashidis were the Shammar tribal nobility, ruling as amirs over the mixed population of Ha'il, which included Shammar tribesmen, Banu Tamim sedentary farmers and merchants, and non-tribal groups of craftsmen, artisans and slaves. Shammar nomads frequented Ha'il for trade and regarded the oasis as falling within their tribal territory. The presence of the Rashidis in the oasis was an extension of the tribe's claim over it. Since the middle of the nineteenth century, Ha'il had served as a base from which the Rashidis had expanded into north Arabia and southern Najd. While the Saʿudi–Wahhabi emirates expanded under the banner of religious legitimisation, the Rashidis spread their influence over other oases and tribal confederations with the support of their own tribe.

The conquests of the Rashidi emirate were in fact a mechanism for spreading Shammar hegemony over others. When this expansion gathered momentum in the middle of the nineteenth century, Shammar tribesmen provided the military force. Shammar tribal sections were the backbone of the force that conquered oases outside Shammar tribal territory, and they also subjugated weaker tribal confederations and turned them into vassals. In the case of the Rashidis, the emirate and the confederation were initially one polity. This was an important factor distinguishing the nature of Rashidi authority from that of the neighbouring Saʿudis in southern Najd. The Rashidis did not have to 'convert' the Shammar to their cause, but acted in conjunction with them to spread the tribe's hegemony. The Rashidi amirs were themselves drawn from the tribe and were tied into it through marital alliances. In contrast, the Saʿudi leadership in Riyadh lacked tribal depth, which obliged it to depend on the alliance with Muhammad ibn ʿAbd al-Wahhab and his followers.

Why the Shammar rallied behind the Rashidi leadership should be understood in the context of mid-nineteenth-century Arabia. It would be simplistic to argue that tribal solidarity was the sole motivating force behind the confederation's support of this newly emerging leadership. The tribe had witnessed the growth of the first Saʿudi–Wahhabi emirate, which had defeated some Shammar sections and forced them to migrate to Mesopotamia towards the end of the eighteenth century. Furthermore, in 1818, the Shammar were attacked by Ottoman Egyptian troops who mistakenly regarded Shammar territory as part of the Saʿudi domain. By supporting the Rashidis, the Shammar were seeking a leadership which would guarantee their security and autonomy *vis-à-vis* both local and foreign rivals. In backing the Rashidis who were connected genealogically to the Shammar, the tribal confederation laid the foundations for organising its own defence and strengthening a unity which had previously been based upon the rhetoric of common origin and tribal solidarity. The centralisation of power in the hands of the Rashidis stemmed from this context of political upheaval, military turmoil and foreign intervention in Arabia. Subsequently, the Shammar were able to resist encroachments on their territory, not only by Egyptian troops but also by the re-established Saʿudi–Wahhabi emirate in Riyadh (Al-Rasheed 1991: 47).

With the consolidation of Rashidi leadership, the amirs began to rely less on the Shammar and more on a mixed force of slaves and conscripts from the oasis. This was a development dictated by the inability of the leadership to control its own tribal sections. The partial shift towards a permanent non-tribal military force was an indication of a change in the power of the amirs. Initially the amirs were tribal shaykhs comparable to other Shammar shaykhs, but later their power increased as they became a sedentary nobility with its own political ambitions. This pattern was consolidated with the leadership of Muhammad ibn Rashid (1869–97), whose domain extended from the borders of Aleppo and Damascus to Basra, Oman and ʿAsir (Musil 1928: 248). The Qasim region and the Saʿudi–Wahhabi capital, Riyadh, were incorporated into this domain. Representatives and governors were appointed in the conquered areas.

The Rashidi emirate relied on four groups for its expansionist campaign in Arabia. First, its leadership summoned the sedentary and nomadic Shammar to fight their rivals, who were designated enemies of the whole tribe. Skirmishes against the Shammar sections acted in favour of Muhammad ibn Rashid in his mobilisation of this tribal force. Second, other non-tribal confederations took part in his campaign as they were motivated by the prospect of booty. Third, the amir's slaves and bodyguard formed the solid core of his military force. And fourth, conscripts from the towns and oases of Jabal Shammar provided a reliable military force which was used regularly for expansion. Their participation guaranteed the predominance of Ha'il, both economically and politically.

This expansion, however, did not lead to the establishment of control. The scanty resources of the region, coupled with the inadequacy of the transport infrastructure, militated against the full integration of these areas into a single unit. In this respect, the Rashidi emirate exhibited a pattern similar to that predominant in the first and second Saʿudi–Wahhabi emirates. Both the Saʿudis and Rashidis engaged in raids and conquest without being able to hold the conquered territories for an extended period of time. While control over the core of the emirate was relatively easy to maintain, the conquered territories represented a periphery difficult to supervise regularly or integrate thoroughly. While in the Saʿudi–Wahhabi emirates the payment of *zakat* was an indication of a group's submission to its authority, the payment of *khuwwa* (tribute) to the Rashidis expressed their control over other groups. Tribute was a tax levied not upon the collector's own community, but rather upon a conquered group which remained more or less autonomous (Pershit 1979: 149–56). Both leaderships, however, resorted to regular raids as a mechanism for ensuring the payment of either *zakat* or *khuwwa*.

While the Rashidi emirate was initially characterised by full integration between the leadership and the Shammar tribal confederation, expansion brought about the recurrent tension between a central power and its diversified and semi-autonomous constituency. At the height of Rashidi power, the constituency included other weakened tribal confederations in addition to the Shammar and the population of oases outside its traditional tribal territory. While frequent raids against rebellious tribes continued, a redistributive economy was also put in place. The amirs of Ha'il collected tribute from weakened groups to be redistributed among others, as rewards for loyalty and participation in the leadership's military campaigns. Tribal shaykhs visited the oasis and received handouts in cash and kind. The subsidy system functioned as a mechanism for the circulation of wealth, thus promising loyalty in return for material gains. Subsidies from the centre to the periphery created economic integration between the Ha'il leadership and its constituency. More importantly, they created dependency on the revenues of the amirs among the sedentary and nomadic populations, who became incorporated into their political realm.

Economic integration between the leadership and its constituency was partially achieved in the Rashidi emirate, but military and political integration were difficult to create and maintain over an extended period of time. Tribal confederations that paid *khuwwa* remained more or less autonomous. The amirs of Ha'il had no monopoly over the means of coercion as it was difficult to break the military strength of the various confederations that came under their authority. The military strength of tribes was occasionally neutralised by frequent raids and subsidies, but in the long term these strategies failed to guarantee loyalty.

Control over the oases in Jabal Shammar was, however, a different matter. Ha'il, the urban core of the emirate, remained loyal to the Rashidi leadership as long as this leadership was capable of defending the wider interests of the emirate. The merchants, artisans and agriculturists supported the leadership because it was able to guarantee the safe passage of trading and pilgrimage caravans, thus allowing the flow of trade between Ha'il and the outside world to continue. An amir who extended his authority over the tribal confederations in the desert created secure conditions for travel between Arabia's trading markets, thus benefiting the merchants and artisans of the sedentary communities. The loyalty of the oasis population was highly dependent on this factor. The Ha'il population withdrew its support only when the Rashidi leadership of the first two decades of the twentieth century became incapable of extending protection outside the walls of the oasis.

After establishing themselves as the rulers of Najd towards the end of the nineteenth century, the Rashidis lost their control over Riyadh when Ibn Saʿud, the son of the exiled Saʿudi ruler in Kuwait, returned to his native town in 1902. Ibn Saʿud killed the Rashidi governor of Riyadh and declared himself the new ruler. Between 1902 and 1921 the Rashidis and Saʿudis competed for control of central Arabia. This competition weakened the Rashidi emirate and led to its demise.

The decline of the Rashidi polity can be attributed to several factors. Rivalry between Britain and the Ottoman Empire in Arabia upset the balance between local Arabian power centres. The Rashidi amirs continued to be allied with the Ottomans even after several tribal confederations and local amirs sided with Britain. After the Ottoman defeat in the First World War, the local Rashidi allies felt the rising pressure of the Saʿudis, who had secured a firm alliance with Britain. This factor alone could not fully explain the demise of Rashidi power in 1921. But the instability of Rashidi leadership, which manifested itself in internal rivalry between the various Rashidi branches, added to their already disadvantaged position in Arabia. A weakened leadership was not able to maintain the loyalty of the various tribal confederations, who shifted their allegiance to a more powerful centre – that of the Saʿudis. The emirate lost control over its tribal periphery;

its leadership witnessed the shrinking of its territories without being able to reclaim them. The Rashidis had no monopoly over the use of coercion. This meant that autonomous and semi-autonomous confederations retained their ability to undermine the Rashidi leadership. These confederations remained a potential threat in the absence of any mechanism to contain their tendency either to challenge Rashidi authority directly or passively resist by withdrawing support needed at times of external threat.

THE SHARIFIAN EMIRATE IN HIJAZ

In Hijaz, the homeland of the most sacred sites of Islam, the Najdi pattern of emirate formation seems to have evolved with some striking similarities (al-Sibaʿi 1984; Peters 1994).[7] The population of Hijaz had always been distinguished from that of Najd by its heterogeneity. Hijazi society included tribal confederations claiming unity through essentially eponymous genealogical links. Ḥarb, ʿUtayba, Billi, Hutaym, Shararat, Banu ʿAṭiya and Ḥuwayṭat were among the best known Hijazi tribal groups (Hogarth 1917: 17; Admiralty 1916: 100). Descriptions of the Hijazi confederations agree that they differed from those in Najd as they had no overarching tribal leadership capable of claiming authority over the whole confederation. It seems that the large Hijazi tribal groups were fragmented into small units under the leadership of a prominent shaykh, who could not claim authority beyond his section. This political fragmentation could be interpreted as a result both of geography and of the presence of an overarching leadership in the person of the Sharif of Mecca (discussed below). Yet Hijazi tribes were territorial groups, similar to those in Najd. Ḥarb, for example, controlled the area between Mecca and Jeddah: ʿUtayba dominated eastern Hijaz, with one section predominate in Taʾif and its environs (Hogarth 1917: 18).

Tribal confederations coexisted with other groups claiming holy descent from Quraysh and the Prophet Muhammad through his grandsons, Ḥasan and Ḥusayn, known as the Ashraf. Descendants of the Ashraf lived in Mecca and Madina, but were also scattered among the Hijazi nomadic population, as well of course as in other parts of the Arab and Islamic world where they had been dispersed since the collapse of the ʿAbbasid Empire (Daḥlan 1993). The holy descent of the Sharifs predisposed them to play a prominent leading role in the emirates of Mecca and Madina from the eighth and ninth centuries, to the exclusion of other 'non-holy' descent groups. They also played a prominent role as religious specialists, for example judges and preachers in the holy cities and as heads of Sufi orders (ibid.).

In addition to Hijazi tribal confederations and Sharifian clans, the population of the Hijaz included Muslims whose ancestors or who themselves had come from Turkey, Africa, India and Asia and who now resided in the major towns and ports. This diversity was extended to the religious domain as the various Islamic legal schools were recognised by the Ottomans. Sufi circles flourished in Mecca and Madina. Sharif Ḥusayn (1908–24) and his sons were Shafiʿi Sunnis. Equally important was the presence of a Shiʿa community, especially in Madina and among some Sharifian clans. According to Ende:

> For many Shiʿite authors, the Sharifs of Mecca and Madina themselves were actually Shiʿites, who for obvious reasons, posed as Sunnites – an attitude considered lawful, as *taqiya*, under Shiʿite Law. Some sections of the Ḥarb (the Bani ʿAli) and Juhaina were also Shiʿa, settled around the date palms of Madina, where another Shiʿa group, the Nakhawla seem to have been living since the days of the early Islamic empire. (Ende 1997: 266–86)

This Hijazi diversity was reflected in a sharper distinction between the urban and rural areas. In Hijaz, the urban–rural divide was more pronounced than in Najd. The cosmopolitan urban centres of Jeddah and Mecca were not comparable in size, specialisation and sophistication to any settlement in Najd or elsewhere in Arabia. These were urban centres where travellers did not fail to draw the boundaries between the desert and the sown. At the beginning of the twentieth century, this sharp divide predisposed Hogarth to claim that 'the Hejazi bedouins are of exceptionally predatory character, low morale, and disunited organisation' (Hogarth 1917: 17). His negative remarks were probably based on views of the population of the urban centres such as Jeddah, which was distinguished from that of the surrounding tribal areas. In Najd the rural–urban continuum would not have justified such representations. In Najd the oasis population and the tribal confederations often belonged to the same social category.

In this diverse region, the Sharifian emirate maintained a rather prolonged presence, predating that of both the Saʿudis and Rashidis in central Arabia. Sharifian authority had fluctuated since the sixteenth century depending on developments outside the region, mainly Ottoman policies towards this vital area. While central Arabian emirates faced the tension between their power and that of the tribal confederations, a further restraining agent burdened the Sharifian emirate, which was capable of both empowering and disempowering its leadership. In Hijaz, the amirs of Mecca were caught between the tribal confederations and the Ottoman Sultan and his representatives. A system of dual authority was established: the Sultan's urban-based representatives dealt with commercial, political and foreign relations; the Sharif dealt with the affairs of the Holy Cities and the tribal confederations, a dualism which was occasionally violated. The two authorities competed without one being able to subdue the other.

This dual authority distinguished Hijaz sharply from Najd. The Ottomans were the official guardians of the holy places, but they could not exercise that privilege without the amir of Hijaz. According to Peters, this dualism provided a perilous equilibrium (Peters 1994: 335). Government in Hijaz differed from that in Najd, the latter being outside the direct control of the Ottoman Empire, although the Ottomans regularly interfered in its affairs. The climax of this intervention was reached with the invasion of Muhammad ʿAli early in the nineteenth century, which was an attempt both to prevent further Saʿudi–Wahhabi expansion and to impose Ottoman rule.

In Hijaz, the Ottoman Sultan retained the power to appoint the amir, whose garrison was funded from the Ottoman treasury. The Ottomans also paid the Hijazi *ʿulama* their salaries (Daḥlan 1993). While Ottoman military and administrative presence was pronounced in the cities, it was virtually non-existent outside them. The duty to control the territories and population in the regions between the major urban centres was delegated to the Sharif. Prominent Sharifs were rewarded for demonstrating exceptional ability to restrain the tribal confederations, especially during the annual pilgrimage season. In return for guaranteeing the security of the pilgrimage caravan from Damascus (using a military force consisting of the amir's police force, slaves and an amalgamation of co-opted tribal groups), the amir of Mecca received regular subsidies and his urban constituency was exempt from Ottoman taxes. Hijaz as a whole was exempt from military service in deference to its special and elevated status among the various Ottoman provinces. Its ports and trade were, however, subject to taxation.

The Sharif of Mecca continued to execute Ottoman policies. Daḥlan, a nineteenth-century *mufti* of Mecca, commented on how, after the withdrawal of Muhammad ʿAli's troops from Hijaz in the 1840s, the Ottomans replaced the Egyptians in the region. The Ottomans confirmed the Sharif's subsidies that had already been put in place by Muhammad ʿAli. They also expected the Sharif to carry out their policies not only in Hijaz, but also in the interior of Arabia. Sharif Muhammad ibn ʿAwn (1856–58) apparently went on an expedition with the Shammar tribe against Faysal ibn Turki, the Saʿudi ruler of the second Saʿudi–Wahhabi emirate. The Sharif imposed an annual tax of 10,000 riyals on the Saʿudi ruler, who continued to pay it until his death in 1865 (Daḥlan 1993). Again Sharif ʿAbdullah, Muhammad ibn ʿAwn's son, together with Ottoman troops conducted an expedition in ʿAsir in 1871, after Muhammad ibn ʿAiḍ rebelled against the Ottoman Sultan (ibid.: 25). The Sharif seized the port of Qunfudah, which had been controlled by the ʿAsiri tribe the Mughaydis (Bang 1996: 30).

Four major differences distinguished Hijaz from Najd: holy Sharifian clans occupying positions of authority, a sharp rural–urban divide, cosmopolitan heterogeneous towns and ports, and an imperial power maintaining a military presence in the major towns and holding the right to appoint the Sharif, who often had been raised and educated in Istanbul under the control and patronage of the Ottoman Sultan (de Gaury 1951: 248). Once appointed in Istanbul, various Sharifs travelled to Mecca, often for the first time, if they had been held hostage in Istanbul. They were expected to rule in Mecca and among Hijazi tribes on behalf of the Sultan. The Sharifs used Ottoman subsidies to control and pacify the various tribal confederations that regularly undermined Ottoman authority by raiding pilgrims.

The Sharifs relied on their prestigious Hashemite descent to extract recognition of their authority both from city dwellers and tribal confederations; in addition their religious authority was sanctioned and backed by the Ottomans. This authority, however, was not sufficient to guarantee obedience. Like the amirs of Ha'il, Dirʿiyyah and later Riyadh, the Sharifs of Mecca resorted to bribes and coercion in their effort to pacify the tribal confederations. The inherent tension between the tribal confederations and the emirates of central Najd was replicated in Hijaz. Neither the religious legitimacy of the Saʿudis and the Sharifs nor the tribal origin of the amirs of Ha'il was sufficient to resolve the tension. The Sharifian emirate was precarious as long as the tribal confederations remained capable of consolidating or threatening the emirate's continuity. The emirate strove to integrate the Hijazi tribes but this was not always possible.

Like Najdi emirates, the Sharifian polity was weakened by succession disputes among various Sharifian clans. Internal rivalries were exaggerated by the regular interference of the Ottoman power. In the 1850s Sharif Muhammad ibn ʿAwn was invited by the Ottoman governor to visit Jeddah, where he was kidnapped and sent to Istanbul. His rival, ʿAbd al-Muṭṭalib ibn Ghalib, who had already been held in Istanbul, was sent as Sharif of Mecca (de Gaury 1951: 248). Although the

Ottomans were often directly involved in setting one clan against another, succession disputes existed even in areas where Ottoman authority was minimal. Such disputes can only be understood by reference to the absence of clear succession rules in these emirates and the fact that legitimacy and authority resided in the lineage as a whole, whether Sharifian, Saʿudi or Rashidi, rather than in the person of the ruler and his immediate descendants. As the centres of the emirates grew in resources, prestige and power, so did competition between rival claimants (Al-Rasheed 1991: 66–74).

HASA IN THE NINETEENTH CENTURY

Hasa was the agricultural region to which Najdi merchants and tribal confederations had turned their attention. The ports of the Persian Gulf and the oases of Hasa were vital for the survival of the Najdi population with its meagre resources.[8] The symbiosis between the nomadic and sedentary groups was clearly manifested in this region. The nomads of Najd brought their animals and animal products (horses, sheep, camels, butter) to the markets of the oases and ports where they exchanged them for agricultural products (mainly grain and dates) and a range of locally manufactured goods and imported items (including weapons). The abundant water resources of the oases of this region had led to the emergence of a specialised peasantry that included landowners, sharecroppers and agricultural labourers. While some Najdi agriculturists were 'part-time' peasants, the Hasawi agriculturists were a specialist group coexisting with the tribal confederations, especially those whose territories bordered Hasa, such as Shammar, ʿAjman, Murra and Muṭayr (Anscombe 1997: 10). This agricultural community was set apart from the rest of the population because of its religious affiliation. The majority of the peasantry consisted of Shiʿa Muslims, a minority among a Sunni majority. They had suffered repression throughout the eighteenth century at the hands of the Wahhabis, who regarded them as the epitome of *ahl al-bidaʿ* (al-Ḥasan 1994; Doughty 1979; Wallin 1854).

Throughout their history, the Shiʿa peasantry suffered a threefold discrimination: one resulted from their religious minority status, one from their despised agricultural specialisation, and one from ignorance of their precise tribal genealogies. In the words of a Shiʿa historian, loss of genealogy does not indicate a foreign or non-Arab origin – an argument often propagated by recent official Saʿudi historical narratives – but should be interpreted as a function of a long history of sedentarisation and commitment to agriculture (al-Ḥasan 1994: vol. I, 27; Al-Rasheed 1998: 130–5). In addition to the peasantry, Hasa had a number of well-known merchant families who traded between the oases of the interior, the ports of the Persian Gulf (e.g. Kuwait, Bahrain, Qatar, ʿUqayr and Qatif) and the outside world (mainly India and Africa). While some merchant families traced their origins to Najd, others were local Hasawis (Fattah 1997: 77–83). Foreign merchants were also noticeable in the region. Indian and British trading companies were established in Qatif in the middle of the nineteenth century (Lorimer 1908: 965).

Before the rise of the Wahhabi movement, the politics of this microcosm were dominated by the confederation of Banu Khalid under the leadership of Al Ḥumayyid (Abu Ḥakima 1967: 67, 157). Banu Khalid supplanted the rule of the Ottomans in Hasa as early as 1670, after which they established their own hegemony. Their control was extended to Najd, which became a territory within their sphere of influence (Fattah 1997: 66; Anscombe 1997: 12). The rise of the first Saʿudi–Wahhabi emirate led to the demise of the Banu Khalid polity in 1795 (Abu Ḥakima 1967: 157). Hasa fell under the influence of the Saʿudi–Wahhabi forces until this emirate was defeated in 1818. The flow of food supplies and goods from Hasa supported the Saʿudis and their followers in the interior, especially in times of drought (Anscombe 1997: 45).

The Saʿudis were able to re-establish a semblance of authority in the region in 1830. In fact the occupation of Hasa was the first attempt to establish Saʿudi rule after the destruction of Dirʿiyyah in 1818. This second Saʿudi–Wahhabi occupation (1830–8) was, however, precarious. Hasa became the territory where the rivalry among Saʿudi contestants was fought out after the death of Faysal ibn Turki in 1865. This rivalry was partially resolved with the Ottoman invasion of 1870, a move planned and orchestrated by the energetic Ottoman governor of Baghdad, Midhat Pasha. Hasa became a *sanjak* of the province of Basra and an Ottoman governor was stationed in Hofuf. In 1874 the Ottomans attempted to revive Banu Khalid's authority against that of the Saʿudis as they appointed Barak ibn ʿUrayʿir as governor of Hasa (Lorimer 1908: 1132). By that time Banu Khalid had already lost their power, and even Ottoman support failed to restore their previous glory. It seems that Shiʿa Hasawis welcomed Ottoman rule as they had suffered continuous mistreatment and repression. Anscombe confirms that the amirs of Riyadh had taxed the people into poverty, taken their possessions and done nothing to stop bedouin depredations (Anscombe 1997: 35–6).

In the nineteenth century the striking contrast between Hasa on the one hand and Najd and Hijaz on the other was the former's failure to produce a local power capable of developing into a regional emirate. After the demise of the emirate of Banu Khalid, it seems that Hasa became desirable to various regional forces (the Kuwaitis, Saʿudis and Rashidis) and foreign imperial states, for example the Ottomans and Britain. Competition for its control was motivated by its agricultural resources, which were incomparably greater than those of Najd, and the diverse trading networks of its inhabitants, a network activated by Ibn Saʿud in the twentieth century for the consolidation of his newly emerging state. The lack of an indigenous emirate does not, however, mean that Hasa lacked local leadership. With the exception of a few studies (al-Ḥasan 1994; Fattah 1997; Anscombe 1997; Steinberg 2001), we still lack a comprehensive micro-historical analysis focusing on local leadership and social history in Hasa. Historical accounts remain concerned with Ottoman and British policies as part of a general preoccupation with 'piracy', 'slavery' and 'international rivalry' in the Gulf.

The question why Hasa failed to exhibit elementary forms of emirate formation cannot be answered with certainty. We can only speculate that this religiously and tribally heterogeneous region became a buffer zone between the powerful southern Iraqi tribal confederations, their Najdi counterparts and the Najdi and coastal emirates of the Persian Gulf. Added to this was the Ottoman and British presence, which led to the crystallisation of various power centres around the region but not among its inhabitants. The fact that a great percentage of those inhabitants were Shiʿa agriculturists among Sunni Muslims must have influenced political development and acted against the crystallisation of power in one of the oases of Hasa.

EMIRATE FORMATION IN ARABIA

The internal dynamics of population movement and sedentarisation (al-Juhany 1983), military force and conquest (Rosenfeld 1965), economic and mercantile interests (Fattah 1997) and religious motivation (Cook 1988) have all been listed as variables responsible for emirate formation in Arabia. None of the above, however, draw our attention to the interaction between the sedentary and nomadic communities of Arabia. The interdependence of these two inseparable communities resulted in an economic, political and social symbiosis at the heart of political centralisation. Some of the oases and towns of Arabia became important centres integrating the pastoral economy of the bedouins with the agricultural and merchant activities of the sedentary population. The Saʿudi–Wahhabi polities and the Rashidi emirate were attempts to regulate this interaction. Both endeavoured to incorporate a nomadic periphery into their sedentary base. They were successful during times of strong leadership endowed with enough surplus to keep a balance between the interests of the bedouins and those of the sedentary communities. This balance was crucial for the durability of these emirates. External factors, diminishing resources and rivalry among members of the ruling groups undermined the stability of the emirates and led to total disintegration at critical historical moments.

However, both the Saʿudi and Sharifian polities were different from the Rashidi emirate because of their leadership. The Ashraf ruled on the basis of their specific holy descent, considered in Hijaz to be above other tribal groups, while the Saʿudis had no clear association with the tribal groups of Najd. Both the Ashraf and the Saʿudis were able to play the role of mediators between various sections of society (nomads and sedentary, tribal and non-tribal), a role that the Rashidis could not successfully accomplish given their association with the Shammar tribal confederation. Rashidi rule rested primarily on the hegemony of a single tribe. The expansion of this emirate was perceived in Arabia as an expansion of Shammar domination over other tribal groups and sedentary communities. In contrast, the expansion of the Saʿudi and Sharifian emirates could not be associated with the domination of a single tribal confederation. In the case of the Saʿudis, expansion took place under the pretext of a religious mission, produced and supported by the *ḥaḍar* communities of southern Najd.

The revival of Saʿudi rule early in the twentieth century and the evolution of their third emirate into a fully fledged state are attributed to the fact that they had no clear or obvious association with a tribal confederation. In all regions, however, the emirate remained the model for political centralisation. During the first three decades of the twentieth century, the Saʿudi state was initially an emirate whose origins, conquests and expansion were very similar to those of its predecessors.

CHAPTER 2

The emerging state, 1902–1932

The early decades of the twentieth century witnessed the disintegration of previous local emirates in Arabia and the rise of ʿAbd al-ʿAziz ibn ʿAbd al-Raḥman Al Saʿud, known as Ibn Saʿud. This chapter describes the military campaigns of Ibn Saʿud that led to the revival of Saʿudi authority as a background to examining the role of two important actors, namely the *muṭawwaʿa*, religious specialists, and the *ikhwan*, tribal military force. The former were active agents in state building; they were also a pre-existing force ready to be mobilised in the service of the state. In contrast, the *ikhwan* were a crucial military force created as a result of the *muṭawwaʿa*'s efforts for the purpose of Saʿudi expansion.

This expansion took place at a time when Arabia was gradually being drawn into the British sphere of influence after the collapse of the Ottoman Empire. By 1900, most of the coastal rulers of the peninsula from Kuwait to Muscat had already signed protection treaties with Britain. However, Britain refused to extend its protection to rulers in the interior until the outbreak of the First World War. The war was a pretext that allowed Britain greater intervention in the interior, which strengthened Saʿudi efforts at state building.

THE CAPTURE OF RIYADH (1902)

As has already been mentioned, Riyadh in 1900 was under the authority of the Rashidi amirs whose domain at the time included most of central Arabia. It stretched from Haʾil in the north, to Qasim in the centre, and reached Riyadh in the south. Muhammad ibn Rashid (1869–97) had already expelled the last Saʿudi ruler of Riyadh, ʿAbd al-Raḥman, to Kuwait, where he lived under the patronage of Al Sabah. Muhammad's successor, ʿAbd al-ʿAziz ibn Mutʿib ibn Rashid (1897–1906), ruled this region through local chiefs and representatives. The amir of Haʾil secured the approval of the Ottomans, who watched his increasing power with suspicion.

From Kuwait, ʿAbd al-Raḥman's son Ibn Saʿud launched an attack on Riyadh to capture the city from the Rashidis. The Al Sabah rulers, who also feared the extension of Rashidi power over their own port, encouraged this. Their fears were compounded by the Rashidi alliance with the Ottoman Empire. It is worth noting that the Kuwaiti rulers signed a protection treaty with Britain in 1899. The Anglo–Kuwaiti Agreement guaranteed the integrity of the Kuwait emirate and promised protection against outside attacks. The agreement also allowed Britain to extend its interests to the upper Gulf (Anscombe 1997). From Kuwait, Ibn Saʿud gathered forty men (Kishk 1981: 277) – in some accounts sixty men (al-ʿUthaymin 1997: 359–61) – and headed towards Riyadh. The capture of Riyadh was effected after surprising the Rashidi garrison at night and killing Ibn Rashid's representative, ʿAjlan, on 15 January 1902 (Vassiliev 1998: 212). It was this surprise attack that brought Ibn Saʿud back to Riyadh.[1] The rest of the Al Saʿud family came later. Ibn Saʿud's father arrived in Riyadh in May to confirm his son in his position as ruler of the town.

From Riyadh, Ibn Saʿud started a series of campaigns in southern and eastern Najd. The small towns of ʿAriḍ, Washm, Sudayr and Kharj fell into his hands. Rashidi troops retreated into Qasim, now a buffer zone between their northern capital and the newly established Saʿudi domain in southern Najd.

After Riyadh and southern Najd, Qasim became the battleground between the Saʿudis and Rashidis between 1902 and 1906. The Ottomans backed Ibn Rashid against Ibn Saʿud, by sending troops and ammunition. Ibn Saʿud secured an alliance with the Kuwaitis and the approval of the British who regarded Ottoman support for Ibn Rashid as threatening to their own interests in Kuwait.

The incorporation of Qasim in Ibn Saʿud's realm was secured after the battle of Rawḍat Muhanna in 1906 during which the ruler of Haʾil, ʿAbd al-ʿAziz ibn Rashid, was killed. By 1906 Ibn Saʿud had extended his control over the major towns of Qasim, ʿUnayzah and Buraydah. The new amir of Haʾil retreated to his capital and what remained of Turkish troops returned to Madina and Basra. The Ottomans confirmed Ibn Saʿud as *de facto* ruler of Qasim and southern Najd. Ibn Saʿud was first appointed *qaʾimmaqam* of Qasim and later *wali* of Najd. The Ottomans seem to have accepted the partition of Najd between Ibn Saʿud and Ibn Rashid.

After Qasim the battleground moved to Hasa, where a substantial Shiʿa community lived. In 1913 Ibn Saʿud launched an attack on Hofuf where the Ottomans had stationed 1,200 Turkish troops after the province's annexation in 1870.[2] Ibn Saʿud nominally acknowledged the Ottoman Sultan but undermined his authority when he appointed a relative of his, Ibn Juluwi, as governor of the region. In May 1913 Ibn Saʿud signed the Ottoman–Saʿudi Treaty, according to which the Ottomans confirmed that "ʿAbdul ʿAziz Pasha was governor of Najd, according to an Imperial Firman' (Leatherdale 1983: 369–70; Vassiliev 1998: 233). It seemed that Ibn Saʿud feared a Turkish invasion by sea following his expulsion of the Ottoman garrison from Hasa (Troeller 1976: 83). The conquest of Hasa brought the Al Saʿud leadership back into this Shiʿa territory where the Ottomans had established their control in the 1870s. According to one source, an agreement was worked out between leading Shiʿa *ʿulama* and Ibn Saʿud in which the latter guaranteed religious freedom for the Shiʿa, who in return pledged loyalty to Ibn Saʿud (Steinberg 2001: 243). Religious freedom remained an unfulfilled promise as Wahhabi Islam defined the Shiʿa as *rafiḍa*, those who reject faith. This became the religious framework guiding the status of the Shiʿa in Ibn Saʿud's territories.

Even after the conquest of Hasa, Britain considered Ibn Saʿud an Ottoman vassal and declined to conclude a treaty that would have conferred British protection status on him (Sluglett and Sluglett 1982: 49). The Anglo–Turkish convention of July 1913 defined the boundaries of the *sanjak* of Najd, which included Ibn Saʿud's new acquisition in Hasa (Leatherdale 1983: 369). Britain, therefore, neither objected to nor recognised Ibn Saʿud's conquest of Hasa. The outbreak of the First World War dramatically changed this situation.

THE FIRST WORLD WAR AND IBN SAʿUD (1914–1918)

With the First World War approaching, Ottoman officials endeavoured to reconcile the two rulers in Najd, Ibn Saʿud and Saʿud ibn ʿAbd al-ʿAziz ibn Rashid, and obtain a promise of their military cooperation. The Ottoman–Saʿudi Convention, signed in May 1914, stated that Najd should remain the territory of Ibn Saʿud and should go to his sons and grandsons by imperial firman. The convention also forbade Ibn Saʿud from entering into treaty relations with foreign powers, or granting concessions to foreigners in his territories (Leatherdale 1983: 370).

Equally, Britain began to search for local allies in Najd whose support was seen as essential to end Ottoman authority in the region (Al-Rasheed 1991: 214–15). The war freed Britain from its previous non-intervention policy in the affairs of the interior. Ibn Saʿud had expressed a wish to enter into negotiations with Britain after he conquered Hasa in 1913. Two years later he received Captain Shakespear, a British envoy whose role was to conclude a treaty with Ibn Saʿud similar to treaties concluded with the Gulf coastal rulers. Shakespear promoted the idea that Britain would gain control of the western littoral of the Gulf, control the arms traffic, and exclude all foreign powers from central Arabia (Troeller 1976: 85). Captain Shakespear was killed in the battle of Jarrab between Ibn Saʿud and Ibn Rashid in 1915, before finalising the terms of the treaty.

While the details of Shakespear's death are not known, his mission was, however, successful, as Ibn Saʿud signed the Anglo–Saʿudi Treaty on 26 December 1915 (Troeller 1976: 86–9; Leatherdale 1983: 372–3). According to this treaty, the British government acknowledged that 'Najd, Hasa, Qatif and Jubayl and their dependencies and territories are the countries of Ibn Saʿud'. Aggression towards these territories 'will result in the British government giving aid to Ibn Saʿud' (Leatherdale 1983: 372). On signing the treaty, Ibn Saʿud received 1,000 rifles and a sum of £20,000 (Vassiliev 1998: 238). In addition, the treaty granted Ibn Saʿud a monthly subsidy of £5,000 and regular shipments of machine guns and rifles (ibid.). Ibn Saʿud continued to receive this subsidy until 1924 (Troeller 1976: 157–67; Sluglett and Sluglett 1982: 50).

In return, Ibn Saʿud agreed not to 'enter into any correspondence, agreement or treaty with any foreign nation or power, and refrain from all aggression on, or interference with the territories of Kuwait, and Bahrain, and of the shaiks of Qatar and the Oman coast, who are under the protection of the British government, and who have treaty relations with the said government' (Leatherdale 1983: 373). This marked the beginning of Britain's direct involvement in the political affairs of the interior of Arabia.

Ibn Rashid, however, distanced himself from Britain as he continued his fragile alliance with the Ottomans, and Haʾil remained within the Ottoman sphere of influence during the war. After recognising Ibn Saʿud as *wali* of Najd (in the Ottoman–Saʿudi Convention of 1914, mentioned earlier), the Ottomans appointed Ibn Rashid as 'Commander of the whole of Najd'. He was sent 25 German and Turkish officers with 300 soldiers in return for his loyalty (Al-Rasheed 1991: 215).

The two rivals in central Arabia, Ibn Saʿud and Ibn Rashid, continued their hostilities during the war. Their rivalry was fuelled by a clearer demarcation of alliances. Britain pushed Ibn Saʿud to attack Haʾil in 1917, now that its rulers were seen as Ottoman allies. While no major victories were recorded, Ibn Saʿud took advantage of the war to request further help from Britain against Ibn Rashid. Ibn Saʿud claimed that the terrain between Qasim and Haʾil was barren ground and this would inevitably make it difficult for his troops to survive. In addition he argued that Haʾil was well fortified and difficult to conquer with the weapons in his possession. Britain agreed to assist him with 1,000 rifles and 100,000 rounds to annex the Rashidi capital (Al-Rasheed 1991: 216). During the war, however, Ibn Saʿud failed to add Haʾil to his realm.

THE CAPTURE OF HAʾIL (1921)

The First World War ended in 1918, but local battles between Ibn Saʿud and his rivals continued. Ibn Saʿud and Ibn Rashid guarded their territories with the hope of extending their dominion to other regions now the Ottoman Empire had disappeared from the political map of Arabia. The war left Ibn Rashid without an ally and contributed to his weakening *vis-à-vis* his rival, Ibn Saʿud. All Ibn Rashid could hope for at the time was to remain in power in Haʾil and its environs. Between 1918 and 1920, the amirs of Haʾil constantly tried to compensate for their losses in central Arabia. They entered into negotiation with the Hashemites in Hijaz and Al Sabah, the amirs of Kuwait, who began to realise the threat that Ibn Saʿud represented – especially after it became clear that Britain's support during the war had greatly strengthened his position. Although these negotiations succeeded in breaking the isolation of the Rashidis after the war, they did not result in any joint military activity against Ibn Saʿud. The Rashidis were not able to prevent Ibn Saʿud's attack on their territories in the 1920s (Al-Rasheed 1991: 223–4). The attack on Haʾil started with economic pressure being applied to the Shammar tribe, strong supporters of the Rashidis, by denying them access to markets in Hasa that had already fallen under Ibn Saʿud's control. Military skirmishes and encroachments on the oases of Jabal Shammar followed.

When military pressure was coupled with internal succession disputes in the Rashidi capital, the decline of Rashidi power in central Arabia became inevitable. The emirate had already been weakened by its alliance with the defeated Ottoman Empire. With British subsidies and ammunition, Ibn Saʿud was able to capture Haʾil in 1921 (Al-Rasheed 1991: 223–4). In August 1921, Ibn Saʿud imposed a siege on the Rashidi capital with 10,000 troops. On 1 November, the Rashidis surrendered to Ibn Saʿud. On 4 November, the gates of the oasis were opened and the people of Haʾil swore allegiance to Ibn Saʿud.[3]

With the fall of Haʾil, Ibn Saʿud's authority stretched to the northern parts of Najd. The fall of the Rashidi emirate ended the prospect of this local power developing into a major political force in twentieth-century Arabia. Moreover, the occupation of Haʾil had far-reaching importance, as it stretched Saʿudi frontiers further north. Gertrude Bell commented on the importance of the capture of Haʾil: 'The conquest of Hayil will have far-reaching consequences. It will bring Ibn Saʿud into the theatre of Trans-Jordanian politics' (in Troeller 1976: 169).

THE CAPTURE OF HIJAZ (1925)

In 1918 and 1919, Hijaz–Najd relations were volatile as rivalry between Ibn Saʿud and King Ḥusayn continued, with the former exerting military pressure on Hijaz. Before the capture of Haʾil, Ibn Saʿud was engaged in an important war. The dispute centred on a small and insignificant village, Khurma, regarded by both Ibn Saʿud and Ḥusayn as falling within their own territories. In Philby's version of the events, the people of Khurma switched allegiance to Ibn Saʿud, an event that led to Ḥusayn sending his troops to reclaim his authority in this village. His forces were defeated and the conflict moved to another village, Turaba, thirty miles south-west of Khurma (quoted in Troeller 1976: 142; Kostiner 1993: 35). Saʿudi forces destroyed the Sharifian regular army led by Ḥusayn's son ʿAbdullah, capturing all his guns. The clashes with the Hashemites resulted in ʿAbdullah being chased out of Turaba. The defeat of the Hijazi army was followed by an armistice between Ibn Saʿud and Ḥusayn, with the arbitration of Britain. Ibn Saʿud insisted that the boundaries of Najd should include Khurma and Turaba and Najdi pilgrims should be allowed to perform the pilgrimage safely (Troeller 1976: 152). Ibn Saʿud's spokesman, Ibn Thunayan, travelled to Hijaz to discuss preliminaries of peace. An armistice was signed between Najd and Hijaz, which suspended hostilities at least for four years (ibid.).

After the armistice with Ḥusayn, Ibn Saʿud siezed the opportunity to expand into the southern Hijaz, namely ʿAsir. It seems that Ibn Saʿud was antagonised by British support for the kingship of ʿAbdullah and Faysal (sons of Ḥusayn) in Mesopotamia and Syria. According to Troeller: 'It appeared to the Najdi ruler that he was being outflanked by his Hashemite adversaries' (Troeller 1976: 152).

ʿAsir had an emirate based in Ṣabiya, founded by a descendant of the nineteenth-century Sufi teacher Aḥmad ibn Idris. Since the late nineteenth century, the Idrisis had opposed Ottoman rule and gathered tribal confederations with the aim of expelling the Ottomans from the land (al-Zulfa 1995). This was an important factor behind the formation of the Idrisi emirate in the twentieth century (1906–34) by Muhammad ibn ʿAli al-Idrisi (1876–1923). The Idrisi emirate became a buffer zone between competing local forces. Both the Sharifian family in Mecca and the Imams of Yemen were trying to expand into this agricultural area, both sought assistance from foreign powers to expand their influence into ʿAsir. The Idrisi state was eventually secured by Britain and Italy, who both had reasons to oppose the Ottomans before the First World War (Bang 1996: 141). Italy declared war on the Ottoman Empire in 1911 following the Italian invasion of Tripolitania and Cyrenaica. Having secured Eritrea, Italy found in Muhammad al-Idrisi, who had opposed Ottoman suzerainty in ʿAsir, a potential ally in the Red Sea area.

The Idrisis maintained a precarious hold over the tribal groups of ʿAsir, especially after the defeat of the Ottomans in the First World War. After the war, tribes loyal to the Idrisis turned to Ibn Saʿud, thus confirming the fragile coalition between the Idrisis and their tribal hinterland. The Idrisis themselves had no tribal roots in the area; they were and remained newcomers among the heterogeneous ʿAsiri tribes (Bang 1996: 135). While the Idrisis continued their fragile rule in ʿAsir, the local amir of Abha offered his allegiance to Ibn Saʿud after Saʿudi troops under the leadership of his son Faysal occupied Abha, ʿAsir's capital.[4] In 1922 Abha became part of Ibn Saʿud's domain, an event that angered Ḥusayn, who regarded the region as an extension of his rule over Hijaz (Vassiliev 1998: 262).

The Saʿudi campaign in ʿAsir was a prelude to a more aggressive military encroachment on Ḥusayn's territories in the heart of Hijaz. Two reasons are identified as background: first, Ibn Saʿud's finances suffered a blow when Britain stopped its monthly subsidy of £5,000 in 1924. He began to look towards the more prosperous region of central Hijaz, where income from the pilgrimage tax and custom duties levied in Jeddah would by far exceed his limited income from Najd and Hasa. Second, on 5 March 1924, Ḥusayn assumed the caliphate which had been abolished by the Turkish assembly two days earlier (Troeller 1976: 216). Ibn Saʿud's attack on Hijaz was a clear indication that he did not recognise Ḥusayn as the new caliph. With his subsidies withdrawn, Ibn Saʿud had little to lose by antagonising Britain, which so far had guaranteed the integrity of Sharifian rule.

In September 1924, Ibn Saʿud's troops appeared at Taʾif, a mountain resort near Mecca. The town was plundered for three days after which its inhabitants succumbed to Saʿudi rule. Under pressure from Hijazi notables Ḥusayn abdicated in favour of his son ʿAli on 6 October 1924. Ḥusayn was sent to the port of Jeddah where the British arranged for him to sail to ʿAqaba. It seems that the British finally decided to recognise the *fait accompli* of the Saʿudi invasion of Hijaz (Troeller 1976: 218). Britain, the mandatory power in Trans-Jordan, refused to allow Ḥusayn to settle with his son ʿAbdullah, for fear that this would encourage Saʿudi raids. Instead, Ḥusayn settled temporarily in ʿAqaba and later moved to Cyprus.

The abdication of Ḥusayn encouraged Ibn Saʿud to march on Mecca. His troops entered the holy city on 5 December 1924. From Mecca Ibn Saʿud insisted on Ḥusayn's successor, Sharif ʿAli, leaving Hijaz as a precondition for peace. Ibn Saʿud declared that the sole purpose of the invasion of Hijaz was to 'guarantee the liberty of pilgrimage and to settle the destiny of the Holy Land in a manner satisfactory to the Islamic world' (Troeller 1976: 220–1).

Ibn Saʿud's troops appeared at the gates of Jeddah in January 1925 and imposed a siege that lasted for almost a year. With British mediation, Sharif ʿAli left Jeddah as the city surrendered on 16 December 1925. The remaining major city in Hijaz, Madina, had already surrendered to Ibn Saʿud. With the main Hijazi cities under his control, Ibn Saʿud declared himself King of Hijaz in December 1925.[5] On 8 January 1926, the notables of Hijaz pledged allegiance to Ibn Saʿud and proclaimed him King of Hijaz and Sultan of Najd and its dependencies. Within three months, he was recognised by European powers who ruled over a substantial Muslim population, namely Great Britain, the USSR, France and the Netherlands (Troeller 1976: 231).

Ibn Saʿud's military campaigns in Arabia guaranteed the expansion of his authority over Najd, Hasa, Hijaz and ʿAsir. This was the first time that these four regions had been held under the authority of a single ruler since the Saʿudi–Wahhabi emirate of the eighteenth century. The military conquests were the background for the formation of the Saʿudi state in the twentieth century. Ibn Saʿud's conquests took place at a time when foreign intervention by Britain reached an unprecedented level. The defeat of the Ottoman Empire in the war was an important catalyst in this intervention, allowing Britain to deal with local amirs rather than the old empire. Britain played a crucial role in Ibn Saʿud's expansion into Haʾil and Hijaz. Its subsidies, ammunition and weapons upset the balance of power between Ibn Saʿud and Ibn Rashid. Moreover, Britain could not openly intervene in the Hijaz war between Ibn Saʿud and Ḥusayn as this would have antagonised its Muslim subjects. This eventually led to the demise of Sharifian rule in Hijaz. It seems that Britain abandoned Sharif Ḥusayn and failed to restrain Ibn Saʿud after promising the Sharif to maintain the integrity of his Hijazi kingdom.

With the conquest of Hijaz accomplished, Britain's main concern was to maintain the integrity of the two territories that fell under its mandate, namely Iraq and Trans-Jordan, where Ibn Saʿud represented a real threat to the newly established Hashemite monarchies. The British government sought to regulate the borders between Ibn Saʿud and his northern neighbours with the signing of the Bahra and Hadda Agreements in November 1925. These two agreements defined the frontiers between Ibn Saʿud and his Hashemite rivals. Moreover, they restricted the movement of nomadic tribes in the north. According to the Bahra Agreement between Ibn Saʿud and Iraq: 'Tribes subject to one of the two governments (Iraq and Najd) may not cross the frontier into the territory of the other government except after obtaining a permit from their own government and after the concurrence of the other government' (Troeller 1976: 227–31; Leatherdale 1983: 375).

A similar article was included in the Hadda Agreement with Trans-Jordan. These restrictions on the movement of tribes between the territories of Ibn Saʿud, Trans-Jordan and Iraq resulted in a serious challenge to Ibn Saʿud's authority by the *ikhwan* tribal force, discussed later in this chapter. Suffice it here to say that this was the first formal attempt to impose restrictions on and control of tribal movement in a region where international conventions and definition of borders by 'states' had so far been alien concepts. In 1925, the northern nomadic population whose subsistence was highly dependent on movement and migration suffered a second blow when Ibn Saʿud abolished the traditional *dira* (tribal territories) and announced that they were from then to be considered state land.

Having secured the upper Hijaz, Ibn Saʿud turned his attention again to ʿAsir when he signed the Treaty of Mecca with Ḥassan ibn ʿAli al-Idrisi in October 1926. Al-Idrisi acknowledged his status under the 'suzerainty of His Majesty the King of Hejaz, Sultan of Negd and its dependencies', and agreed not to 'enter into political negotiations with any Government or grant any economic concession to any person except with the sanction of His Majesty'. Ibn Saʿud agreed that the 'internal administration of ʿAsir and the supervision of its tribal affairs were dealt with by the Idrisis' (Leatherdale 1983: 379). This treaty allowed the semi-autonomous emirate of ʿAsir to coexist with Ibn Saʿud's dominions for a short while, but this status came to an end in 1930, as will be shown in the following chapter.

After the conquest of Hijaz, Britain was the main foreign power regulating the relationship between the newly emerging dominions of Ibn Saʿud and its mandated territories in the north. It was precisely after this conquest that the British government realised that its first treaty with Ibn Saʿud, signed in 1915, was 'patently inappropriate to the circumstances of 1926' (Leatherdale 1983: 63). The Treaty of Jeddah, signed in May 1927, recognised 'the complete and absolute independence of the dominions of his Majesty the King of the Hejaz and of Nejd and its Dependencies', and stipulated that Ibn Saʿud should undertake 'that the performance of the pilgrimage will be facilitated to British subjects and British protected persons of the Moslem faith'. The treaty reiterated that Ibn Saʿud should maintain 'friendly and peaceful relations with the territories of Kuwait and Bahrain, and with the Sheikhs of Qatar and the Oman Coast' (ibid.: 381). According to Leatherdale, Ibn Saʿud made sure that the treaty referred to the legality of his secular and historical rights, ensuring his right to choose his successor. Britain, however, did not include 'most-favoured-nation treatment, nor did it provide for a commercial treaty with Ibn Saʿud's dominions' (ibid.: 71). Britain's treaty with Ibn Saʿud, acknowledging his full and absolute independence, was almost unique in that it was not aimed at a state, such as Egypt or Iraq, but at a man (ibid.: 73). Britain limited the validity of the treaty to the reign of Ibn Saʿud.

However, Britain's intimate relationship with Ibn Saʿud remained ambiguous. Up to 1929, the British government, 'while taking heed of the exploits of Ibn Saud and the need to adapt relations with him, still had not come round to viewing him as a critical factor in Britain's position in the Arab world. Ibn Saud was still seven or eight years from achieving that kind of prominence' (Leatherdale 1983: 89). When Ibn Saʿud declared his realm the Kingdom of Saudi Arabia in 1932, this kingdom, like other Gulf states, was not a colony. They existed vaguely within the British Empire in special treaty relations with Britain. Although 'ambiguous', this special relationship with Britain remained absolute until the arrival of Americans *en masse* during and after the Second World War (Sluglett and Sluglett 1982: 54).

While Ibn Saʿud's special relationship with Britain was beginning to be formalised after the conquest of Hijaz, there were important local mechanisms that facilitated the Saʿudi expansion during the first three decades of the twentieth century. The story of the consolidation of Saʿudi rule is not complete without an assessment of local actors who played an equally important role in state formation. We turn our attention to the *muṭawwaʿa* and *ikhwan* of Najd.

THE *MUṬAWWAʿA* OF NAJD

Najdi men of religion were known in the local dialect as *muṭawwaʿa*. Although today the term *muṭawwaʿa* refers to a specific profession within the religious establishment, at the beginning of the twentieth century the term had a wider meaning than the contemporary, often negative, connotation.[6] In 1900 a *muṭawwaʿ* was a member of the *ḥaḍar* who had acquired a religious education after a period of study with a distinguished member of the *ʿulama*, based in the main towns of southern Najd (mainly Riyadh) and Qasim (ʿUnayzah) after which he became a specialist in jurisprudence and matters relating to *ʿibada* (Islamic rituals). The term *muṭawwaʿ* embodies both obedience and compulsion. A *muṭawwaʿ* was a volunteer who enforced obedience to Islam and performance of its rituals.

The *muṭawwaʿa* were a Najdi phenomenon. They differed from religious scholars in other parts of the Islamic world, commonly referred to as *ʿulama*. Historically Najdi men of religion often studied, taught and applied Ḥanbali *fiqh* only, and considered other branches of the religious and linguistic sciences as intellectual luxuries that were not needed in their own society (al-Juhany 1983: 252). As they were *fiqh* and *ʿibada* experts, it is more accurate to describe them as 'religious ritual specialists', or simply 'ritual specialists'. The term *ʿulama* evokes an image of religious scholars whose knowledge and expertise often encompassed other branches of religious science in addition to *fiqh*. With the exception of perhaps some of the descendants of Muhammad ibn ʿAbd al-Wahhab, known as Al Shaykh, and a handful of other Najdi personalities who had maintained a tradition of wide religious scholarship since the eighteenth century, the majority of Najdi men of religion were of the *muṭawwaʿ* type. They were preoccupied with ritualistic Islam and exhibited limited expertise in theology. They practised their expertise in conjunction with agriculture and trade.

Most Saʿudi chroniclers of Najdi *ʿulama* do not make the distinction between the *ʿulama* and the *muṭawwaʿa* (al-Bassam 1978). In their accounts, all Najdi men of religion are referred to as *ʿulama*. However, to call early twentieth-century Najdi *fiqh* specialists *ʿulama* would be misleading. Najd did not have an important centre for religious learning comparable to Mecca, Cairo and Najaf. With the exception of a handful of *ʿulama* in Riyadh and Qasim, the majority of religious specialists were in fact *muṭawwaʿa*.

The enforcement of ritualistic Islam by the Najdi *muṭawwaʿa* was significant in the process of state formation. Between 1902 and 1932 the regime of 'discipline and punishment' enforced by the *muṭawwaʿa* who were constantly preoccupied with ritualistic Islam was essential for domesticating the Arabian population into accepting the political authority of Ibn Saʿud after he captured Riyadh in 1902.

Najdi ritual specialists needed a politico-military figure, a symbolic *imam* to endorse their cause. Who would be better suited for this mission than Ibn

Saʿud, whose ancestors had continuously supported them since the famous alliance of 1744? When Ibn Saʿud entered Riyadh, they declared him their *imam*, hoping to develop their own ascendancy. The symbolic title of *imam* granted him a most needed legitimacy.[7] In return, the *muṭawwaʿa* were assured of sympathetic political and military leadership. It is important to note that Ibn Saʿud was not perceived as their amir or tribal shaykh. He could only be their *imam*, a title impregnated with the same religious symbolism that had already been granted to his ancestors. The *muṭawwaʿa* were not only his instructors during his years of exile in Kuwait, but also his maternal kin and later his affines. From the age of seven, the young Ibn Saʿud had been placed under the religious authority of several religious figures, most famous of whom was ʿAbdullah ibn ʿAbd al-Laṭif Al Shaykh, a descendant of Muhammad ibn ʿAbd al-Wahhab. This specialist taught him 'the doctrine of *tawḥid* and *fiqh* through a pamphlet especially prepared for him' (al-Zirkili 1972: 17). Ibn Saʿud himself was initiated in these two areas, considered the most important by the *muṭawwaʿa* (Ḥamza 1936: 13). His instructor, the maternal grandfather of King Faysal (1964–75), became his father-in-law.

The majority of the *muṭawwaʿa* were drawn from among the sedentary population of the oases of Najd. They did not emerge within a short period of time, nor did Ibn Saʿud bring them into existence. They were an already existing socio-religious group which had been brought up on the teachings of the reformer Muhammad ibn ʿAbd al-Wahhab since the eighteenth century. Such religious specialists had existed in almost every town and oasis in Najd even before the reform movement had gathered momentum in the eighteenth century (al-Juhany 1983). Najdi settlements had mosques where religious scholars taught the principles of faith and Islamic rituals. Their students became mosque *imams* and preachers. Those with more sophisticated religious knowledge acted as judges who administered the *shariʿa* under the patronage of local amirs.

The holy alliance between Ibn Saʿud and the Najdi ritual specialists is important for understanding the origins of the Saʿudi polity in the twentieth century. This alliance was also the mechanism that contributed to its continuity. Ritual specialists performed important functions in the process of state formation. Their Wahhabi training predisposed them towards an idea of the state as a partnership between the symbolic *imam*, 'leader of the community', and the religious specialists, the former enforcing the religious rulings of the latter. It is important to note that this idea of partnership was not the outcome of the *muṭawwaʿa*'s own intellectual activity, but had already been developed by more established men of religion, several of them descendants of Muhammad ibn ʿAbd al-Wahhab, who were of the *ʿulama* type.

Wahhabi religious specialists accepted the doctrine that power is legitimate however it may have been seized, and that obedience to whoever wields this power is incumbent upon all his subjects (al-Azmeh 1993: 107). Wahhabi specialists were thus pragmatic in the sense that they were able to switch allegiance from one ruler to another without doctrinal difficulties.

In the Wahhabi idea of the state Ibn Saʿud found a conceptual framework crucial for the consolidation of his rule. He was granted legitimacy as long as he championed the cause of the religious specialists, becoming the guardian of ritualistic Islam. His legitimacy sprang from the recognition and enforcement of the *shariʿa*, a divine law above him and independent of his will (al-Azmeh 1993: 230). As long as he allowed himself to be governed by this law and the way it was interpreted by the Riyadh *ʿulama*, he was able to rule. Such concepts of authority and power were crucial for promoting ambitious leadership.

Often the *muṭawwaʿa* arrived among the tribal confederations before Ibn Saʿud's raiding troops.[8] Among the sedentary population, the *muṭawwaʿa* were already part of the community as a socio-religious group. They facilitated Saʿudi expansion by familiarising the population with the above-mentioned ideas. However, one should not imagine that between 1902 and 1932 the *muṭawwaʿa* were engaged in elaborate discussions of the nature of the Islamic state with their audience. The people they indoctrinated were not concerned with theological debates on the nature of the Islamic theory of the state and the just ruler, partly because they were illiterate, but more importantly because the majority of the *muṭawwaʿa* themselves had no expertise in such theoretical matters. It is more likely that the *muṭawwaʿa* were confined to teaching the Qurʾan and *ʿibada*, in which they had a distinct specialisation. In addition, they preached the importance of obedience to *wali al-amr*, leader of the Muslim community. Obedience should be manifested in readiness to pay him *zakat* and respond to his call for *jihad*. Both *zakat* and *jihad* were at the heart of the Wahhabi idea of the state, and were considered crucial mechanisms for its consolidation.

Moreover, religious specialists were an indigenous community specialising in the administration of *fiqh*. Their main concern was with the disciplining of the others in the pursuit of the main Islamic rituals such as prayer, fasting, *jihad*, payment of *zakat* and *ḥajj* (pilgrimage). They were religious teachers with a sacred knowledge. Among other things, they taught people how to perform ablution without water, to pray without literacy, to recite the Qurʾan without understanding, to practise true Islam without innovations, to bury the dead without marking their graves, and to worship God without mediators. The list was long indeed. In addition to launching a regime of 'discipline', they were also, as the self-appointed guardians of true Islam, concerned with 'punishment'. These ritual specialists became the nucleus of the Committee for the Propagation of Virtue and Prohibition of Vice.

The *muṭawwaʿa* of Najd initiated whole communities in the art of obedience and submission. Although this submission was meant to be to a higher authority, that of God, in practice they implied that without submission to the political authority of Ibn Saʿud, the faith and deeds of Muslims would be threatened. Najdi religious ritual specialists were dispatched to sedentary communities and tribal confederations alike. Although they openly practised their preaching and peacefully invited people to 'return' to the true path of Islam, they often had to use violence against those who refused to submit to their authority. They themselves were permitted to carry out physical punishment.

This often took the form of publicly lashing those who violated their code of behaviour. The *muṭawwaʿa* were often remembered as wandering with a long stick, which they used now and then to punish any reluctance to perform the prescribed rituals. Among the public, they used methods of punishment mastered in their own small *madrasa*s, schools where they taught the sons of local notables, merchants and landowners. Almana described their methods of punishment in 1926 when he arrived in Riyadh. He mentions that a senior member of the royal court had been lashed in public because a *muṭawwaʿ* suspected he did not perform communal prayers. The *muṭawwaʿa* were also known to have cut, in public, the hair and shirts of men who exceeded the prescribed 'Islamic' length. Ibn Saʿud was not spared public punishment when the *muṭawwaʿa* criticised him for wearing a long shirt. On one occasion they ordered his shirt to be shortened while he was wearing it. Scissors were fetched and the act was completed (Almana 1980: 111–12).

The same methods of punishment continued afterwards. A Najdi notable who had been the student of a notorious Riyadh ritual specialist in the 1940s recalled his experience when he arrived at his religious school one morning wearing a wristwatch, a gift from Ibn Saʿud himself to his father. The young boy was not capable of containing his joy over this unusual new acquisition. The *muṭawwaʿ* pulled him over and with a long stick smashed the watch on his wrist. The rest of the pupils watched with horror. This public display of punishment was justified by the *muṭawwaʿ*, who told him the wristwatch was *bidʿa*, of the devil's work. The boy was told that he should not have worn it on his wrist, but should have put it in his pocket, as the *muṭawwaʿ* did. The boy returned to his parents who could not utter a word of protest. Instead, the boy was reprimanded for defying the sacred authority of this famous Riyadh *muṭawwaʿ*. If this was the method of enforcing religious knowledge and practice among the notables of Riyadh in the 1940s, we can only begin to speculate on how those ritual specialists treated the commoners, whether in the oases or among the tribal confederations of the Arabian Peninsula during Ibn Saʿud's military campaigns.

Historically the majority of those described here as ritual specialists originated in the small settlements of southern Najd and Qasim. In local terminology they were *ḥaḍar*, who had not retained genealogical links with the tribal confederations. Some ritual specialists claimed descent from well-known sedentary groups in the Arabian social hierarchy (for example Banu Tamim), while others had lost both the connection and the memory of such descent.

Their religious specialisation was combined with worldly endeavours such as trade and agriculture (al-Bassam 1978). While a minority of specialists attained wealth as a result of involvement in the trade network between Najd, Iraq, the Arabian Gulf and India, the majority remained poor and provincial. One of their chroniclers, al-Bassam, describes them as men whose genealogy and wealth were *'al-ʿilm wa al-khuluq'*, knowledge and morality (ibid.).

Although religious specialists did not exhibit the same kinship and genealogical structures as those among the tribal confederations, it is accurate to describe them as a closely knit group, united by religious knowledge and practice. Their knowledge was derived from well-known religious scholars, for example the descendants of Muhammad ibn ʿAbd al-Wahhab. This knowledge emanated from one source, the teachings of the eighteenth-century reformer. This was the backbone of their unity as a group. After their apprenticeship, they practised their calling in various settlements in northern Najd, Qasim and southern Najd. A common source of knowledge enhanced their loyalty to each other, and created everlasting bonds of friendship and camaraderie.

Their solidarity also stemmed from family connections. Some Najdi families produced several ritual specialists, who were often close kinsmen. For example, the families of Al Shaykh, al-ʿAngari, ibn ʿAtiq, ibn Blayhid, al-Salim, al-Sayf and al-ʿIssa were all Najdi religious families with several members dedicating their life to *daʿwa* (al-Bassam 1978: vol. I, 745: ʿAbdullah 1995: 53). It was not uncommon to find several brothers from one family specialising in religious study. Some of these families had been associated with religious knowledge since the eighteenth century, whereas others were initiated into it at a later date.

It seems that before Ibn Saʿud captured Riyadh, the *muṭawwaʿa* were lacking in prestige and authority. Among their own people, that is the sedentary population, religious specialists enjoyed a certain esteem in return for performing important practical functions, for example mediation, dispute settlement and religious guidance relating to *awqaf* (religious endowments), marriage, inheritance and divorce. However, when they showed excessive zeal, a higher political authority was often capable of undermining their rulings. Their decisions could not always be enforced without the consent of the local amir. The story of the expulsion of Muhammad ibn ʿAbd al-Wahhab from ʿUyaynah in the eighteenth century was a classic case of a religious specialist coming into conflict with the political leadership over excessive application of the rules of *shariʿa*.

Among the tribal confederations, neither sacred knowledge nor piety granted ritual specialists an elevated status. They were at best tolerated and at worst dismissed with ease. During the first two decades of the twentieth century, in Haʾil, the capital of the Rashidi emirate, religious specialists coexisted with sedentary Shammar tribesmen, none of whom would have considered a career in religious learning. It was simply a job that those without a tribe would find appealing. Salih Salem al-Banyan, a Haʾil *muṭawwaʿ*, was described as a man whose genealogy was '*al-din wa al-khuluq*' (religion and morality). Having studied with ʿAbdullah ibn ʿAbd al-Laṭif Al Shaykh when this scholar was summoned to Haʾil by the Rashidi amir during the late years of the nineteenth century, al-Banyan was described as a 'dedicated man of religion'. The ruler of Haʾil once said that if this specialist was sent to Satan, he would have succeeded in converting him to Islam. After several disagreements with other scholars in Haʾil, al-Banyan became unpopular with its ruler, who expelled him to the neighbouring oasis of Taymaʾ (al-Bassam 1978: 349). Another Haʾil *muṭawwaʿ*, Ibn Khalaf, was also not tolerated by the Rashidi amir. Ibn Khalaf demanded the expulsion of the Mashahida, a Shiʿa merchant community resident in the oasis for decades, but was himself expelled to Taymaʾ (ibid.: 537). The amir of Haʾil could not expel this important community of taxpayers even though the *muṭawwaʿa* considered them outside the realm of true Islam.

Among the nomadic sections of the tribal confederations, religious specialists were virtually unknown, and were often not consulted if there was an alternative value system deriving from tribal custom, tradition and law. If a nomad wanted religious counsel, he would visit the nearest oasis. In most cases he would wait until he needed to visit the oasis for more urgent matters, for example the purchase of dates or the selling of his sheep and wool.

The *muṭawwaʿa* enjoyed a limited authority in Arabia on the eve of Ibn Saʿud's return to Riyadh. They retained, however, a vivid memory of their fortunes during the first Saʿudi emirate of the eighteenth century, when they became active participants in political, financial and military issues. This was their first experience of living in the court of the *imam* (ʿAbdullah 1995). They benefited from the emirate's expansion in an unprecedented manner. Political stability meant increased religious knowledge and scholarship, prosperous trade and growing state revenues, which they shared with the political head of the emirate. The treasury was shared between them and Saʿudi rulers. Their eminence in the eighteenth century is in sharp contrast with their decline in the nineteenth century.

The *muṭawwaʿa* suffered a serious disaster with the Egyptian invasion of Arabia at the beginning of the nineteenth century. The deportation and slaughter of several religious specialists accompanied the capture of the Saʿudi ruler of Dirʿiyyah by Ibrahim Pasha in 1818, the majority belonging to Al Shaykh (al-Bassam 1978). Najdi religious knowledge was almost eradicated. After the sacking of Dirʿiyyah the monopoly of the Al Shaykh was partially weakened as new religious specialists began to emerge. While Ibn Saʿud's chief judge, Muhammad ibn Ibrahim, was a member of the Al Shaykh family, for the large-scale 'domestication' of the tribal confederations Ibn Saʿud relied on a wider circle of specialists, often drawn from less well-established Najdi religious families.

The demise of the religious specialists, especially members of Al Shaykh, at the hands of the Egyptian troops in 1818 weakened them. The *muṭawwaʿa* obviously did not want to fall victim to such a disaster again, an annihilation from which they did not fully recover until the twentieth century. After the collapse of the first Saʿudi–Wahhabi emirate, those *muṭawwaʿa* who survived lagged behind in religious scholarship as they desperately tried to guard the legacy of Muhammad ibn ʿAbd al-Wahhab. Several descendants of this scholar lived and died in exile, in Egypt (Bligh 1985: 38). The exiled Wahhabi scholars remained in Egypt where they taught the principles of the Ḥanbali school of Islamic jurisprudence at the Azhar mosque, thus leaving the Najdi *muṭawwaʿa* with no important sources of religious authority throughout most of the nineteenth century.

Having lost their material wealth, prestige and status in the nineteenth century, the *muṭawwaʿa* were predisposed to accept a political figure who promised not only their salvation but also a reversal of their misfortune.

This is not to undermine their genuine determination to revive the religious message of their ancestor and his reforms. There is no doubt about their commitment to deliver the rest of Arabia from its recurrent state of 'ignorance and savagery'. They aspired towards an era whereby the rule of the *shariʿa* would be supreme, which would among other things restore their own status and authority.

It is not surprising that between 1902 and 1930 the *muṭawwaʿa* exercised their newly acquired authority with zeal and dedication. When Ibn Saʿud arrived in Riyadh, he invested them with prestige as he showed them respect in return for their success in extracting recognition of his rule from rebellious groups that would not willingly accept his government. In return for 'disciplining' and 'punishing' the people of Arabia, they would be rewarded materially and symbolically. Traditionally, ritual specialists did not receive salaries from local amirs; the more fortunate among them made their livings as farmers and merchants while the rest lived off charitable donations and endowments for mosques. Others asked for money in return for religious services, judgment and advice, a practice which Muhammad ibn ʿAbd al-Wahhab considered a kind of bribe, compromising their impartiality (al-Juhany 1983: 252). Ibn Saʿud enlisted them in the service of his domain as he employed them and paid their salaries in cash and kind. He thus transformed them into full-time religious ritual specialists, loyal to him and dependent on his resources. In return, Ibn Saʿud was guaranteed the political submission of the Arabian population under the guise of submission to God. The *muṭawwaʿa* were expected to 'flog all persons who were caught smoking, wearing fine adornment or procrastinating in their religious duties . . . They were also responsible for the collection of *zakat* for the central government' (Helms 1981: 131). Both the regime of moral discipline and the collection of *zakat* were important mechanisms behind the consolidation of Saʿudi authority in Arabia.

A new holy alliance between Ibn Saʿud and the religious specialists began with the 1902 *bayʿa*, the oath of allegiance. This oath was given to Ibn Saʿud after he captured Riyadh and killed its governor, who had ruled the city on behalf of the Rashidi amirs of Ha'il. After the Friday prayer, religious specialists, notables and ordinary residents of Riyadh assembled to hear the confirmation of Ibn Saʿud as the new *imam*. Ibn Saʿud's father, ʿAbd al-Raḥman, remained a revered figure. To show his approval of the new arrangement, ʿAbd al-Raḥman presented his son with the sword of Saʿud al-Kabir (an ancestor of Ibn Saʿud), with its sharp Damascene edge, a handle decorated with gold, and a silver case (al-Zirkili 1972: 32). The 1902 *bayʿa* had a symbolic significance, similar to the pact of 1744 between the Saʿudi amir of Dirʿiyyah and Muhammad ibn ʿAbd al-Wahhab.

Riyadh immediately became a centre of attraction for scholars from all the towns in Najd. Already established Najdi ritual specialists and newly emerging ones found Riyadh a safe haven under the auspices of Ibn Saʿud. Most Najdi religious specialists had already had contact with their counterparts in Riyadh through periods of study with them or regular visits. From now on, religious students came to Riyadh for periods of training and instruction. They were later dispatched to spread the call among the tribal confederations and the sedentary communities.

An anecdote from the Shammar, the tribal confederation that initially resisted the indoctrination programme of the *muṭawwaʿa* and continued to oppose Ibn Saʿud until 1921, indicates the contradiction between what the religious specialists preached and the social and cultural background of the confederations. The scene was an encounter between two Shammar shaykhs to discuss how to resist the threat of Ibn Saʿud's forces, which were approaching Haʾil with the objective of terminating the rule of the Rashidis and their tribal confederation. Nada ibn Nuhayer, the shaykh of the Waybar Shammar, suggested that to save the autonomy of the tribe, the Shammar 'should wear their ʿ*amaym* [the head gear of the *ikhwan*]', implying that the Shammar should adopt the message of reformist Islam, become *ikhwan*, and wear the distinctive head-cloth of those who had already become *ikhwan*. The other Shammar shaykh present, ʿOkab ibn ʿAjil, replied: '*ḥina ma khadhinaha bi ba wa ta, ḥina khadhinaha bi al-sayf*' (Shammar supremacy was not achieved with knowledge of the ABC; it was achieved with the sword). After the demise of Haʾil in 1921, some Shammar sections preferred to flee to Iraq rather than become subject to the regime of discipline and punishment, and the political submission this entailed.

Those who were subjected to this regime experienced an everlasting change. Descriptions of the character of the Muṭayr tribal chief as a result of his indoctrination by the *muṭawwaʿa* indicate the scope of this process: 'Faysal al-Duwaysh, shaykh of Muṭayr, was a savage, arrogant and shrewd bedouin. He became shaykh after his father. When he lived in ʿArṭawiyyah, his behaviour and concerns changed as a result of the effort of the ʿ*ulama*, *qaḍis*, and *muṭawwaʿa*' (al-Zirkili 1972: 166). In conjunction with the 'discipline and punishment' programme, al-Duwaysh, like many other tribal shaykhs, was 'invited' to reside in Riyadh in order to receive religious education from its most esteemed practitioners, whose elevated status meant that they remained closer to the centre of power. The so-called invitation was another mechanism for control, to ensure the submission of tribal confederations. If a shaykh refused the 'invitation', his position would be undermined as Ibn Saʿud would elevate another member of the shaykh's lineage to the post of tribal shaykh. Among tribal confederations, there was often no shortage of eligible lineages.

After the capture of Riyadh, the *muṭawwaʿa* of Najd were the first instrument used by Ibn Saʿud to conquer Arabia. Under the guise of religious education, enforcing the *shariʿa* and guarding public morality, the *muṭawwaʿa* ensured the submission of most of the population that came under the authority of Ibn Saʿud between 1902 and 1932. This included the sedentary people of the oases of Najd and the nomadic tribal confederations. The *muṭawwaʿa* also played a crucial role in the creation of the *ikhwan* fighting force.

THE *IKHWAN*

Between 1902 and 1912, Ibn Saʿud's army consisted mainly of the townsmen of southern Najd, who saw their participation in his raids as a mechanism for defending their own commercial interests. The most loyal fighters were from ʿAriḍ in southern Najd. They formed the core of the royal guard and were considered *jihad* warriors. They were distinguished from others, for example tribal confederations, by their permanent service with Ibn Saʿud (Vassiliev 1998: 307).

It was only in 1907–8, when Ibn Saʿud was threatened by the rebellion of the ʿAraʾif branch of his own family (descendants of Ibn Saʿud's uncle, Saʿud), together with some ʿAjman tribesmen, that the idea of a tribal force began to take shape. The ʿAraʾif rebellion was assisted by a nomadic tribal confederation. Ibn Saʿud realised that his conquests in Qasim and southern Najd could be easily undermined by the confederations as long as they continued to practise nomadism and maintain their political autonomy.

Thanks to the education programme of the *muṭawwaʿa*, Ibn Saʿud was able to create a semi-permanent fighting force drawn from among the tribal confederations. The role of the *muṭawwaʿa* in state formation has to be understood in conjunction with another instrument, the *ikhwan*, the tribal military force with which Ibn Saʿud conquered Hasa, Haʾil and Hijaz. The literature on the formation of the present Saʿudi state gives us a detailed analysis of this force with which Ibn Saʿud conquered various regions (Habib 1978; Kostiner 1985; Lackner 1978; Helms 1981; ʿAbd al-ʿAziz 1993; al-Yassini 1985). In this literature, there is a strong emphasis on the prominent role of the *ikhwan*, a religio-tribal corps that subjugated Arabia for Ibn Saʿud. The *ikhwan* were

> those Bedouins who accepted the fundamentals of orthodox Islam of the Ḥanbali school as preached by Abdl-Wahhab which their fathers and forefathers had forgotten or had perverted and who through the persuasion of the religious missionaries and with the material assistance of Abdl-Aziz abandoned their nomadic life to live in the Hijrah which were built by him for them. (Habib 1978: 16)

After the sedentary people of the Najdi oases, the *ikhwan* were the first organised military force to be subjected to the *muṭawwaʿa*'s education programme among the nomadic population. The *ikhwan* were recruited from among the tribal confederations of Arabia. They initially received the *muṭawwaʿa* in their nomadic camps, but later some confederations consented to settle in *hujjar*, village settlements that emerged around wells where agricultural work was possible. The word *hujjar* evokes the early migration of the Prophet Muhammad from Mecca to Madina where he established the first Muslim community in the seventh century. The *muṭawwaʿa*'s instruction required a sedentary lifestyle where preachers and judges could function according to the authentic Islamic tradition of the Prophet. The tribal confederations were therefore required to abandon their nomadic existence, settle in the *hujjar* and practise Islam as preached by the *muṭawwaʿa*. They were also expected to practise agricultural work. Sedentarisation was obviously more suited for religious indoctrination, military enlistment and control. Those who agreed to settle and endorse the *muṭawwaʿa*'s teaching became known as *ikhwan*. They were taught to obey the legitimate *imam* and respond to his call for *jihad* (ʿAbd al-ʿAziz 1993: 105).

With the *ikhwan*, the tension between central power and the tribal periphery, which had plagued previous Saʿudi emirates and had often led to their demise, was partially overcome. Ibn Saʿud incorporated the tribal confederations in a semi-permanent force, which was not meant to disperse after raids against settlements or confederations. Habib argues that what Ibn Saʿud needed was a fighting force that had the mobility of the bedouins and the loyalty, bravery, dedication and stability of the townsmen (Habib 1978: 15). In this respect, the emerging Saʿudi polity differed from previous emirates because it demanded from the very beginning the commitment of tribal confederations to sedentary life, under the guise of religious education.

As the sedentarisation of the tribal confederations was expected to lead to the practice of agriculture, the *hujjar* settlements clustered in central

Najd where arable land and water were available. The first most famous *ikhwan* settlement, ʿArṭawiyyah, north of Riyadh, was founded in 1912 as the settlement of the Muṭayr tribal confederation under the leadership of Faysal al-Duwaysh. This settlement received ʿAbdullah al-ʿAngari from Tharmadah who was sent to educate the Muṭayr confederation. By the age of sixteen al-ʿAnghari had acquired his religious scholarship in Riyadh under the patronage of ʿAbdullah ibn ʿAbd al-Laṭif Al Shaykh (al-Bassam 1978: 582; ʿAbd al-ʿAziz 1993: 104). In addition to his religious instruction among this tribal confederation, al-ʿAngari was also a judge in Sudayr. After al-ʿAngari, another religious scholar by the name of ʿOmar ibn Muhammad ibn Salim was dispatched to continue the indoctrination of the Muṭayr confederation. The military importance of the Muṭayr was perhaps the reason why Ibn Saʿud chose more distinguished religious scholars rather than ordinary *muṭawwaʿa* to instruct them and complete their indoctrination.

In 1913, sections of the ʿUtayba tribe, under the leadership of their chief Sultan ibn Bijad, were settled in al-Ghaṭghaṭ (ʿAbd al-ʿAziz 1993; Habib 1978). The pattern of ʿArṭawiyyah was followed. ʿUtayba tribesmen received the *muṭawwaʿa* who instructed them in matters relating to fasting, prayers and other Islamic rituals. They were also instructed to obey Ibn Saʿud as the legitimate *imam* of the Muslim community and to pay him *zakat*. Each of these settlements attracted on average 1,500 people.

According to Habib almost 150,000 tribesmen were settled by 1926 (Habib 1978). By 1930, it was hard to find a tribal confederation that did not have tribal sections associated with settlements. While some tribal sections voluntarily accepted settlement because of hardships caused by a combination of climatic factors and the economic pressures associated with the First World War, others were forced to settle after being defeated by the forces of Ibn Saʿud. The *ikhwan* accepted the authority of Ibn Saʿud as *imam* of the Muslim community who was responsible for negotiations with foreign powers and the call for *jihad*. They also accepted the authority of the Riyadh ʿ*ulama* as guardians and interpreters of the divine law (Helms 1981: 131). However, both Ibn Saʿud and the ʿ*ulama* of Riyadh were remote. The *muṭawwaʿa* lived among the *ikhwan* in the settlement and had closer direct contact with them. Not only did the *muṭawwaʿa* instruct in matters relating to religion, they also distributed various material benefits from Ibn Saʿud. As agricultural work in the settlements was neither productive nor successful, the allegiance of the *ikhwan* depended on a continuous flow of subsidies from Ibn Saʿud's treasury. The *muṭawwaʿa* distributed regular and annual gifts among the *ikhwan* and their families (Habib 1978; Helms 1981; ʿAbd al-ʿAziz 1993). Together with a share of the booty gained after raids and military conquests, these subsidies strengthened the allegiance of the *ikhwan* to Ibn Saʿud.

While the *muṭawwaʿa* exerted mental coercion among those whom they were meant to educate in Islamic rituals, the *ikhwan* practised physical coercion against people in Arabia. In Hasa, Haʾil and Hijaz, they exercised their powers without restraint.[9] They terrorised people under the guise of enforcing the *shariʿa*, Islamising Arabia and reforming religious practices. Their worst atrocities were committed in Hasa against the Shiʿa population in 1913 and in the Hijazi resort of Taʾif in 1924.[10] The *ikhwan* carried out public prosecutions and looted and plundered the towns and their inhabitants. They became known in Arabia as *jund al-tawḥid*, the soldiers who enforced the doctrine of the oneness of God. They distinguished themselves by their dress and manners. They wore short white shirts and white headgear, reflecting their puritan and austere interpretation of Islam. They refused to greet both non-Muslims and Muslims whose Islam was regarded as corrupt, such as for example the Shiʿa and the Hijazis. Their uncompromising attitude and ability to inflict severe punishment created an atmosphere of fear and apprehension among people. Their reputation travelled fast in Arabia even before they arrived at the gates of oases and towns. The *ikhwan* were anchored in historical memory as 'ignorant and ferocious'. It seems that the *ikhwan* endorsed fully the teachings of their mentors, the *muṭawwaʿa*, and acted according to a literal interpretation of these teachings.

Both the *muṭawwaʿa* and the *ikhwan* operated a system of terror difficult to evade as long as they had the full support of Ibn Saʿud and the ʿ*ulama* of Riyadh. It seems that after they secured the conquest of Hijaz in 1926, their power was beginning to be resented in Riyadh. The holy alliance that began with the *muṭawwaʿa* and the *ikhwan* was reversed when they staged a rebellion against Ibn Saʿud's authority.

AN ALLIANCE NOT SO HOLY: IBN SAʿUD, THE *MUṬAWWAʿA* AND THE *IKHWAN*

Ibn Saʿud himself was 'domesticated' by the *muṭawwaʿa* in a manner similar to that experienced by the rest of the Arabian population. It is alleged that he once admitted that when he came across the most senior member of the ʿ*ulama*, ʿAbdullah ibn ʿAbd al-Laṭif Al Shaykh, in the narrow streets of Riyadh, he used to sweat from fear (al-Zirkili 1972: 197). It is also alleged that when this important Wahhabi scholar died in 1922, Ibn Saʿud declared: 'Today I am the ruler of Najd.' It is unlikely that Ibn Saʿud feared him for religious reasons. Ibn Saʿud was renowned for his piety and religious observance, which he regularly displayed in public. It is certain, however, that he feared the ʿ*alim*'s withdrawal of support. Such withdrawal had historical precedents.

The scholar's decisions during the internal strife among the Saʿudi brothers in the 1870s demonstrated the ease with which he switched allegiance from one brother to another (Crawford 1982). He granted the oath of allegiance to whoever happened to conquer Riyadh at the time. This continued to haunt Ibn Saʿud in the 1920s.

We cannot take for granted that the Riyadh ʿ*ulama*, especially the descendants of Muhammad ibn ʿAbd al-Wahhab, were automatically predisposed to grant the oath of allegiance to Ibn Saʿud on the basis of his descent or his ancestors' marital alliances with Al Shaykh. In 1891, ʿAbdullah ibn ʿAbd al-Laṭif swore allegiance to a Rashidi, Muhammad ibn Rashid, the new master of Najd who had resolved the power struggle among the Saʿudi ruling group and expelled the last Saʿudi ruler, ʿAbd al-Raḥman, to Kuwait (Crawford 1982: 235). The scholar was acting in accordance with the principle that 'a tyrannical Sultan was better than perpetual strife' (ibid.). The scholar was taken to Haʾil for two years where he taught several local Haʾil students (al-Bassam 1978: 349, 537), after which he returned to Riyadh. Moreover, when Ibn Saʿud appeared on the outskirts of Riyadh in 1900 during his first failed attempt to recapture the town, ʿAbdullah ibn ʿAbd al-Laṭif sided with the Rashidis and helped defend the town against him (Bligh 1985: 45). It was only in 1902 when it became clear to him that Ibn Saʿud had actually captured Riyadh and killed the Rashidi governor that he was prepared to offer Ibn Saʿud the oath of allegiance.

After the 1902 oath of allegiance, Najdis began to refer to Ibn Saʿud as *imam*. His expanding domain was referred to in local parlance as an emirate. Both the sedentary population and the tribal confederations had already been familiar with the notions of imamate and emirate. While the imamate was anchored in religious discourse, the emirate was tied to a perception of power specific to the context of Arabia. After the capture of Haʾil, Ibn Saʿud became the regional power in central Arabia. He emerged as the undisputed ruler of a large territory. Hasa, Qasim and northern Najd succumbed to his leadership to the detriment of local power centres. Ibn Saʿud adopted the title *imam* to distinguish his realm from the tribal emirates of Arabia and minor local oasis/town amirs.

During the summer of 1921, Ibn Saʿud declared himself 'Sultan over the whole of Najd and its dependencies' (Kostiner 1993: 18–35). Religious specialists sanctioned the new title. 'Sultan' seemed acceptable to both the

Najdi population and its men of religion since it was based on a familiar concept well developed in religious discourse. As such it was not perceived as a deviation from the imamate. However, the title of sultan remained a formality, an irrelevance to the majority of those who became Ibn Saʿud's subjects. In 1921, Ibn Saʿud was still perceived by the sedentary population and the tribal confederations as the regional ruler of Najd who managed to eliminate a number of power centres and impose his own hegemony over vast territories, a scenario too familiar to them. By November 1921, southern Najd, Jabal Shammar and Hasa had become part of his realm. Their local leaders had already been eliminated.

The title 'sultan' was meant for external consumption, to impress external powers, mainly Britain, with his achievements. Ibn Saʿud adopted the title immediately after Faysal, the son of King Ḥusayn of Hijaz, became King of Iraq. While Arabia had known several amirs, in 1921 there was undoubtedly only one sultan in central Arabia. In their Arabian Affairs correspondence, British officers could dispatch letters pointing to the Sultan of Najd, from now on an easily identifiable figure above other local Najdi power centres. As far as Britain was concerned, there remained in Arabia Ibn Saʿud, the Sultan of Najd, and Sharif Ḥusayn, the King of Hijaz. In August 1921, Britain confirmed Ibn Saʿud's title.

When Ibn Saʿud captured Hijaz from its Sharifian rulers in 1926, religious specialists confirmed him as King of Hijaz and Sultan of Najd. Hijazis were familiar with the idea of kingship, since Sharif Ḥusayn had adopted the title in 1916. Already familiar with both the Hijazi Shafiʿi and Ottoman Ḥanafi schools, Hijazi *ʿulama* had no problem with the concept of kingship. After the capture of Mecca, Ibn Saʿud came into immediate contact with such *ʿulama*. He summoned the Hijazi notables and asked them to 'designate a time when the most senior and most distinguished *ʿulama*, notables, merchants and people of opinion could be present to discuss their government under his supervision' (Ḥamza 1936: 98).

The title 'King in Hijaz and Sultan in Najd' implied a duality, reflecting Ibn Saʿud's reluctance to put the loyalty of the Najdi *ʿulama*, who were perhaps not ready for such a political innovation, to the ultimate test in 1926. Najdi *ʿulama* aspired to have an *imam*-turned-into-sultan championing their cause. They found such a person in Ibn Saʿud. The imamate was a concept well developed in Ḥanbali theology. The sultanate was a concept which was closely linked to the imamate in their own religious texts. In 1926 the transfer from imamate to kingship, however, would have been premature. It took a further round of events to predispose the Najdi *ʿulama* to accept the idea of a king in their own territory.

In 1926 Najdi ʿ*ulama* were still euphoric after the capture of the two Hijazi holy cities, a victory promising the extension of their regime of punishment and discipline to the holiest of all provinces. At that time they were still concerned with issues relating to the 'purification' of Islamic practices from all innovations. If Hasa was considered by the Wahhabi ʿ*ulama* to be a breeding ground for innovations due to the practices of its Shiʿa population (al-Ḥasan 1994), Hijaz had a similar status in their minds due to its association with Ottoman Islam. Najdi ʿ*ulama* were happy to see their pupils, the *muṭawwaʿa*, actively involved in 'Islamising' the Hijazi population.

With the capture of Hijaz, Najdi ʿ*ulama* immediately began debating whether the Hijazi telegraph and other technological innovations in the province could be adopted without jeopardising Islamic principles. At the same time, the *ikhwan* and their mentors, the *muṭawwaʿa*, were busy 'purifying' the landscape from traces of what they regarded as religious innovations. This included the destruction of shrines built on the tombs of the Prophet, his relatives and Companions. This also involved the 'Islamisation' of public space in Hijaz, for example the enforcement of the ban on smoking in public (Wahba 1964: 22).

Perhaps this would have been an appropriate moment for Ibn Saʿud to declare himself King of Najd, while the Riyadh ʿ*ulama* were busy debating the legitimacy of a technology which was as yet unknown to them but well established in Hijaz. Ibn Saʿud, however, felt the early warning signals of an imminent and serious rebellion.

While Ibn Saʿud's alliance with the Riyadh ʿ*ulama* was well established, the allegiance of the *ikhwan* was shrinking. The *ikhwan* of Najd under the leadership of al-Duwaysh, Ibn Bijad and Ibn Ḥithlayn were beginning to resent their subordinate status. During the conquest of Hijaz, Ibn Saʿud exercised his authority to restrain both the *muṭawwaʿa* and the *ikhwan*. The *ikhwan* of Muṭayr, ʿUtayba and ʿAjman had already been well initiated into ritualistic Islam as they had been the first to be subjected to the *muṭawwaʿa*'s education programme. This initiation was beginning to have serious, unexpected consequences.

The capture of Hijaz brought to the surface contradictory perceptions of Ibn Saʿud's expansion. Ibn Saʿud himself thought of it as 'restoring his ancestors' glory and domination over most provinces of the Arabian Peninsula'. His *muṭawwaʿa* perceived it as an expansion of the boundaries of the Muslim *umma*, faithful to the principles of *shariʿa*, under the auspices of an *imam*, the guardian of the Islamic legacy and prosecutor of their will. Though subordinated by the religious specialists, the *ikhwan*, however, did not abandon their well-established views on political leadership and autonomy. Faysal al-Duwaysh, the most celebrated *ikhwan* rebel, exemplified the contradiction between the three ideas of the state, that of Ibn Saʿud, the *muṭawwaʿa* and the tribal confederations. Al-Zirkili described al-Duwaysh thus: 'When he came to Riyadh to visit Ibn Saʿud, he was accompanied by 150 armed men. He used to sit next to Ibn Saʿud; he was too arrogant to greet anybody in the *majlis* except the *ʿulama*. He perceived himself Ibn Saʿud's equal' (al-Zirkili 1972: 107–8).

So far al-Duwaysh had been a tribal shaykh. The capture of Madina, Mecca, Taʾif and other Hijazi towns gave him and other tribal chiefs the prospect of being elevated to the rank of amir of one of the newly conquered settlements. Al-Duwaysh was determined to become amir of Madina, while ibn Bijad looked towards Taʾif (al-Zirkili 1972: 108). While Ibn Saʿud was aspiring to concentrate power in his own hands, the tribal chiefs exerted pressure on him to share it. The leaders of the *ikhwan* rebellion continued to regard themselves as legitimate partners in the newly created realm, rather than 'instruments' for its expansion, to be used and dismantled after the mission had been accomplished (Kostiner 1985). Al-Duwaysh's ambitions were well understood by the amir of Kuwait, who, unlike al-Zirkili, was not concerned with al-Duwaysh's 'bedouin' and 'savage' nature. Amir Aḥmad of Kuwait described al-Duwaysh:

> Al-Duwaish is a great politician . . . there is no question of din [religion] behind this rebellion; what Duwaish is playing for is the downfall of the house of Saud and the rise of himself, al-Duwaish, in Bin Saud's place. With success his horizon has become widened and now he hopes to become master of Nejd, and in the process does not care if the Hijaz returns to the Shereefian family or Hail to Bin Rashid. (Kostiner 1993: 139)

While the details of the 1927–30 *ikhwan* rebellion are well documented,[11] it is important to grasp the ritualistic aspect of its resolution, for this sheds light on the tension and accommodation in the holy alliance between Ibn Saʿud, the *muṭawwaʿa* and the *ikhwan*. Immediately after the capture of Hijaz, the *ikhwan* leaders held a 'conference' in ʿArṭawiyyah, at which they criticised Ibn Saʿud on several grounds. The most important criticism centred on relations with Britain, the nature of kingship, the Islamic legitimacy of Ibn Saʿud's taxes and his personal conduct, for example his serial marriages with daughters of tribal shaykhs and slaves and his luxurious lifestyle. Other issues of contention were related to the status of the Hasa Shiʿa community and the necessity of 'Islamising' them, and the annual arrival of the Syrian and Egyptian pilgrims with certain practices considered outside Islam, for example their use of music and singing. Ibn Saʿud was also criticised for limiting the prospect of *jihad* against a whole range of groups, such as tribes in Iraq, Jordan and Kuwait (Shamiyyah 1986: 195). This complaint was directly related to the Hadda and Bahra Agreements with Britain (mentioned earlier), which regulated tribal movement between Ibn Saʿud's domain, Trans-Jordan and Iraq.

Ibn Saʿud responded to the *ikhwan* criticism by calling for a conference to take place in 1927. It was the first time that the resolution of these urgent matters was delegated to the *ʿulama* of Riyadh. Ibn Saʿud could not resolve these issues without consultation with the *ʿulama*. The *ʿulama* gave their opinion on each item of criticism. They accepted the *ikhwan*'s criticism of Islamic practices in Hijaz. They recommended that tombs on graves should be destroyed. They also recommended that the Shiʿa of Hasa, under Ibn Saʿud's authority since 1913, should become 'true Muslims' and abandon their innovations. They demanded that Syrian and Egyptian pilgrims stop their 'un-Islamic practices', a reference to using music and chanting during the pilgrimage season, and recommended that Iraqi Shiʿa tribes should be prevented from grazing their animals on Muslim land, a reference to Ibn Saʿud's territories.

On the more important issue of *jihad*, the *ʿulama* confirmed that this remained the prerogative of Ibn Saʿud, the *imam* of the Muslim community, who was also free to impose taxes as long as they were Islamic. The *ʿulama* negated any knowledge of un-Islamic conduct on his behalf. The *ʿulama*'s opinion was crucial for Ibn Saʿud. From now on he could act against the rebellious *ikhwan* with the full support of the Riyadh *ʿulama*. The 1927 *ʿulama* conference was a critical moment for the relationship between Ibn Saʿud and the Najdi men of religion.

The *ikhwan* rejected the opinions of the Riyadh *ʿulama* and continued to challenge Ibn Saʿud's authority. In 1928, when it seemed that the *ikhwan* rebellion was getting beyond his control, Ibn Saʿud sent letters to all parts of Najd announcing his abdication. Immediately Riyadh became a 'pilgrimage' centre for his most loyal supporters, among them tribal chiefs, *ʿulama* and other Najdi notables. In a meeting with several hundred attendants, Ibn Saʿud made a famous speech. After invoking emotive notions of *niʿma* (divine abundance) and *badawa* (bedouin tradition), he reminded his audience of his achievement of having conquered Riyadh with only 'forty men'. In this speech the rhetoric of economic gains, the chivalry of his first conquest, the noble bedouin tradition and religious observance accomplished in the provinces were all combined to create a metaphor of power difficult to resist. He asked both the *ʿulama* and *muṭawwaʿa* to 'clarify the relationship between *raʿi* (shepherd/leader) and *raʿiyya* (followers) and the obligations of one towards the other'. He invoked the famous well-developed Wahhabi concept of submission to the leader of the Muslim community. Finally he asked the *ʿulama* and the notables present to choose another ruler from among his own family to replace him if they were not satisfied with his style of government (al-Zirkili 1972: 112).

This was extremely significant, as Ibn Saʿud could not possibly have contemplated another family ruling Arabia. There was also an indication that al-Duwaysh could not possibly become ruler. Ibn Saʿud's speech implied that while he himself might be replaced, the hegemony of his family was sacrosanct. Once again the religious specialists were preoccupied with matters relating to whether the telegraph was a form of sorcery to be rejected. The final verdict was established that neither the Qurʾan nor the Prophet's tradition indicated that the telegraph was illegitimate. On the more important issue of the *ikhwan* rebellion, the religious specialists declared that the *ikhwan* leadership had strayed outside the consensus of the *umma*, and were to be fought until they came back to wisdom. Al-Duwaysh himself was labelled *baghi* (usurper), whose elimination and curtailment were Islamically legitimate. Finally they renewed the oath of allegiance to Ibn Saʿud, who was eventually given religious authorisation to terminate what could have developed into a crucial setback to his rule.

The Riyadh meeting of 1928 confirmed the status of the Riyadh *ʿulama* that had already begun to take shape in 1927. From now on, they were confined to giving their opinions regarding matters of Islamic ritual and technological innovation, of which the country would have no shortage in the coming years. The *ʿulama* accepted this limited role in the newly created realm, as it was a continuation of their ancient specialisation in matters relating to *ʿibada*. They were in fact predisposed to play this comfortable role which had been in line with their own well-developed concerns. To involve them in the daily affairs of politics would be a violation of an ancient division of labour between the political *imam* and his men of religion. This division had developed with the first alliance between Al Saʿud and Muhammad ibn ʿAbd al-Wahhab in 1744. In 1928 the Riyadh *ʿulama* were not ready to challenge or attempt to change this arrangement. By 1928 they had accomplished the rather difficult task of recruiting a large number of *muṭawwaʿa* emissaries who were dispatched to domesticate the rest of the population of Arabia for Ibn Saʿud. After that their role was to become state apologists to be called upon when need arose and to guard public morality in the realm. The more senior among them were to specialise in initiating legitimising charters, *fatwas* which would give Islamic legitimacy to state practice. In 1928, it became clear to those distinguished among them that if they were to continue to play a role in the country, they would have to accept the subordination of religion to politics. They also understood that their eminence was dependent on restraining their former students, the *muṭawwaʿa*.

With the approval of the *ʿulama*, Ibn Saʿud was able to pacify the *ikhwan* and terminate their rebellion. This pacification became more urgent as the *ikhwan* leaders drew up plans to divide Ibn Saʿud's realm among themselves. Vassiliev reports that al-Duwaysh, ibn Bijad and ibn Ḥithlayn aspired towards becoming rulers in Najd, Hijaz and Hasa respectively (Vassiliev 1998: 277).

THE COLLAPSE OF THE *IKHWAN* REBELLION

By March 1929, Ibn Saʿud assembled a fighting force consisting mainly of men from Najdi oases with which to end the *ikhwan* rebellion. War against the *ikhwan* rebels began with the battle of Sibila, followed by several military attacks on their *hujjar*, mainly in ʿArṭawiyyah and al-Ghaṭghaṭ (Kostiner 1993: 136). Britain found itself helping Ibn Saʿud to restrain the *ikhwan*, who began to be pursued by the Royal Air Force (Sluglett and Sluglett 1982: 45). This was a crucial element in the pacification of the *ikhwan*, the majority of whom fled over the Kuwaiti frontier. According to Leatherdale: 'Reports spoke of panic-stricken people rushing in terror from both the RAF and Ibn Saʿud . . . the British feared that the *ikhwan* would seek refuge with Kuwaiti tribes and eventually merge with them' (Leatherdale 1983: 119).

This must have been an important factor behind British deployment of the RAF. The last thing Britain wanted to see was *ihkwan* sympathisers among the Kuwaiti tribes, some of whom shared common descent with their Saʿudi counterparts. However, it was not until January 1930 that the *ikhwan* leaders surrendered to the British in Kuwait. Britain was reluctant to hand them over without conditions, 'fearing either summary execution of large numbers, possibly including women and children, or alternatively, a free pardon, enabling them to raid again in the future' (Leatherdale 1983: 119). Britain eventually agreed to return the *ikhwan* leaders to Riyadh after Ibn Saʿud promised to spare their lives and pledged that there would be no further raids into Kuwait and Iraq (ibid.: 120). The *ikhwan* rebels were returned to Ibn Saʿud, who put them in prison first in Hasa and later in Riyadh. The most prominent of the *ikhwan* rebels, Faysal al-Duwaysh, died a year later. The defeat of the *ikhwan* marked the end of a turbulent era in Saʿudi history. The *ikhwan* proved to be an efficient fighting force for the expansion of Ibn Saʿud's realm, but turned out to be problematic in the consolidation of his authority.

Ibn Saʿud, the *muṭawwaʿa* and the *ikhwan* formed an alliance that was not dismantled until the conquest of Arabia was terminated. After the capture of Hijaz in 1926, Ibn Saʿud could expand no further in the north and east because this would have antagonised Britain, the mandate power in Trans-Jordan and Iraq, and the protector of Gulf rulers from Kuwait to Muscat. There remained a small opportunity on the Saʿudi–Yemeni border. In 1930 Ibn Saʿud annexed ʿAsir and announced that its Idrisi ruler was permitted to remain only as a nominal head of the province. The formal annexation of ʿAsir after its capital, Abha, had been part of Ibn Saʿud's realm for almost eight years was the final territorial acquisition (Leatherdale 1983: 136). The annexation of ʿAsir did not result in major clashes with local or foreign powers, for example, Britain or Italy whose influence in the Red Sea was being consolidated in the 1930s. However, it brought Ibn Saʿud and Imam Yahya of Yemen close to a serious military confrontation in 1934.[12]

Military expansion reached its limits in the north, east and south-west. The Saʿudi realm bordered territories where Britain had already guaranteed the integrity of two newly created Hashemite kingdoms, that of King ʿAbdullah in Trans-Jordan and King Faysal in Iraq. The *ikhwan* rebels had made the serious mistake of not recognising the political realities of the new situation. Driven by political ambition and religious zeal, they continued to raid tribal groups and towns in the north in areas where Ibn Saʿud had no authority or claim recognised by Britain. Ibn Saʿud and Britain co-operated in dismantling the *ikhwan* force after they had fulfilled the rather difficult task of expanding Ibn Saʿud's realm within the boundaries that were possible. The holy alliance between Ibn Saʿud, the *muṭawwaʿa* and the *ikhwan* collapsed under new pressures that demanded a cessation of military expansion. The Riyadh *ʿulama*, the early mentors of the *muṭawwaʿa*, were called upon to justify the suppression of the *ikhwan*, whose eclipse was achieved with the surrender of their leaders.

The *ikhwan* rebellion was not only a religious protest against Ibn Saʿud, but was also a tribal rebellion that exposed the dissatisfaction of some tribal groups with his increasing powers. The *ikhwan* rebels refused to remain the instruments of Ibn Saʿud's expansion and expected real participation as governors and local chiefs in the conquered territories. Ibn Saʿud refused to share with them the political rewards their conquests had brought. More importantly, the *ikhwan* rebellion demonstrated that the emerging state was from the very beginning a non-tribal entity whose expansion and consolidation could only progress at the expense of the tribal element. Given the scholarly attention devoted to documenting and interpreting the *ikhwan* rebellion, it is surprising that the Saʿudi state is still mistakenly considered by some scholars as the epitome of the tribal state.[13] This misconception continues to be propagated despite evidence to the contrary. While substantial sections of the population were certainly tribal in the 1930s, the state was definitely a non-tribal entity that gradually undermined and broke the cohesion of the various tribal groups.

Having pacified the *ikhwan* and restrained the *muṭawwaʿa* with the approval of the small circle of senior Riyadh *ʿulama* and the valuable assistance of Britain, Ibn Saʿud declared his realm (so far called the Kingdom of Hijaz and of Najd and its Dependencies) *al-mamlaka al-ʿarabiyya al-saʿudiyya* (the Kingdom of Saudi Arabia) on 22 September 1932. The new name emphasised the merging of the two main regions, Hijaz and Najd, and, more importantly, 'commemorated Ibn Saʿud's part in creating a unified state under his authority' (Leatherdale 1983: 148).[14]

CHAPTER 3

Control and loyalty, 1932–1953

As the Kingdom of Saudi Arabia was declared in 1932, Ibn Saʿud endeavoured to consolidate a royal lineage to provide continuity at the level of leadership. The consolidation of a Saʿudi royal lineage was achieved as a result of two parallel processes. First, Ibn Saʿud marginalised members of his own generation (his brothers and nephews). Second, he consolidated his own line of descent (his sons), which eventually developed into a distinct royal group. This chapter investigates processes of control and explores the mechanisms underlying loyalty to the state in the pre-oil period. It then moves on to introduce an important landmark event in the history of Saudi Arabia in the twentieth century, namely the oil concession of 1933, which resulted in the discovery of oil in commercial quantities.

MARGINALISING SAʿUDI COLLATERAL BRANCHES

The strategy of marginalisation involved the containment of potential claims to the throne from within the Al Saʿud group. Immediately after the capture of Riyadh, Ibn Saʿud endeavoured to resolve the threat of his own paternal uncles and their descendants.

During the period of early expansion in Arabia, Ibn Saʿud faced the challenge of the so-called ʿAraʾif, his paternal cousins, under the leadership of ʿAbd al-ʿAziz ibn Saʿud ibn Faysal ibn Turki (al-Dakhil 1982: 103–4; Rihani 1928: 182).[1] These paternal cousins were the descendants of Saʿud, who challenged the authority of the Saʿudi ruler, ʿAbdullah, in the 1870s. After the collapse of the Saʿudi leadership in the 1890s, Ibn Saʿud's paternal cousins were hostages in Ibn Rashid's court in Haʾil. During a battle with Ibn Rashid, Ibn Saʿud secured their release in 1904, but did not win their allegiance (Samore 1983: 38).

In 1908 the ʿAraʾif allied themselves with their maternal kin the ʿAjman tribe, and staged a rebellion against Ibn Saʿud in the eastern province. The ʿAraʾif were pacified only after a series of military campaigns. Their pacification was sealed with a marriage between Saʿud ibn ʿAbd al-ʿAziz (the rebellious paternal cousin later known as Saʿud al-Kabir) and Ibn Saʿud's sister Nura (Bligh 1984: 17; al-Qaḥṭani 1988: 65). Al-Kabir's brother Muhammad married Munira, another sister of Ibn Saʿud (Samore 1983: 38). With the pacification of the ʿAraʾif, a potential threat from Ibn Saʿud's paternal cousins was eliminated. Members of this group continued to live under Ibn Saʿud's supervision and control.

Other potential rivals belonged to collateral branches of the Al Saʿud. For example, Al Juluwi could have been a potential threat had they not been incorporated in the process of state building from the very beginning. A member of this branch, ʿAbdullah ibn Juluwi, assisted in Ibn Saʿud's capture of Riyadh in 1902. ʿAbdullah ibn Juluwi was active in the military campaigns following the fall of Riyadh. In return for his military assistance, Ibn Saʿud rewarded him first with the governorship of Qasim in 1908 and later moved him to Hasa in 1913. ʿAbdullah ibn Juluwi remained governor of Hasa until his death in 1936. His son Saʿud succeeded him (Bligh 1984: 38). Another member of the Juluwis, ʿAbd al-ʿAziz ibn Musaʿid, was rewarded with the governorship of Haʾil in 1925. ʿAbdullah ibn Juluwi governed the eastern province as his own, almost autonomous, emirate. He exercised a free hand in disciplining both its sedentary Shiʿa population and nomadic tribal confederations (al-Ḥasan 1993). According to one account, he ran the province with an iron fist. Rihani described how the name ʿAbdullah 'strikes terror in the heart of the Bedu; with it mothers frighten their babes' (Rihani 1928: 219). The Juluwis were politically neutralised by Ibn Saʿud as they were drawn into government. Having become functionaries of Ibn Saʿud, they shared political power as they became almost independent governors in his most important territorial acquisitions, Qasim, Haʾil and Hasa.[2]

There remained the challenge from Ibn Saʿud's brothers and half-brothers. Ḥamza lists seven brothers of Ibn Saʿud: Saʿad, ʿAbdullah, Muhammad, Saʿud, Aḥmad, Musaʿid and ʿAbd al-Moḥsin (Ḥamza 1936: 77). During thirty years of military campaigns (1902–32), several of Ibn Saʿud's brothers contributed to his military expansion in Arabia. His only full brother, Saʿad, was particularly useful in a series of campaigns in Qasim. He was captured by the forces of Sharif Ḥusayn during the early military skirmishes in Hijaz. Ibn Saʿud secured his release after accepting humiliating conditions imposed by the Sharif.[3] Saʿad died in battle and consequently did not pose a threat to Ibn Saʿud's leadership. It is known that Saʿad's premature death was a blow to Ibn Saʿud as he was his only full brother, an ally against his half-brothers. Ibn Saʿud married the deceased's widow, Jawhara bint al-Sudayri.

While the rest of Ibn Saʿud's brothers were still junior members of the family, his main rival brothers remained ʿAbdullah and Muhammad. Ibn Saʿud's half-brother ʿAbdullah was commander of the Saʿudi army that conquered Hijaz in 1924–5 and pacified the *ikhwan* during their 1927 rebellion. When the military campaign came to an end, ʿAbdullah became a ceremonial figure, holding court in his house in Riyadh; a kind of respected sage of the family (Yizraeli 1997: 63). ʿAbdullah died in 1976; throughout his life he was politically marginalised, but continued to be a respected symbolic figure, a member of the same generation as Ibn Saʿud himself.

Ibn Saʿud's third brother, Muhammad, was active in military campaigns against the Rashidi emirate in 1921. Muhammad was the one least happy with the appointment of Ibn Saʿud's son Saʿud as Crown Prince in May 1933 (Ḥamza 1936: 50–1). Between 1933 and 1943, he posed a serious challenge to Ibn Saʿud's monopoly over power and tried to promote his own son Khalid as potential rival to Saʿud. Bligh suggests that Muhammad had been an ally of Sultan ibn Bijad, the famous *ikhwan* rebel, who was also his father-in-law. Muhammad was described as someone who sympathised with the *ikhwan*. He was later nicknamed *muṭawwaʿ*. He was disappointed with the pacification of the *ikhwan*, which led to the demise of his father-in-law.

It is alleged that in 1927, Muhammad's son Khalid tried to assassinate Ibn Saʿud's son Saʿud (later Crown Prince) (Bligh 1984: 33).[4] Both Muhammad and his son resented Ibn Saʿud's severe treatment of the *ikhwan* rebels. Following the appointment of Saʿud as Crown Prince, Muhammad wrote to the King complaining about the succession. It is known that Muhammad refused to vow allegiance to Saʿud (Samore 1983: 46). He and his son remained in Mecca for a while, away from Ibn Saʿud's court in Riyadh. Khalid died in 1938 in mysterious circumstances. Bligh suggests that Ibn Saʿud possibly had him assassinated during a hunting trip (Bligh 1984: 37). Muhammad died in 1943, leaving Ibn Saʿud without a serious potential rival in his own generation. Ibn Saʿud had marginalised Muhammad when he limited succession to his own sons at the expense of his brothers. The death of Muhammad brought a revealing comment by a British diplomat: 'The King, while grieving over the loss of an old companion, was glad, as a ruler, to see a possible cause of future trouble disappear' (Bligh 1984: 37).

CONSOLIDATING IBN SAʿUD'S LINE OF DESCENT

The marginalisation of members of Ibn Saʿud's generation, that is, his paternal cousins and half-brothers, was accompanied by consolidating his own line of descent through an active strategy of polygamy and concubinage. By 1953 this resulted in the birth of forty-three sons and over fifty daughters, important for the creation of a royal lineage. Ibn Saʿud wanted to ensure that kingship remained confined to his own sons. After the kingship of Saʿud, he wanted his second most senior son, Faysal, to become king. Kingship was to remain a reward for his own sons, especially those early ones who had participated in his conquest of most of Arabia, namely Saʿud and Faysal.

Ibn Saʿud's polygamous marriages and the number of his children astonished foreign and local observers. Among others Philby, Rihani, Ḥamza, al-Zirkili and Wahba documented Ibn Saʿud's marital unions with subtle references to them being rather excessive, even in a polygamous society such as Arabia. Philby described an informal gathering with the King:

> The king then confessed to having married no fewer than 135 virgins, to say nothing of 'about a hundred' others, during his life, though he had come to a decision to limit himself in future to two new wives a year, which of course meant discarding two of his existing team at any time to make room for them. (Philby 1952: 111)

It is interesting that Philby described the King's words as a 'confession' rather than mere informative statements about his marital affairs. Ibn Saʿud 'confessed' in the context of a private meeting with his most trusted companions in his summer residence in Taʾif. Apparently the King repeated such 'confessions' during his more relaxed retreats during the summer months.

Tribal shaykhs who were contemporaries of Ibn Saʿud also commented on his polygamy. Although these tribal shaykhs would have had polygamous marriages themselves, the majority regarded Ibn Saʿud's practices as excessive. A narrative of a verbal exchange between the King and one tribal shaykh indicates how unusual Ibn Saʿud's marital practices were in Arabian society, even among the tribal shaykhs and amirs. In a private meeting, it seems that Ibn Saʿud 'confessed' that he had married over a hundred women. A tribal shaykh present asked Ibn Saʿud, '*wa kuluhum bi layla waḥda ya maḥfuẓ?*' (and all of them in one night, your majesty?) (oral tradition). This anecdote is repeated to highlight several things: the ignorance of the tribal shaykh of court life, his limited horizons, and his lack of imagination. But perhaps the anecdote is still remembered because it reflected how Ibn Saʿud's marriages were perceived as extraordinary even in a society that allowed a mixture of both polygamy and concubinage. Ibn Saʿud stretched the practice to its limits.

How can we interpret the 'extraordinary' number of the King's marital unions? The number of Ibn Saʿud's wives, concubines and children outnumbered those of his contemporaries in Arabia and elsewhere. Neither King Ḥusayn of Hijaz, nor Imam Yaḥya of Yemen, nor the Sultan of Oman was a match. Perhaps only his son Saʿud exceeded him in the number of his marriages and children. Saʿud had fifty-three sons and fifty-four daughters (Shamiyyah 1986: 243).

Ibn Saʿud's marital practices have been interpreted in different ways. His opponents attribute his serial polygamy and concubinage to his insatiable lust and limitless appetite for women. They find at their disposal abundant written evidence, similar to that of Philby cited earlier, and local oral narratives. While Ibn Saʿud's diet, dress and several other personal habits remained simple and in line with Arabian patterns (Ḥamza 1936: 31; al-Zirkili 1972: 181; Benoist-Mechin 1957: 243), in the area of marriage he exhibited a rather unusual inclination. His 'confessions', cited by several authors, were considered to be a reflection of a corrupt nature, in the guise of Islamic puritanism.[5] While not ruling out such interpretations altogether, one should not see the King's marital practices only in terms of choices rooted in sexual potency and personal overindulgence, both of which could have been exaggerated by power. It is possible that after 1932, the King felt sufficiently comfortable and secure in his realm to be able to turn his attention to the satisfaction of his desires. Such interpretation, however, is based on a narrow understanding of Arabian marriages, especially in the case of those conducted by political leadership. It reduces the meaning of marriage to a single dimension, while failing to acknowledge the fact that it is a social institution with a wider significance.

Another interpretation prominent in the literature on the emergence of the modern Saʿudi state anchors the King's exogamous/polygamous marriages in the realm of political strategy. His marriages are seen as a mechanism for cementing alliances with various sections of the population, especially well-known tribal groups, the religious elite and the sedentary nobility.[6] Marriage as a mechanism for alliance does not obviously explain the vast number of concubines whom the King kept. Concubines were often foreign slaves of African, Circassian or Yemeni origin, so the alliance theory cannot explain the significance of such unions. Nevertheless, the King's numerous exogamous marriages were seen as a reflection of his strategic thinking, whereby marriage became a means to a political end, namely drawing the population into kinship relations with the ruling group. Marriage became a political strategy for state building and consolidation.

It is extremely difficult to construct a comprehensive list of the marriages conducted by the King over almost half a century. Some marriages were of such short duration that they escaped both memory and historical records. Women who failed to produce children were often easily forgotten. Nevertheless, some marriages are still remembered for their social and political significance. According to one source, Ibn Saʿud had twenty-two wives (Lees 1980: 36; Holden and Johns 1981: 14). Some of Ibn Saʿud's unions were with daughters of famous Arabian tribes (Banu Khalid, Shammar, ʿAniza, ʿAjman), tribal nobility (Al Shaʿlan, Al Rashid), sedentary families of religious learning (Al Shaykh), sedentary Najdi families (Al Sudayri) and branches of the Al Saʿud (Al Thunayan, Al Juluwi). These marriages are taken as evidence to support the argument that alliances with various important power centres were the underlying rationale. It should be noted that several of Ibn Saʿud's sons were born to concubines, who were freed of their slave status after the birth of a male child.[7]

For marriages to cement already existing alliances or initiate new ones, important preconditions need to be present. First, husband and wife need to belong to groups who are equal at least in power and wealth.

Second, marriages need to be monogamous in order to foster long-term political alliances. For a union to be of any political value, it cannot be combined with several others, all meant to be serving the same purpose. In theory polygamy can increase the network of alliances, but in reality it creates rivalry and competition between groups. Polygamy devalues the political significance of any single marriage (Samore 1983: 5). It can only facilitate the possibility of wife-receivers manipulating several groups of wife-givers. If wife-receivers happen to be politically dominant, dependency – rather than alliance – is more likely to follow.

Third, easy divorce militates against a marriage being a vehicle for long-term political agendas. A marriage of a short duration cannot be a pillar upon which loyalty between wife-receivers and wife-givers is established.

Fourth, for marriages to promote an alliance, wife-receivers will have to reciprocate and themselves become wife-givers to the group that supplies them with wives. Situations in which a dominant group receives wives from other groups but keeps its own daughters for internal circulation cannot expect solid political loyalty from its wife-givers.

The majority of Ibn Saʿud's marriages did not meet these preconditions. While he married into Arabia's nobility, the majority of these groups had already been rendered powerless and politically subordinate. The King took women from such groups precisely at that moment when their power, wealth and prestige were undermined by his own military conquests.

Examples to illustrate this point are numerous. One of Ibn Saʿud's early marriages while he was still in Kuwait was with a member of the Banu Khalid tribe, Waḍḥa bint ʿUrayʿir, who became the mother of the future King Saʿud. The hegemony of Banu Khalid had already been declining since the eighteenth century. It was unlikely that this union would have fostered an important alliance, for Banu Khalid had already become marginal political players.

Immediately after the capture of Riyadh in 1902, Ibn Saʿud married Tarfa, the daughter of ʿAbdullah ibn ʿAbd al-Laṭif Al Shaykh. She became the mother of Faysal, the third King. This marriage was considered as an important strategy enhancing the allegiance of the religious family of Al Shaykh to the Saʿudi leadership. Yet this allegiance had already existed long before Ibn Saʿud married into the family and, as argued in the last chapter, the Al Shaykh's loyalty could not be taken for granted.

Furthermore, Ibn Saʿud's serial marriages with Shammar women and in particular members of their Rashidi ruling group took place precisely at the moment when Shammar hegemony was beginning to decline. The King married Fahda bint ʿAsi al-Shraym, a member of the Shammar, after the tribe's hegemony had been broken. Similarly, his marriages with Rashidi women took place after he conquered Haʾil and forced its rulers to move to Riyadh in 1921. By the time Ibn Saʿud married Jawhara bint Muhammad ibn Rashid and his son Musaʿid married her sister Waṭfa, the Rashidis were already captives in Ibn Saʿud's court (Al-Rasheed 1991: 250–1).

While most of Ibn Saʿud's marriages were with prestigious Arabian nobility, in the majority of cases these groups had already lost their power prior to the marriages. Needless to say the other preconditions for alliance were not met. Ibn Saʿud abided by the Islamic tradition, which allows a man four wives at the same time and an unlimited number of concubines. The King often divorced one of his four wives in order to enter into a new union. As mentioned before, Philby stated that 'the king had come to a decision to limit himself in future to two new wives a year, which of course meant discarding two of his existing team at any time to make room for them' (Philby 1952: 111). Several daughters of important nobility were removed from the list to enable him to receive a new wife. There was, however, the possibility of divorcing a woman, marrying her again, and divorcing her for the second or third time. After the third time, the same woman had to marry someone else, then get divorced to allow the first husband to remarry her for the fourth time. Although this may appear complicated, it was easily practised. The King divorced a woman to make room for a new fourth wife, sometimes the divorcée's sister. He would remarry the divorced woman at a later time, if he so wished. Although divorce was normal practice, its disruptive social aspects could not be favourable for long-term political alliances: for a sedentary group or tribal nobility to have their daughters 'discarded' could not have maintained the desired long-term alliance. To wait in the hope that a daughter would be brought back to wedlock with Ibn Saʿud or one of his brothers (such practices were also common) could not be congenial to political ends. Nothing could be so remote from generating or maintaining loyalty than divorcing a wife in order to marry her sister. The marriage choices of the King were such that it is doubtful whether the concept of alliance could be invoked here let alone applied to some of his marital unions.

Furthermore, while the King practised both endogamy and exogamy, his daughters circulated among a close network of paternal cousins and collateral branches of the Al Saʿud. Several daughters married their paternal parallel cousins, some of them potential rivals of Ibn Saʿud. His daughters' marriages were meant to ease off the pressure of internal power struggles. It is doubtful whether this strategy was successful. However, what is relevant here is the fact that with the consolidation of the kingdom, the Al Saʿud emerged as wife-receivers without allowing their women to be part of an exogamous network, thus limiting the scope for genuine political alliances to be formed.

Ibn Saʿud's marriages were an efficient divisive mechanism, maintaining and enhancing already existing social hierarchies. They also created new ones. Ibn Saʿud's marriages could not have generated a web of political alliances with important power centres because these marriages had none of the preconditions that would have disposed them to play that role. The King's marriages could only be seen in terms of a general policy to subordinate the Arabian population through a systematic appropriation of its most cherished and valued members, women. Marriages were part of a political strategy to dominate and control in a country where as yet there were very few resources to achieve this objective.

In the majority of cases, Ibn Saʿud married the ex-wives or daughters of his ex-rivals and enemies. Such unions could not easily turn them into allies. These marriages were an extension of the political domination of groups following their military defeat. In such contexts neither the bride nor her relatives could express an opinion or refuse a marriage. Most women qualified for the status of *sabaya*, captives. A commentator on the King's marriages with his defeated enemies rightly described these marriages as 'a sure sign to the world that the king was the conqueror' (McLoughlin 1993: 123).

The survival of wife-givers became dependent on their being part of the network of the King's affines. This status was not even secure, as frequent divorce undermined its durability. Upon marriage, a group could become the recipient of various gifts and favours, but these benefits could be disrupted. Moreover, the system encouraged groups to compete with each other for the status of being the King's affines. Competition between groups and within groups to provide wives resulted from vigorous polygamy exercised by the highest authority in the kingdom. Marriage sealed the subordination of Arabian nobility to the Al Saʿud. In the words of van der Meulen, 'the king created privileged classes' (van der Meulen 1957: 255). While the majority of these 'classes' had previously enjoyed independent political and economic power, they became totally dependent on Saʿudi royal largesse with the consolidation of the Saʿudi state. Marriages with Arabian nobility enabled them to be part of the patronage networks woven around the King and his sons. From a political perspective, the marriages of the royal lineage extended the domination of the ruling group. Marital strategies sealed what had already been achieved politically and militarily.

POWER AND POMP IN THE PRE-OIL ERA: THE *MAJLIS*

Having contracted several marriages with Arabian nobility, and having fathered a large number of sons, Ibn Saʿud conferred on his line of descent the status of royalty by a series of symbolic acts and practices. The royal lineage distinguished itself from its subjects, thanks to its resources, which were meagre in the pre-oil era, but were nevertheless impressive in a society that had experienced austerity. Power had to be represented and visualised in order for the populace to fear and respect it. This became an urgent matter especially after the cessation of Ibn Saʿud's military campaigns, which had impressed his allies and frightened his enemies. The display of power became important at a time when the state was not able to impress with public works, administration or bureaucracy. In a society where communication technology was virtually non-existent, the power of royalty had to be displayed directly to the subjects.

Royal power was exhibited in the *majlis*, that traditional meeting known in Arabia for centuries. Traditionally oasis amirs, tribal shaykhs and men of authority held public meetings where they received both their own subjects and outside visitors. The *majlis* was an arena for mediation, dispute settlement, the renewal of allegiance, but most importantly the representation of power (Al-Rasheed 1999a: 152–5). Attending the *majlis* of a local amir gave subjects the opportunity to assess the magnitude of his power. Amirs displayed their wealth through regular feasts, which often attracted a hungry population. Slaves and retainers indicated the military might of a ruler. The physical surroundings, a large room in the amir's residence furnished with imported rugs and comfortable cushions, often impressed both the sedentary and nomadic population of Arabia.[8] The legacy of the *majlis* survived with the consolidation of the Saʿudi state, but its magnitude and functions deviated from the patterns associated with previous emirates.

The King presided over several regular daily gatherings where he demonstrated his consolidated power. In 1932 Ibn Saʿud was King of Arabia and his *majlis* reflected this status. One of his regular gatherings, called *majlis ʿamm*, was held in the morning. This *majlis* was in theory open to everybody, but in practice only those who had business to discuss or a request to make were expected to attend:

> There was a clear understanding among the king's subjects that a man did not go to the palace unless he had particular business with the king or the visit was a traditional right such as the annual visit of the bedouins. The townspeople of Riyadh for instance never came to the palace unless they had a special reason to do so. (Almana 1980: 178)

The King sat in the central part of the *majlis*, surrounded by his brothers, relatives and children according to their seniority. In addition to visiting tribal shaykhs, the *majlis* was attended by his recently defeated rivals, who were required to reside in Riyadh under strict supervision. They attended the King's regular *majlis*; especially the one held after the *ʿaṣr* (afternoon) prayers. This group often included a number of Arabian notables. The King once said to Philby with a smile: 'I already have many guests from all over the country: the Rashids, for instance, and the Ashrafs, and the Bani Aidh, and others' (Philby 1952: 107). The presence of such notables in Ibn Saʿud's *majlis* was important. It was a proof of their defeat and also a sign of the King's generosity and forgiveness. As his previous enemies sat with him and enjoyed his largesse, his political wisdom was displayed in public.

The King was distinguished by his double *ʿuqal* (head-rope), indicating the status of royalty. Early photographs of the King show him wearing the royal double head-rope as early as 1910 (Saudi Arabia 1996c: 22–3). Covering his white shirt was the Arabian brown or black *bisht*, a cloak embroidered with gold. Such items of clothing had been in the past the reserve of distinguished rulers in Najd. Neither tribal shaykhs nor ordinary oasis amirs wore them.

In the *majlis*, a space on the King's right hand side was always left vacant for special visitors. Upon the arrival of such visitors, the King rose to shake hands with them. The King himself was an imposing figure, taller than most of his relatives and populace. His physical appearance, 'which impressed both local and foreign visitors, bestowed on him an air of casual but profound authority' (Holden and Johns 1981: 99). As the King rose to greet distinguished guests, the audience followed suit. The murmuring of greetings by the King marked the entry into the *majlis* of commoners (al-Zirkili 1970: 517).

The King always initiated conversation in the *majlis*. Philby noted: 'The conversation generally resolved itself into a royal monologue, punctuated by murmurs of assent from all present; and the session would come to a quick or less quick end in proportion to the king's own interest in the subjects under review' (Philby 1952: 105). He added: 'In public and in private it is always he who does all the talking to a silent audience, which often does not listen to his words of wisdom or hear them, but is always ready with agreeable phrases in the event of His Majesty deigning to solicit an opinion on his remarks' (ibid.: 225).

In the public *majlis* the King's power was demonstrated by the silence of his audience. The latter remained quiet until they were asked to present their cases. Some presented the King with lengthy letters in which they described their requests or reported injustices. Others addressed the King directly. In both cases, a decision would often be taken then and there unless further consultations were needed to settle the case. In such gatherings, the King was mediator and judge. His word was final and uncontested: 'Twice a day, the king held a more private gathering, *majlis khaṣṣ*, once before noon and once after the *ʿaṣr* [afternoon] prayers. His brother ʿAbdullah and Crown Prince Saʿud attended this, in addition to other advisers' (al-Zirkili 1970: 353).

Another meeting, called *majlis al-dars* (study session), was held after the evening prayers.[9] This meeting was devoted to reading the Qurʾan, followed by commentary and interpretations. Al-Zirkili described this gathering:

> There is a *majlis* between *khaṣṣ* [private] and *ʿamm* [public]. It starts after evening prayers. The Saʿudi amirs seldom appear at this gathering. The King's high employees and some local guests usually attend it. Its purpose is the study of the Qurʾan and *sharʿia*. A reader from among the *ʿulama* reads a section of the Qurʾan in front of a lamp for half an hour. Then he offers some interpretations

and comments. I asked the King's brother, ʿAbdullah, about the origins of this *majlis*. He explained that it is a tradition in their family. (al-Zirkili 1970: 519)

While public meetings displayed the King's power, *majlis al-dars* anchored his realm in religion. It demonstrated his commitment to the *shariʿa* and its interpreters. Once again, power in this world was tightly linked to the realm of the sacred. Commitment to the sacred was also enforced through regular public prayers, where the King was visible in a state of humility, kneeling to his creator.

The King's private entertainment revolved around a private gathering, *majlis al-rabʿ*, where a limited number of the most trusted personalities attended. They sat on the floor cross-legged and chatted until the King retreated to his private quarters (al-Zirkili 1972: 210). Among the attendants were Philby and other close advisers and employees. It is in this setting where the King talked about women, marriage, worldly pleasures and politics: 'Women and world politics continued to divide the honours as prime subjects of conversation at the king's private sessions' (Philby 1952: 111).

At a time when the Saʿudi state was otherwise invisible, it was personified in the context of several public and private meetings. These were important repetitive rituals consolidating the emerging power of the royal lineage. When military campaigns ceased, the *majlis* became the stage on which the drama of power was acted for the populace to see. Those who came to Riyadh for business were exposed to it. But the royal power drama was also mobile.

Occasional desert excursions were part of the royal routine. The King, his sons and his entourage would leave the royal palace and head towards the nearby sand dunes around Riyadh. Before the car made its appearance in the country, the King used 'a carriage, an old one horse Victoria, – the only one in Ar-Riyad, – which squeaked and lurched most disgracefully' (Rihani 1928: 175).

When motor cars were finally available in the capital in the late 1920s, the King used one for his occasional rides into the desert. It impressed local bedouins and added to his aura. Rihani witnessed the arrival of the car and was invited by the King to join him during one of his desert excursions: 'We were going on an outing, I realised; for the Sultan on such occasions takes the children – his own and the Rashids – with him. About a hundred people that day, including the *rajajil*, accompanied us riding horse-back; and some of them raced with us, when the speedometer was registering two, three, four above forty miles' (Rihani 1928: 182).

Such excursions often involved horse races. Saʿudi princes and Arabian notables engaged in racing while the King watched through binoculars in amusement (Rihani 1928: 176). The King's sons participated in these races together with the sons of notables; Ibn Saʿud's army had defeated most of them. Winners were rewarded with prizes, which were paid in English gold on the spot by the King's treasurer (ibid.).

The expansion of the Saʿudi realm, especially after the conquest of Hijaz, allowed the King to travel to this cosmopolitan region. The entire royal court had to be transported initially on camels and later by car. The King resided in the Sharifs' palaces and also used the large houses of the merchants of Jeddah, who occasionally made them available to him.[10] During these visits not only the King and his entourage made the journey to Hijaz, but also his letters, stored in wooden chests. In the 1930s and 1940s the state had no archives or documents. It was only after the Second World War that an attempt was made to store these letters and create modern archives (Vitalis 1999: 659). The King's interpreter Almana described the royal procession as it travelled outside Riyadh:

> When the King travelled, he would take with him most of the staff in the Domestic and Foreign Courts, numbering in total about twelve clerks and six servants. We would take with us not just the usual supplies and weapons, but also all the Court records, files and correspondence. They were stored in huge wooden chests and were carried first on camel-back but later by car over countless thousands of miles of desert, following the King's caravan wherever it went. (Almana 1980: 181)

The travelling royal court made occasional stops *en route* for rest and food. Nomadic tribes and their shaykhs would visit the King's camp and renew their allegiance. The shaykhs would bring gifts of animal produce and would be rewarded with gold and silver coins from the royal *ṣurra* (purse) (al-Zirkili 1972: 365). The King travelled with his purse and had the privilege of distributing its contents himself: 'Now and again, from a bag always ready at his side for the poor and needy he might meet on the way, the royal hand would scatter a shower of silver coins on the rugs, and there would ensue a general scramble, in which all present would join' (Philby 1952: 112).

Whether in Riyadh or elsewhere, visiting guests would join the feast of lamb and rice, followed by coffee. Important guests would depart after being perfumed with incense, thanking God for peace and abundance. The memory of the event would linger in the minds of those who witnessed it. The news of the King's court would travel beyond those who were present.

The organisation of hospitality was one of the early measures to be formalised in the kingdom. One of the functions of the royal court was to deal with the requirements of feeding huge numbers of royal guests, retainers and tribal shaykhs. A special budget was set up for catering in the royal palace. The sophistication of palace life required that guests should not be mixed, hence the establishment of three hospitality divisions, *muḍif*, one to feed special foreign delegations, one for the bedouins and one for the townspeople (al-Zirkili 1970: 354). During the King's inspection of the oil installations in Hasa, a royal banquet was held in the residence of the local governor, Ibn Juluwi:

> American guests were confronted with a whole cooked camel, legs, head and all, 280 whole cooked sheep on the customary mounds of rice, two thousand chickens and six thousand eggs, and roughly ten thousand side dishes of fruit and vegetables and puddings. When the first sitting of five hundred guests had made what impression they could, servants and soldiers had their fill, five hundred at a time, and finally, early the following morning, the citizens of the town were let in to eat what was left and wrap what they could not eat in their skirts and take it away. (Howarth 1964: 222)

While the accuracy of Howarth's figures is doubtful, royal feasts impressed the King's guests and attracted a flow of bedouins. In the 1930s and 1940s it was not uncommon for hungry bedouins to pitch their tents around the capital during the summer months as they would be guaranteed a meal in *muḍif* Khraymis, the hospitality section responsible for feeding the bedouins, named after Khraymis, the slave in charge (oral tradition). A special neighbourhood in Riyadh, Baṭḥa, was designated for the serving of food, as ordinary bedouins were not welcomed in the royal palace, the grounds of which were reserved for distinguished tribal shaykhs and foreign guests.

These were the mechanisms by which the emerging Saʿudi state made itself visible to the people at a time when its machinery was still primitive. The consolidation of the state was highly dependent on a series of ritualised acts performed in the public *majlis*. The power of the ruling lineage had no outlet for display apart from that traditional institution, which was in theory open to a large section of the population. The seating arrangement, the silence of the audience, and the development of a sense of royalty among the ruling group shattered the myth of the *majlis* as the archetype of 'Arabian tribal democracy' because the 'ability to express views to the decision-maker is not equivalent to having a share in determining what decisions are made' (Niblock 1982b: 89). One might add that only a select group had regular access to the royal *majlis*. In those contexts, there was no doubt that a hierarchical and absolutist monarchy was in the process of being consolidated. While the *majlis* gave the impression that the monarch was easily accessible to his subjects, the reality of the gathering was far from it.

Royalty was made visible through ostentatious feasts, which fed the population and developed among them a sense of the political realm that was in the process of being established. Royal hospitality ensured the allegiance of the population at a time when neither national mythologies, nor a common sense of history and destiny, nor a well-developed welfare programme tied subjects to rulers. With the exception of some Najdi sedentary communities who willingly supported Ibn Saʿud, the majority of the subjects in other parts of Najd, Hijaz, Hasa and ʿAsir became part of the realm as a result of conquest. While the *majlis* was the arena where undisputed Saʿudi power was represented, both marriages and feasts resulted in the forging of a bond between the Saʿudi royal lineage and the population of Arabia. Marriages and feasts created relations of dependency and acquiescence. State–society relations revolved around personalised contacts with the King and other senior members of the royal lineage. When oil revenues began to pour into the royal purse, the same principles were maintained, but the magnitude of the process exceeded previous patterns.

STATE AFFAIRS

While such ritualised dramas of power made the Saʿudi royal lineage visible to the people, the affairs of the state were conducted behind closed doors. When the Kingdom of Saudi Arabia was declared in 1932, the King, together with a small circle of princes (mainly his sons Saʿud and Faysal) and foreign advisers and employees dealt with urgent matters of state affairs. A division of the royal court called *al-shuʿba al-siyasiyya* (the Political Committee) was established. At one time the committee consisted of eight members among whom were an Egyptian, Ḥafiẓ Wahba, two Syrians, Khalid al-Ḥakim and Yusuf Yasin, a Lebanese, Fuʾad Ḥamza, a Libyan, Khalid al-Ghargini, and H. St John Philby (Almana 1980: 191–2). Philby rarely attended the meetings of the committee as he preferred to see the King during his relaxed evening *majlis*. Ibn Saʿud's Arab entourage ran the daily affairs of the state. It seems that Ibn Saʿud trusted them with this job and felt relaxed in their company (Philby 1955: 294).

These individuals were Arabs of a certain standing. They had already acquired administrative skills in their own countries, which they put at the service of the King at a time when local expertise was lacking. Some had been driven away from their homelands by colonial pressure and found refuge in Saudi Arabia away from direct foreign rule. It is worth noting that in the 1920s and 1930s the King's employees initially did not receive regular salaries, but were rewarded with annual gifts; some of them resided in special sections of the royal palaces and were fed among the King's entourage. This informal arrangement tied them to the King, upon whom they became completely dependent.

A regular daily meeting with the King took place, usually after the midday prayers, to discuss a variety of issues such as correspondence with foreign powers and pilgrimage affairs. The committee dealt with both local and foreign matters. Its role was advisory; it had no executive power.

> The King would raise a subject upon which he wished to have advice. A general discussion then followed, in which every member of the committee was quite free to give his true opinion and make any suggestion he wished. The King would end the discussion when he thought that enough had been said and he would then make up his own mind about what to do. No member of the committee would ever have considered suggesting a topic for discussion on his own initiative; this was entirely the prerogative of the King. (Almana 1980: 179)

The committee did not discuss or deal with financial matters. Those were secretly discussed between the King and his most loyal and trusted finance minister, ʿAbdullah ibn Sulayman. In his youth, Ibn Sulayman had left his native town, ʿUnayzah, for Bombay, to seek employment with a leading Najdi merchant. After an unsuccessful business venture in Bahrain, he returned to Najd and was asked by his uncle, who had already been looking after court finances, to help as an assistant. When his uncle died, Ibn Sulayman was elevated to the status of finance minister, to deal with all state revenues and expenditure. He remained in this post until the death of Ibn Saʿud (Almana 1980: 192–3). One of his early preoccupations was to manage the grant of £5,000 paid to Ibn Saʿud by the British government until 1924 (Vassiliev 1998: 298).

On several occasions, Ibn Sulayman was the King's messenger to the merchants, whose resources were drawn upon during times of scarcity. When the King was preparing to terminate the *ikhwan* rebellion in 1927 and the royal purse was virtually empty, it was Ibn Sulayman who was dispatched to 'milk' the merchants. He came back with gifts of cash and loans to sponsor the military campaign (Almana 1980: 194). He had the contacts and skills to persuade merchants to invest some of their profit in financing the King's military ventures, which were portrayed as beneficial to commerce and trade: 'While Ibn Saud emptied the exchequer, it was Abdullah al-Sulaiman's duty to replenish it' (Vassiliev 1998: 299).

There was also the tradition of expecting the merchants to 'donate' money and provisions for particular purposes and provide regular supplies for the royal household (Niblock 1982b: 93). Ibn Sulayman's discussions with the King remained strictly private, away from the people and the Political Committee, but also away from Ibn Saʿud's sons, who were increasingly demanding money from their father's treasurer to finance their own endeavours:[11] 'But the real business of the state was done in the cool of the early morning, when Suleiman used to come with his books, alone and unobserved, to His Majesty's private chamber immediately after the morning prayer' (Almana 1980: 197).

In the 1920s and 1930s most state revenues came from *zakat*. In 1925 Ibn Saʿud issued a decree to regulate the collection of this Islamic tax. His decree stipulated that *zakat* paid in kind should be taken from among livestock of average quality. *Zakat* paid in cash should be based on the average price of livestock. Other taxes were imposed on agricultural produce calculated at 5 per cent of crops growing on irrigated land and 10 per cent of crops growing on non-irrigated land. Both silver and gold were taxed at 2.5 per cent of their price (Vassiliev 1998: 304–5).

Among the bedouins it was the duty of local shaykhs and district amirs to see that those taxes were paid. In the *hujjar* settlements, mentioned in the last chapter, it was the duty of the *muṭawwaʿa* to collect the taxes. Tax collectors were paid a fixed salary or received commissions, calculated as a percentage of what they extracted from people.

In addition to these taxes, Ibn Saʿud imposed 8 per cent customs duties in Hasa and Hijaz. He also enforced the payment of *jizya* (an Islamic tax imposed on non-Muslims). This included the Shiʿa of Hasa and non-Muslims, mainly Christian and Hindu merchants.

However, before the discovery of oil, state revenues were drawn mainly from the pilgrimage. Ibn Sulayman resided in Hijaz to supervise the tax collectors and levy duties on imported goods and pilgrims. It was estimated that he employed some 400 officials, slaves and guards for what became the Ministry of Finance (al-Zirkili 1970: 910). In 1913, Ibn Saʿud's revenues did not exceed £100,000. In 1923 they reached £210,000 (al-Zirkili 1970: 709). After the conquest of Hijaz, they rose to £1.5 million in 1927 (Vassiliev 1998: 305). Although these revenues could not establish a state infrastructure, when they were distributed as gifts, subsidies and feasts, they were impressive.

With the state treasury safely in the hands of ʿAbdullah ibn Sulayman, other state functions had to be formalised. After the conquest of Hijaz in 1926, a directorate dealing with foreign affairs was set up. In 1930 this was renamed the Ministry of Foreign Affairs. Its functions were separated from those of the Political Committee. The King's son Faysal headed it. Several Arab deputies dealt with its daily affairs. Among them were Yusuf Yasin, Fuʾad Ḥamza and Ḥafiẓ Wahba. The ministry employed an interpreter, Almana, to deal with foreign correspondence (Ḥamza 1936: 117–18).

In the 1930s, the Ministry of Foreign Affairs initially relied on loyal Saʿudi merchants to represent the country abroad. Members of Najdi and Hijazi commercial families who had already been prominent in establishing merchant houses and companies in major ports and towns abroad served the King as his representatives, in addition to carrying out their own commercial activities. Prominent merchants came from the families of Mandil, Nafisi, Fawzan and al-Goṣaybi, all belonging to the *ḥaḍar* communities of Najd, Hasa and Hijaz (Almana 1980: 191). With the growth of state bureaucracy in later years, these families became the nucleus of the Saʿudi civil service.

One of the ministry's practical functions was to regulate the entry into Saudi Arabia of foreign nationals by issuing a special visa. This was important for the regulation of the annual pilgrimage to Mecca and the taxing of the pilgrims. This taxation was gradually abandoned as the state treasury began to receive revenues from oil.[12]

Representatives of foreign missions resided in Jeddah. The USSR was among the first to recognise the kingdom, in 1926.[13] Britain, the Netherlands, France and other countries followed suit. In the 1930s the number of foreign embassies did not exceed a dozen. The Ministry of Foreign Affairs dealt with all correspondence with such missions and reported urgent matters to the King (Ḥamza 1936: 114–39).

In addition to the Political Committee, Ministry of Finance and Ministry of Foreign Affairs, the formalisation of military arrangements was deemed necessary immediately after the kingdom was declared in 1932. The Saʿudi forces included members of the Hijazi army and police force, which became the nucleus of the Saʿudi army after the capture of Hijaz in 1925. A *wikala* (agency) was established in the early 1930s and the finance minister, ʿAbdullah ibn Sulayman, headed it (Ḥamza 1936: 257). In 1944, this became the Ministry of Defence.

In the 1930s and even 1940s, a formal Saʿudi army was virtually nonexistent. As mentioned in the last chapter, Ibn Saʿud's conquests between 1902 and 1932 resembled *ghazu* (raids) by a permanent core force drawn from ʿAriḍ (or Wadi Ḥanifa, the region around the capital, Riyadh) and other oases in Najd, supplemented by the *ikhwan* tribal force. The *ikhwan* tribal force was never counted as part of a Saʿudi army; what was left of the *ikhwan* force became the nucleus of the National Guard, a separate paramilitary force often deployed for internal security.

While the Saʿudi army and National Guard were still not fully organised in the early 1930s, the most important military force consisted of the *jihad* warriors and the Royal Guard, an amalgamation of urban conscripts from Najdi oases and ʿAriḍ *ḥaḍar* communities: the first formed the flanks in battle while the latter fought in the centre (al-Dakhil 1982: 123). Ibn Saʿud kept a substantial number of slaves for his own security, but these slaves also participated in battle. His most loyal slave, who stood behind him at the *majlis* meetings and watched him when he prayed in the mosque, guaranteed his personal security (Vassiliev 1998: 308).

While no proper Ministry of Religious Affairs was established in the 1930s, the King held a formal weekly meeting with the *ʿulama*. This was a regular event whose purpose was to inform members of the *ʿulama* of major events and to seek their advice regarding innovations in the kingdom. Like the informal daily *majlis al-dars*, the meeting was important as it showed that the King was committed to the opinion of the *ʿulama*, although the latter had already been co-opted in the service of the state. After 1932, no serious clashes with the *ʿulama* were reported. The introduction of the car, aeroplane and telegraph, and even the arrival of the first American oil-exploration mission in 1933 (discussed below), went without serious challenges. The *ʿulama* seemed to have accepted Ibn Saʿud's authority and justifications for major innovations. Their meeting with the King remained a formality to which future Saʿudi monarchs remained faithful.

THE OIL CONCESSION (1933)

The day was Friday, the time for noon prayers at Riyadh's main mosque. Shaykh ibn Nimr, the imam of the mosque in Riyadh, was delivering his usual khuṭba [sermon] *to a large audience. Ibn Saʿud was listening. The shaykh recited several Qurʾanic verses including 'And incline not to those who do wrong, or the fire will seize you; and ye have no protectors other than Allah, nor shall ye be helped'* [Qurʾan, *sura* 11, verse 113]. *Ibn Saʿud was furious. He asked Shaykh ibn Nimr to step down. Ibn Saʿud began to recite* sura al-kafirun: *'Say: O ye that reject faith. I worship not that which ye worship, nor will ye worship that which I worship. And I will not worship that which ye have been wont to worship, nor will ye worship that which I worship. To you be your way and to me mine'* [Qurʾan, *sura* 109, verses 1–6]. (Oral narrative)

Several months after that Friday in 1933, Ibn Saʿud's finance minister, ʿAbdullah ibn Sulayman, signed an agreement with the American company Standard Oil of California (SOCAL) to start exploration for oil.[14] The pacification of the *ikhwan* and royal pomp left Ibn Saʿud with a debt of over £300,000, so he accepted an American initiative to search for oil in his territories. In public and during communal prayers he had already invoked a famous Qurʾanic verse. With the oil negotiation in the background, a Qurʾanic verse defining relationships between Muslims and 'infidels' (*sura al-kafirun*, recited by Ibn Saʿud) seemed more appropriate than the *sura* recited by Ibn Nimr. The first allowed the possibility of separation/cooperation between Muslims and non-Muslims as long as each party kept its religion to itself. A justification for negotiating with the 'infidels' was important.

A year before the signing of the oil concession, Saudi Arabia had fewer than fifty non-Muslim residents. After the oil concession, their number rose to 134, including 50 Americans, 11 Dutchmen, 44 Britons, 19 Italians, 5 Russians and 5 Frenchmen. Non-Muslims worked in consulates, petrol-pump stations and centres selling repair parts and pharmaceutical products (Ḥamza 1936: 144). While early 'infidels' were largely based in the cosmopolitan Hijaz, the American exploration team ventured into territories where they had never been seen, for example, in Najd and the desert between its main oases and those of the Eastern Province.[15] This was the beginning of a process that not only brought an increasing number of 'infidels' to the country, but also laid the foundation for a major material transformation.

The American SOCAL offered Ibn Saʿud what the Anglo-Persian Oil Company had declined. Under the supervision of Stephen Longrigg, the Anglo-Persian Oil Company rejected Ibn Saʿud's demands for a yearly rental of £5,000 in gold and an immediate loan of £100,000. The company proposed paying rent in Indian rupees instead of gold.[16]

SOCAL's chief negotiator, Lloyd Hamilton, won the contract according to which the King received an immediate loan of £20,000 and an annual rental of £5,000 (al-Shaykh 1988: 92). Ironically, with the American government's embargo on gold export during the 1930s economic depression, SOCAL bought the gold in London and shipped it on a P&O steamer to Jeddah, where it was deposited at the only bank in the country, the Netherlands Trading Society. At the office of the bank manager, ʿAbdullah ibn Sulayman counted the gold on the table while preparations for SOCAL explorers to fly to Jubayl with their pipes, cranes, drums, wrenches, cars and lorries were made (Holden and Johns 1981: 118; al-Shaykh 1988: 123). In 1933

SOCAL placed the oil concession with Saudi Arabia under a wholly owned subsidiary, California Arab Standard Oil Company (CASOC). This company was the precursor of Arabian American Oil Company ARAMCO, established in 1944 (Long 1997: 63).

From Saudi Arabia's side the key personality behind the agreement was Philby (Brown 1999: 45). According to Monroe, Philby's biographer, SOCAL paid him $1,000 a month, $10,000 if SOCAL won the concession, a further $25,000 if commercial oil was found, and a royalty of 50 cents per ton exported until a second $25,000 was reached (Monroe 1974: 204–5; al-Shaykh 1988: 71–4). While securing substantial commissions for himself, Philby would now begin to anticipate Ibn Saʿud paying off the debt to his company, Sharqiyyah, amounting to over £50,000. Ibn Saʿud was able to pay off this debt in 1943 (Brown 1999: 54).[17] Philby played the British and American oil companies off against each other in the interests of Ibn Saʿud and himself. His negotiations with SOCAL won Ibn Saʿud the best deal at the time and introduced Saudi Arabia to American commercial interests. This was followed by greater political involvement on behalf of the American government, an issue discussed later in this book.[18]

The terms of the 1933 agreement with SOCAL eased the immediate financial pressures resulting from the decline in pilgrimage revenues during the world economic depression. While an estimated 100,000 pilgrims arrived in Mecca in 1930, the number dropped to 20,000 three years later (Ḥamza 1936: 216–19). The oil concession came at a time when the state 'lurched from one financial crisis to another. Officials' salaries were substantially in arrears and the government borrowed money from most of the commercial companies in Jeddah' (Sluglett and Sluglett 1982: 47). It was estimated that Ibn Saʿud's debts at the time were £30,000 to the government of India, £4,000 to the Eastern Telegraph Company and £6,000 to the Banking and Marine Company, as well as £80,000 to ʿAbdullah al-Quṣaybi, the King's private banker (ibid.: 48). The oil concession resulted in immediate relief.

OIL IN COMMERCIAL QUANTITIES

It took some time before it became clear that the initial investment by SOCAL's subsidiary CASOC would yield future profit. Drilling for oil began in 1935 and after several disappointments oil well Dammam No. 7 started to produce oil. In 1938, the valves were turned on to pump oil in commercial quantities. On 1 May 1939, the first tanker with liquid fuel

Table 1. *Government revenues 1946–1952*

Year	Revenues in $US
1946	13.5 million
1950	113 million
1951	165 million
1952	212 million

Source: al-Zirkili 1970: 709.

sailed from Ra'’s Tannura (Vassiliev 1998: 318). Oil well Dammam No. 7 produced more than 1,500 barrels per day, in excess of what most oil wells in the USA were producing at the time (Long 1997: 62).

The outbreak of the Second World War came at a bad time both for ARAMCO and for Saudi Arabia. While oil production was not brought to a complete halt, it was difficult to reach a high level of extraction given restrictions on further exploration, human resources, drilling and shipment. In 1938 oil extraction started with 0.5 million barrels. By 1945 it had increased to 21.3 million barrels (Vassiliev 1998: 319).

The King was able to enjoy the beginning of oil wealth, some of which was used to build new royal palaces for himself and his sons. The Muraba' palace was built in 1936 out of the first cheque paid by the oil company and was completed in 1937 (Facey 1992: 311).[19] The palace accommodated the royal household, consisting of 1,000 persons at the end of the Second World War (ibid.: 312). Foreign guests from the Jeddah-based consulates and important shaykhs were hosted in another palace, Badi'a, a holiday retreat for the King and his household. Senior brothers and sons of Ibn Sa'ud were accommodated in new buildings and annexes, part of the royal complex. Riyadh became a large construction site, attracting bedouins who sought work and royal largesse. Its population rose from an estimated 47,000 in 1940 to 83,000 in 1950 (ibid.: 300). In 1938 it was estimated that state revenues were £1,300,000 in gold mainly from Hijaz customs and pilgrims (Sluglett and Sluglett 1982: 46). State revenues continued to rise steadily after the Second World War (see table 1).

The Riyadh construction boom was disrupted with the outbreak of the Second World War. The war reduced the number of pilgrims, upon whom state finances were still partially dependent, and the material and skilled personnel needed for further oil exploration and production.[20] Saudi Arabia experienced food shortages and with the efforts of ARAMCO's managers exerting pressure on Washington, the country qualified for the American Lend-Lease fund as Roosevelt declared the kingdom 'vital for the defense of the USA' in 1943 (Holden and Johns 1981: 128). After maintaining official 'neutrality' during the early years of the war, Saudi Arabia declared war on Germany.[21] American aid, together with a British subsidy of £1 million per year, helped Saudi Arabia towards the last years of the war. By the end of the Second World War oil contributed $10 million out of total government revenue of £13.2 million in sterling (Philby 1955: 197; al-Shaykh 1988: 120).

In 1946 the King visited Cairo where he had his first experience of a railway. Upon his return to Saudi Arabia, he asked ARAMCO to construct a railway line from Dammam to Riyadh via Hofuf, Ḥarad and Kharj. The line was inaugurated in 1951 (Facey 1992: 305). ARAMCO also started the drilling of water in deep wells with mechanical pumps, thus catering for royal palaces and the increasing population of Riyadh.

In 1953, oil extraction reached 308.3 million barrels (Vassiliev 1998: 319). Between 1945 and 1953 the King enjoyed what a Saʿudi writer described as *istiraḥat al-muḥarib* (a state of peace and tranquillity) (ʿAbdullah 1990). This peace was occasionally disrupted by the behaviour of some members of his own household who 'overindulged themselves in the new personal wealth and the luxuries it brought, both had never been experienced before' (Holden and Johns 1981; Howarth 1964).[22]

During his last years the King witnessed the expansion of Riyadh, the mushrooming of royal palaces, water pumps, electricity, cars, aeroplanes, the reintroduction of the train after a short-lived experience during the First World War[23] and the initiation of Saudi Arabia into international and Arab politics. In addition to his meeting with King Faruq of Egypt, Ibn Saʿud met American President Franklin D. Roosevelt and British Prime Minister Winston Churchill in 1945: the first presented him with a Douglas DC-3 airliner, followed by an agreement with TWA to provide pilots and air-support services. Several months later Churchill sent a Rolls Royce car.[24] By that time Saudi Arabia had already been slipping away from Britain.

The King also had a glimpse of the timid expansion of his government. In addition to the ministries created in the 1930s and 1940s (Foreign Affairs and Finance) mentioned earlier, five more were inaugurated in the early 1950s: Interior (1951), Health (1951), Communication (1953), Agriculture and Water (1953) and Education (1953). In October 1953, a month before his death, Ibn Saʿud agreed to establish the Council of Ministers. This remained a formality that later threatened the balance of power between his sons Saʿud and Faysal (Shamiyyah 1986: 243). In 1950, the so-called ministries had 4,653 employees (al-Zirkili 1970: 378); the majority neither received regular salaries nor kept systematic records of their operations (Vitalis 1999: 660: ʿAbdullah 1990: 36). Public works and state machinery remained underdeveloped partly because financial resources were meagre during the war and partly because substantial sums were spent on the construction of royal palaces and covering the expenditure of the royal lineage. The country had twenty-seven state schools and twenty-two private schools; the biggest and most prestigious of all schools (Falaḥ School in Mecca) had fewer than eight hundred pupils (Ḥamza 1936: 227–8).

OIL AND SOCIETY IN THE 1940S AND 1950S

Despite the gradual proliferation of state bureaucracy, Ibn Saʿud remained an absolute monarch. He delegated some responsibilities to his sons Saʿud and Faysal and retained a number of functionaries. ARAMCO was involved in most public works undertaken during the last decade of his life. It is absurd to imagine a state 'bureaucracy' or 'administration' during this period, in spite of the creation of the above-mentioned ministries. ARAMCO's involvement in building the country's infrastructure to facilitate oil extraction and shipment to overseas markets extended beyond the construction of roads, pipelines, ports and airports in the oil regions and elsewhere to providing schools, hospitals and quasi-state administration. ARAMCO filled a gap where public services, education and health facilities were underdeveloped and in some parts of the country virtually non-existent. In the absence of a state apparatus, ARAMCO was the state subcontractor. It provided vital services (water and health provisions) for the royal household in addition to highly visible public projects, consolidating royal authority. The railway project was one among several initiatives undertaken between 1945 and 1953. Given the company's initial role in building the material infrastructure it is ironical that neither its early contribution nor its later 'Saudisation' feature in official historical narratives (Vitalis 1997: 17 and 1998: 3–25), a theme dealt with later in this book.

It is important to note, however, that in the 1940s and early 1950s not many Saʿudis came into contact with the company and its American managers and their families (Brown 1999: 140). This was partly because of the isolation of its high-ranking personnel in what was referred to as the Dhahran 'American Camp'. In this camp 'a system of race and caste segregation was exported by oil men and managers' (Vitalis 1997: 17).

By 1950 Dhahran, the headquarters of ARAMCO's American employees, developed into a 'town' where 'one may buy stamps and post a letter, get a hair cut or a beauty treatment, buy groceries, household supplies, and essential personal items' (Brown 1999: 140). This area was physically separated from other quarters of the camp by barbed wire, beyond which Saʿudi and Arab workers lived, commonly referred to as 'Saʿudi Camp'. Saʿudi camp was 'open and unfenced, and, at first, bereft of all basic services; water, power, sewers, and so on. These came later, and slowly, after a series of strikes by non-American workers and in the wake of the 1948 Palestine war, when the Aramco officials believed that the company's concession was in danger' (Vitalis 1998: 14).

Although this segregation was part of ARAMCO's ethos, Saʿudis had neither the inclination nor the power to challenge it. *Sura al-kafirun*, recited by Ibn Saʿud during the Friday prayer, remained the background against which Saʿudis perceived the flux of 'infidels' into the 'land of Islam', an understanding that has lasted until the present day. In the meantime, Dhahran 'began to acquire the appearance and aura of an American company town. It was said to resemble Bakersfield on the edge of the Mojave Desert in California, as it was in the 1950s – a little world of split-level houses with outskirts of dreary tin-roofed shacks, cement block bars, and filling stations' (Brown 1999: 139–40).

Saʿudis were recruited from among the indigenous Shiʿa population of the oases of Hasa, who in 1954 constituted 60 per cent of the ARAMCO Saʿudi workforce (Vitalis 1998: 10). Others came from among the sedentary population of the oases in the eastern province and Najd. Bedouins were also attracted to menial jobs revolving around drilling, construction, driving, clearing and cleaning sites. Hasawi, Qaṣimi and Hijazi merchants, for example the Goṣaybis and ʿOlayan, acted as subcontracting agencies for transport, labour contracting, laundries and supplies (Vitalis 1998: 11; Field 1984: 217, 311).

In the early 1950s, of the 20,400 people ARAMCO employed, 4,000 were Americans, 13,400 were Saʿudis and 3,000 were of other nationalities – African, Arab and Mediterranean (Brown 1999: 140). Americans constituted about one-third of ARAMCO's workforce. The number of Saʿudi workers might be small among the population, estimated at the time to be 2.5 million (al-Zirkili 1970: 709), but the consequences of their recruitment spilled beyond those who were stationed at the camp.

It was those tin-roofed shacks that housed Saʿudi and Arab workers employed in the four oil fields that had been discovered at the time: Abu Ḥadriyya, Abqaiq, Qatif and Dammam (Vassiliev 1998: 329). Their 'barrack-like dwellings consisted of concrete cement-block structures, offering modest recreational facilities, a market for buying food and other items, and one or more mosques' (Brown 1999: 141). Sheep and camels intermingled with workers. Between 1945 and 1960, the turnover in Arab employees reached a level of 75 per cent, and stayed at that level for years (ibid.: 150). While bedouins from different parts of the country would come and go, the Hasawi Shiʿa peasantry proved to be the least fluctuating bloc in this newly created heterogeneous entity called 'ARAMCO workforce'. According to Brown, they came to work for one reason: 'Word spread to the desert and townspeople that in exchange for some physical effort the blue eyed foreigners would give a man a handful of silver' (ibid.: 147).

Yet the 'slums' of ARAMCO feature in the popular memory of the early Saʿudi workers. A Saʿudi ex-ARAMCO worker described his experience:

> During the second war we almost starved in Qasim. Members of my family were poor peasants who looked after the palm groves of a wealthy local. We had already heard from people that some *naṣranis* [Christians] were offering jobs in Hasa for cash. My father decided that I should go and try my luck. I travelled with a bedouin caravan to 'American Camp' and was offered a job to carry goods and material. I did all sorts of jobs. For the first time in my life I found myself with other tribesmen from ʿUtayba, Shammar and Qaḥṭan, each had their stories and dialect. We worked together. I met people from ʿAsir and other parts of Najd. It was amazing. We had a communal kitchen, it was our 'restaurant'. We called it *maṭʿam abu rubʿ*, because they charged a quarter of a riyal for the meal. The food was awful. But the Najdis would not say anything. They were shy; they would not complain. They would not ask for more money or food. They just left the Indians to eat there. Later in the 1950s they began to demand things from ARAMCO. When *al-lajna al-ʿummalyya* [the Workers' Committee] told us to ask for more cash and better food, we did not respond. People were not beggars. But when they told us to ask for political rights, we all responded and joined the strikes in 1953. I sent money to my family. All I wanted to buy for myself was a radio. I wanted to hear about what was going on in Palestine and Egypt. Palestinian workers told us about their problems. We listened to the news together. (Interview, March 1999)

The radio did have its effect in altering the consciousness of some of those early Saʿudi workers, together with the wages they received. As Saʿudis intermingled with Palestinian, Syrian, Egyptian and Lebanese workers, they came face-to-face with the turbulent historical moment in the Arab world following the 1948 Palestine war. Saʿudi workers listened to the news with the Arab co-workers and debated the events in male dormitories. Ibn Saʿud's cautious policy towards Palestine, which he had maintained in the 1930s, could no longer be sustained in the late 1940s.

A new kind of awareness began to develop among ARAMCO Saʿudi workers. It was different from that generated as a result of the previous encounters between Arabian nomads and merchants crossing, for example, the northern boundaries of the country into areas that had become increasingly well-defined territories belonging to newly created 'nation-states'. While the crossing of boundaries had already been gradually contained by the emerging states to the north, the flow of immigrant workers into Saudi Arabia began to take shape. This flow supplemented the already-existing Arab functionaries whose employment in the country started in the 1920s. With the exception of the transient pilgrims, Saudi Arabia became a host country for immigrant labour for the first time.

In the early 1950s a limited number of Saʿudis in Hasa began to benefit from public health work, hospitals and schools. ARAMCO managers ventured outside the camp enclosure to supervise the drilling for water, among other things, in Riyadh and elsewhere. They were often remembered as 'big and red-faced; they wore big hats. People used to say that they wore them because they did not want to see Allah of the Muslims' (oral tradition). Saʿudi workers sent wages to families as far as Najd, ʿAsir and Hijaz. While individual contributions and remittances from the Hasa-based ARAMCO industry travelled to other parts of the country, the infrastructures of those parts remained virtually untouched. In the case of ʿAsir, the remotest hinterland of Saudi Arabia, real economic development did not begin until several decades later.

Only a few Saʿudi workers moved out of menial and unskilled job categories as they began to demonstrate managerial skills. Rudimentary training schemes were introduced by ARAMCO. Literacy classes began to attract workers. Saʿudis who distinguished themselves during their employment with ARAMCO were later sent abroad, initially to Egypt and later to Europe and the United States to pursue higher education.

The Saʿudi dissident Naṣir al-Saʿid (born 1923) had a short career in ARAMCO that was terminated in 1957 after he claimed to represent the Arab workforce through his activities in the Federation of Arab Trade Unions. Al-Saʿid had travelled to ARAMCO camp from his native town, Haʾil, in search of employment. Through his contact with Arab workers and an alleged visit to the Soviet Union, he became politicised and was behind the 1953 riots and later the 1956 strikes organised by ARAMCO workers (al-Saʿid 1981; Abu Dhar 1982; Lackner 1978; Abir 1988). These riots pushed ARAMCO to reconsider the material and social conditions of the camps and raise wages. By 1957, ARAMCO's basic wage scale had more than doubled, and the average annual income among all Saʿudi employees had risen to $1,300 (Brown 1999: 154). The involvement of al-Saʿid, among others, in issues relating to improvement of the conditions of work regarded by both the government and ARAMCO as revolutionary at the time led to his imprisonment. When he was released, he left Saudi Arabia to spend his life in exile in Lebanon, Syria and Iraq. In 1979, al-Saʿid was kidnapped in Lebanon, allegedly by agents of the Saʿudi government, and never appeared again (Abu Dhar 1982). His wife and children are still living in Libya.

The oil industry generated forms of opposition previously unknown in Saudi Arabia, and also provided much of the background for the Saʿudi dissident literature of the early 1950s. For example, in his *Cities of Salt* trilogy, Saʿudi novelist ʿAbd al-Raḥman Munif captured the spirit of that unique historical experience. His novels represented the first serious attempt to show the effect of oil and Americans on Saudi Arabia. They were set in Mooran, an imaginary city isolated in the desert but transformed beyond recognition within a short time. In *The Trench*, Munif writes:

> Within a few years Mooran was a wondrous city. Due to the journeys its people had made to a variety of countries, the magazines they brought back with them, the blue prints they planned for the houses they saw on these trips, and the existence of the al-Gazal Villa and Palace Construction Company, palaces began to appear like creeping plants, like Japanese gardens: an assemblage of colors, shapes and forms the eye could not stand: houses so spacious that one could only wonder what they could be used for or who would live in them . . . Cars had come to Mooran, air conditioners, jewels and ever-rising numbers of foreigners. (Munif 1993: 412–13)

ARAMCO not only facilitated the emergence of the first wave of Saʿudi administrators, technocrats, civil servants and oil millionaires, but also the first political prisoners, dissidents, exiles and opposition literary figures. What was described as tribal conspiracies or religious opposition during the reign of Ibn Saʿud was replaced by a new discourse drawing on the 1950s fashionable Arab political trends. In 1953 Saudi Arabia had its own timid Nasserites, Arab nationalists, and communists, all bred near the oil fields and inside 'Saʿudi Camp'. While Ibn Saʿud did not live long enough to see the unfolding of new forces in Saʿudi society, his son Saʿud was haunted by new political developments that had their origins near the oil fields, discussed in the next chapter.

SAUDI ARABIA AND BRITAIN

The oil concession with ARAMCO marked the beginning of the decline of Britain's influence in Saudi Arabia, which came to its final phase after the Second World War. In the early 1930s Ibn Saʿud constantly appealed to Britain for aid, but no direct subsidy was given. Instead, the British government decided to send arms on very easy terms and aeroplanes for the Saʿudi air force (Sluglett and Sluglett 1982: 47). Britain was, however, anxious that Ibn Saʿud's financial difficulties might encourage the Italians, who had established a base on the African side of the Red Sea, to bale him out (ibid.: 48).

In November 1930, Ibn Saʿud announced the annexation of ʿAsir while allowing the Idrisi (mentioned in the last chapter) to remain in nominal charge of the province. This was well received in London (Leatherdale 1983: 146). However, the annexation of ʿAsir brought Ibn Saʿud closer to the territories of Imam Yaḥya of Yemen, who also had strong ambitions in ʿAsir.

In 1932, a plot, involving simultaneous attacks on Hijaz, from the south and from the north, was discovered. The plot was orchestrated by Ibn Rifada, the chief of a Hijazi tribe, together with Hijazi notables from the Dabbagh and al-Khaṭib families, who had fled to Yemen and Trans-Jordan after the conquest of Hijaz in 1925. This plot drew Ibn Saʿud's attention to the danger ʿAsir could pose for the security of his realm. Later the Idrisi, with Yemeni support, rebelled against the Saʿudi governor of ʿAsir. The uprising was put down in 1933, after which the Idrisi himself fled to Yemen (Leatherdale 1983: 150). Yemeni troops immediately entered the inland town of Najran and other parts of ʿAsir, demanding the return of all Idrisi dominions.

Ibn Saʿud lacked the financial means to purchase arms for what appeared an inevitable war with the Imam of Yemen. Once again, Britain rejected his request for arms and tried to dissuade him from any hostile enterprise (Leatherdale 1983: 151). The conflict that originated in ʿAsir turned into a confrontation between Saudi Arabia and Yemen, with Italy and Britain being drawn into this conflict. Between March and May 1933, Saʿudi forces marched on the disputed areas of the Saʿudi–Yemeni borders and, after several military confrontations, Ibn Saʿud announced a ceasefire in May. This was followed by the Treaty of Taʾif in June 1934. Ibn Saʿud and Imam Yaḥya appealed to 'Islamic friendship and brotherhood'. Imam Yaḥya agreed to Ibn Saʿud's demands to release Saʿudi hostages, the settlement of disputed regions, and the surrender of the Idrisi and his followers (ibid.: 160). Ibn Saʿud formally acquired ʿAsir, but failed to reach a final agreement with Imam Yaḥya on the Saʿudi–Yemeni borders.

While Britain had supported Ibn Saʿud in suppressing the 1927 *ikhwan* rebellion, it seems that its support during the Saʿudi–Yemeni war was not so forthcoming. According to Leatherdale, 'Yemen was not Iraq: Britain having no comparable interest at stake' (Leatherdale 1983: 160). Britain's policy in the 1930s revolved around the maintenance of Ibn Saʿud as the principal source of political authority. Britain saw the Saʿudi–Yemeni war as a local conflict over the disputed buffer territory of ʿAsir. It is not unlikely that Ibn Saʿud interpreted Britain's reserved attitude towards this war as a failure to help him. This may have been one of the reasons why he agreed to sign the oil concession with an American company, whose government was considered to be neutral and without obvious imperial ambitions in Arabia.

In the 1930s, the question of Palestine did not become an issue between Ibn Saʿud and Britain. Prior to the 1936 disturbances in Palestine, it seems that Ibn Saʿud had paid little attention to events in this part of the Arab world, perceived as both physically remote and culturally alien to his realm: 'Ibn Saʿud had been noticeably unwilling to allow himself to be used by either Palestinian or Syrian agitators, although the Grand Mufti of Jerusalem had complained to Ibn Saʿud about Britain's Zionist policy, which was depicted as being calculated to destroy the Arab nation' (Leatherdale 1983: 268).

Britain made it clear that 'the Saʿudi King would neither promote his friendship with Britain, nor enhance his prestige in the Arab world at large if he concerned himself with a purely British problem in Palestine' (Leatherdale 1983: 268). In 1937, it became obvious that the British mandate in Palestine was entering its final phase and the territory was going to be partitioned into an Arab and a Jewish state. Britain informed Ibn Saʿud of the decision, but no Saʿudi reaction comparable to those of other Arab countries was noticeable. In fact, Ibn Saʿud's initial response to the partition of Palestine was muted (ibid.: 274). It seems that 'Ibn Saʿud was more concerned with the ambitions of the Hashemite ʿAbdullah, who was actively intriguing with the Palestinian Arabs and who, with the support of Iraq, made no secret of hoping to absorb Palestine into a greater Jordan' (ibid.).

Ibn Saʿud's policy towards Palestine in the 1930s was cautious; he

> was determined not to open up his Kingdom for the benefit of pan-Arab conferences. Neither did he send a delegate to the Arab Conference at Bludan, in Syria, in 1937. It was one thing for Ibn Saʿud to outwardly support Muslim

1 Street scene, Riyadh. © Popperfoto

solidarity movements: it was quite another to encourage the popular xenophobia, intellectual agnosticism, and reformist ideals which could permeate his Kingdom. (Leatherdale 1983: 282)

Ibn Saʿud's indifference towards the Palestinian problem was maintained until the outbreak of the Second World War. This attitude was summed up by his famous saying: '*ahl filiṣṭin adra bi shiʿabiha*' (Palestinians know better their own valleys) (*al-Yamama*, 31 March 2001: 24). While this saying implies reluctance to interfere in the Palestinian conflict, it reflected both a deep-seated reservation and a desire to remain aloof from an Arab crisis that Ibn Saʿud considered irrelevant to the preservation of his realm. Saudi Arabia did not take a serious part in the Arab–Jewish war of 1947 although it sent one battalion which acted as a unit of the Egyptian army (Vassiliev 1998: 349). The declaration of the state of Israel in 1948 resulted in the expulsion of thousands of Palestinians, who fled as refugees to neighbouring Arab countries. Ibn Saʿud made a concession to the Palestinian problem when in 1949 he informed ARAMCO of his desire that the company should employ at least a thousand Palestinian refugees (Seccombe and Lawless 1986: 571). ARAMCO immediately sent officials to recruit Palestinians in Beirut where they received more than 5,650 applications. In December 1949

ARAMCO employed 100 Palestinians; a year later their number rose to 826 (ibid.: 572).

In the late 1940s Ibn Saʿud's main concern was the two Hashemite kingdoms of Iraq and Trans-Jordan, both of which had important tribal populations that originated in Saudi Arabia. Also, both monarchs had legitimate claims to leadership on the basis of their holy descent. Saudi Arabia opposed King ʿAbdullah's ambition to annex eastern Palestine and used the Arab League, which it joined in 1945, to curb Hashemite influence in the Arab world.

Saʿudi Arabia remained convinced that Britain's policy in the Middle East strengthened its Hashemite rivals, and this conviction was behind Ibn Saʿud's desire to develop a closer relationship with the United States. In 1942 the United States appointed a chargé d'affaires in Jeddah. Between 1944 and 1946 the American diplomatic mission was headed by W. A. Eddy, an experienced intelligence officer and Arabist, and later an ARAMCO consultant (Vassiliev 1998: 325). ARAMCO officials remained the main driving force behind Saʿudi–American relations during the last years of the Second World War. In 1943, ARAMCO officials facilitated visits by Saʿudi princes Saʿud and Faysal to Washington. ARAMCO officials convinced Washington that Saudi Arabia's oil reserves amounted to 20 billion barrels, which was equal to all the explored deposits in the United States (ibid.).

ARAMCO's efforts to draw Washington's attention to Saudi Arabia culminated in a meeting between Ibn Saʿud and American President Roosevelt in 1945. Ibn Saʿud was brought from Jeddah to the Suez Canal, where Roosevelt was waiting for him on board the *Quincy*, a US cruiser (Miller 1980: 128–31). The meeting resulted in the establishment of stronger relations with the United States, at the expense of Britain. Ibn Saʿud agreed to allow American ships to use Saʿudi ports and to the building of an American large air-force base. An area was leased to the US army for a period of five years; thereafter it was to be returned to Saudi Arabia with all the structures erected on it (Vassiliev 1998: 327). Ibn Saʿud confirmed that the 1933 oil concession with ARAMCO was still valid and granted his consent to the building of the Trans-Arabian oil pipeline between Hasa and the Mediterranean (ibid.). Washington sent a military mission to investigate the construction of military airfields in Dhahran. For Ibn Saʿud, the meeting held great significance as he journeyed beyond his borders in search of an ally to guarantee the independence of his newly created realm. The United States was in search of oil deposits and military air bases.

The main factor behind Saʿudi–American relations during the Second World War was oil and the commercial interests of American oil companies. After the oil concession of 1933, Saudi Arabia became the first independent Arab state to develop important relations with the United States (Leatherdale 1983: 211). Also, Saudi Arabia was the first area outside the western hemisphere where American political and strategic influence replaced that of Britain (ibid.: 212). The oil concession marked the beginning of a relationship that matured only after the Second World War. During the war, Britain retained Saudi Arabia within her sphere of influence, a position which the United States never sought to challenge until after the war (ibid.). Saudi Arabia, however, received arms and military equipment from the United States under the Lend-Lease Program, which created favourable impressions in Saudi Arabia and facilitated the development of an intimate relationship when the Second World War ended.

THE END OF AN ERA

While objections to ARAMCO camp conditions were fermenting hundreds of miles from Riyadh, Ibn Saʿud spent his last years in a state of tranquillity, caused by old age and illness and surrounded by his most loved sons. While his most senior sons, (Crown Prince) Saʿud and Faysal, had already been involved in running the affairs of the politically most important regions (Najd and Hijaz) and ARAMCO's empire growing steadily and simultaneously in Hasa, this tranquillity gradually gave way to withdrawal from public life. Ibn Saʿud retreated among his most intimate relatives while nurturing his younger sons, those born in the 1930s and 1940s to ex-concubines with whom he had developed an intimate affinity. Prince Ṭalal ibn ʿAbd al- ʿAziz Al Saʿud and his later political career were products of that intimate encounter between the ageing father/king and a son whose loyalty was not tainted by maternal kin drawn from Arabian nobility.[25] Ibn Saʿud promoted the career of Ṭalal and his full brothers, an act that later fuelled internal rivalries among his sons and threatened the kingdom's survival. Van der Meulen visited Riyadh before the King died in November 1953. He described the famous *majlis*:

> The failing spring has failed. I heard nothing new, no sparkling comments, no vigorous views on Arab-Muslim policy or the affairs of the outside world. The audience-Chamber was no longer a place of inspiration for his people. The voice that used to resound there no longer raised an echo in the hearts of men. Before long it would be stilled. Ar-Riadh was waiting for that moment and out of respect due to the great old man it waited in silence. (Van der Meulen 1957: 229–30)

CHAPTER 4

The politics of dissent, 1953–1973

A fierce power struggle between Ibn Saʿud's most senior sons, Saʿud and Faysal, erupted immediately after he died. Throughout the 1950s, the Saʿudi state came close to collapse on several occasions and the future of the country seemed uncertain as a result of the volatile internal political struggle between the two Saʿudi brothers.

Throughout this period, the political upheavals of the Arab world (the Suez Crisis of 1956 and the Arab–Israeli war of 1967) influenced political and social events in Saudi Arabia. Various external ideologies, for example, Naṣir's pan-Arabism and socialism and later Iraqi/Syrian Baʿthism threatened the very foundation of Saʿudi rule and became the impetus for the development of Faysal's Islamic politics in the early 1960s. Faysal highlighted the Islamic credentials of the Saʿudi state. This became a counter-strategy with which Saudi Arabia aimed to undermine the wider claims of Arab nationalism and establish itself as an important player in Arab regional politics after decades of remaining on the margins of an Arab world dominated by Egypt.

This chapter is a chronological account of the internal political struggle within the Saʿudi royal family against the background of the Arab regional context. While the internal rivalry between Saʿud and Faysal had its own local reasons, the political struggle cannot be fully understood without exploring Saudi Arabia's relationship with the Arab world in the 1950s and 1960s.

THE REIGN OF KING SAʿUD (1953–1964)

Crown Prince Saʿud (born 1902) was declared King shortly after his father died and his brother Faysal automatically became Crown Prince. Saʿud was ill-suited to succeed his father and did prove extremely incompetent when the time came.

During his first year as King, Saʿud's oil revenues rose to $236 million. They reached $340 million in 1954 and dropped to $290 million in 1956.

They remained static in 1957 and 1958. The increase in oil revenues did not solve the financial problem associated with the debts Saʿud had inherited from his father, estimated to have been $200 million in 1953. In fact this debt more than doubled by 1958, when it reached $480 million (Shamiyyah 1986: 243). The Saʿudi riyal lost half of its official value against the dollar. Both ARAMCO and international banks declined Saʿudi demands for credit. Saʿud suspended the few government projects he had initiated, but continued his spending on luxurious palaces (Safran 1985: 87). In fact, in 1953 he fixed the annual salaries of the royal princes at $32,000 plus an allowance for miscellaneous spending in spite of the government debt (Shamiyyah 1986: 244). Previously, princes had been dependent on Ibn Saʿud's largesse and informal arrangements whereby they negotiated various cash and land gifts with their father, whose instructions were executed by the finance minister.[1]

This was the background of the political crisis that made the reign of Saʿud associated with the most turbulent period in the history of the nascent Saʿudi state. Government finances, or more accurately its plundering, became the umbrella under which a fierce struggle for power between Saʿud and his ambitious brother Faysal was unfolding. Saʿud and Faysal fought an internal battle over the definition of political responsibilities and the division of government functions.

The limited historiography of the period paints a picture of Saʿud and Faysal as binary opposites. In these accounts Saʿud is often associated among other things with 'traditional tribal government, plundering of oil revenues, palace luxuries, conspiracy inside and outside Saudi Arabia, and vice'. Faysal is associated with 'sobriety, piety, puritanism, financial wisdom, and modernisation' (Yizraeli 1997; Safran 1985; Shamiyyah 1986; al-Shaykh 1988; ʿAbdullah 1990). Moreover, the conflict between the two brothers is often described as originating from the desire of Faysal to curb his brother's spending and solve Saudi Arabia's financial crisis. Government finances were believed to have been the motivation behind Faysal's successive attempts to marginalise the King and limit his various powers. The crisis, however, was not only economic and financial, but also political and social. While not underestimating the magnitude of the financial crisis, an understanding of those turbulent years should go beyond the Saʿudi debts, and investigate the internal rivalries among Ibn Saʿud's sons that erupted immediately after he died.

With the death of Ibn Saʿud, a political crisis at the level of leadership followed. How to divide the patrimony of Ibn Saʿud among his various sons became an urgent matter among his immediate descendants. The sharing of power among the most senior princes who had been directly involved in the creation of the realm had to be institutionalised. A division of labour between Saʿud and Faysal had already been in place, but the creation of the Council of Ministers a month before the death of Ibn Saʿud in 1953 did not solve the problem of power sharing between the King and the Crown Prince. In fact, this council became the platform for this internal struggle. The Council of Ministers was meant to be the executive organ of the government. It had the authority to issue ministerial decrees, but had no power separate from the King, who approved all its decisions.

During his lifetime, Ibn Saʿud had relied heavily on his Arab advisers and managed to post members of his own generation to distant provinces as governors, while promoting only a limited circle of his own sons. Once the council was created, internal rivalries over its membership and role erupted. Ibn Saʿud did not leave behind a historical precedent to be followed by his descendants. For although he delegated some responsibilities to his two senior sons, there was no doubt that he was the ultimate authority. His death removed the implicit understanding among his descendants that the Saʿudi King was an absolute monarch.

The battle between the two brothers was fought over the role to be assigned to the Council of Ministers. Saʿud abolished the office of prime minister by royal decree, thus enforcing his position as King and *de facto* prime minister. Saʿud thought of himself as both King and prime minister whereas Faysal envisaged more powers in his own hand as Crown Prince and deputy prime minister. Had the power struggle between Saʿud and Faysal been resolved, a smooth incorporation of royal princes in government would have been possible. Several ministries emerged in less than a decade: Communication (1953), Agriculture and Water (1953), Education (1953), Petroleum and Mineral Resources (1960), Pilgrimage and Islamic Endowments (1960), Labour and Social Affairs (1962) and Information (1963). The expansion of government bureaucracy, however, exposed the underlying tension between Ibn Saʿud's descendants.

Saʿud began to promote his own sons, as his father had done at the expense of his brothers (Shamiyyah 1986: 244). Between 1953 and 1964, the eight ministries were partly meant to contain the fermenting demands for political participation among members of the royal lineage. But in 1957 Saʿud placed his son Fahd in the Ministry of Defence, his son Musaʿid in the Royal Guard, his son Khalid in the National Guard and his son Saʿad in the Special Guard (ibid.: 245). Having secured control over defence, he appointed his brother Ṭalal (mentioned in the last chapter) to the Ministry of Transport. Saʿud also promoted his father's Syrian doctor, Rashad Firʿun, to run the Ministry of Health. He appointed a Hijazi from an established merchant family, Muhammad ʿAli Riḍa, to run the Ministry of Commerce and ʿAbdullah ba al-Khayr to run the Ministry of Communication. With this configuration, the government profile did not take into account the claims of Saʿud's brothers and, most importantly, Faysal, the most senior.

Between 1953 and 1964, three royal power blocs began to crystallise. One group developed around Saʿud, consisting of his own sons. A second group revolved around Faysal, his half-brothers (Muhammad and the group later known as the Sudayri Seven) and paternal uncles led by Musaʿid ibn ʿAbd al-Raḥman and ʿAbdullah ibn ʿAbd al-Raḥman (both brothers of Ibn Saʿud). A third group of relatively younger sons of Ibn Saʿud (born around the 1930s), notably Ṭalal whose maternal connections were outside Arabia, Badr, Fawwaz, and ʿAbd al-Muḥsin, began to take shape (Gause 1990: 60; Abir 1988: 92). These coalitions exposed the wisdom behind Ibn Saʿud's marital practices discussed in the last chapter. The rhetoric of patrilineal descent was put to the first ultimate test during the reign of Saʿud. In an attempt to carve a niche for themselves after the death of their father, the young princes oscillated in their allegiance between the bloc of Saʿud and that of Faysal. They initially co-operated with Saʿud, but were also willing to switch allegiance to Faysal, when he promised to listen to their demands. The game was carefully played until they began to distance themselves from both.

Having surrounded himself with an emerging group of educated Saʿudis who had already been incorporated in the various newly created ministries, in 1958–9 Ṭalal surprised the King when he proposed the formation of a National Council, a consultative rather than a legislative assembly (Yizraeli 1997: 112). The proposal was presented to the King while Faysal was outside Saudi Arabia, perhaps because of Ṭalal's anticipation that Faysal would object to it. Saʿud's response was to resort to the *ʿulama* in an attempt to evade a direct confrontation. He 'transferred Ṭalal's request to the *ʿulama* in order to give an opinion whether a National Council was a legitimate institution in Islam' (Shamiyyah 1986: 250).

Several Hijazi and Najdi civil servants were behind the proposal, for example Muhammad ʿAli Riḍa, ʿAbd al-ʿAziz Muʿamar and ʿAbdullah al-Ṭariqi. Ṭalal expected the National Council to be the first step towards a constitutional monarchy. When these demands fell on deaf ears, Ṭalal became more radical, after being dismissed from government in 1961. He moved to Cairo and Beirut where he announced the establishment of a royal opposition group, *al-umara' al-aḥrar*, the Free Princes. The group consisted of Ṭalal and his full brothers, together with a coterie of educated Saʿudis, influenced by current political trends in the Arab world, especially Nasserism. The Free Princes' main demand revolved around the establishment of a constitutional monarchy in Saudi Arabia. The Egyptian and Lebanese press closely followed their activities, centred at the Saint George hotel in Beirut, a cosmopolitan international tourist attraction long associated with disenchanted Arab exiles of all persuasions. The Saint George hotel was far removed from the lives of the majority of Saʿudis in the early 1960s, when female education had not yet started.

While the princes were engaged in a fierce battle over power sharing and its institutionalisation, only a small section of Saʿudi society was beginning to experience a social transformation associated with the oil industry in the eastern province and the new wealth this brought. Between 1950 and 1960 a small group of indigenous educated technocrats was beginning to appear. An educated coterie crystallised around the King, Crown Prince and other senior princes. The first wave of Saʿudis with formal education from universities abroad returned to the country. They were placed in the various ministries created during that decade. Some Saʿudis were also elevated to military ranks in the army after several years of training in Egypt. Oil wealth, coupled with the expansion of state administration, allowed such individuals to be recruited into the civil service, thus partially replacing the Arab functionaries of Ibn Saʿud. Some of those indigenous civil servants were influenced by current political ideologies in the Arab world that were associated with Gamal ʿAbd al-Naṣir's version of Arab nationalism.

The career of ʿAbdullah al-Ṭariqi (born 1925) illustrated the social changes that began to unfold in Saudi Arabia and their political ramifications (Duguid 1970: 197). In his youth al-Ṭariqi left his native Najdi oasis, Zilfi, to seek secondary education in Kuwait (al-Shaykh 1988: 368). Later most of his early higher education took place in Egypt, where he acquired a Bachelor of Science degree from Fu'ad I University. He returned to Saudi Arabia and found employment in the nascent Saʿudi administration with the Ministry of Finance, under the patronage of the finance minister, ʿAbdullah ibn Sulayman. Initially he worked as translator for Ibn Saʿud in his dealings with ARAMCO officials. He secured a grant from the King's treasury to study geology in Cairo and Texas where he married an American woman, whom he later divorced in Saudi Arabia. Upon his return, he was appointed director of Petroleum and Mineral Resources.

During the reign of King Saʿud, he became oil minister in 1960 with the creation of the Ministry of Petroleum and Mineral Resources (al-Shaykh 1988: 368; Brown 1999: 151). Influenced by the Arab political atmosphere of the 1950s, particularly Nasserism, al-Ṭariqi attacked ARAMCO when he demanded its nationalisation. It is alleged that the source of his antagonism was the bigotry that he faced when in the 1950s he was not admitted to the senior staff camp as his rank entitled him (Brown 1999: 153).

Al-Ṭariqi participated in the first Arab Petroleum Congress, which met in Cairo in 1959 (Duguid 1970: 207). In this meeting he proposed that all petroleum agreements should be periodically renegotiated when they no longer suited one of the parties. Al-Ṭariqi argued that all oil concessions with Arab countries were negotiated at a time when these countries were either under foreign occupation or were too unsophisticated in such matters to fully comprehend the importance and intricacies of the agreements (ibid.: 206).

Al-Ṭariqi was also behind the establishment of an organisation consisting of the oil-producing countries. The Organisation of Petroleum Exporting Countries (OPEC) was born in September 1960. The background to establishing such a forum was the post-Second World War oil glut that did little to increase the oil revenues of the oil-producing countries. In an attempt to prevent a total collapse of oil prices, oil companies reduced production, which in turn affected the economies of countries dependent on oil. Al-Ṭariqi envisaged OPEC playing a leading role in stabilising markets, preventing economic waste and conserving this irreplaceable natural resource (Duguid 1970: 209). While al-Ṭariqi was oil minister, Saudi Arabia gave its full support to OPEC. However, in the 1960s OPEC failed to influence oil prices, as several oil-producing countries had little control over their natural resources under oil concessions signed with foreign oil companies in previous decades. OPEC became a tool in the hands of the oil companies (Long 1997: 66–8; Duguid 1970: 209).

Al-Ṭariqi's radical views made him unpopular with Faysal, his early patron. Faysal dismissed al-Ṭariqi from his post in the Council of Ministers in 1962. One reason for this dismissal was al-Ṭariqi's increasing nationalist feelings and liberal outlook (Duguid 1970: 210). When his career in Saudi Arabia ended, al-Ṭariqi moved to Beirut, where he established an independent petroleum consulting firm to supplement his $2,000-per-month stipend, paid to all ex-ministers at the time (ibid.: 211). Al-Ṭariqi's desire to see oil under complete Saʿudi control did not fully materialise until the

1980s. Saudi Arabia acquired 25 per cent of ARAMCO in 1973; this was increased to 60 per cent in 1974. ARAMCO became Saudi ARAMCO in the 1980s when Saudi Arabia took full ownership of the company (Long 1997: 67).

Al-Ṭariqi and a few others were influenced by the turmoil of the Arab world in the 1950s and early 1960s that shaped the aspirations of a small educated group in Saudi Arabia. The loss of Palestine in 1948 and the Suez Crisis of 1956 led to the radicalisation of a few members of the Saʿudi ARAMCO workforce, evidence of which were the series of demonstrations, riots and strikes in 1953 and 1956.[2] Most important was the Egyptian coup of 1952 that set a precedent for how monarchies could be overthrown by 'Free Officers', not only elsewhere in the Arab world (for example Iraq, Yemen and Libya had their own home-bred Free Officers in 1958, 1962 and 1969 respectively), but also in Saudi Arabia. In 1955 a plot by Egyptian-trained Saʿudi army officers to overthrow Saʿud was discovered days before the coup was to take place, sending shock waves among the Saʿudi royal family, who blamed Saʿud personally for the aborted coup.

Moreover, while Ṭalal's young Free Princes struggled to acquire power within the post-Ibn Saʿud government, they clothed this struggle with the current rhetoric of Arab nationalism, socialism and constitutional monarchy. Naṣir's pan-Arabism remained their source of inspiration. In the late 1950s and early 1960s a new political vocabulary was appearing in Saudi Arabia. It was the language of 'coups' and 'revolutions', all far removed from the social context of Arabia at the time. As the Saʿudi army was still in a state of infancy, incapable yet of training its own officers, let alone produce 'Free Officers', Saudi Arabia had its home-bred 'Free Princes'. In the early 1960s, there was no shortage of the latter.

An oral narrative about how King Saʿud's era was fraught with political uncertainty illustrates the King's obsession with such new political vocabulary. According to this narrative:

> King Saʿud was sitting in his *majlis* one afternoon. The peace was disturbed by the sound of trucks drilling in a nearby construction site. The King asked his servant about the noise. The servant informed the King that it was noise generated by a *qallabi* [truck]. The King misheard the word *qallabi*. He confused it with *inqilab* [*coup d'état*]. Suddenly the King rose up in panic and retreated to his private quarter. He returned when his panic subsided. (Oral narrative)

During the turbulent years of Saʿud's reign, however, it was difficult to imagine an organised opposition. Although the discourse of coups and revolutions haunted Saʿud, this discourse circulated among individuals who, by virtue of their exposure to Arab politics and education, expressed 'dissident' opinions. Prince Ṭalal, ʿAbdullah al-Ṭariqi and Naṣir al-Saʿid (mentioned in the last chapter) among others remained scattered voices that nevertheless made Saʿud's reign the most uncertain period in modern Saʿudi history. Ordinary dissidents did not represent their own regions, let alone Saʿudi society at large. In the 1950s and early 1960s 'Hijazi' and 'Najdi' interests, for example, could not have been expressed without royal patronage. Individual Hijazis and Najdis became identified with Faysal and Saʿud respectively, but it would be absurd to imagine that people in those regions thought of political activists as their representatives.

Most of those who can be described as 'political activists' were not drawn from major tribal groups. In fact, their activisim was motivated by a desire to overcome their marginality in a society that still defined people's status and achievements along the old tribal lines. Neither the training of Saʿudi army officers (mainly from lower Hijaz and ʿAsir) in Egyptian military academies nor the acquisition of prestigious higher education from Arab and Western universities elevated people to high social ranks. Those who were recruited to Saʿud's various ministries remained civil servants (with the accent put strongly on 'servants'). In the words of one observer, among the civil servants there were individuals who represented a 'new man' in Saudi Arabia (Duguid 1970), a self-made educated person without the privilege of genealogy, but with a much-needed education in a society where people with formal and technical training were in short supply.

While cultural, social and economic differences between the regions existed, these differences were not yet endowed with any political significance. With the exception of Prince Ṭalal and his royal entourage, dissident voices came from the newly educated Saʿudis in a society that still cherished descent and tribal origin. Evidence of this was the political career of Naṣir al-Saʿid. Although this dissident belonged to Banu Tamim in Ha'il, an oasis associated with the rival Rashidi emirate (incorporated in Ibn Saʿud's realm in 1921), his political rhetoric failed to inspire the Shammar tribe, known for its opposition to Saʿudi hegemony since the eighteenth century. Like other tribal groups, several Shammar lineages seemed to have found a comfortable niche for themselves in the Saʿudi National Guard, a paramilitary force that had survived the *ikhwan* rebellion of 1927. It was basically a tribal force that absorbed a substantial section of Saʿudi society, mainly those historically associated with nomadism, the *badu*.[3]

During Saʿud's reign, the majority of Saʿudis were still far removed from the rhetoric of political dissent that had become fashionable in the Arab world. Dissidents among ARAMCO workers found it difficult to attract followers from among the workforce, let alone from a wide base outside the camps. The comment of one of those early workers (mentioned in the last chapter) about how 'shy they were to ask for more money or better food in their local canteen' attests to the difficulties encountered by some members of the politicised 'leadership'. While an attempted coup was discovered in 1955 and strikes did take place in 1956, there was no visible grass-roots support among the Saʿudi population. The strikes did result in the amelioration of ARAMCO work conditions and the introduction of more vigorous training schemes, but that remained confined to the camp boundaries.

With the Free Princes in the background, Saʿud and Faysal continued their power struggle until 1962, when Faysal formed a cabinet in the absence of the King, who had gone abroad for medical treatment.[4] Faysal brought into government his half-brothers Fahd and Sultan, both of whom had been his close allies. Faysal's new government excluded the sons of Saʿud. He promised a ten-point reform that included the drafting of a basic law, the abolition of slavery and the establishment of a judicial council (Gause 1990: 61; Abir 1988: 94).

Upon his return Saʿud rejected Faysal's new arrangement and threatened to mobilise the Royal Guard against his brother. Faysal ordered the mobilisation of the National Guard against the King. With the arbitration of the *ʿulama*, and pressure from senior members of the royal family, Saʿud gave in and agreed to abdicate on 28 March 1964. He left Saudi Arabia for Cairo, and died in Greece in 1969. With his abdication, the turbulent years between 1953 and 1964 came to an end. Saʿud's abdication also ended the short-lived opposition of Ṭalal and the Free Princes.

SAUDI ARABIA AND THE ARAB WORLD IN THE 1950S

In the early 1950s the Arab world witnessed the collapse of the Egyptian monarchy, with whom Ibn Saʿud had in the 1940s maintained friendly relations to counter the influence in Iraq and Jordan of the Hashemites, historical enemies of the Saʿudis. The Free Egyptian Officers under the leadership of Gamal ʿAbd al-Naṣir declared Egypt a republic in 1952. Saʿud preferred to keep up an appearance of friendship, and signed a mutual-defence treaty with Naṣir in 1955. This initiative was mainly against Hashemite Iraq, which had joined the Baghdad Pact, a coalition of Britain, Iran and Pakistan, the main purpose of which was to transfer military assistance to countries vital for 'Western interests, While internal political struggle among the royal family was intensifying, Saʿud not only adopted Naṣir's rhetoric of Arab nationalism but also felt compelled to accept his emerging alliance with the Soviet Union. Saʿud also sent two princes to Prague in search of new sources of military equipment (Shamiyyah 1986: 261; Safran 1985: 79). In 1954, against ARAMCO's will, Saʿud negotiated an agreement with the Greek shipping magnate Aristotle Onassis to transport Saʿudi oil, thus antagonising the oil company that so far had had complete control of Saudi Arabia's most precious and only economic resource. Saʿud and Naṣir were unlikely allies given their backgrounds and political orientation, but they agreed to oppose the Hashemites in Iraq and Jordan, although for different reasons. Saʿud was still threatened by the Hashemites whose ancestry guaranteed in the Arab world a kind of legitimacy which he did not enjoy.

Most Saʿudis were surprised when Saʿud supported Naṣir's nationalisation of the Suez Canal, which led to the Suez Crisis in 1956, while ARAMCO was still in full control of Saʿudi oil. Britain and France joined arms against Egypt when the latter closed the canal and claimed ownership of this important waterway. Saudi Arabia severed diplomatic relations with Britain following the crisis. Britain's influence in Saudi Arabia had already sunk to its lowest level.

British–Saʿudi relations had been tense over the Buraymi border dispute with Abu Dhabi and Oman before the death of Ibn Saʿud in 1953 (Peterson 1976). Britain, the main external power in Abu Dhabi and Oman at the time, supported their claims to the oasis against those of Saudi Arabia. Saʿud supported Imam Ghalib of the interior of Oman against the Sultan of Muscat, Saʿid ibn Taymur, at a time when Oman was still ruled as two separate countries. The Imam's rebellion was crushed in 1959 by the forces of the Sultan, who was assisted by the British. Saʿud allowed Imam Ghalib and his entourage to settle in Dhahran, while waiting for the right moment to reverse the sequence of events (Vassiliev 1998: 345–8; Wilkinson 1987: 286–95). Throughout the 1950s Saʿud continued to support the tribal rebellion in Oman against the British-backed Sultan Saʿid ibn Taymur.

In an attempt to prevent the joining of the two Hashemite kingdoms in a coalition that would threaten the Saʿudi royal group, Saʿud, together with Naṣir, supported Jordanian demonstrations in 1956 against the Baghdad Pact. King Ḥusayn of Jordan remained outside the Baghdad Pact.

Saʿud's early alliance with Naṣir culminated in an invitation to an Egyptian military mission to train Saʿudi recruits. This was a mistake, as Saʿud learned later that Egyptian indoctrination resulted in an attempted coup in 1955 led by a Saʿudi by the name of ʿAbd al-Raḥman al-Shamrawi and twelve officers who had been sent to Egypt for training (Safran 1985: 81).

However, the alliance with Egypt continued and Naṣir arrived first in Dhahran and later in Riyadh in September 1956 on a state visit to discuss a union that would include Egypt, Syria and Saudi Arabia. He was met with popular support that spread alarm signals among the Saʿudi royal family, especially Saʿud and Faysal (Shamiyyah 1986: 265). After this visit, Saʿud realised that his alliance with Naṣir masked important differences that could not be concealed indefinitely. Naṣir was pursuing a vigorous campaign against the Egyptian Muslim Brotherhood, a group that maintained close contacts with Saudi Arabia. Also, Naṣir's anti-imperialist and pan-Arab rhetoric soon exposed the underlying tensions between his leadership and that of Saʿud. By 1958 the semblance of a Saʿudi–Egyptian alliance was shattered, and the relationship turned sour following the February announcement of the union between Syria and Egypt. Saʿud's conspiracies embarrassed the royal family. It was revealed in the Lebanese press that Saʿud had given Syrian intelligence officer ʿAbd al-Ḥamid al-Sarraj a cheque for £1.9 million to assassinate Naṣir (ibid.: 267). This incident was perceived by Saʿud's brothers as most damaging to the country's reputation and credentials. His failed attempt to have Naṣir assassinated took place when the latter's popularity was rising in the Arab world after the Suez Crisis of 1956.

Saʿud visited Baghdad in 1957, the first ever visit by a Saʿudi king to the Hashemites of Iraq. Faysal II, the King of Iraq, welcomed the Saʿudi King. Both anticipated a new relationship that ignored past enmities. Saʿud began to see the Hashemite Kingdom of Iraq as a counter-force against Naṣir. Friendship with Iraq did not last long, as the Hashemites were deposed in July 1958 by Colonel ʿAbd al-Salam ʿArif and Brigadier ʿAbd al-Karim Qasim, still unknown quantities as far as Saʿud was concerned (Tripp 2000: 149). Later it transpired that the *coup d'état* was initially supported by diverse groups consisting of Free Officers, Baʿthists and Communists.

Conflict and competition between Saʿud and Naṣir moved to Yemen when an Egyptian-backed officer, ʿAbdullah al-Sallal, deposed Imam al-Badr of Yemen in September 1962 (Shamiyyah 1986: 273). The Yemen Arab Republic became the first non-monarchical regime in the Arabian Peninsula (Gause 1990: 57). As such, it became a major Saʿudi security threat. Saudi Arabia's primary concern was to secure the removal of the Egyptian military presence, estimated at 20,000 troops in 1963 (ibid.: 57).

The struggle between Yemeni royalists (supporters of the imamate) and republicans became a proxy battle between Saudi Arabia and Egypt (Dresch 2000: 89). Saudi Arabia supported the royalists without being able to match what the Egyptians offered the republicans. Three Saʿudi pilots seized their opportunity, and flew to Cairo in protest. Saʿud immediately banned the use of aeroplanes by Saʿudi officers and pilots (Shamiyyah 1986: 273). Saudi Arabia broke off diplomatic relations with Egypt in November 1962 (Gause 1990: 60). Saʿud was deposed in 1964 before the Yemeni revolution and civil war were over. Saʿudi–Egyptian relations remained tense throughout the early 1960s (Detalle 2000).

In an Arab world dominated by Naṣir and Egypt, Saʿud remained a marginal figure in regional politics. His manoeuvres and his rapprochement with Naṣir were mainly motivated by his desire to contain the Hashemites in Iraq. In the 1950s the most consistent element in Saʿudi foreign policy was the obsession with the two Hashemite monarchies created by the British in neighbouring countries. Even the question of Palestine, which dominated Arab concern, became secondary to Saʿud, as it had been for his father.

SAUDI ARABIA AND THE UNITED STATES IN THE 1950S AND EARLY 1960S

Although Saudi Arabia signed the oil concession with an American company in 1933, Saʿudi–American relations did not develop until after the Second World War. During the war, as far as Saudi Arabia was concerned, ARAMCO was the 'United States'. As mentioned in the last chapter, ARAMCO was responsible for facilitating contact between the USA and Saudi Arabia.[5]

After the Second World War the United States strove to replace Britain as the dominant power, especially when oil changed from being a commercial product to a strategic commodity of prime importance (Vassiliev 1998: 324). While the United States did not depend on Saʿudi oil after the war, it considered Middle East oil, including that of Saudi Arabia, as an essential resource for the reconstruction of Europe's devastated economies. From the United States' perspective, access to Middle East oil came to be viewed as critical to the success of the Marshall Plan and the reconstruction of Europe (Anderson 1981: 162). America's interest in Saudi Arabia and its oil should be seen as part of its concern to maintain its superpower position after the Second World War.

Added to the European dimension, the United States was beginning to be concerned with the threat of communism.[6] Washington was convinced that 'the Soviet Union seems to be determined to break down the structure which Great Britain has maintained so that Russian power and influence can sweep unimpeded across Turkey and through the Dardanelles into the Mediterranean, and across Iran and through the Persian Gulf into the Indian Ocean' (Anderson 1981: 168).

This was the background to Saʿudi–American relations in the 1950s. The Eisenhower Doctrine was based on the assumption that a vacuum had been created in the Middle East after the defeat of France and Britain in the Suez war in 1956. The doctrine promised that American armed forces would be deployed to protect countries threatened by communism (Vassiliev 1998: 351). In 1957 Eisenhower asked Congress to approve use of American military forces to assist 'any nation in the Middle East which requested such help to oppose aggression by any state dominated by international Communism' (Grayson 1982: 89).

In an attempt to counter the threat of Naṣir and communism, Saʿud visited Washington in 1957, after stopping in Cairo where he met Naṣir and several other Arab leaders who were opposed to the Eisenhower Doctrine. In Washington Saʿud was promised military assistance and economic support amounting to $180 million. He won a commitment from the Americans to supply Saudi Arabia with aircraft and naval equipment, train Saʿudi pilots and send technicians (Vassiliev 1998: 352). In return, Saʿud promised the Americans that he would suspend all aid to Egypt. He signed two agreements during the trip, granting the United States the use of the Dhahran base for an additional five years and providing for America to extend additional military assistance to strengthen the Saʿudi armed forces (Grayson 1982: 90). The right to use the Dhahran air base was terminated in 1962.

Saʿud had to moderate his enthusiasm for the Eisenhower Doctrine after Naṣir made his objections clear. On his way back from the United States, Saʿud stopped in Cairo to brief Naṣir and soften his objections to the Eisenhower Doctrine. Saʿud failed in his mission (Grayson 1982: 90).

As Saʿud returned to Riyadh, Crown Prince Faysal announced that 'the views of the Saudi Arabian government are in full agreement with the views of Egypt on all problems' (Vassiliev 1998: 352). The announcement, however, did not mask the growing rift between Egypt and Saudi Arabia especially after the latter moved closer to the United States and the Hashemite monarchy in Iraq.

Faysal came to play an important role in enlisting American support even before he became King in 1964. In 1962, Egyptian planes began a series of daily attacks on the Saʿudi border with Yemen. American combat planes based in Dhahran made demonstrative sorties to warn the Egyptians (Safran 1985: 96; Gause 1990: 60). Faysal asked the United States for help after announcing a general mobilisation against Yemen. The United States immediately sent warships and aircraft to Saudi Arabia. The United States also agreed to establish an air defence system along the Yemeni border near Najran. In February 1963, joint exercises between American and Saʿudi paratroopers started near Jeddah; they were joined by 100 American paratroopers sent from Germany (Vassiliev 1998: 372). But America interpreted American 'protection' at the time as limited to the oil fields. President Kennedy's reticence was based on the United States's desire to work with Naṣir. It seems that the American administration was 'mending fences with ʿAbd al-Naṣir, seeing him as a progressive non-Communist local counterweight to Soviet expansions' (Gause 1990: 60).

In 1963, Faysal restored relations with Britain, which promised to modernise and upgrade the Saʿudi National Guard. In June 1963, a British military mission arrived in Saudi Arabia to help train the National Guard, together with a number of planes, pilots and surface-to-air missiles (Gause 1990: 62). This was an attempt by the Saʿudis to enlist an alternative support after sensing America's reluctance. Saudi Arabia must have been worried by the response of the USA, its superpower ally and ultimate guarantor of its security (ibid.: 60), especially after the Kennedy administration recognised the Yemeni Republic in December 1962.

However, Faysal realised that a closer relationship with the United States offered protection against communism and Arab revolutionary trends in the 1960s. Faysal's 'diplomatic maneuvering elicited an effective American deterrent against outright Egyptian invasion of Saudi Arabia or raids on oil facilities, but it did not constrain Egyptian border attacks and active efforts at subversion, nor did it prevent the United States from recognising the republican regime in Yemen' (Safran 1985: 111). During the early 1960s Saʿudi–US relations were tense as Faysal rejected Kennedy's proposal to withdraw support from the Yemeni royalists. Faysal insisted on the withdrawal of the Egyptian military forces as a precondition for suspending support to Yemeni royalists. The relationship with the United States remained tense in 1962–3, although later Faysal drew closer to the United States in an effort to strengthen his country against the threats of Arab nationalism and socialism. As Crown Prince and Prime Minister Faysal

Table 2. *Volume of petroleum export and GDP 1965–1975*

Year	Volume of petroleum export billion SA riyals	GDP billion SA riyals
1965	22.2	10.4
1966	26.5	11.4
1967	28.4	13.14
1968	31.5	14.6
1969	44.1	15.9
1970	49.7	17.4
1971	146.5	28.2
1972	78.5	40.5
1973	98.9	99.3
1974	110.6	139.6
1975	92.2	164.5

Source: IMF 1999: 798–9.

also saw the United States as the main superpower capable of guaranteeing the security of the kingdom against the rising influence of the Soviet Union in the Middle East.

THE REIGN OF KING FAYSAL (1964–1975)

The reign of King Faysal (born 1906) was associated with a steady increase in oil revenues (see table 2). This allowed the previous financial crisis of the Saʿudi government to sink into historical oblivion. Between 1965 and 1975, the Saʿudi GDP rose from a mere 10.4 billion riyals to 164.53 billion. By 1974, government revenues from petroleum exports reached an unprecedented level of 110 billion riyals.

Faysal inherited from his brother a country with a remarkably underdeveloped material infrastructure. While ministries had proliferated during the reign of Saʿud, they had been crippled by fluctuating and limited budgets, allocated as royal gifts. During the first month of his reign, Faysal designated his half-brother Khalid Crown Prince, and Sultan minister of defense and aviation, a post he still held in 2002. He confirmed Muhammad Zaki Yamani as the replacement for al-Ṭariqi as minister in the Ministry of Oil and Petroleum (al-Shaykh 1988: 397–400). Faysal dismissed al-Ṭariqi because of his 'radical views' on matters relating to ARAMCO and Saʿudi oil. Al-Ṭariqi had demanded more Saʿudi control over this vital resource, and later he even contemplated the nationalisation of ARAMCO.

Although a planning agency had been established during the reign of Saʿud, no serious projects materialised. In 1965, planning was formalised in the Central Planning Organisation, which in 1975 became the Ministry of Planning. The age of five-year development plans began with the first initiative (1970–5). According to the first plan gross domestic product was to increase by 9.8 per cent per year. Planned budget allocations for the five years were $9.2 billion, 45 per cent of which was to be spent on capital projects. Planned expenditures were concentrated on defence, education, transport and utilities. As oil revenues grew, budget allocations increased, amounting to about $27 billion for the five years, while actual budget expenditures amounted to $21 billion.

The first five-year plan was meant to create and develop the material infrastructure, including the construction of roads, airports and ports, the extension of electricity supplies, telephones and communication in general. Social services, hospitals and medical centres multiplied and began to reach a wider section of the population.

Elementary education was virtually absent in some regions. Several Saʿudis from prominent families in Najd, Hasa and Hijaz sent their young boys to boarding schools in Egypt and Lebanon. Girls' education remained unknown in the central part of Saudi Arabia and ʿAsir. Armed with a steady increase in government oil exports, Faysal made the education of girls a priority.

Expenditure on education increased to an annual level of approximately 10 per cent of the budget. During Saʿud's reign, a new university carrying his name was opened in 1957. Faysal later changed its name to Riyadh University and drew plans for more institutions to mark his commitment to education. Vocational training and institutions of higher education were built in addition to more than 125 elementary and secondary schools for girls. The University of Petroleum and Minerals was opened in Dhahran in 1969. Two Islamic higher education institutions were also established under Faysal's patronage: the Madina-based Islamic University (founded in 1961) and Imam Muhammad ibn Saʿud Islamic University (founded in 1974). In the eastern province, King Faysal University was established in 1975 (al-Salloum 1995: 65–72). These universities began to produce the first wave of formally and indigenously educated Saʿudis. The proliferation of higher-learning institutions overstretched the capacity of the Ministry of Education (established in 1953) and resulted in a lack of co-ordination and communication. In 1975, a segment of this ministry became a separate government body, the Ministry of Higher

Education, under the recommendation of an American team of education experts (ibid.: 63).

Faysal's promotion of education in general, and female education in particular, made his name synonymous with modernisation. Faysal features as a 'modernist', whose reforms were represented in Saʿudi historiography as part of *al-nahḍa*. His wish to develop the economic infrastructure was promoted by the biggest ever increase in oil prices as a result of the oil embargo in 1973. In 1975, oil revenues contributed over 75 per cent of total government income. The sudden increase in oil revenues allowed the expansion of state machinery and bureaucracy. It is not an exaggeration to describe the 1970s as an era of the consolidation of the state of 1932. While a royal lineage had already been part of the political scene of Saudi Arabia since the 1930s, the 'state' in its modern configuration was a later development associated with the sudden increase in oil prices in the 1970s.

Faysal's economic, social and bureaucratic reforms were initiated amidst a climate of political conservatism. The promise made in 1962 to introduce a Consultative Council (*majlis al-shura*) was abandoned with the abdication of Saʿud in 1964. Furthermore, the Council of Ministers that led to the political struggle between 1953 and 1964 fell under the full control of Faysal, who assumed the role of both King and prime minister. Faysal re-merged the two responsibilities in a fashion similar to that desired by Saʿud. He institutionalised the merger of the two posts after having secured the placement of the most loyal senior princes in the most important ministries, namely Interior (Nayef) and Defence (Sultan). Muhammad Zaki Yamani was appointed oil minister; he remained in his position until 1986. Faysal's most important contribution to the consolidation of the Saʿudi state stemmed from his division of state functions among his loyal half-brothers, thus merging important branches of the royal lineage with state machinery.

Having dismissed Saʿud's sons from state service, Faysal also consolidated his father's vague vision of succession to kingship. He designated his half-brother Khalid Crown Prince. While seniority was not respected, there was no doubt that succession should remain confined to Ibn Saʿud's sons, rather than his grandchildren, some of whom were as old as their paternal uncles (if not older). While the deposed Saʿud continued to threaten this arrangement from his exile in Egypt under the encouragement of Naṣir, the threat ceased to be realistic with his death in 1969. Saʿud's sons seemed to have accepted their political marginalisation. The group associated with Ṭalal ibn ʿAbd al-ʿAziz also failed to challenge Faysal's new arrangement, as Ṭalal himself remained in exile. The Free Princes and their vision of a constitutional monarchy had no success among other senior princes and virtually no grass-roots support. Their discourse of 'constitutional monarchy', 'Arab nationalism' and 'socialism' proved to be alien to both the majority of royalty and to commoners.

Faysal's political conservatism was combined with a vision that Saudi Arabia can import technological expertise and modernise economically while remaining faithful to authentic Islam. While Faysal had been socialised into Islamic education from an early age under the influence of his Al Shaykh maternal kin, his Islamic rhetoric came to the forefront mainly as a counter-discourse to current Arab political trends associated with Arab nationalism in both its Nasserite and Baʿthist versions. He perceived Gamal ʿAbd al-Naṣir's pan-Arabism as a direct threat to the survival of the Saʿudi ruling group. Naṣir's intervention in Yemen was the background. Furthermore, in the 1960s the rhetoric of Baʿth ideologues, for example Mishel ʿAflaq, concerning 'unity, freedom and socialism' and the call for 'a single Arab nation with eternal mission' became most threatening after the establishment of Baʿth regimes in Iraq (1968) and Syria (1970). Faysal adopted the discourse of modernisation within an Islamic framework. In Saʿudi media, he began to be represented as the authentic Muslim king.[7] The 'corrupt' Saʿud disappeared from public imagination, while a historical amnesia relating to his era was encouraged.

Growing up in Riyadh in the late 1960s and early 1970s, one was led to imagine that Ibn Saʿud was succeeded by Faysal, the Muslim modernist. Saʿud was hardly mentioned in school history textbooks. While Arab teachers (mainly Egyptians) concerned with outlining a chronological history of 'modern Saudi Arabia' mentioned Saʿud's name in passing, they devoted several sessions to discussing the glorious period of Ibn Saʿud and Faysal's reigns. Saʿud's portraits ceased to be displayed in teachers' offices, government buildings, airports and other public places. The university that carried his name was renamed Riyadh University. Saʿud's memory was confined to his immediate descendants, who had to accept a second-class status among royalty. The people of Riyadh continued to pass by his famous abandoned Naṣiriyya palace that had been left to go to ruins, while in the privacy of their homes stories about his extravagance, concubines and debauchery flourished.

Under Faysal's patronage and part of his bureaucratic reforms, the Saʿudi *ʿulama* were formally co-opted. The Ministry of Justice was established in 1970. The most senior *ʿulama* became state functionaries. The informal arrangement that had been part of a loose holy alliance (described in chapter 2) was to be formalised. The timing coincided with increasing modernisation and development that began to touch the basics of life. Female education, the introduction of new communications technology (for example, the television broadcasting station in Riyadh) and the influx of foreign labour not only to the eastern province but also to other parts of the country posited serious problems for the King. It was only after reassuring the ʿ*ulama* that girls would have a solid religious education under a separate ministry (the Ministry of Education for Girls, supervised directly by the ʿ*ulama*) that the King was able to embark on a massive schooling programme for girls. Also, the television broadcasting station was inaugurated only after pacifying demonstrators, which resulted in the shooting of the leader of the demonstrators, the King's nephew, Prince Khalid ibn Musaʿid ibn ʿAbd al-ʿAziz, in 1965. This proved a tragedy not only for the prince but also for the King himself. In 1975 the King was assassinated by the victim's brother, a prince also called Faysal.

Technological innovations proved to be costly in a society that was still resistant to a whole range of innovations under the influence of Wahhabi doctrine. Faysal strove to incorporate the ʿ*ulama*. He made them part of the state and endeavoured to reward the most moderate among them, who were willing to endorse his reforms in return for concessions. Their religious knowledge began to be formally transmitted with the establishment of religious universities that gradually replaced informal centres of learning around the mosque school. Since the 1970s, the number of students at such institutions has more than tripled. Concessions to the ʿ*ulama* were made in return for *fatawa*, religious decrees casting authenticity and legitimacy on almost every aspect of social and economic reform. While this interpretation does not question the King's personal religiosity, it highlights the historical context whereby his private commitment to faith became a political strategy to counter a series of internal and external threats.

While Ibn Saʿud's early expansion in Arabia was assisted by the *muṭawwaʿa*, oil revenues allowed Faysal not only to increase their numbers, but also privilege the most scholarly among them and those whose education, lineage and piety elevated them to higher ranks. Faysal consolidated a system that had already been put in place, albeit informally, by his father. The most uncompromising among the ʿ*ulama* were ousted and denied the privilege of becoming civil servants at a time when employment in the public sector was one of the opportunities resulting from the oil boom of the 1970s. With the exception of the 1965 confrontation between Faysal and the ʿ*ulama* over the Islamic nature of television broadcasting, he was granted the support of the majority of the ʿ*ulama*, whose formal education in state-owned religious universities and regular salaries ensured an acquiescence that most kings ruling under Islamic rhetoric aspire to.

Oil revenues allowed the Saʿudi state to consolidate an old mechanism – the redistributive role of central power in Arabia. Before the oil era, Ibn Saʿud had access to foreign subsidies, very similar to the later oil rents that he used to reward allegiance. When he formalised pilgrimage taxes, he appropriated them from both local and foreign pilgrims only to use them to cement political alliances with indigenous tribal shaykhs. It had always been the case that one category of people (foreign pilgrims and local merchants) subsidised political relations in a society with no wide base of taxation. On the odd occasion that oasis dwellers paid their dues to the treasury, these were redistributed among groups that were not easily reached for the purpose of taxation. The redistributive economy behind political centralisation in Arabia had been in place before oil wealth. Surplus appropriated from one group as a result of tribute/*zakat* or raids had always been partially redistributed among other groups, while keeping a portion for the maintenance of chiefly lineages and their military force. The rest had always been used to buy loyalty.

The novelty of the situation in the early 1970s was related to the magnitude of the surplus and the diversity of the rewards. Furthermore, oil revenues made it possible for the limited circle of previous 'tax payers' (for example, foreign pilgrims, old merchant families and wretched peasants) to escape the burden of *ad hoc* taxation, as it was no longer necessary for the state to impose taxes on those groups. With oil, local merchant families lost all semblance of their previous bargaining power *vis-à-vis* the state, a power that should not be exaggerated as merchants had always been one source among others in the consolidation of centralised authority in Arabia.[8] Subsidies from the British, and the Ottomans before them, created polities that lasted for a long time. The perception of the ruler as a provider was not novel in the Arabian context. Oil only consolidated what had already been the foundation of rule, namely 'generosity'.

Oil revenues allowed generosity to surpass the regular feast of lamb and rice and the occasional gifts of cloth, dates and weapons. Under Faysal's rule, the state became the source of welfare benefits, medical treatment, new houses, travel documents, legal deeds, birth and death certificates, places at school or university, scholarships to the USA, terrain for agricultural production, construction sites and cash gifts for weddings and hardship. The list was long. More importantly, the state became a gatekeeper that mediated the existence of all citizens. Its influence penetrated all aspects of economic and social life.

Ordinary Saʿudis and royalty entered the age of commissions, extra hidden payments that accompanied contracts for all development projects, the construction boom and military expenditure. The state paid its citizens directly as it became the major employer, and also indirectly in benefits, commission and land-distribution schemes.[9] Saudi Arabia began to produce its own 'businessmen', some direct descendants of Ibn Saʿud. Princes who were excluded from the state political machinery or had no political ambitions found an economic niche with great material rewards. This was a novelty in Saudi Arabia. It is alleged that Ibn Saʿud advised his sons before his death: 'Do not compete with the merchants so that they do not compete with you' (Shamiyyah 1986). The scale of economic and financial opportunities in the late 1970s made such advice difficult to adhere to. Princes who served as ministers together with those who had no place in Faysal's political administration were the first to seize the new economic opportunities. They became state subcontractors, thus receiving vast commissions on projects and material they sold to the state.

Oil revenues allowed the consolidation of a cohesive royal family now united by real economic interests rather than vague genealogical and blood links. Royal solidarity among Ibn Saʿud's sons needed more than the rhetoric of descent: they had already been weakened by divisive matrilineal links immediately after his death. The struggle between Saʿud, Faysal and the Free Princes was evidence of a fragile coalition that erupted in 1953 and could not be contained without sacrificing Saʿud's throne. From the 1970s, the maximisation of private wealth rather than blood ties was behind the cohesiveness of the royal group.[10] As the majority of princes benefited from commissions, it became increasingly less attractive to engage in idealised visions of the polity without serious risks that would undermine the survival of the whole royal group.

Old tribal nobility could not easily challenge a realm that was consolidated with oil revenues. Tribal shaykhs and previous amirs had already been co-opted, initially by marriage (in the 1930s and 1940s) and later by economic benefits (in the early 1970s). Far from becoming allies, they developed into a 'parasite' group whose survival was highly dependent on royal handouts. As those shaykhs were the maternal kin of some princes, they lost their independence and bargaining power with the state. Princes operated a patronage system that touched not only their maternal kin but also ordinary members of the tribes (Al-Rasheed 1991: 254). Government monthly stipends were extended to a wider circle than that of the Al Saʿud and their maternal kin. Tribal shaykhs as far as Tarabjal and al-Jawf in the north, and Abha and Najran in the south-west, received benefits from state agencies. A closer circle of tribal shaykhs accompanied princes during their hunting trips first in Saudi Arabia and later in other parts of the Arab world. They also accompanied princes on regular European tours as part of a royal entourage. The most loyal amongst them were granted the status of *khawi*, a quasi-brotherhood between two unequal partners. Regular cash handouts, representing tokens of generosity from private/public royal purses, supplemented direct benefits (Al-Rasheed 1991: 254–8).

Ordinary Saʿudis became recipients of rewards that were distributed as both government subsidies and as salaries for employment in state bureaucracy, the army and the National Guard. In their daily *majalis*, princes received their *khawi* and other ordinary guests who presented petitions for *maʿuna* (help) and requests for *sharha* (an annual cash handout).

The first wave of bureaucrats, technocrats, professionals and merchants had no bargaining power. Region, tribe, dialect, family and unequally distributed benefits divided them. Wealth and education could not easily override social and regional differences. While lifestyles, above all consumerism, united the newly educated Saʿudis, neither economic interest nor education allowed the establishment of a homogenous group. Saʿudi professionals remained dependent on a state that fragmented them through unequal access to wealth.

Allegiance to family, tribe and region continued to be important divisive mechanisms in the 1970s. The social prohibition on female exogamous marriages illustrated the social divisions within the country and the barriers that were still erected. Najdi women could not marry Hijazi, Hasawi or ʿAsiri men. Within Najd itself, the tribal groups would not give their daughters to *khaḍiris*, the non-tribal population of the towns and oases. In Hijaz, daughters of Sharifian descent would not marry ordinary Hijazis nor would they marry into Najdi noble tribal groups.

Restrictions on female marriages were accompanied by a trend of male exogamy. Men belonging to the old tribal nobility, professional Saʿudis and even princes married women from neighbouring Arab countries, mainly from Egypt, Lebanon and Syria. In addition to marrying a first paternal/maternal parallel cousin, princes and tribal nobility sought second or third wives from established elite families in the Arab world.[11]

After acquiring education abroad, ordinary Saʿudi men often returned with non-Saʿudi wives: al-Ṭariqi was one. These marriages were products of both the internal restrictions that prohibited marriages across tribe and region and the new wealth that made Saʿudi men an attractive match for

Arab women. Oil wealth inflated Saʿudi women's dowries, making them beyond the reach of men with limited means (Yamani 1998).

The increasing number of these exogamous marriages prompted the Saʿudi government to respond in the mid-1970s, and it became necessary for Saʿudi men to obtain the permission of the Ministry of Interior before they married non-Saʿudi women. Also at this time it became illegal for Saʿudi women to marry non-Saʿudi men, a category that included Muslim Arabs and non-Arab Muslims (Yamani 1998: 164). The ban on marrying non-Saʿudis was accompanied by reluctance to grant women scholarships that would enable them to travel abroad for education.

Education and oil under Faysal did little to alter old social hierarchies and prejudices among the various groups that constituted Saudi Arabia. In the 1970s Saʿudi society began to immerse itself in consumerism. The real issues for all Saʿudis was how to consume without losing an authenticity that had been defined in Islamic terms since the beginning of Faysal's reign.

FAYSAL AND THE ARAB WORLD

Saʿudi involvement in the Yemen war of 1962 that started during the reign of King Saʿud continued when Faysal became King in 1964. Naṣir came to Jeddah on 24 August 1965 and promised to withdraw Egyptian troops from Yemen by November 1966. Under the terms of the Jeddah Agreement Faysal promised to stop all assistance to the Yemeni royalists (Gause 1990: 68). Both Saʿudi and Egyptian interventions in Yemen officially came to a halt with the outbreak of the Arab–Israeli war of June 1967 (Dresch 2000: 114). Naṣir shifted his troops and attention to a more serious conflict.

The Arab–Israeli war of 1967 was very short compared to later military conflicts in the region. A Saʿudi brigade of 3,000 soldiers was sent to southern Jordan during the war. It was deployed far from the front, but close enough to the capital to support King Ḥusayn. Faysal may have seen Jordan as a buffer state between Saudi Arabia and Israel (Vassiliev 1998: 384). Within six days, Egypt lost Sinai and Gaza; Jordan lost Jerusalem and the West Bank, Syria lost the Golan Heights and Naṣir lost his claim to Arab leadership, although his popularity remained unaffected.

Reactions in Saudi Arabia to the war were mild compared to those elsewhere in the Arab world. Nevertheless, anti-American demonstrations took place in Hijaz and the capital. Important demonstrations, however, were reported in the eastern province, mainly in Qatif, Khubar and Dammam. Students of ARAMCO's College of Petroleum and

2 King Faysal in the Regents Park mosque, 1967. © Popperfoto

Minerals attacked the company's installations, the American airbase and the United States consulate (Abir 1988: 111).

In August 1967, following the humiliating defeat, Arab leaders, including Faysal, declared in Khartoum their three famous slogans: *la iʿtiraf, la mufawaḍa, la ṣulḥ* (no recognition of the state of Israel, no negotiations with Israel, and no peace with Israel). Moreover, Khartoum was important for the Arab–Israeli conflict as Saudi Arabia, Kuwait and Libya, the main oil producers at the time, committed themselves to financing the so-called front-line Arab states, namely Egypt, Syria and Jordan (Shamiyyah 1986: 274). Saudi Arabia warned that it would start payment only after the Egyptians had completed the withdrawal of their forces from Yemen (Vassiliev 1998: 277). After Khartoum Saudi Arabia became an exporter of capital and a source of financial aid for the states that confronted

Israel (ibid.: 384). Saʿudi oil brought Saudi Arabia from the margin to the centre of Arab politics.

In a side meeting, Faysal and Naṣir decided to leave Yemen to the Yemenis before the end of 1967. While Naṣir had no bargaining power in Khartoum, Faysal emerged triumphant. As far as Saudi Arabia was concerned, Nasserism and a defeated Naṣir no longer posed a real threat to Saudi Arabia. Faysal accommodated a weakened Naṣir until the latter's death in September 1970. With the removal of Naṣir from the Arab scene, Saudi Arabia could now contemplate playing a central role that matched its oil resources. Its desire for leadership in the Arab and Muslim world on the basis of its Islamic heritage and the claim to protect the holy sites in Mecca and Madina had been constantly frustrated by Egypt. A defeated Egypt offered an important opportunity.

During the reign of Faysal, Iraq surfaced again as a source of worry for Saudi Arabia after the Baʿth takeover of 1968. While Nasserism dominated Arab politics in the 1950s, in the late 1960s Baʿthism in both its Syrian and Iraqi versions was perceived as a threat to Saudi Arabia. Arab nationalism, now in its Baʿthist version, undermined the legitimacy of the Saʿudi ruling group. Nothing was more unacceptable to Faysal than the discourse of Arab unity and socialism. Claims to unity on the basis of secular culture, history and civilisation were bound to be considered un-Islamic by Faysal. Iraq's first venture into Kuwait in 1961 was still remembered by Faysal, who could not express joy over the takeover by the Baʿthists Aḥmad Ḥasan al-Bakr and Saddam Husayn in July 1968 (Tripp 2000).

While in the 1950s and early 1960s Cairo had been a centre for anti-Saʿudi activities, in the late 1960s Baghdad became an alternative destination for Saʿudi Baʿthists and Shiʿa dissidents, mainly from the eastern province where the oil industry was based. Saʿudi Baʿthists were allowed to broadcast to Saudi Arabia from Baghdad. Dissidents published a journal, *Ṣawt al-Ṭaliʿa*, which became popular among leftists and Baʿthists alike (Abir 1988: 112).

In 1969 Faysal faced a major internal plot to overthrow him.[12] Saʿudi army officers, police and pilots together with a handful of civilians plotted a *coup d'état* that was discovered in June and was immediately suppressed (Buchan 1982: 115). Faysal was alarmed, as it was revealed that his own pilot, together with Dawud al-Rumaiyḥi, an officer at the Dhahran military base, and Yusif al-Ṭawil from Jeddah, were behind a plan to assassinate him on his first aeroplane trip (Shamiyyah 1986: 279; Buchan 1982: 116; Cordesman 1984: 137–40). A major campaign of arrests followed and several Saʿudis suspected of taking part in the plot fled the country to Egypt and Lebanon.

It was estimated that by the end of 1969 the Saʿudi authorities had arrested almost two thousand dissidents and suspects (Abir 1988: 114). Most of those who left the country did not return until after Faysal's death, when his successor, King Khalid, issued an amnesty to all those political dissidents who had left Saudi Arabia for neighbouring Arab countries in the 1950s and 1960s.

Faysal supported the Palestinian cause and clothed this support with Islamic rhetoric. His wish was to pray in Jerusalem, the third holy site in Islam after Mecca and Madina. In 1969, Faysal attended the Arab meeting in Rabat where the Palestinian Liberation Organisation (created in 1964) became the sole legitimate representative of the Palestinians. Saʿudi financial commitment to the PLO was a crucial factor in bringing the country into the centre of Arab politics. Saudi Arabia joined other Arab countries in trying to manipulate factions within this umbrella organisation. A close relationship with sections of the PLO resulted in huge sums being transferred from Saudi Arabia to Palestinian training camps in Lebanon, Syria and Jordan (Vassiliev 1998: 387).

In the 1960s Faysal envisaged an Islamic conference organisation in an attempt to widen the scope of regional politics and to include non-Arab Muslim states such as Iran and Pakistan to dilute Egypt's influence. Both Iran and Jordan supported his diplomatic efforts (Gause 1990: 69). He became associated with pan-Islamism, especially when he tried to revive the non-governmental World Muslim Congress (Sindi 1980: 184). Faysal's pan-Islamism had three objectives: to promote inter-governmental cooperation among Muslim states; to eliminate Soviet threats and communist trends in the Arab world; and to mobilise Muslim countries for the struggle against Israel (ibid.: 189). In May 1962 he sponsored a conference in Mecca whose main purpose was to devise ways to fight radicalism and secularism in the Arab and Muslim worlds. The conference declared that 'those who disavow Islam and distort its call under the guise of nationalism are actually the most bitter enemies of Arabs, whose glories are entwined with the glories of Islam' (ibid.: 186). Aversion to nationalism and secular trends dominated not only Faysal's policy but also the national history textbooks of the Saʿudi state, as will be shown later in this book. The Mecca meeting resulted in the establishment of *rabiṭat al-ʿalam al-Islami*, the World Muslim League, with its headquarters in Mecca (Piscatori 1983).

As the al-Aqsa mosque in Jerusalem was set on fire in 1969, King Ḥusayn of Jordan called for an Arab summit. Faysal suggested an Islamic summit, perhaps to undermine further the weakened Naṣir. In 1970 twenty-three foreign ministers of Muslim countries met in Jeddah to establish the General Secretariat of the Muslim League under Saʿudi patronage (Vassiliev 1998: 387). Foreign ministers agreed to meet once a year to 'promote cooperation among the Islamic states and establish institutional bases for pan-Islamism' (Sindi 1980: 191). In subsequent meetings. Muslim states proposed the establishment of an Islamic international news agency and Islamic cultural centres around the world. Saudi Arabia agreed to provide funds for such initiatives.

At a second meeting in 1972, the conference decided to create a 'fund for the holy war' against Israel. The conference denounced Israel for its annexation of the Arab part of Jerusalem (Vassiliev 1998: 388). Throughout the 1970s the Muslim World League and the Organisation of the Islamic Conference became a platform for Saudi Arabia to spread its influence in the Muslim world. The Saʿudis used their status as the guardians of the holy sites and their oil wealth to consolidate their presence in the wider Islamic world. In the 1970s, it seemed that identifying with this Muslim world offered protection against secular and socialist threats from within the Arab world (Piscatori 1983; Fraser 1997).

At the international level, Faysal's popularity in the Islamic world reached a level never granted to previous Saʿudi kings. If Saʿud was regarded as a source of conspiracy in the 1950s and early 1960s, Faysal in the 1970s became the symbol of Islamic politics not only in the Arab world but also among Muslims in Africa and Asia. Faysal turned to Islam to find an authentic alternative to Arab nationalism (Vassiliev 1998: 385). Saudi Arabia began a campaign to support Muslim education, religious centres and mosques abroad (Piscatori 1983). Several Muslim countries in Africa and Asia benefited from Saʿudi aid, distributed as part of the country's commitment to spread Islam and strengthen Muslim countries. In 1974 Faysal contributed $10.2 million to the Islamic Solidarity Fund. He was also behind the establishment of the Islamic Development Bank, with permanent headquarters in Jeddah (Sindi 1980: 195–6; Piscatori 1983: 47).

As Faysal pursued his pan-Islamic policy, the involvement of Egypt and a final reconciliation with its leadership was important, given Egypt's importance in the Arab world. This became possible after the death of Naṣir. An intimate relationship developed with Egyptian President Anwar al-Sadat, who expelled Soviet military advisers in 1972, sought an alliance with the United States and abandoned pan-Arabist strategies and revolutionary rhetoric (Fraser 1997: 221). Saudi Arabia began to see Egypt as an ally rather than a threat. It provided Egypt with important financial help and continued to import Egyptian labour. Faysal also facilitated the close relationship with the United States that Egypt began to develop in the 1970s. Saʿudi financial aid was expected to replace Egypt's dependence on the USSR.

Faysal seemed to have succeeded in rescuing Saudi Arabia from its internal political turmoil that coincided with the upheavals of the Arab world. At home, the King restored confidence in the Saʿudi economy and was even able to launch a planning programme for economic and social modernisation. While Faysal is remembered for his social and economic reforms, he is also remembered for brutal suppression of dissident voices in Saudi Arabia, which in the 1960s consisted of an amalgamation of Nasserites, Arab nationalists, Baʿthists, socialists and even communists. By the 1970s Faysal had tightened his internal security measures and succeeded in suppressing various opposition groups, which never recovered from brutal force at a very early stage in their political evolution. The so-called secular opposition came to an end in Saudi Arabia.

At the regional level, Faysal succeeded in subverting the threat to Saudi Arabia of revolutionary regimes in the Arab world. Behind the scene diplomacy guaranteed the survival of the Saʿudi state against a background of serious Arab–Israeli conflicts and revolutionary rhetoric. Saudi Arabia's main rival in the Arab world remained Naṣir's Egypt. So far Saudi Arabia's role as the guardian of the two holy sites of Islam had had only symbolic significance. In international and Arab politics, this guardianship remained fairly unimportant until it was backed by the new wealth of the 1970s. In the 1960s, however, Faysal promoted Islamic rhetoric in a desperate attempt to counter threatening secular and socialist ideologies in the Arab world, which appealed to sections of Saʿudi society.

Having at their disposal ample evidence, Faysal's enemies among dissidents of the 1960s pointed to his conservatism and autocratic rule. His failure to introduce a basic law and a consultative council, both promised during his struggle against his brother Saʿud, shattered the myth of his progressive government. However, there is no doubt that the consolidation of the Saʿudi state of 1932 and even its survival during the turmoil of the Arab world in the 1960s were products of his efforts. Faysal's success in stabilising Saʿudi internal politics and his popularity in the Islamic world developed against the background of a new wealth that he began to possess. The dramatic rise of oil prices in the early 1970s allowed Saudi Arabia to become an important player not only regionally but also internationally. The new wealth also made radical and secular dissidence less appealing in Saudi Arabia, as we shall see in the next chapter.

CHAPTER 5

From affluence to austerity, 1973–1990

The short-lived oil embargo that Saudi Arabia together with other Arab oil-producing countries imposed on the United States and Europe, in support of Egypt's 1973 war with Israel, brought Saudi Arabia to the attention of the world. The embargo led to dramatic increases in oil prices, allowing Saudi Arabia to enjoy an unprecedented affluence, which facilitated internal modernisation, strengthened the ability of the regime to extend services, enforced state control over the population and created dependency on its resources. Faysal's economic and social reforms in the late 1960s could now be implemented and even expanded with his increased revenues.

However, the new wealth of the 1970s increased the vulnerability of the Saʿudi regime and pushed its leadership to search for 'patrons' to protect it against internal and external threats. Saudi Arabia continued to look towards the United States to play the role of protector and guarantor of its security. While Saudi Arabia had been enjoying a close liaison with the United States since after the Second World War, this relationship became increasingly 'troubled' in the 1970s. Partnership with the United States became more urgent in the aftermath of the new wealth in a country that lacked the human and technological resources to guarantee its own security. Saudi Arabia had the financial means to purchase security, but at a very high price.

While a sense of vulnerability accompanied the boom of the 1970s, this became exaggerated in the mid-1980s when oil prices decreased sharply, leading to a serious decline in Saʿudi revenues. Regional development in the 1980s (the Iranian revolution of 1979, the Soviet invasion of Afghanistan in 1979, and the Iran–Iraq war in the 1980s) did little to alleviate Saudi Arabia's sense of insecurity. In the 1980s, as tension moved from the Mediterranean to the Persian Gulf region, Saudi Arabia was caught in the mounting instability. Both the siege of the Mecca mosque (1979) and the Shiʿa riots (1979–80) created serious internal challenges and convinced the regime of its precarious position in a volatile region.

During both the affluence of the 1970s and the austerity of the 1980s, one theme seemed dominant in Saʿudi politics; a deep-rooted vulnerability, itself a product of demographic/economic factors (the combination of small population, large territory and immense wealth), developmental factors (a combination of weak human resources and dependence on foreign labour) and the responsibilities of geography that made the Saʿudi regime the guardian of the two holy Muslim shrines. Geography imposed on Saudi Arabia certain responsibilities in the Arab and Islamic worlds, and rendered its partnership with a foreign power such as the United States even more problematic.

AFFLUENCE: THE OIL EMBARGO (1973)

Before 1973, it seems that Saʿudi government rhetoric, in particular that of Faysal, assured the international community that 'oil and politics should not be mixed', implying that Saudi Arabia would not use its oil resources to push the West to put pressure on Israel to withdraw from Palestinian territories. In press releases Saudi Arabia insisted that it did not intend to use oil as a weapon in the Arab–Israeli conflict (al-Sowayyegh 1980). However, in spite of government rhetoric, oil and politics had been inseparable (Golub 1985: 15). As oil prices began to increase in the early 1970s, Saudi Arabia called for lower prices to cement a closer relationship with the United States – it used oil for a political end.

In July 1973 OPEC raised the price of oil by 11.9 per cent (Grayson 1982: 110). The outbreak of the Egyptian–Israeli war in October 1973 led to further increases in oil prices. During the months leading to the October war, Saudi Arabia began to warn that it would use oil as a weapon in case of a new war with Israel. On 31 August 1973, Faysal announced that 'he cannot continue to maintain shipment of oil if the United States continued its cordial relations with Israel' (ibid.). These warnings went unheeded in both the United States and Europe (Peck 1980: 240).[1] In October 1973 the Western world seemed surprised when Saudi Arabia joined other Arab oil-producing countries and declared an embargo on the shipment of oil to countries that supported Israel.

It is worth pointing out that Saudi Arabia did not spearhead the drive for the oil embargo and oil-production cuts, nor did it seek or even expect the massive oil-price increases that the oil embargo produced (Golub 1985: 8). Saudi Arabia delayed its commitment to join the embargo with other oil-producing Arab states until it could no longer 'delay and delay, hoping to ride out conflict without being forced to play the oil card' (ibid.: 10).

After a successful surprise attack on Israel on 6 October 1973, Egypt began to experience military difficulties that were more likely to reverse the early success. It was at this juncture that Saudi Arabia decided to give up the 'waiting game' and institute an embargo on the West (Golub 1985). Saudi Arabia found itself under pressure to respond to a call by the Palestine Liberation Organisation (PLO) on 7 October 1973 urging oil-producing Arab states to use their wealth as a weapon (Grayson 1982: 15).

Ten Arab oil ministers met in Kuwait on 17 October and agreed to reduce oil production by 5 per cent every month until the Middle East conflict was resolved. They also agreed to raise oil prices by 17 per cent (Grayson 1982: 111). On 18 October Saudi Arabia went further than the decision taken at the Kuwait meeting by announcing a 10 per cent reduction in oil production, with a complete ban on petroleum shipment to the United States (ibid.). This coincided with the United States military 'air bridge' to compensate Israel for its arms losses. Saudi Arabia declared that it would cease oil supplies to all countries that had adopted a pro-Israeli stance (Vassiliev 1998: 393). The Saʿudi decision to use the 'oil weapon' against the West 'catapulted Saudi Arabia to the center of Arab politics at the expense of an Egypt that became even more dependent on Saudi Arabia and the West after the 1973 war' (Fraser 1997: 222).

Even after a decision to use the oil card was made, Saudi Arabia delayed the enforcement of the embargo. It took two weeks to raise the initial cut in oil export from 2 to 25 per cent. Golub argues that Faysal's repeated delays and his obvious reluctance to bring the Kingdom into its first-ever conflict with the United States appear to indicate that the intention of the Saʿudi moves was to avoid raising prices, as this would have further antagonised the United States (Golub 1985: 12).[2]

When it was finally enforced, the oil embargo shocked the international community as the price of oil rose by almost 70 per cent (Safran 1985: 161). Europe and Japan in particular had been dependent on Middle East oil since the end of the Second World War. They were more threatened by the embargo and the rise in oil prices than was the United States. Both oil shortages and the increase in oil prices were expected to cripple European economies and eventually lead to a world economic recession.

The effect of the oil embargo on Western economies was exaggerated in both Arab and Western media at the time. The embargo lasted less than six months and was partially enforced. Crude-oil production declined during the six months of the embargo by only 4.5 per cent (Safran 1985: 160). The United States had been purchasing some 500,000 barrels of Saʿudi oil daily, or about 3 per cent of total American consumption. If one is to count reductions and bans on shipment by other Arab states, the United States suffered a deficit of about 12 per cent of its total supply (Grayson 1982: 112).

Saudi Arabia and other Arab oil-producing countries began to be seen as threatening to Western interests. The image of the 'greedy oil shaykh' became dominant in the West and the United States. Saudi Arabia reacted to reports that the United States might use military means to break the oil embargo with the warning that 'If pressed Saudi Arabia could reduce its oil production by 80 per cent, and that if America resorted to military action, the oil fields would be blown up' (Grayson 1982: 112). In the heated atmosphere of the last months of 1973, the United States threatened to suspend food shipment to Arab countries.

In Saudi Arabia the oil embargo resulted in a dramatic increase in oil revenues, thus allowing Faysal to launch his economic transformation and increase his government spending on infrastructure. In 1972 Saudi Arabia's GDP was 40.5 billion Saʿudi riyals. In 1973, it reached an unprecedented level of 99.3 billion riyals (IMF 1999: 798). Saudi Arabia entered the age of affluence. Its new wealth allowed Faysal to accelerate the internal modernisation programme. His reign began to be associated in popular imagination with *al-nahḍa* (awakening/renaissance). While Faysal had been determined to modernise the economy and create an infrastructure that was still virtually non-existent in the 1960s, he was now able to increase government spending on the first five-year plan (mentioned in the last chapter). He expanded education and health services, improved transport and communication facilities, implemented bedouin sedentarisation schemes and, most importantly, increased Saʿudi military capabilities through the purchase of arms from the United States.

The new wealth generated an unresolved contradiction in the way Saudi Arabia began to be perceived by outsiders. A country with a very small, lightly distributed population, lagging behind in training and skills, and completely dependent on foreign labour began to control vast new resources which it used to dictate policy and influence international opinion. Moreover, Faysal had already promoted the country as guardian of Islam and supporter of Muslim causes, above all the Palestinian problem, which he continued to link to the religious significance of Jerusalem.

However, Saudi Arabia so far had not supported this rhetoric with any significant action. The opportunity came in 1973 when Faysal used his only vital resource in the service of the Palestinian cause. With the oil embargo, Saudi Arabia's commitment to Muslim and Arab causes was demonstrated at the international level.

Regardless of whether the oil embargo had a real or exaggerated influence on Western economies, its symbolic significance for Arabs in general and Saudi Arabia in particular was paramount. Oil was used for the first time as a potential weapon in the Arab–Israeli conflict. Previous disruptions of oil supplies during the Suez Crisis in 1956 and the Arab–Israeli war in 1967 had been unimportant – oil shortages at the time failed to attract the attention of the world media because of the oil glut of the 1960s, or lead to a world economic crisis similar to the one in 1973 (Peck 1980: 234). Since the 1970s there has been no shortage of pleas among revolutionary Palestinian groups and radical Arab regimes in favour of 'trying the oil card again'. These pleas constituted the dreams of the Arab masses, many of whom had not recovered from the so-called *naksa*, the humiliation of June 1967. The Saʿudi regime, however, was more concerned with maintaining its control over its own population and remained unwilling to undermine its long-term economic and military relations with the United States and Western Europe.

As a weapon, the oil embargo failed to bring Jerusalem back into Arab jurisdiction. However, Saudi Arabia's image in the Muslim and Arab world was altered beyond recognition. The country and Faysal in particular became symbols of defiance in the eyes of many Muslims. The oil embargo 'underscored the Kingdom's pivotal position within oil producing countries, brought it into open confrontation with the United States for the first time, and thrust upon it an unprecedented leadership role in the Arab World' (Safran 1985: 176). Furthermore, Saudi Arabia became the critical player in international oil diplomacy (Fraser 1997: 222). Having promoted Islamic rhetoric and capitalised on Saudi Arabia's role as guardian of Islam's holiest shrines, Faysal had to maintain his country's Islamic credentials by joining the oil embargo (ibid.: 224). While the oil crisis enhanced the status and influence of Saudi Arabia, it also created a wider web of responsibilities: 'If the oil crisis helped to move Saudi Arabia to a position of unprecedented influence in the Arab state system, it also placed the monarchy at the centre of the conflicts that wrecked that system' (ibid.: 224–5). It is this new situation that prompted Saudi Arabia's sense of vulnerability and its increased reliance on its relationship with the United States.

VULNERABILITIES: SAʿUDI–AMERICAN RELATIONS IN THE 1970S

One would imagine that a country whose economic resources multiplied during a very short period of time would emerge triumphant, as it was in a position to convert its economic wealth into political influence and enhance its stature in the international arena. After the embargo Saudi Arabia did emerge with an inflated image of itself, an image that was endorsed and popularised internally, regionally and internationally. But a deeper sense of vulnerability accompanied this inflated image. This was apparent in the country's relationship with the United States and its increasing reliance on American military resources, purchased at a very high price.

Saudi Arabia's open confrontation with the United States during the oil crisis was a short-lived experience. This confrontation was different from the early conflict over recognition of the republican regime in Yemen in 1962. In the 1970s the rhetoric of confrontation over the oil crisis and the Arab–Israeli conflict masked a partnership that had been developing behind the scenes. So far the United States had regarded Israel and the Shah of Iran as its main allies in the Middle East. After the oil crisis, ironically, Saudi Arabia emerged as another potential ally.

In the 1970s Iran and Saudi Arabia had a tacit alliance to contain the secular and radical Arab states, which coincided with American interests (Fraser 1997). By 1974, Saudi Arabia seemed to have returned to an old bargain with the United States. The bargain was rooted in Saudi Arabia's vulnerability. Relations with the United States were based on Saudi Arabia's commitment to apply a moderate oil policy that would ensure low oil prices for the benefit of the United States and Europe. In return, the United States would pursue a comprehensive Middle East peace, guarantee Saudi Arabia's economic and military development and ensure regional security (Golub 1985). These three objectives remained the underlying rationale behind Saudi Arabia's desire to maintain a friendly partnership with the United States.

The more the Saʿudis appeared to rely on this partnership, the more troublesome the relationship became in a region where in October 1973 the Americans made it crystal clear that they were the main ally of Israel, a state that threatened the security of several Arab countries. This violated the first objective of the Saʿudi–United States bargain, the pursuit of a just Middle East peace. Saudi Arabia could not have an open alliance with the United States without invoking hostility (both verbal and real) from several neighbouring Arab states. In the 1970s, Libya, Syria, Iraq and

Southern Yemen were generating revolutionary anti-imperialist rhetoric that was directed mainly towards the United States. In the eyes of those regimes, for a Muslim country with enormous oil wealth to be identified with American imperialism, which was sponsoring Zionist expansion at the expense of the Arab world, was not acceptable. The Saʿudi–United States relationship invited the wrath of revolutionary regimes and the hatred of the Arab masses in the late 1970s. Saudi Arabia's vulnerability to the attacks of those revolutionary regimes made it even more necessary for the country to seek protection from the United States and buy huge quantities of weapons from the same source. As most of those regimes were in close alliance with the communist Soviet Union, Saudi Arabia seemed to have no other option but to continue to develop a careful but steady partnership with the United States.

The vulnerability of Saudi Arabia, combined with the contradictions behind its relationship with the United States, remained a constant feature of this relationship. This was so because 'although its financial power and religious character give it definite forms of influence in the Arab world and beyond, Saudi Arabia is in certain essential aspects an extremely weak country' (Halliday 1982: 127). Weakness manifested itself demographically, socially, militarily and economically (ibid.). As such, Saudi Arabia had not been able to seriously influence the United States policy on Israel, even after the oil embargo.

While Faysal reluctantly joined the Arab oil embargo in October 1973, he was determined to put an end to the oil crisis in order to assure Washington of his good intentions. In March 1974, a Saʿudi threat to leave OPEC was decisive in persuading other members attending the OPEC meeting in Vienna to keep oil prices low. OPEC members agreed to freeze prices for three months at $11.65 per barrel. Saudi Arabia later announced that it would increase its own oil production by 1 million barrels per day, thus compensating for previous oil shortages in the West (Grayson 1982: 114).

Saudi Arabia's push for low oil prices was rewarded with the signing of several economic and military agreements with the United States. In April 1974 the Saʿudi defence minister, Prince Sultan, signed a contract to purchase some $270 million worth of missiles and other related military equipment (Grayson 1982: 115). In the same month, Prince Abdullah, commander of the National Guard, signed an even greater agreement for the United States to assist in the modernisation of this para-military force to the extent of $335 million (ibid.). Two months later, the Saudi interior minister, Prince Fahd, arrived in Washington to sign an agreement that led to the establishment of two commissions, one responsible for expanding bilateral cooperation in the economic area and one in the military area (ibid.). The Joint United States–Saʿudi Committee for Economic Cooperation initiated contracts worth $650 million, and in 1978 Saudi Arabia imported nearly $4.4 billion worth of US goods, making it the seventh-largest US export market (Halliday 1982: 132). The United States also became a market for Saʿudi investment. By 1979 $35 billion were held in American government securities, and another $24 billion in other US investments (ibid.)

Military cooperation was one of the main objectives behind building a close relationship with the United States. In 1976 the US Corps of Engineers set up a special Middle East division that became involved in a massive construction programme, leading to the establishment of three 'military cities' in Saudi Arabia: al-Baṭin (near the Iraqi border), Khamis Mushayt (near the Yemeni border) and Tabuq (near the Jordanian border) (Halliday 1982: 137). The locations reflected Saʿudi insecurities and its perception of its 'troublesome' neighbours. Moreover, between 1971 and 1980 Saudi Arabia purchased military equipment worth over $34 billion (ibid.). These purchases were followed by the acquisition of highly developed military aircraft (F-5 and F-15 fighters).[3] The availability of sophisticated military equipment generated a false sense of security, as it became clear in 1977 that if Saudi Arabia were to receive no more military equipment it would take six years for existing personnel to be able to use already bought technology (ibid.: 141).

King Faysal died in 1975, before various Saʿudi–US military and economic commissions developed into a fully fledged partnership. He was assassinated on 25 March 1975 by his nephew Prince Faysal ibn Musaʿid ibn ʿAbd al-ʿAziz. After much speculation regarding the motives of the assassin, the government informed its citizens that the assassination was an 'individual act'. Most Saʿudis remembered the assassin's brother Prince Khalid, who in 1965 led a demonstration against the opening of the television broadcasting station, as a result of which the Saʿudi police shot him. While the government offered no explanation for the King's assassination, Saʿudis made their own interpretations (al-Shamrani 1988b: 33–53). Some commented on the linkages between the 1965 and 1975 incidents, while rumours about 'American and Zionist conspiracies' against Muslims flourished. In the popular imagination his assassination was depicted as revenge by the West for the oil embargo of 1973.

The assassination had been a personal act of revenge. It took place at a time when Saudi Arabia was beginning to experience the tension between the rhetoric of Islamic authenticity that King Faysal promoted and the increasing material and technological transformation associated with oil wealth. A second contradiction resulted from the incompatibility of this Islamic rhetoric with the increasing reliance on American technology and military personnel for the training of Saʿudi forces and general economic development. After establishing that the assassin, Prince Faysal, was in command of all his mental abilities, the Riyadh *ʿulama* authorised his beheading. The execution took place in Riyadh's public square after the Friday noon prayer (al-Shamrani 1988b: 17–31).

THE REIGN OF KING KHALID (1975–1982)

Khalid (born 1912) became King within three days of Faysal's death. His half-brother Fahd was named Crown Prince. During the eight years of King Khalid's reign (1975–82) the contradiction between Faysal's Islamic rhetoric on the one hand and the increasing affluence and materialism of Saʿudi society on the other began to unfold.

King Khalid's reign might have been uneventful had it not been for several external factors that had ramifications in Saudi Arabia. First, the Iranian revolution of 1979 influenced internal political developments and inspired Islamic activism in several Arab states, including Saudi Arabia. Second, the Soviet invasion of Afghanistan exaggerated Saʿudi fears of communism and offered the rationale behind a closer partnership with the United States. And third, the Iran–Iraq war in the 1980s brought a regional conflict closer to Saʿudi borders. This conflict became extremely threatening to Saudi Arabia especially as the Islamic Republic of Iran regularly criticised and exposed the contradiction underlying Saʿudi–American relations: the Saʿudi regime came under attack from a fellow Muslim country which had important social and military capabilities exceeding those of Saudi Arabia. Saʿudi vulnerabilities seemed to have worsened while the country was still enjoying a period of affluence. We shall start with the domestic scene.

While during Faysal's reign technological innovations had occasionally been sanctioned by the leading senior *ʿulama*, excessive wealth, corruption of the ruling group, the changing landscape of Saudi Arabia and the expansion of religious education in universities created by King Faysal in the early 1970s triggered the return of the *ikhwan*. Faysal was responsible for promoting an Islamic world-view, together with an Islamic foreign policy, but both undermined his growing partnership with the United States and rendered the behaviour of members of the royal family that deviated from

Islam more problematic. His Islamic policy was a double-edged sword. It enhanced Saudi Arabia's position internally and internationally, but also invited criticism whenever the Islamic ideal was perceived to have been violated.

During the annual pilgrimage season on 20 November 1979, the siege of the mosque in Mecca by Juhayman ibn Muhammad al-ʿUtaybi and Muhammad ibn ʿAbdullah al-Qaḥṭani, together with several Saʿudi and non-Saʿudi followers, was the most open manifestation of an underlying tension in Saudi Arabia. The leader of the siege, Juhayman, had been an active preacher who ventured into giving opinions on the just Muslim ruler, relations with 'infidel powers', materialism and corruption, and the relationship between the *ʿulama* and power (Buchan 1982: 122). He declared the spiritual leader of the movement, al-Qaḥṭani, the true *mahdi* (the one who guides), and demanded the removal of the corrupt royal family. By the time he organised the siege, he had attracted around two hundred followers (ibid.), in some accounts between four and five hundred (Abir 1988: 151). The group included wives and children who were participating in the pilgrimage during the 1979 season, which corresponded to the year 1400 AH in the Muslim calendar. The majority of Juhayman's rebels had been students at the Islamic University of Madina, where the Egyptian Muslim Brotherhood's influence had been strong. In his attempt to undermine Naṣir in the 1960s, Faysal had welcomed members of this brotherhood who became active in several newly established Saʿudi religious universities.

Juhayman and his followers represented an Islamic uprising in protest at what its members described as the religious and moral laxity and degeneration of the Saʿudi rulers (al-Yassini 1985: 124: Al-Rasheed 1997: 76; Ayubi 1991: 99–104; Buchan 1982: 120–4). This was the first time the Saʿudi royal family had been openly attacked for improper personal conduct and corruption since the reign of Ibn Saʿud.[4]

This tension manifested itself at three levels: how to reconcile sudden and immense wealth, as well as rapid economic modernisation, with adherence to Islam; the incompatibility between religious dogma and royal politics; and the vulnerability of the royal family to attack from the neo-*ikhwan*, the successors of those who staged the rebellion against Ibn Saʿud between 1927 and 1929. Juhayman himself was born in the *ikhwan* settlement of Sajir in Qasim (Buchan 1982: 121; Abir 1988: 150).

The government mobilised the *ʿulama*. The Institution of *Ifta*ʾ and Scholarly Research, headed by Shaykh ʿAbd al-ʿAziz ibn Baz, issued a

3 The Kaʿba, Mecca. © Popperfoto

fatwa supporting the ruling group and authorising military intervention in the sacred sanctuary. The siege was brought to an end after the killing of the proclaimed *mahdi*, and the capture of the military leader and theoretician of the movement as well as 170 followers (Al-Rasheed 1997: 76). Crushing the rebellion took two weeks and led to several deaths among the rebels. On 3 December 1979 the last rebels emerged from the Kaʿba.[5]

The political messages of the rebels were overshadowed by their proclamation of the spiritual leader of the movement, Muhammad al-Qaḥṭani, as the *mahdi*, a controversial concept in Sunni Islam. The government capitalised on this controversy to discredit the rebels and their self-styled *mahdi* (al-Qaḥṭani 1988a: 83). The senior *ʿulama* embarked on a theological debate regarding the characteristics of the true *mahdi*, thus overshadowing the political opposition underlying the rebellion. The *ʿulama* concluded that al-Qaḥṭani could not be the true *mahdi*, thus justifying the brutal suppression of the movement inside the holy mosque, a sacred precinct where the shedding of blood had been prohibited before the rise of Islam. Whether al-Qaḥṭani was a true or false *mahdi* is beyond the scope of this book – what is relevant here is how the theological debate among the Saʿudi *ʿulama* assisted the government in shifting the focus of attention away from the magnitude of the political opposition underlying the siege of the mosque. However, both the ruling group and ordinary Saʿudis understood that the rebellion was not about a false or true *mahdi*, but was about a development that unleashed contradictory social outcomes and tensions not anticipated by a government that championed modernisation in the process of creating new grounds for legitimacy. The mosque siege was part and parcel of the material modernisation of the 1970s. It was a political awakening drawing on religious rhetoric that became more articulate under the sponsorship of religious centres of learning, education and literacy. Juhayman was distinguished from Faysal al-Duwaysh, the *ikhwan* rebel of 1927, by his religious education and theological treatise, all developed during a long period of study in an Islamic university established by the Saʿudi state.

The same social tensions that led to the siege of the mosque were unfolding in the eastern province, where the majority of Saʿudi Shiʿa lived. Most Shiʿa in Saudi Arabia worked in the oil fields, but they faced various forms of discrimination.[6] The fact that Wahhabi doctrine branded the Shiʿa as heretics only fuelled a discrimination that was grounded in the fact that the majority of the Shiʿa had been peasant farmers in a society that held such occupation in low esteem. The Shiʿa were discriminated against not only because they were Shiʿa but also because they constituted a community that was regarded as a social 'anomaly' in Arabia (Al-Rasheed 1998: 131).

In the 1970s a further contradiction emerged. The oil industry was based in Shiʿa territory, where they contributed the bulk of semi-skilled and unskilled labour. This was not translated into better economic, educational and social opportunities for the population. Outside ARAMCO camps, the majority of the Shiʿa did not benefit from the expansion in health and social services. They were banned from certain professions, for example the army and educational institutions. They were also banned from performing their special *ʿashura* mourning rituals in public and building their own mosques. Under Faysal's patronage Wahhabi *ʿulama* issued several *fatwas* condemning the Shiʿa. Some *ʿulama* went as far as to declare that meat slaughtered by Shiʿa butchers was not fit for consumption by Muslims. The state did little to suppress extreme religious opinions that denounced the Shiʿa (al-Ḥasan 1993).

The success of the Iranian revolution in 1979 turned several Shiʿa activists into 'Muslim rebels'. In 1979, the Shiʿa took to the streets during the *ʿashura* season, when they usually mourn the death of their martyrs, Ḥasan and Ḥusayn, a practice forbidden by the state and confined to the private domain since the incorporation of Hasa into the Saʿudi realm in 1913. The government dispatched 20,000 National Guard soldiers to disperse the mourners.

In 1980, the Shiʿa organised a large demonstration and a series of strikes in Qatif to celebrate the first anniversary of the return of Khomeini to Iran. This became an occasion to voice their discontent over their status as second-class citizens in Saudi Arabia. The National Guard dispersed demonstrators, killing several participants. The Shiʿa remember the events as *intifaḍat al-minṭaqa al-sharqiyya*, the uprising of the eastern province (al-Shaykh, al-Dakhil and al-Zayir 1981). The Organisation of the Islamic Revolution (*munadhamat al-thawra al-islamiyya*), a clandestine Shiʿa organisation representing the community in the eastern province, began to take shape as the political outlet for the group following the spontaneous events of 1979–80 (Al-Rasheed 1998: 122). Members of the organisation were drawn from students in the University of Minerals and Petroleum (Dammam) and workers at the oil fields. The organisation began broadcasting from Iranian radio stations in an attempt to reach the community in Saudi Arabia, and an information office was opened in Tehran to coordinate political activities.[7] King Khalid realised the volatile nature of this new opposition that gathered momentum as a result of the anti-Saʿudi rhetoric of the Islamic Republic of Iran. After a series of violent confrontations with the Shiʿa, their leadership went into exile.

Following the 1979 and 1980 riots, the Saʿudi government adopted a pragmatic approach and promised a series of economic reforms. Officials visiting the region immediately after these events openly recognised the social and economic privation of the community and promised to improve the educational, health and economic infrastructures of Shiʿa towns. However, these *ad hoc* measures failed to pacify the Shiʿa. It was only in 1993 and under the pressure of the Gulf War of 1991 that a fragile reconciliation was achieved (Al-Rasheed 1998).

Both the Mecca mosque siege and the Shiʿa riots were manifestations of the underlying tensions that were created during the reign of King Faysal and materialised during the reign of King Khalid. The first disturbance represented the discontent of some Wahhabi religious scholars over the material transformation of Saʿudi society and the risk of losing Islamic values. Juhayman's rebellion highlighted the contradiction between the Islamic rhetoric and credentials of the Saʿudi state and its prolonged relationship with the West. The Shiʿa opposition resulted from the unequal distribution of oil wealth that had been produced in the eastern province since 1938. The riots were products of the success of the Iranian revolution whose leadership began to attack Saudi

Arabia for corruption, alliance with the West, and above all questioned the Saʿudi leadership's claim to protect the two Muslim shrines in Mecca and Madina. Both the mosque siege and the Shiʿa riots took place at a time when Islamic political rhetoric was beginning to undermine previous leftist and nationalist political trends in the Arab world.

At the level of the ruling group the reign of King Khalid was marked by stability resulting from Faysal's institutionalised division of tasks and ministerial jobs among the senior princes. It was during Khalid's eight-year rule that the group often referred to in Western literature as the 'Sudayri Seven', the sons of a Sudayri mother, became more consolidated as a political force among the Saʿudi ruling group. The group consisted of Fahd (Crown Prince during Khalid's reign), Sultan (second deputy prime minister and minister of defence and aviation), Nayef (minister of the interior), Salman (governor of Riyadh), ʿAbd al-Rahman (vice-minister of defence and aviation since 1962), Aḥmad (vice-minister of the interior) and Turki (vice-minister of defence until 1978). This group established its monopoly over key government posts, namely defence and interior affairs. In 1982, Khalid died after a short illness. With his death the Sudayri brothers were confirmed in their ministerial offices under the kingship of Fahd.

During Khalid's reign, Crown Prince Fahd assumed more responsibilities while Khalid became a ceremonial figure. This was attributed to an internal power struggle within the Saʿudi royal family between Fahd and his full brothers on the one hand, and Khalid and other half-brothers on the other hand, mainly ʿAbdullah, commander of the National Guard. However, this struggle in the late 1970s was not comparable to that between Faysal and Saʿud in the 1960s. Fahd and Khalid seemed to have coexisted in a manner that did not threaten the survival of the ruling group. Khalid's ill-health did little to strengthen his position within the royal family. He accepted his honorary role as a ceremonial king while letting his brother Fahd run state affairs and make major decisions.

AUSTERITY: THE REIGN OF KING FAHD (1982–2005)

Crown Prince Fahd (born 1921) became King following the death of Khalid in 1982. This was a smooth transition, as Fahd had already assumed great powers during the last years of Khalid's rule. The King, together with his six full brothers, consolidated control over key government positions, mainly defence and interior. Their half-brother ʿAbdullah, commander of

Table 3. *Volume of petroleum export and GDP in billion SA riyals 1982–1997*

Year	Volume of petroleum export	GDP
1982	80.6	415.2
1983	56.5	372.0
1984	47.9	351.4
1985	35.2	313.9
1986	52.6	271.0
1987	43.5	275.4
1988	55.4	285.1
1989	56.1	310.8
1990	47.0	391.9
1991	96.6	442.0
1992	103.7	461.4
1993	101.3	443.8
1994	99.9	450.3
1995	100.0	470.7
1996	100.3	511.33
1997	99.6	547.41

Source: IMF 1999: 798–9.

the National Guard, became Crown Prince and first deputy prime minister. In 1986 King Fahd adopted a new title, Custodian of the two Holy Mosques.

Fahd's early years as King coincided with a sharp decrease in oil prices, which reached their lowest level in 1986. The oil price dropped from $32 per barrel to $15 in the early 1980s, thus reducing Saʿudi oil revenues by over 30 per cent. Within six months, between January and July 1986, oil prices dropped from $26 to $8 per barrel (Birks, Seccombe and Sinclair 1988: 272). In 1982 Saʿudi gross domestic product reached an unprecedented level of over 400 billion Saʿudi riyals. In 1986 it dropped to 271 billion (see table 3).

The affluence experienced during the reigns of Faysal and Khalid could no longer be taken for granted, while the Saʿudi government tried to adjust to decreasing oil prices that exposed the vulnerability of an economy based on a single commodity. Fahd's early years as monarch were often described as the age of austerity, and contrasted with the years of affluence during the reigns of Faysal and Khalid.

In the 1980s a slower modernisation of the country's infrastructure was deemed necessary as a result of successive budget deficits. Saudi Arabia met deficits by drawing on reserves and borrowing from the local economy (Gause 1994: 148). Overambitious projects were stopped or abandoned in response to growing economic uncertainty. The fourth development plan (1985–90) reduced expenditures on infrastructures and shifted more resources to developing economic and human resources. Real GDP growth averaged 1.4 per cent per annum, far below the 4 per cent anticipated. Spending on prestige construction projects fell by 8.5 per cent. Plans to construct an oil refinery in Qasim and a new international airport in the eastern province were abandoned (Vassiliev 1998: 453). Completed high-rise office buildings in the major cities remained unoccupied reflecting low demand, declining revenues and slow economic growth. The construction sector of the economy suffered most as reflected in the decline of the number of foreign workers employed (Birks, Seccombe and Sinclair 1988: 268).

The government, however, was reluctant to cut spending on public services and benefits among a population that had grown accustomed to free hospitals, schools and social benefits. While the government continued to subsidise agriculture, in 1985 electricity and gas rates were increased by 70 per cent for the first time since 1972 (Vassiliev 1998: 454). Ordinary Saʿudis began to resent paying exorbitant gas, telephone and electricity bills. With decrease in cash flow, only a few Saʿudis could afford luxury holidays abroad or the consumer goods that were saturating the market. Saʿudis remember the 1980s as a decade of austerity alien to the generation that prospered during the oil boom of the late 1970s.

The government could not contemplate taxing the population during times of declining oil revenues for fear of the consequences. The idea that citizens pay taxes remained unacceptable among a population used to receiving state benefits rather than contributing to public funds. In a desperate attempt to raise revenues, the government announced its intention to introduce income tax on foreign workers, a decision that had to be revoked when highly skilled expatriates threatened to resign. Instead, higher fees for residence and exit visas were introduced to raise extra cash. Throughout the 1980s, it was estimated that roughly 30 per cent of the Saʿudi population was foreign, but non-nationals constituted 60 per cent of the labour force (Cordesman 1997: 71).

Saudi Arabia began to feel the pressure of high population growth with an estimated birth rate of 3.68 per cent and a fertility rate of 6.48 children per woman (Cordesman 1997: 31). It had and still has one of the fastest-growing populations in the world. If birth rates continue at this level, it is predicted that its population will reach 22 million early in the twenty-first century (ibid.: 34). Almost 50 per cent of the population are under the age of sixteen, making it also one of the youngest.

The number of students in schools and universities stretched the capacity of the education system to absorb pupils while struggling to maintain reasonable standards. Students in higher education continued to receive generous monthly allowances (amounting to $300 per month), introduced in the 1970s as an incentive to increase higher education enrolments (Mosa 2000: 24). Pressure on general services and infrastructure mounted together with an increase in demand for employment in an economy that was not developed enough to absorb the growing number of young educated Saʿudis aspiring to secure jobs with inflated salaries.

The government remained the major employer, attracting over 40 per cent of the labour force. Industry, construction and oil absorbed 25 per cent of the labour force while services provided opportunities for 30 per cent. Only 5 per cent of the workforce were engaged in agriculture.

These percentages conceal the fact that the economically active workforce included a substantial expatriate community consisting of Western, Arab and Asian employees, estimated in the 1980s to be 4 million (Cordesman 1997). In 1985 it was estimated that non-nationals accounted for more than 71 per cent of the Saʿudi workforce (Birks, Seccombe and Sinclair 1988: 267). They dominated three economic sectors: construction, manufacturing, and utilities. In 1985 Arab workers remained the largest group among foreign workers, estimated at 1.12 million, followed by 1.1 million South Asians (ibid.: 274). Arabs came mainly from Egypt, Lebanon, Palestine, Syria and Jordan, with a small minority from North Africa. The largest and most longstanding group of Arab workers had been the Yemenis, whose expulsion *en masse* from the kingdom in 1990 caused serious economic problems in Yemen.[8]

The decline in Saʿudi revenues in the 1980s encouraged the government to promote the rhetoric of 'Saʿudisation', a programme aimed at the gradual replacement of foreigners with Saʿudis as the latter acquired education, training and skills. This was a stated objective of the fourth five-year plan (1985–90). Reliance on foreign labour had long been regarded as a necessary evil during a period of transition. Saʿudisation, however, remained limited. A shortage of local candidates for highly skilled jobs together with the reluctance of Saʿudis to engage in menial work meant that the country remained dependent on Western expertise for specialised industries and Asian labour for construction and other unskilled and menial jobs. The number of work permits issued to non-nationals rose from 523,000 in 1977 to an initial peak of 687,000 in 1979. A small drop in 1980 was followed by a 16 per cent increase in 1981 and further small increases in 1982 and 1983 to a new peak of 790,000. It was only in 1984 that the number of permits issued fell by 5 per cent (Birks, Seccombe and Sinclair 1988: 269). The Saʿudisation programme was accompanied by stricter immigration controls and the deportation of clandestine or undocumented immigrants. During 1985 and 1986 the number of deported immigrants rose to 300,000, compared with 88,000 in 1979 (ibid.: 270). By the mid-1980s Saudi Arabia saw the departure of more than 360,000 South-East Asian workers (ibid.: 272). While those non-nationals working in the construction sector (estimated at 1,021,600 in 1985) were the first to leave, Saudi Arabia remained dependent on Asian labour in the services sector (estimated at 859,550 in 1985) (ibid.: 275).

During the 1980s, the participation of Saudi women in the economy remained limited amidst debates about whether their employment would decrease the country's reliance on foreign labour. During this period Saudi women did take jobs in the newly created all-female banks, services and education. Members of the wealthy elite invested their capital in small all-female businesses. Female-owned and managed boutiques, sports centres and beauty salons in prestigious shopping malls mushroomed in Riyadh and Jeddah. It was estimated that in 1980 there were 11,847 Saʿudi women on the government payroll, working mainly in the fields of education, health, administration and social services (Bahry 1982: 505). There were even debates about allowing women to drive, to facilitate their mobility and decrease their reliance on foreign drivers for transport – a luxury that some Saʿudi families would have preferred not to pay for during times of rising living costs and less cash.[9]

Debates about the right of women to work began to appear in the Saʿudi press in the late 1970s and early 1980s. Suhaylah Zayn al-ʿAbdin, a journalist, defended strict limitations on the jobs women should be allowed to hold and advocated that a special school curriculum for women should be introduced. This generated a response from another female journalist, Khayriyyah al-Saqqaf, who advocated education for women and called for the extension of job opportunities to include the wider economy (Bahry 1982: 505).

The economic uncertainty of the late 1980s failed to change attitudes and loosen social and cultural restrictions on full female participation in the economy. In fact, the increasing visibility of women in the public sphere led to tighter controls and greater vigilance on behalf of the religious police. In the 1980s it was common for the *muṭawwaʿa* to raid all female services in search of 'immoral behaviour' and to smash headless plastic models displaying the latest fashion in shop windows. The importation of dolls was banned in response to criticism from religious circles. While many observers were anticipating greater freedoms under the rule of Fahd, thought of as a progressive king, economic hardship was not enough to loosen restrictions on women or bring about their greater visibility in the economy. Highly successful businesswomen were tolerated but remained dependent on male relatives for all their dealings with government bureaucracies. Some female businesses continued to function amidst frustration and fear that one day they would be closed down.

It was the newly urbanised population of the cities that felt the strain of limited opportunities and the rising cost of living. Young educated Saʿudis who had no close ties with royal networks or government bureaucracy came to realise that employment immediately after a university education could not be taken for granted. Some young Saʿudis found that degrees in the humanities and from religious universities did not prepare them to seek employment in the highly specialised oil industries or services. A division between those who were educated in local institutions of higher learning and those who returned with degrees from foreign universities began to cause resentment. Locally educated Saʿudis were channelled into low-ranking jobs in the civil service where they received modest salaries.[10] Those who returned from American and European universities where they had acquired technical and linguistic skills were predisposed to occupy well-paid jobs in prestigious ministries.

In the 1980s the population of Najd, which had been lagging behind that of Hijaz in education and expertise, began to catch up. While in the 1970s the Hijazi commercial elite was the first to seize the new economic opportunities under the patronage of King Faysal, the newly educated Najdis pressed for greater opportunities under Fahd's rule. In 1986 the Hijazi oil minister Zaki Yamani was removed from office after several years of service, sending alarm signals among the Hijazi elite who had grown accustomed to close ties with the government thanks to their highly valued expertise at times when the country had limited human resources.[11] Employment in various government ministries reflected the shift towards recruiting people from Najd, a region that had been historically more relevant to the foundation of the Al Saʿud rule than any other region in the country. The diminishing resources fuelled the competition among groups in Saʿudi society to gain access to government contracts, commissions and other favours.

The 1980s saw the beginning of sharp social and economic divisions. The wealthy elite consisted of a close circle of royalty, tribal nobility, and a class of commercially successful educated Saʿudis. The growing population, although achieving higher levels of education, was handicapped by its limited access to influential circles as a result of regional background, lack of family connections or social marginality. Recently urbanised bedouins and the traditional peasantry of the oases fell into this category of politically and economically marginalised Saʿudis. The rising literacy and aspirations of such groups contributed to their awareness of their disadvantage. It was among this group that the economic crisis was most strongly felt.

It was no surprise that some young Saʿudis in this category responded favourably to Islamic preachers calling for a denunciation of the West, materialism, corruption and consumerism. Non-government religious organisations started to proliferate in the late 1980s. A strong Islamic rhetoric promoting a return to Islamic authenticity attracted people who had grown frustrated with a truncated modernisation, inequality, corruption of the government and close ties with the West, which began to be increasingly defined as the source of social and economic evils. In addition to the West, sections of Saʿudi society itself were held responsible for the social problems that were being experienced at the time, for example drug abuse and alcoholism, social ills that in the past had never been acknowledged in public. The Western-educated elite began to be referred to as liberals/secularists, who were regarded as dominant in the media and senior government posts. Prominent Saʿudi literary figures and intellectuals reflected on the relationship between Islam and modernity on the pages of the Saʿudi press. The writings of Shaykh ʿAwad al-Qarni and Saʿid al-Ghamdi included attacks on the so-called liberals who were accused of undermining the Islamic foundation of Saudi Arabia (al-Ṣafadi n.d.: 78; Fandy 1999: 48). Such debates were popular among many Saʿudis who saw in Islam a solution to their growing social and economic problems. While the erosion of traditional lifestyles was accelerating, intensive debates about the future of the country, its Islamic heritage and relations with the West flourished in the press, mosques, lecture halls and private domains.

In the late 1980s a clearer division emerged between those who cherished a return to tradition, authenticity and a stricter application of Islamic values and morality and those who aspired towards greater freedoms, openness towards the outside world and an immersion in modernity. It was not uncommon for a single Saʿudi family to have its own members divided along these lines. A relative would be labelled *muṭawwaʿ* if he internalised the rhetoric and discourse of the new Islamist groups. He would be identified by his constant preaching among family members, listening to religious cassettes, regular denunciation of Western culture, music and luxury goods, and his enforcing of a strict moral code among his female relatives. The era witnessed the emergence of a new generation of self-appointed literate and articulate *muṭawwaʿa*. They coexisted with less conservative members of their families who were more comfortable with a relaxed lifestyle and a personal religiosity that did not demand interference with the lives of others. Within families, tolerance and tension progressed hand in hand. Some members of the older generation who had benefited from the oil boom of the 1970s were puzzled by the radicalisation of their own children in the 1980s. While this older generation had never questioned its own religiosity, it did not anticipate this development.

SAUDI ARABIA AND THE GULF CONTEXT IN THE 1980S

This background of social and economic uncertainty coincided with Saudi Arabia's continuous involvement in regional Arab politics. It reluctantly joined Arab efforts to isolate Egypt following the Camp David peace treaty with Israel signed in 1978. Together with other Arab states, Saudi Arabia supported the expulsion of Egypt from the Arab League, and severed diplomatic and economic relations. However, Saudi Arabia was not prepared to go as far as expelling Egyptian migrant workers or cutting airline services (Long 1985: 121). Two years after the Camp David agreement, more urgent developments overshadowed the Arab–Israeli conflict and the Middle East peace process. As far as Saudi Arabia was concerned, conflict in the Gulf region was now more threatening.

The major concerns of Saudi Arabia in the 1980s were in a geographical area closer to its border and more vital for its interests. Two successive developments in the Gulf were perceived as threatening to Saudi Arabia's security: the Iranian revolution (1979) and the Iran–Iraq war (1980). These events gave previous Arab–Israeli conflicts a secondary importance. A third, relatively distant, threat, but of concern to Saudi Arabia, erupted in Afghanistan with the Soviet invasion of that country in 1979.

As Egypt was temporarily and superficially marginalised in the Arab world following the Camp David agreement, there emerged a window of opportunity for Saʿudi leadership aspirations. A second window of opportunity arose with the fall of the Shah of Iran, long considered by the United States the most suitable leader to police the Gulf, keep the Soviets out of this strategic region, and check revolutionary regimes in the area. While Saudi Arabia was shocked to see the quick departure of the Shah, with whom it had developed friendly but tense relations, its fears of Iran became more pronounced with the establishment of an Islamic regime. The Islamic Republic in Iran distinguished itself from its predecessor regime by adopting anti-Western rhetoric and attacking Muslim countries allied to the West, including Saudi Arabia. Furthermore, Iran aimed to export its model of Islamic government and revolutionary experience to other countries, especially those with considerable Shiʿa minorities.[12] Several Gulf states (especially Kuwait, Bahrain and Saudi Arabia) were targeted in Iranian government propaganda.

The anti-Saʿudi rhetoric of the Islamic regime in Tehran that inspired Shiʿa riots in the eastern province was part of the global impact of the Iranian revolution. This rhetoric convinced the Saʿudi government that Iran under an Islamic leadership represented a serious threat to its internal security. The pilgrimage season brought thousands of Iranian pilgrims who used the occasion to organise demonstrations and repeat anti-American slogans denouncing Muslim rulers who co-operated with the West in general and the United States in particular. Clashes with the Saʿudi police and security forces during the pilgrimage season became regular annual events throughout the 1980s. One major clash occurred in 1985 when more than 400 people were killed, including 275 Iranians (Vassiliev 1998: 471). This incident fuelled the hostile rhetoric of the Iranian leadership, who decided to boycott future pilgrimage seasons in response to a low quota set by the Saʿudis. Saudi Arabia introduced the quota system partly to reduce the number of Iranian pilgrims to a level that could be easily contained by the Saʿudi police and partly as a strategy to deal with the rising number of Muslim pilgrims. Saudi Arabia accused Iran of using pilgrims for its own propaganda purposes. Relations between Iran and Saudi Arabia over pilgrimage matters remained antagonistic throughout the 1980s.[13]

The decade-long Iran–Iraq war (1980–90) represented another serious threat to Saudi Arabia. Both the Baʿthist Iraqi regime and the Iranian Islamic Republic were seen as undermining Saʿudi security. Both had populations and military capabilities greater than those of Saudi Arabia. In addition, both had seen themselves as playing important leadership roles in the region.[14] Both had expansionist territorial claims, geographically close to Saudi Arabia. Iraq had long maintained ambitions towards Kuwait, while Iran looked towards Bahrain, not to mention the border disputes between the two countries in the Shatt al-Arab area. Saudi Arabia perceived both Iran and Iraq as rival regional powers and also as potential threats to its own internal security. Saddam Husayn's pan-Arab rhetoric was not appealing to Saudi Arabia, as this rhetoric undermined the legitimacy of the Saʿudi regime. Equally the Islamic Republic in Iran exposed Saudi Arabia's close alliance with the United States and openly called upon Muslims to denounce this relationship.[15]

Saudi Arabia, however, preferred to back Baʿthist Iraq, as it saw Iran as more threatening in the 1980s, given its open criticism of what it considered conservative Muslim regimes and its commitment to 'export' its experience of Islamic republicanism to other Muslim countries. The Saʿudi Shiʿa riots in 1980 were a constant reminder of the new threat not only in Saudi Arabia but also in other Gulf states that had substantial Shiʿa populations, namely Kuwait and Bahrain. Saudi Arabia was not directly involved in the military operations of the Iran–Iraq war but provided, together with other Gulf states, enormous financial support for Iraq. Saʿudi financial aid to Iraq amounted to $25.7 billion, according to King Fahd. This consisted of a combination of grant aid, concession loans, military and transport equipment and industrial products, oil aid, and development loans (Kechichian 1993: 9). Iraqi debts to Saudi Arabia and other Gulf states caused resentment in Iraq and precipitated a major conflict when Saddam Husayn invaded Kuwait in 1990, two years after the Iran–Iraq war was brought to an end (discussed in the next chapter).

In an attempt to mobilise other Arab Gulf states to consider a common policy on security and other issues of common interest (for example, education and economic cooperation) Saudi Arabia was one of the Gulf states behind the foundation of the Gulf Cooperation Council (GCC) in May 1981. In addition to Saudi Arabia, the council included Kuwait, Bahrain, Qatar, the United Arab Emirates and Oman.[16] While cooperation over social, economic and educational matters among other things was a motivation behind the formation of the GCC, the security of the Arab Gulf states and military coordination between its members were the primary concerns of the founding states. This security became an urgent matter, especially after the Iranian revolution and the outbreak of the Iran–Iraq war. In the 1980s, the priorities of GCC states focused on regional cooperation, a policy of non-alignment, Islamic solidarity and keeping a foreign military presence out of the Gulf (Braun 1988: 225).[17]

In all joint public statements, GCC states emphasised 'harmonisation, collaboration, and cooperation', thus moving away from notions of 'unity, merger, or structural integration' (Anthony 1984: 84). According to the GCC charter, the council had three objectives:

> First, it sets out the desire of the six member states to reinforce their common links through co-ordination, cooperation, and integration. Second, it defines such cooperation within the larger frameworks of Arab and Islamic interests and emphasises that the system is not intended to replace but rather to strengthen those interests. Third, the charter calls for cooperation in all fields. This approach underscores the pragmatism underlying the GCC programme from its very inception. (Peterson 1988: 106)

Furthermore, in order not to provoke Arab criticism, the six governments avoided any rhetoric that would imply that the council was a move towards a security alliance (Braun 1988). Council members were also keen not to be seen as undermining the Arab League. According to supporters of the GCC, the council's birth was the 'logical culmination of a decade-long movement to impose a degree of order on the dozens of bilateral and multilateral agreements and understandings among these states' (Anthony 1984: 87).

In the field of military cooperation, Saudi Arabia entered into discussion with other GCC states in order to establish a unified air-defence strategy. Central to this project was the airborne warning and control system (AWACS) stationed on the eastern coast of Saudi Arabia (Braun 1988: 256). The GCC states, however, dismissed a proposal for arms standardisation. The Saʿudi defence minister declared in 1982 that arms standardisation was inadvisable, in particular because of common dependence on one arms supplier for resupply and spare parts in a crisis (ibid.: 257). The GCC states opted for a rapid deployment force, now called the Peninsula Shield Force, a small force composed of units from all six states and stationed at King Khalid military city in the north-east of Saudi Arabia. The force was initially put under Saʿudi command (ibid.: 258). Saudi Arabia's military capabilities exceeded those of other founding members of the GCC, and smaller states in particular saw the council as an institutional tool for spreading Saʿudi hegemony over the region. While such criticism did not feature in the public sphere, it was often expressed at the grass-roots level. It was obvious from the very beginning that the GCC had no political or military viability without Saudi Arabia, which was the only member with modern military capabilities sufficient for an integrated GCC defence system (Hameed 1986: 96). Added to that was Saudi Arabia's political and economic influence, both a function of its control over the holy places and enormous oil reserves.

Saʿudi security became increasingly urgent in the mid-1980s. Saudi Arabia was geographically far from the centre of the battleground between Iran and Iraq, but military operations in the Gulf waters threatened the security of its own oil fields. In 1984 Iranian missiles hit Kuwaiti and Saʿudi cargo ships and tankers outside the war zone on their way to and from Saudi Arabian and Kuwaiti ports (Braun 1988: 269). Saudi Arabia did not retaliate. Instead, it increased its financial contribution to Iraq's war efforts, a measure that further drained its diminishing revenues in the late 1980s. When the Iran–Iraq war ended in August 1988, Saudi Arabia was relieved to see a weakened Iran but was increasingly becoming fearful of the Iraqi regime. In spite of triumphalist rhetoric, Iraq emerged from the war with great debts and a drained economy. Saudi Arabia watched Saddam's claims to leadership of the Arab world with suspicion.

In addition to the regional instability caused by the Iran–Iraq war, the Soviet invasion of Afghanistan in 1979 and the consolidation of a communist government sent alarm signals to Saudi Arabia, which had always considered the Soviet Union and communism as enemies of Islam and a threat to its security. The invasion of a Muslim country by the communist superpower confirmed Saʿudi fears. Saudi Arabia responded by providing financial support for the Afghan *Mujahidin* resistance fighters, and allowed its own citizens to join their training camps in Pakistan as volunteers and sponsors.

Saudi Arabia's support of the Afghan resistance, however, became problematic when Saʿudi volunteers returned home after the Soviet withdrawal from Afghanistan in 1989. Several of those activists turned their attention to their own government. Their military training and indoctrination with the Afghan resistance predisposed them towards Islamist politics upon their return. They had developed good networks and friendships that continued to be cherished after the war was over. These networks, coupled with lack of employment opportunities, strengthened the discontent of the so-called 'Saʿudi Afghans', who expected to be given due respect upon their return to the country, in appreciation of their efforts.

SAʿUDI–AMERICAN RELATIONS IN THE 1980S

The rapid fall of the Shah and the failure of the United States to rescue its close ally undermined the credibility of the United States. Saudi Arabia began to see it as unwilling or unable to save its close friends. The Saʿudi leadership wondered whether the United States would accord similar treatment to the Saʿudi regime in similar circumstances (Long 1985: 123).

The credibility of the United States was also undermined by the Soviet invasion of Afghanistan, which rekindled the threat of communism. This invasion led to fears in Washington of a possible Soviet move into the Gulf, especially if there were no conventional forces to prevent such a move. The same fears were surfacing in Saudi Arabia. In December 1979, the United States created the Rapid Deployment Force to prepare for such a scenario, while Saudi Arabia intensified its close contacts with Washington, in a desperate search for commitments to protect its oil fields.[18]

The Carter administration sent firm signals that in the event of Soviet encroachment, 'American military forces will be used to gain control of the Persian Gulf region, and any assault on the Gulf will be regarded as an assault on the vital interests of the United States'. This became known as the Carter Doctrine (MacDonald 1984: 100–1).

Saudi Arabia had always wanted US military protection; however, when the offer was made in the early 1980s, Saudi Arabia refused to permit American combat forces in the country. It was regarded as too dangerous to accept (Grayson 1982: 142). In April 1980 Foreign Minister Prince Saʿud Al Faysal stated that the establishment of American military bases would only serve to jeopardise the host nation (ibid.). Saudi Arabia, however, reportedly supported the thrust of the Carter Doctrine (MacDonald 1984: 101).

Saudi Arabia tested the merit of its liaison with the United States by pushing for more arms sales, while at the same time diversifying its sources. With the Soviet threat in the background, the outbreak of the Iran–Iraq war left Saudi Arabia with less bargaining power as far as its partnership with the United States was concerned. It sent an urgent request to the United States to dispatch four AWACS aircraft in September 1980 to help direct Saʿudi air defence against possible Iranian attack. The sale of the AWACS to Saudi Arabia in 1982 was an attempt to restore both United States' credibility as a reliable security partner and Saʿudi faith in US commitment to regional Gulf security (Cordesman 1984: 269–99; Long 1985: 63).

In the 1980s Saudi Arabia increasingly became a partner of the United States, upon whom it depended for vast quantities of arms, economic development and above all security. The AWACS package was considered vital for protecting Saʿudi oil fields against Iran and countries in which the Soviet Union had military presence (for example, South Yemen). During the Reagan administration, the Soviet Union was projected as the main threat in the Gulf. Reagan moved to improve America's credibility by professing a strong commitment to friendly governments, including Saudi Arabia.[19]

Saʿudi vulnerabilities in the 1980s were behind attempts by Fahd (first as Crown Prince and later as King) to strengthen relationships with the United States during the Reagan administration: 'Fahd, more than any other Saudi leader, pursued a special relationship with the United States. He was the driving force for closer military, political, and economic relations' (Long 1985: 119). Faced with instability in the Gulf resulting from the overthrow of the Shah and the Iran–Iraq war, Saudi Arabia sought support from the United States to protect itself against what it considered the menace of the Islamic regime in Tehran and a possible threat from the Soviet Union. However, given the political climate in the Gulf, which was dominated by revolutionary Islamic rhetoric emanating from Iran and creating disturbing echoes in Saudi Arabia and the Gulf, the Saʿudi–American partnership looked more troubled and problematic than ever before. By the end of the 1980s, the Saʿudi regime sensed hostility from important sections of society which criticised its close liaison with the United States. Early warning signals were given during the siege of the mosque in 1979. Throughout the 1980s Saudi Arabia had no option but to adopt a policy based on 'a balance of dangers' and opt for the least dangerous path. The country sought important military assistance from the United States, but continued to promote itself as a non-aligned Islamic country, resisting all US efforts to establish military air-base facilities on its soil. Saudi Arabia was under the illusion that this resistance would conceal the intimate relationship with the United States that had been developing since the Second World War. Military equipment and American military advisers were a constant reminder of both the country's dependence on the United States for security and its deeply rooted sense of vulnerability to internal and external threat.

Saudi Arabia preferred what became known as 'over the horizon' US military support, as a deterrent against instability (Braun 1988; Long 1985). The Reagan administration insisted on the neutrality of the United States during the Iran–Iraq war, but found itself drawn into planning security strategies for the Gulf region. The United States declared that it would not get involved in military confrontations in the Gulf without the explicit invitation and assurance that landing rights and other facilities would be placed at its disposal (Braun 1988: 260). Saudi Arabia, however, remained reluctant when it came to granting military air-base facilities to the United States. This would have invited further criticism from Iran and other Muslim countries. The Saʿudis were opposed to foreign intervention in the Gulf unless absolutely necessary. However, US arms transfer had a high political cost even if Americans maintained a minimal visibility (MacDonald 1984: 109).

By 1990 Americans could no longer remain 'invisible' in Saudi Arabia. Iraq's invasion of Kuwait in August 1990 dramatically altered the situation, as Saudi Arabia could no longer conceal its dependence on the United States for security. It was obliged to invite American troops to defend its territory, a decision that shattered the myth of Saʿudi non-alignment, Islamic politics and self-reliance.

CHAPTER 6

The Gulf War and its aftermath, 1990–2000

Two major challenges faced the Saʿudi government in the 1990s. Saddam Husayn's invasion of Kuwait on 2 August 1990 proved to be problematic not only for the Kuwaitis but also for their Saʿudi neighbours.[1] The war was an unprecedented event in that, for the first time, Saudi Arabia felt that it was under imminent threat of invasion by a neighbouring Arab state (Al-Rasheed 1996b: 361). Although an 'annexation' of Saudi Arabia by the Iraqis was highly unlikely, the Saʿudi government and the United States could not rule out the possibility of military action near the important oil fields of the eastern province. The liberation of Kuwait became a priority for the Saʿudis not only to restore the exiled Kuwaiti ruling family to government but also to push the Iraqi army beyond its immediate borders. Saudi Arabia became the territory from which the liberation of Kuwait was to take place. This liberation was dependent on the assistance of American troops under the umbrella of a multinational force. This important development brought about King Fahd's second problem, the strengthening of Islamist opposition immediately after the Gulf War. The causes of the Islamist opposition predated the Gulf War, but the war itself was a catalyst that the opposition used to voice their general discontent with the government over important issues.

During the 1970s and 1980s Saudi Arabia spent from $14 to $24 billion a year on defence (Cordesman 1997: 105). This expenditure amounted to 36 per cent of the budget in 1988 and 20 per cent of the GDP throughout the 1980s. Military imports reached $52.4 billion between 1985 and 1992 (ibid.: 107). Saʿudi military force was estimated at 162,500, including the regular forces and the National Guard.[2] This, however, was no match for Saddam's army (ibid.: 98). Immediately after the occupation of Kuwait, it became clear that Saudi Arabia could not face the Iraqi forces alone, in spite of the country's massive military expenditure. Within days, King Fahd was advised to apply to the US for protection. Washington immediately dispatched air and additional naval forces to Saudi

4 US army tanks deployed in the Gulf War, 1990. © AFP/Popperfoto

Arabia and the Persian Gulf. Over 500,000 American troops arrived later.

The Gulf War created a crisis of legitimacy among the Saʿudi ruling group. Above all the war led to serious questioning of the right of a government to rule after having mismanaged the economy and overspent on an inefficient defence system. Saʿudi defence forces could not be trusted during the Gulf crisis as Saudi Arabia could not have stood up to Iraq in any circumstances.

One of the major decisions that the Saʿudi government had to make after the occupation of Kuwait was how to justify the 'invitation' of foreign troops to defend Saʿudi territory from a possible invasion by Saddam Husayn. On 9 August 1990 King Fahd denounced the Iraqi invasion and stated that the US military presence in Saudi Arabia was a necessary and a temporary measure. He also appealed to Arab countries for help (Abir 1993: 174). The invitation of foreign troops exposed the rationale behind military expenditure and Saudi Arabia's dependence on the United States. A small number of Egyptian, Syrian and Moroccan troops were called upon as part of the multinational force, which consisted mainly of US troops supplemented by smaller British, French and Italian forces. Saddam Husayn was given the deadline of 17 January 1991 to withdraw his troops from Kuwait. In the meantime the allied forces began to arrive in Saudi Arabia. While the international community was busy finalising the terms of economic sanctions to be imposed on Iraq and the American military build-up was proceeding very quickly in the Gulf, Saudi Arabia was to enter a period of intensive public debate. Autumn 1990 witnessed unprecedented discussions that in the past had been confined to private domains. The debate revolved around several issues, some directly related to the Gulf War, while others touched upon the very foundation of the Saʿudi political system and the legitimacy of the ruling group.

One of the most heated issues was the presence of American troops on Saʿudi soil and the dependence of Saudi Arabia on the United States for security. While Saʿudis were aware of their country's intimate relationship with the United States, not many had anticipated the arrival of such massive American military manpower. In the eyes of many Saʿudis, this amounted to a humiliation brought about by government mismanagement. While the majority accepted American military support as a necessary strategy, a substantial minority regarded it as a violation of Islamic principles. But Saʿudis had never thought of defending themselves against anything as large as the threat posed by Saddam.

The strongest criticism of the government over this issue originated from the rank and file of young religious scholars. Mosque preachers used their Friday sermons to criticise the government's decision to invite 'infidel' Americans to defend the land of Islam. The debate centred on several questions: is it legitimate for Saʿudis to resort to non-Muslims in order to fight fellow Muslims? Can a government that has to resort to such measures be viewed as a legitimate Islamic government?

In September 1990 Islamic scholar Dr Ṣafar al-Ḥawali, dean of the Islamic College at Umm al-Qura University in Mecca, released one of his most critical tapes. His reinterpretation of the political crisis concluded that the real enemy was not Iraq; it was the West. This was followed by the publication of pamphlets and booklets commenting on the Gulf crisis and relations between the USA and the Muslim world (Al-Rasheed 1997; Fandy 1999). Al-Ḥawali's views on the Gulf War were expressed in a letter to the highest religious authority, Shaykh ʿAbd al-ʿAziz ibn Baz (died 1999), head of the Council of Higher *ʿUlama* and the Institution of *Ifta*ʾ and Scholarly Research (al-Ḥawali 1991). In this letter al-Ḥawali asked Ibn Baz to respond to several questions. One of the questions related to the presence of foreign troops on Saʿudi territory. Al-Ḥawali interpreted this development as a manifestation of the increasing dependency of Saudi Arabia, both government and society, on the West. The Gulf War, in his opinion, confirmed this dependence and extended it in terms of the creation of stronger military ties with the USA. The Gulf War provided the opportunity for foreign domination and intervention. While it was obvious that al-Ḥawali was not a supporter of the Iraqi regime, he nevertheless questioned the legitimacy of resorting to 'an evil greater than Saddam, that is the USA', in order to liberate Kuwait.

Another Islamic scholar, Salman al-ʿAwdah, a faculty member at Imam Muhammad ibn Saʿud University in Riyadh, became prominent among a small circle of preachers and scholars who used the background of the Gulf War to publicise their discontent and sharpen their criticism of the Saʿudi government. Al-ʿAwdah's Friday sermons and lectures were taped and circulated in Saudi Arabia during the Gulf War, especially those that denounced the West and its intervention during the crisis. In his sermons, he envisaged an Islamic moral order where the rule of the *shariʿa* was supreme. Like al-Ḥawali, al-ʿAwdah objected to the use of non-Muslim troops to fight Saddam's army. He was critical of the government's incompetence that led, in his opinion, to greater reliance on the West. This reliance was detrimental to the unity of Muslims.

Both al-Ḥawali and al-ʿAwdah have been prominent in the debate in Saudi Arabia about Islam, modernity and the West. The Gulf War provided an opportunity for a wider coverage of their activities and ideas, thanks to the influx of 1,500 foreign reporters and journalists, whom the Saʿudi government tried unsuccessfully to contain (Wilson and Graham 1994: 63). The Gulf War only intensified what had already been fermenting in Saʿudi society, namely the increasing polarisation over issues related to the country's rapid modernisation and close relations with the West, and the incompatibility with Islam of this close relationship. Despite the rising Islamist discontent, the Gulf War created a climate of *infitaḥ* (openness) that encouraged some Saʿudis to voice aspirations towards greater freedoms and liberalisation.[3] The women's driving demonstration in Riyadh was a manifestation of the rising hopes of a section of Saʿudi society that saw the Gulf War as an opportunity to press the government for reform. On 6 November 1990, forty-five women belonging to the educated elite violated the ban on female driving when they drove their cars into the centre of Riyadh. They were noticed by the police and the *muṭawwaʿa* who ordered their arrest. They were taken to the nearest police station for interrogation, and were later released under guarantees from their male guardians. The women were suspended from their jobs (Doumato 1992; Fandy 1999). It is doubtful whether these women chose the right moment for such public defiance. They were perhaps under the illusion that with

5 Women shopping in downtown Jeddah. © AFP/Popperfoto

500,000 male and female American troops already in the country, together with hundreds of reporters and journalists, the government would respond favourably and lift the ban on women driving. They were wrong. They lost the battle over the right to drive, but they will no doubt feature strongly in historical imagination as the first initiators of female public defiance in Saudi Arabia.

The incident confirmed the fears of the Islamists, who thought that Saudi Arabia, its tradition and morality were now under greater threat than ever before. Criticism of the government in mosques and university lecture halls proceeded hand in hand with increasing vigilance on the part of the religious police. In an attempt to minimise contact between this force and foreign troops, the government transferred some members of the religious police from the eastern province, where most foreign troops were stationed, to Hijaz and other parts of the country. The most prominent among them issued letters to the King, minister of interior and governor of Riyadh, requesting harsh punishment to be inflicted on the women drivers. Some *muṭawwaʿa* did not hesitate to call them 'Communist whores' (Fandy 1999). The female driving incident did nothing to calm the Islamist tide. In fact, it confirmed their suspicions that Saudi Arabia was now heading towards serious changes that ignored their demands and aspirations. In their minds, this change would only be accelerated as a result of the presence of foreign troops and increasing dependency on the United States.

SAʿUDI RESPONSES TO THE GULF WAR

In December 1990 there was no sign that Saddam Husayn was about to withdraw Iraqi troops from Kuwait. It became more likely that the foreign troops that assembled in the eastern province were going to be deployed in a battle to liberate Kuwait.[4] It became more urgent for the Saʿudi government to establish the legitimacy of its decision to invite foreign troops to defend the country. In January 1991 Shaykh ʿAbd al-ʿAziz ibn Baz, the most eminent religious figure in the country, issued a *fatwa* authorising *jihad* against Saddam Husayn even if this required the assistance of non-believers. This *fatwa*, however, did little to silence the voices of dissent that had been clamouring since August 1990. The war against Saddam broke out as anticipated, a few hours after the deadline passed. Neither the swift victory of the allied forces nor the humiliating defeat of the Iraqis brought about an end to the internal political crisis in Saudi Arabia.

During the first months of 1991, the government was to enter the age of petitions, open letters addressing the King and asking for general reforms. The first letter, described as a 'secular petition' to distinguish it from a later petition, was signed by forty-three public figures, including former cabinet ministers, prominent businessmen, writers and university professors (Abu Ḥamad 1992: 59). The signatories proposed ten reforms. Their demands included 'the formation of a consultative council comprising the elite from among the qualified and knowledgeable opinion makers', 'the revival of municipal councils', 'modernising the judicial system', 'commitment to total equality among all citizens', 'greater freedom of media to preach good over evil', 'reform of the Committee for the Propagation of Virtue and the Prohibition of Vice', and 'greater participation of women in public life, within the scope of the *shariʿa*' (ibid.: 60).

These demands were presented after a lengthy preamble in which allegiance to the government and the royal family was declared. The petitioners did not form an organised group with a clear political agenda nor did they represent a 'secular' trend in Saʿudi society. Their demands reflected a general dissatisfaction with certain issues – for example, inequality before the law, the inadequacy of the judiciary and the limited role of women. Perhaps their denunciation of the excessive powers of the *muṭawwaʿa* in the petition inspired the label *ʿalmaniyyun* (secularists), to distinguish them from later trends. However, to call the signatories of this petition 'secularist' would be a misrepresentation. The fact that they were not religious scholars did not necessarily mean that they were secularists. It is ironical that in the early 1990s both Western reporters and Saʿudi Islamists used the label 'secularists' to describe people outside the Islamist circles who demanded reform. Among others, Ghazi al-Goṣaybi, the Saʿudi ambassador to Britain, was labelled a secularist by an Islamist, a label that provoked al-Goṣaybi to write a book defending himself (al-Goṣaybi 1991).

In May 1991, a different kind of letter, the so-called 'religious petition', was sent to King Fahd. It was signed by fifty-two Islamists including Ṣafar al-Ḥawali, ʿAiḍ al-Qarni, Naṣir al-ʿOmar and Salman al-ʿAwdah (AbuḤamad 1992: 61; Dekmejian 1994: 632; Abir 1993: 189). The signatories demanded several reforms within an Islamic framework. These reforms covered several areas: the role of the *ʿulama* and preachers, laws and regulations, the judicial system and the courts, public administration, the economy and finance, social institutions, the army, the information system and foreign policy. The proposed reforms implied that in those ten areas the government was not applying the *shariʿa*, and demanded the 'Islamisation' of politics in Saudi Arabia. Whereas the secular petition demanded the regulation of the role of the religious police, the Islamists' letter asked the government to lift restrictions on religious clerics, scholars and preachers. The Islamists' petition also demanded that the *ʿulama* play a greater role in all government agencies, including ministries and embassies.

The ten points raised in the May petition became the background to a lengthier petition under the title 'Memorandum of Advice' (*Mudhakarat al-naṣiḥa*), a pamphlet submitted to ʿAbd al-ʿAziz ibn Baz in September 1992 and signed by over a hundred Islamists. The memorandum reiterated the ten points raised in the Islamists' petition and expanded on several themes (Fandy 1999: 50–60). The memorandum raised the objection that mosque preachers were restricted to dealing with general moral issues and prevented from discussing politics and current affairs (*Mudhakarat al-naṣiḥa* n.d.: 11). This was obviously a response to the curbing of sermons by Ṣafar al-Ḥawali and Salman al-ʿAwdah that were critical of the Gulf War. Both had used the mosque and lecture halls to voice their objections to the invitation of foreign troops.

The memorandum demanded respect for human rights as defined by the *shariʿa*. An independent judiciary was seen as the mechanism for applying the *shariʿa* in a manner that did not undermine the rights of Muslims. The memorandum argued that only a Muslim judge should give authorisation to detain individuals and that all forms of torture, intelligence and detention should be forbidden (*Mudhakarat al-naṣiḥa* n.d.: 49).

According to the memorandum the Saʿudi media should promote Islamic principles and allow freedom of opinion to be expressed regarding current affairs and the behaviour of rulers, and ensure that public opinion was not corrupted by Western influences. It was critical of the manipulation of the media by Saʿudis who were described as distorting the image of Islam and its principles. The media was criticised for promoting the biographies and messages of 'actors and singers' whose artistic works diverted the youth of Saudi Arabia from fulfilling their religious duties and responsibilities (*Mudhakarat al-naṣiḥa* n.d.: 84–5). A ban on the display of unveiled women on television screens should be put in place to counter Western trends of corruption and immodesty.

It called for the establishment in Saudi Arabia of a strong Islamic army whose spirit should be kept alive by the call of *jihad*. According to the authors of the memorandum, the Gulf War exposed the general weakness of the armed forces. The government's overspending on defence failed to ensure the ability of Saudi Arabia to defend itself during times of crisis. When outside help was needed, the government should have relied on other Muslim armies (Fandy 1999: 58). The memorandum suggested increasing the size of the army and ensuring that all Saʿudis undergo military training.

The government, according to the memorandum, should promote an Islamic foreign policy and show greater commitment to Islamic concerns. It was critical of the government's reluctance to support the Algerian and Sudanese Islamists. The Westernisation of Saʿudi embassies, manifested in the increasing employment of women, was denounced as un-Islamic (*Mudhakarat al-naṣiḥa* n.d.: 92).

The memorandum included a chapter on the economy in which it was clear that its authors were critical of the increasing disparity in wealth that had become apparent in Saudi Arabia. It demanded that more money be spent on social welfare, education and health to replace the current spending on aid to regimes and governments that did not comply with Islamic teachings. Islamic banking should be applied where Western banking systems had become dominant. The document was critical of commissions and spending by government agencies where there were no means to establish accountability.

In short, the Memorandum of Advice called for substantial reforms of Saʿudi society, politics and government. The tone of the memorandum was highly critical of the government, which was held responsible for allowing the rule of the *shariʿa* to weaken in the country. The document called for a return to an Islamic moral order that formed the basis of government. It envisaged a greater role for the *ʿulama* in government. According to one source, the memorandum represented the Islamists' quest for power. They demanded structural changes that would result in a major loss of power for the royal family and the economic elite (Dekmejian 1994: 637). Islamists hoped that their request for an independent consultative council to determine both domestic and foreign policies would translate into greater involvement in political decisions on the part of religious scholars.

The Memorandum of Advice assumed greater importance as it was published outside Saudi Arabia, to the embarrassment of the government.[5] The government demanded an apology from the *ʿulama*. Ibn Baz denounced the publication of the memorandum, but not its content. He argued that advice to the ruler of the Muslim community was a duty that the *ʿulama* should respect and engage in, but this advice should not have been publicised. The publication of the memorandum could lead to *fitna* (dissent); its content should have been circulated only among those who deserve to engage in the act of *naṣiḥa* (advice).[6]

Rather than strengthening state–society relations, the Gulf War exposed the fragile foundation of this relationship. Saʿudi society responded to the external threat posed by Saddam's invasion of Kuwait not by renewing its allegiance to the government and the ruling group, but by launching a series of opposition opinions that undermined the legitimacy of the government at a time when this legitimacy was most needed. The war precipitated several reactions from Saʿudis whose anger was directed almost entirely at their own government and its ambiguous relationship with the West rather than at the invading Iraqi army. The internal political situation in Saudi Arabia became the focus of debate and criticism. During the war the government failed to rally the population behind its policies. When the battle for the liberation of Kuwait was over, the Saʿudi government had to deal with a deep rift that now began to separate it from its own constituency. The constituency itself seemed to be more polarised. New terminology of political dissent and labels such as 'secularists and Islamists' became part of the political vocabulary of most Saʿudis. Increasing demands for change pressurised the government to deliver a programme of reform in an attempt to contain the rising tide of criticism.

STATE RESPONSES: THE REFORMS OF MARCH 1992

Faced with public manifestations of discontent such as direct petitions to the King, public sermons criticising the government, tapes circulating rapidly among people in the country and petitions signed by hundreds of *ʿulama*, the state mobilised its machinery to deal with the new challenge. The first step taken by the King in an attempt to pacify and contain opposition voices was to announce in March 1992 three important reforms: the Basic Law of Government, the Law of the Consultative Council, and the Law of the Provinces.[7]

The Basic Law of Government contains several chapters each discussing an aspect of government (Aba-Namay 1993). After stating that Saudi Arabia is a sovereign Arab Islamic state, the Basic Law proceeds to specify the system of government as a monarchy. According to article five, rule passes to the sons of the founding king, ʿAbd al-ʿAziz ibn ʿAbd al-Raḥman Al Saʿud, and to his children's children. The most upright among them is to receive allegiance in accordance with the principles of the Holy Qurʾan and the tradition of the Prophet. The King chooses the Crown Prince and can relieve him of his duties by royal order. The Crown Prince takes over the powers of the King on the latter's death, until the oath of allegiance has been given. Article six states that citizens are to pay allegiance to the King in submission and obedience, in times of ease and difficulty, fortune and adversity. This is a clear response to the Gulf crisis and the opposition that followed. The focus on the Saʿudi royal family is interpreted here as a reinforcement of the right of the Al Saʿud to rule at a time when the voices of opposition had succeeded in creating an atmosphere in which this could no longer be taken for granted.

The Basic Law of Government invokes the role of the family as the kernel of Saʿudi society. It highlights that members of the family should be brought up according to the teachings of Islam. The state will endeavour to strengthen Islamic and Arab values and create the right conditions for the development of resources and capabilities. While the family is seen as crucial for the consolidation of national unity, the state is responsible for preventing disunity and dissent.

Economic and financial matters, relating to the prospect of imposing taxes whenever needed, are alluded to. One article states that taxes and fees are to be imposed on the basis of justice and only when the need for them arises. The Basic Law establishes that economic resources are the property of the state and that public money is sacrosanct. The state is responsible for the protection of private property, the public confiscation of which is prohibited.

On the rights and duties of the state, the Basic Law stresses the responsibility of government to protect Islam and preserve the holy places in the country. Human rights and their protection in accordance with the *shariʿa* are also the responsibility of the state. The state is to provide employment, education and health facilities, and develop the armed forces for defence. The law guarantees access to the King's court and to that of the Crown Prince for making a complaint or a plea against injustice.

The Basic Law specifies that the judiciary remain independent, but the appointment of the judges and the termination of their duties are carried out by royal decree, an important factor in maintaining state control over the religious establishment. The law states that there is no control over judges except when the judges themselves transgress the *shariʿa*. Citizens and residents of Saudi Arabia have the right to litigation on an equal basis.

One of the most important aspects of the Basic Law relates to the establishment of a consultative council. Article sixty-eight states that the statute will specify how it is formed, how it exercises its powers and how its members are selected. The King has the right to convene both the Consultative Council and the Council of Ministers (established in 1953) for joint meetings. The creation of a consultative council was a direct response to the demands that were expressed in the petitions mentioned earlier.

The Law of the Consultative Council announces the establishment of a sixty-member council (this was increased to ninety members in 1997) and a chairman, all appointed by the King who chooses scholars and men of knowledge and expertise. The duties of members are defined by royal decree. A member must be known to be a good and competent Saʿudi national over the age of thirty. The council is endowed with the power to interpret laws as well as to examine reports referred to it by state ministers and agencies. An issue to be considered by the council has to have the signatures of ten members, and proposals have to be approved by at least thirty members before being forwarded to the King for a decision.

Upon its formation, former Justice Minister Shaykh Muhammad ibn Ibrahim ibn Jubayr headed the council. The council's deputy speaker was ʿAbdullah ʿOmar Naṣif, former secretary general of the Mecca-based Muslim World League. Thirty-three of the sixty members appointed by the King held doctorates, only nine of whom were *shariʿa* specialists, eleven others held masters degrees in various subjects. The remaining members were diploma holders. The educational background of the council members reflected the desire of the government to strengthen its alliance with the professional elite. Technocrats and people with expertise in areas other than religious education were overrepresented in the first Saʿudi Consultative Council. Over 60 per cent of members were educated at Western universities (Dekmejian 1994; Al-Rasheed 1997;

Fandy 1999). The regional background of the council members mirrored the hegemony of the central province in government. Although council members were selected from among 'people of expertise and knowledge' in Najd, Hijaz, ʿAsir and Hasa, Najdis occupied almost 40 per cent of the seats. This perpetuates not only the Al Saʿud's hegemony but also that of their traditional supporters in this region.

In addition to the Basic Law of Government and the Law of the Consultative Council, a third reform, relating to the government of the provinces, was introduced. The Law of the Provinces was concerned with reforming local government. Before 1992, Saudi Arabia did not have a clear local administration. It was the amir of the province and his relation with the King that defined the relationship with central government. The new law defined the duties of the provincial governors and affirmed the role of the interior minister in supervising regional administration. The law divided the kingdom's fourteen provinces into governorates, which were in turn divided into districts and precincts. It also created provincial councils, comprising the governing prince, his deputy and other local representatives of government ministries, and at least ten well-qualified and experienced local citizens appointed by the King. The local amir/governor is charged with maintaining security and order, carrying out judicial rulings and guaranteeing the rights and liberties of individuals. The regional amir is also responsible for welfare and economic development. He should discuss the affairs of his region with the ministers. As for the regional councils, the law gives them the power to decide priorities on spending and development plans. The councils have the power to review, advise and propose reforms in the regions, and improve public utilities after defining needs.

The Law of the Provinces was meant to curb corruption at the regional level and establish tighter controls over financial matters. It is argued that this regional reform, with its accentuated semi-autonomy for the major urban areas, represents a vertical division of functions within the administration. The local council, composed of ten appointed locals and the appointed amir with a rank of minister, are accountable to the Ministry of the Interior, and thus will tend to be controlled by the authority that flows from the centre, that is from the King, the final point of authority (Aba Namay 1993).[8]

The government reforms went hand in hand with the augmentation of state control through the use of violence against suspected dissidents. The Ministry of the Interior and the intelligence services were mobilised to contain any activity considered a threat to state security. This included greater surveillance of public discussions, mosque preachers and sermons, and enforcing a prohibition on the circulation of opposition literature and tapes containing messages deemed hostile to the government or critical of the ruling group. Reports following the announcement of the reforms indicated that arrests and intimidation were used against suspected Islamists and those who were involved in issuing statements critical of the government.[9] Between 1992 and 1994, Saudi Arabia witnessed one of its fiercest campaigns against Islamic dissidents. During this period, al-Ḥawali and al-ʿAwdah were arrested after they called for a more vigorous application of the *shariʿa* and openly criticised the royal family. In 1994 the minister of the interior, Prince Nayef, admitted that 110 Saʿudi citizens had been arrested for 'actions that undermined national security' (*Middle East International*, 28 November 1994). Opposition sources gave an inflated figure of over a thousand arrests. Nayef's declaration showed the extent of the operation and how difficult it was for the government to deny the existence of dissent in the country. The government's previous policy of denial and silence became difficult to maintain in the post-Gulf War period.

In addition to direct violence against outspoken members of the Islamist opposition, the government mobilised its own media to discredit the opposition. Articles in praise of religious moderation appeared in the official press. In one publication, the religious affairs editor wrote that 'extremism means being situated at the farthest possible point from the centre. Figuratively it indicates a similar remoteness in religion and thought, as well as behaviour. Islam recommends moderation and balance in everything; in belief, conduct and legislation. Extremism is too disagreeable for ordinary human nature to endure or tolerate' (*Saudi Gazette*, 8 July 1994). While the author did not name groups of extremists, it was obvious that he was describing and criticising a general atmosphere in the country following the Gulf War. This kind of rhetoric became increasingly more apparent in official publications and speeches delivered by members of the government. While in government-controlled media there were usually no direct references to the demands of the opposition, vague messages condemning extremism and extremists, *ghulat*, tended to dominate the Saʿudi press. An explicit and direct response to these demands (such as for example those contained in the two petitions discussed earlier) would involve an implicit recognition of their existence and validity.

State-sponsored publications by Saʿudi and Arab intellectuals represented another arena in which the government tried to discredit the opposition. A booklet entitled *Explicit Reading of the Memorandum of Advice* (Raḍwan n.d.) appeared shortly after the Gulf War. Its author launched an attack on the Islamists' main petition, *Mudhakarat al-naṣiḥa*. *Explicit*

Reading established the Islamic credentials of the Saʿudi state by listing the Islamic projects sponsored by the government in the country and abroad. The author gave details of Saʿudi spending on Islamic aid, the establishment of Islamic charitable organisations abroad, and the funding of Islamic education. The author's aim was to discredit the allegations made in the original memorandum that the Saʿudi state did not support Muslim causes and that its political, legal, social, economic and military apparatuses were in need of substantial reforms. Such publications indicated that, after the war had been brought to a halt, a war of rhetoric began in a country not accustomed to such public exchanges relating to sensitive and almost taboo topics, including the nature and legitimacy of Saʿudi rule. The intensification of public debate was a real outcome of the Gulf War.

THE ISLAMIST OPPOSITION

The Gulf War brought back the memory of exiled opposition, with one important difference. While the exiled opposition of the 1960s and 1970s relied on ideologies produced in the Arab world,[10] the opposition of the 1990s was predominantly an indigenous response with a strong Islamic rhetoric. Three decades before, Saʿudi dissidents had found refuge in neighbouring Arab countries sympathetic to their demands and aspirations. It is ironical that this later Islamist opposition opted for exile in the West, the main target of their criticism. This is the story of the Committee for the Defence of Legitimate Rights in Saudi Arabia (CDLR).

The CDLR was initially established in Riyadh in May 1993. Six Saʿudis were involved in signing a letter that declared the foundation of the organisation (Al-Rasheed 1996a). The group included two university professors, a retired judge and religious scholars. In their foundation document they declared that their general intention was to lift injustice, and establish the rights of individuals according to the principles of the *shariʿa*. In this first letter, no criticism of the government or the ruling group was mentioned. Supported by Qurʾanic verses and several *aḥadith* (sayings of the Prophet), the signatories invited people to provide the committee with information on cases related to injustice. In a second communiqué (signed by five members of the committee as one early signatory withdrew his support allegedly under government pressure), the group stressed again that their programme was derived from the *shariʿa* and that their intention was not to form a political party, as had been mistakenly reported in the media. They refuted allegations that they were encouraging 'discord and chaos' and insisted that their intention to propagate virtue and prohibit vice is an Islamic duty (CDLR 1994: 19–26).

While only six Saʿudis put their names on the first document, the organisation relied on several activists, mainly professionals with Islamic orientation (Fandy 1999: 119). Two activists became the driving force after the committee ceased to operate in Saudi Arabia. Muhammad al-Masʿari (the son of ʿAbdullah al-Masʿari, a retired judge who had signed the committee's first letter) was appointed spokesman after he distinguished himself in his dealings with Western media (ibid. 121). The second personality was Saʿad al-Faqih, who played an important role in the early stages and later when the committee moved its headquarters to London in 1994. While the founders were religious scholars, these two activists were professionals. Al-Masʿari is a professor of physics and al-Faqih a medical doctor.

The CDLR was immediately banned in Saudi Arabia, reflecting the serious threat this movement represented in the eyes of the government. The highest religious authority, the Council of Higher *ʿUlama*, denounced the organisation as illegitimate in a country ruled according to the principles of Islam. Some of the committee's members, including its spokesman, Muhammad al-Masʿari, were imprisoned and later released. Al-Masʿari later appeared in London where in April 1994 he and al-Faqih established the CDLR's headquarters. With the establishment of the CDLR in London, a new phase in Islamist opposition began. The committee relied heavily on free access to Western and Arab media to launch its campaign. It established a web site and began to use telecommunication technology, including faxes and electronic mail, to communicate with its supporters in Saudi Arabia and abroad. Its messages and language became more critical of the government and the ruling group.

A reading of the committee's various publications, pamphlets, booklets, faxes and communiqués, all produced in London, points to a number of features. In the letter of introduction that announced the establishment of the CDLR in exile, the committee projected a dual image of its purpose and function. The first image anchored the organisation in the domain of humanitarian organisations; the second in Islam, understood to be the framework for all its actions and motivations. The committee emphasised that its understanding of 'legitimate human rights' stemmed from Islam rather than from other current formulations, believed to be illegitimate – a subtle reference to Western perceptions of the concept, although the CDLR statement did not directly specify these alternative perceptions.

The committee, however, refrained from spelling out these Islamic legitimate rights, the definition of which was believed to be the responsibility of 'people of knowledge', a reference to the *ʿulama*. In a subsequent communiqué, the committee reiterated that it was not *ḥizb siyasi*, a political party with political goals. This rhetoric located the organisation in a sphere removed from a secular understanding of political behaviour. Furthermore, the committee added that its highlighting of issues such as arrests, abuse of human rights and torture should not be understood as an infringement on the domain of the judiciary, the courts and the Council of Grievances. Such statements had defined a specific sphere of activity for the organisation, rooted in its understanding of what was permissible, possible and recommended by Islam. The committee was also careful not to antagonise the majority of Saʿudi *ʿulama* and did not want to be seen as an alternative source of authority.

While maintaining that it was an Islamic humanitarian organisation, CDLR members did make statements that can only be described as political. Several communiqués were devoted to criticising the King and members of the royal family. In an interview, spokesman al-Masʿari described the royal family as 'dinosaurs' who should die out. He declared that 'the government is the monarchy, the state, the family, and the mafia'. Similarly, the committee's director, al-Faqih, announced that 'leaders of an Islamic state should be elected and accountable', thus implying that the Al Saʿud did not fall in this category (Al-Rasheed 1996a: 19).

Throughout its campaign, the CDLR adopted the language of reform rather than revolution. In several communiqués, it called for the establishment of an independent judiciary, an economy in which wealth is equally distributed, a foreign policy more sensitive to Islamic concerns, and a strong army capable of defending the country in times of crisis. In the opinion of the committee, the Saʿudi *ʿulama* had become state apologists. This was a reference to the situation in which the religious establishment, mainly the Council of Higher *ʿUlama*, continued to issue religious decrees in support of government policies. The CDLR's reform programme did not deviate from that proposed in the Memorandum of Advice mentioned earlier.

The CDLR continued to insist that criticism and advice stem from an important Islamic principle, *naṣiḥa*, which is a duty of every Muslim. In the modern world, however, this advice could not be secretive. The situation in Saudi Arabia, in the committee's opinion, required criticism to become public through the establishment of the right to free assembly and free expression (al-Masʿari 1997a: 81). In an open letter to the Council of Higher *ʿUlama*, the committee demanded:

> We ask you to declare your truthful opinion on this government, especially its economic policy and its position *vis-à-vis* preachers and religious scholars. The Muslim community knows that its leaders are allied to the enemies of Islam, for example the Communists in Yemen. Our leaders imprison preachers, torture them and prevent them from saying the word of truth. Our leaders have mismanaged our economic resources and stolen our wealth. (CDLR 1994: 68)

The acquiescence of the *ʿulama* was criticised by al-Masʿari. He described their silence over important policy issues as amounting to their death. In his opinion, Saudi Arabia became the *ʿulama*'s cemetery (al-Masʿari 1995: 156). He encouraged them to break the silence and engage in the debate about the legitimacy of a government that reduced their intellectual vigour and confined them to controlling public morality and issuing approval statements that cost the government a few millions (ibid.: 157). He later distinguished between the truthful *ʿulama*, later known as *ʿulama al-ṣaḥwa*, the *ʿulama* of the awakening, and those *ʿulama* who 'sold their religion and faith'; the first paid a high price as they were imprisoned and tortured while the latter prospered in the comfortable role of approving government policy.

In addition to criticising the traditional *ʿulama*, the CDLR became a source of information on government corruption, abuse of human rights, and the torture and imprisonment of dissidents in the country. The committee followed the plight of important outspoken members of the *ʿulama*, especially the imprisonment of al-ʿAwdah and al-Ḥawali. It publicised their case by publishing and distributing leaflets that highlighted their messages and preaching. *Ḥuquq* (Rights) became a regular newsletter that informed those who received it about issues including the disappearance of dissidents, the mismanagement of pilgrimage affairs, economic hardship and the failure of public services. Within a year of its establishment in London, the CDLR became a commentator on the shortcomings of public affairs, the private lives of princes and their scandals and corruption. In this process the CDLR was assisted by the mastery of its founders over new communication technology. The CDLR, however, soon faced the challenge of dissent within its own ranks.

In March 1996 the CDLR faced a serious internal schism. Al-Masʿari announced in a communiqué that the committee had decided to terminate the role of al-Faqih, and offered several reasons. First, he alleged that al-Faqih had refused to publish some literature that was strongly critical of the ruling group. Second, he stated that al-Faqih had had contact with

Crown Prince ʿAbdullah without discussing in detail the nature of this contact. Al-Masʿari implied in a subtle way that al-Faqih had been co-opted by the government. Third, he alleged that al-Faqih, who had been in charge of managing the committee's finances, refused to pay solicitors' bills with respect to al-Masʿari's request for asylum in Britain.[11] These public accusations revealed a deepening rift between al-Faqih and al-Masʿari, not only over matters relating to finance, but also more important differences. The dispute was interpreted as a function of differences over principles. Al-Masʿari tried to build bridges with other pan-Islamist groups in London, for example, ʿOmar Bakri and the al-Muhajirun Organisation, while al-Faqih struggled to persuade his colleague to confine the committee's concerns to Saudi Arabia (Fandy 1999: 146).

This story is confirmed by al-Faqih, who claimed that the dispute with al-Masʿari was related to the fact that the latter was building bridges with the British branch of Hizb al-Taḥrir and ʿOmar Bakri, described by al-Faqih as 'an ignorant shaykh'. Al-Faqih also commented on the 'clash of personalities' between him and al-Masʿari who was described as a highly educated man with a flamboyant personality (interview, March 1999). He praised al-Masʿari's general knowledge and ability to communicate with the press during the early days in London when these qualities strengthened the image of the CDLR, but his 'flamboyance' became a liability for the organisation (ibid.).

When al-Faqih established the Movement for Islamic Reform in Arabia (MIRA) in 1996, it became clear from his communiqués that he did not envisage his organisation becoming a pan-Islamist opposition movement, a development which al-Masʿari had been trying to achieve since his exile in London. Al-Faqih may have sympathised with other Islamist groups in the British capital, but nothing in his newsletters and publications suggested that this was a policy eagerly pursued by MIRA. The split in the CDLR proved to be detrimental to the organisation, as it lost its credibility both in Saudi Arabia and abroad. Al-Masʿari's communiqués became irregular and in late 1996 disappeared altogether. The most active spokesman of CDLR turned his attention to writing lengthy pamphlets documenting the genesis of the Islamist opposition in Saudi Arabia since the Gulf War. After 1996 al-Faqih, now director of MIRA, continued to send weekly bulletins, under the title *Iṣlaḥ* (Reform). The content of *Iṣlaḥ* did not differ from the previous CDLR publication, *Ḥuquq*. The one-page newsletter of MIRA combined a commentary on current affairs in Saudi Arabia with the highlighting of cases of injustice and abuse of human rights. It offered regular interpretations of social, political and economic developments. In the late 1990s, MIRA seemed to be the most efficient Islamist organisation operating outside Saudi Arabia. Its web site, Arabic newsletter and special monthly publications (*Arabia Unveiled* and *Arabia in the Media*), in addition to several booklets written by al-Faqih, revealed a high level of planning and effort on the part of its director and his highly skilled computer assistants.

MIRA drew heavily on the content of the Memorandum of Advice and sought to promote the reforms endorsed in this important document. Al-Faqih perceived MIRA as a media outlet for the post-Gulf War Islamist opposition. He insisted that MIRA was not an independent organisation with a new vision. He continued to endorse and support reform within an Islamic framework that would guarantee a greater role for the *ʿulama* in Saudi Arabia. He saw himself as acting on behalf of the *ʿulama* who refused to support Saʿudi policies during the Gulf War, a decision that led to the imprisonment of several mosque preachers and religious scholars.

MIRA endorsed the cause of *al-ʿulama al-shabab*, a loosely organised group of young *ʿulama*. One of al-Faqih's pamphlets, *The Earthquake of Al Saʿud*, indicated his association with this group and his endorsement of their criticism during the Gulf War. This pamphlet offered an account of the Islamist opposition that confirmed his involvement in drafting the early *ʿulama* petition and the Memorandum of Advice and the formation of the CDLR in Saudi Arabia. According to al-Faqih the young *ʿulama* developed into an important source of inspiration as they delivered their sermons in religious universities and mosques. They continued to show deference to their mentors, the old *ʿulama* generation, although they differed in their interpretations and analysis. This fact allowed a degree of tolerance on behalf of the government that was later shattered with the open criticism of government policies during the Gulf War.

Like the CDLR, MIRA continued to launch a campaign against the Al Saʿud. In a booklet written by al-Faqih, *How the Al Saʿud Think: A Psychological Study*, the Saʿudi ruling family was portrayed as illegitimate (al-Faqih n.d.a). According to al-Faqih, their absolutism, arrogance and personal style of government created peculiar conditions that are counterproductive. Moreover, al-Faqih highlighted the Al Saʿud's inferiority complex in their relations with the West, and their total reliance on money to solve problems. In his words, 'the dollar has become the solution. It is used to dilute criticism, to bribe people inside the country and abroad: it is also used to silence criticism and cement alliances with foreign governments' (ibid.: 41–7).

Despite his criticism of the royal family, al-Faqih was hesitant about the future of the country without the Al Saʿud leadership. He said: 'I am not ready to say that we need to pull the tree [the Al Saʿud] out of the soil because at the moment there is no alternative in Saudi Arabia. Only the *ʿulama* can run government affairs during a transition period, otherwise we will return to the era of local warlords' (interview, March 1999). 'Warlords' refers here to tribal shaykhs, whom al-Faqih rejected as an alternative leadership.

It is difficult to assess whether this statement implies that by the late 1990s al-Faqih had reached the conclusion that the Al Saʿud could continue to rule under the authority of the *ʿulama* provided that the latter group included *al-ʿulama al-shabab*. He envisaged temporary chaos and civil war in a situation whereby the Al Saʿud cease to rule. He claimed that 'Saʿudis will not follow al-Masʿari or al-Faqih; they will follow the *ʿulama* who can restore peace and order' (ibid.). Al-Faqih did not project himself as someone with personal political ambitions; he perceived himself as a vehicle promoting and publicising Islamist reform on behalf of religious specialists and scholars.

Al-Faqih's articulation of an Islamic government brings to mind the Shiʿa concept of *wilayat al-faqih*, the rule of religious scholars, but the parallels have never been explicitly drawn by al-Faqih. According to MIRA's political programme document, the Consultative Council does not reflect the demands of the Islamists. The real *shura* (consultation) is established 'when members are chosen according to the consensus of the Muslim community and when such members are elected. One of the duties of the council should be to supervise public spending and enforce the accountability of rulers' (MIRA n.d.a). This vision of the Consultative Council provokes a reversal of current roles whereby the King appoints members, whose authority is limited. MIRA's political programme demands that the Consultative Council becomes a political authority higher than the King and members of the ruling group, who become accountable to the council. MIRA's demand that the *ʿulama* should play a more prominent role in determining Saʿudi internal and external political affairs invokes a renegotiation of the Saʿudi–Wahhabi pact of 1744. During the last hundred years of Saʿudi history, the pact was understood to imply a clear division of labour between the Al Saʿud and the *ʿulama*: the first dominated political decisions while the latter were in charge of religious affairs. MIRA's message undermined this understanding of the pact when it called for the *ʿulama* to participate directly in the political process and social affairs. The Islamists are no longer happy with the limited role of the *ʿulama* as guardians of public morality in the realm. This role followed the defeat of the *ikhwan* by Ibn Saʿud in the 1930s and was institutionalised by King Faysal in the 1970s. With education under the auspices of the state, the *ʿulama* have become more articulate and vocal in demanding greater involvement in politics.

In addition to the CDLR and MIRA, Saudi Arabia faced the challenge of a more global Islamist opposition, the group associated with Usama Bin Laden (born 1957), known as the Advice and Reform Committee (ARC). Bin Laden came from a Hadrami family that made its fortunes in the construction business in Saudi Arabia. Bin Laden's political career originated in Afghanistan where he supported the Afghan resistance movement in its struggle against the Soviet army. He used his personal wealth to sponsor Saʿudi and Arab volunteers who were willing to join the Afghan resistance. He set up several guesthouses and training camps inside Afghanistan where those volunteers were hosted, the most famous being al-Qaʿidah (the Base), established in 1988. These activities were initially acceptable to Saudi Arabia, but after the Gulf War they became threatening. Like other Islamists in Saudi Arabia, Bin Laden objected to the invitation of American troops, and made his criticism of the Saʿudi decision public. Saudi Arabia withdrew his citizenship in 1994. Since then he has intensified his criticism of Saudi Arabia and its close alliance with the United States. It is believed that the ARC has become an umbrella organisation for radical Islamist groups that include Saʿudis and others (Fandy 1999). According to a MIRA pamphlet, Bin Laden has two circles of followers. The first is a closed core of followers, who are related to him by a chain of command and take orders like a secret organisation. Most of these are probably in Afghanistan, but others are in Saudi Arabia and possibly in other Muslim countries. A second wider group consists of people who are not part of the secret organisation but are sympathisers. They would 'look at Bin Laden as [a] godfather and would regard themselves as obliged to perform some of his general orders' (MIRA n.d.e). It is difficult to assess the magnitude of an organisation such as the ARC. Bin Laden has been declared an international terrorist by the United States. On 11 September 2001, two hijacked aeroplanes hit the World Trade Center in New York and a third one crashed into the Pentagon in Washington. The United States immediately declared Bin Laden the prime suspect. In spite of vast numbers of subsequent media reports and information about Bin Laden and his network, it seems that hard evidence remains at this point very elusive. Described as the 'godfather of terror' (*The Independent*, 15 September 2001) and as 'the world's most wanted man' (*The Independent*, 16 September 2001), Bin Laden is believed to be in Afghanistan, under the protection of the Taliban regime. Saudi Arabia severed diplomatic relations with the Taliban in September 2001.

A decade after the Gulf War, it seems that the Islamist opposition both inside the country and abroad has succeeded in capturing the imagination of Saʿudis and outsiders, thanks to wide international media coverage. Since the mid-1990s the north London headquarters of MIRA, and the CDLR before it, have not only become a centre of Islamist activism, but also a source of information on a country not known for openness and transparency. Opposition spokesmen have acted both as activists and sources of information on internal political affairs. Western human rights organisations, journalists and academics have flooded to their offices in search of insights into Saʿudi politics and society. In addition to publicising their messages, the opposition has actively engaged in the dissemination of knowledge relating to Saudi Arabia, a fact that is often ignored in the literature on the development of Islamist activism in exile. This was an outcome of the opposition's presence in the West and, of supreme importance for their activities, their ability to manipulate new forms of communication technology.

The functional transformation of information technology from education and entertainment to embodying and facilitating political resistance has been remarkable in Saudi Arabia. A university student with access to computers may not only use them for his mathematical models, but can also receive messages and communicate with political groups in his spare time without even moving out of his university campus. This has given rise to a new brand of person, capable of expressing his political views against central power and away from state control. Access to these new technologies has a tendency to empower citizens. The question at this juncture is whether this empowerment is real or illusory. While it is too early to give a definite answer – Saudi Arabia allowed wide access to the Internet only in 1999 (Human Rights Watch 1999: 51) – young Saʿudis can and will develop a consciousness of their empowerment. Access to information and the ability to share and debate news are real outcomes of new communication technologies. New technologies have become efficient vents for political protest, but political change is not so self-evident (Al-Rasheed 1999a: 160). The major outcome of this new political protest so far has been the politicisation of citizens, long slowed down through oil prosperity, generous welfare benefits and state control. It is too early, however, to jump to conclusions and predict the political future of Saudi Arabia on the basis of the wide availability of fax machines, electronic mail, the Internet and satellite dishes.

It is equally difficult to assess whether the Islamist opposition will turn into a mass movement in the future. It is clear from the previous exposition that the opposition can be organised and can claim supporters among high-ranking religious scholars and lay professionals. It is also clear that the establishment of an opposition in exile had the financial support of people in Saudi Arabia, although it is difficult to discover the sources. The theological expertise of the young *ʿulama* combined with the organisational skills of a young generation of educated Saʿudis who sympathise with their opinions can potentially create a volatile situation in Saudi Arabia. Religious rhetoric continues to inspire a young generation whose economic security and prosperity remain uncertain as the government tries to recover from debts incurred during the economic crisis of the 1980s and the Gulf War.[12]

Neither state reforms nor the creation of the Consultative Council in the early 1990s were sufficient to silence the voices of Islamic dissent. Given the right moment, these voices can become loud again. The country has already experienced several terrorist attacks, for a long time rare in Saudi Arabia. In 1996 bombs exploded near the American military mission in Riyadh and in al-Khobar Towers, killing several Americans. Both terrorist attacks were linked to Bin Laden. In October 2000 a Saudi Arabian aeroplane, carrying ninety passengers from Jeddah to London, was hijacked by two Saʿudis, Faysal al-Bluwi and ʿAish al-Faridi, both members of the Hijazi Billi tribe, who sought asylum in Iraq (*al-Quds al-ʿArabi*, 24 October 2000). Most of their demands related to the improvement of social welfare services, schools and hospitals. It is not clear whether the hijackers were part of an Islamist group. In November 2000 a British citizen, mistaken for an American, was killed in a terrorist attack in Riyadh. This was linked to expatriate drug and alcohol circles operating in the kingdom (*al-Quds al-ʿArabi*, 9 May 2001). Social ills, coupled with possible succession disputes and economic uncertainty, can generate future discontent that might find expression in Islamist politics.

SUCCESSION

Although in 2000 the Islamist threat appears to have subsided, succession to the throne is still a matter of speculation. An internal power struggle within the royal family may reactivate Islamist discontent and threaten to destabilise Saudi Arabia.

An open dispute over succession following the death of ailing King Fahd could easily reactivate the Islamist opposition, now that it has gained important skills in dealing with the media, organising networks of support and launching campaigns against the government. Since 1998 it has often been revealed in the press that the Saʿudi royal family has delayed the assumption of full powers by Crown Prince ʿAbdullah (born 1923) in spite of the fact that King Fahd is no longer in control of government due to his deteriorating health (*al-Quds al-ʿArabi*, 9 June 1998). Perhaps the royal family is hesitant to declare ʿAbdullah king because there is no apparent consensus among themselves. Since the mid-1990s Crown Prince ʿAbdullah has represented the King in various government functions but has yet to be officially declared king. King Fahd still makes an appearance on Saʿudi television after holidays in Marbella and visits to other cities in Saudi Arabia. He is seen seated in his wheel-chair, receiving well-wishers at Riyadh airport. Members of the royal family, the *ʿulama* and army officers line up to kiss his hand, shoulder or nose, depending on their rank and status. On 23 September 2000, for example, during the celebration of the Saʿudi national day, King Fahd's return from a trip to Jeddah was televised.

While rumours abound that Fahd's full brothers (Sultan, Salman, ʿAbd al-Raḥman, Nayef, Turki and Aḥmad) are plotting to bypass ʿAbdullah for the succession, there seems to be no agreement over who should become king. The fact that there is no historical precedent of a Saʿudi king abdicating for 'health reasons' made the end of the twentieth century an era of speculation as far as royal politics is concerned. Fahd's brothers will not be restrained by the 'seniority principle', as this has never been fully respected in the past. What can be potentially restraining is the possibility of dissent among members of the royal family if they bypass ʿAbdullah altogether and choose a king from the so-called Sudayri seven (Henderson 1994; Kechichian 2001). What would complicate succession even more is the possibility that, given the age of the second generation (Fahd and his brothers), the royal family might choose a king from among the third generation (Ibn Saʿud's grandchildren). This scenario seems unlikely as there is no obvious candidate given the size of the third-generation royal group. While royal politics remains a top secret, foreign newspapers reported that a 'Royal Family Council' has been established to discuss 'family and succession matters'. As these discussions take place behind closed doors, Saʿudis wait for the king who would lead them in the twenty-first century. It remains to be seen whether they wait in silence.

CHAPTER 7

Narratives of the state, narratives of the people

> Heritage is not a hearth made of mud, its fire turned to ashes in a gas burner. Heritage is not a *dalla* (coffeepot) or *mat'ouba* (brass water container) or *es'hala* (milk container) or *mehmass* (roasting container) or a *zinbeel* (straw basket) with broken handles. Heritage is not a nabti poem or a Najdi dance. Heritage is not houses made of hay and mud or *okt* (cheese snacks) made of a racing camel's milk . . . *Turath* (heritage) is the people in their joy and sorrow, defeat and victory, in their dreams that take refuge in the future.
>
> (Fawziyya Abu-Khalid, translated in Arebi 1994: 57–8)

Although the Saʿudi state is now highly visible, thanks to the infrastructure it has created, its relations with its people and history remain contentious. For this reason, state-sponsored representations of the past, embedded in official historiography, political rhetoric and festivities create a historical memory that serves to enforce obedience to the ruling group. Oil wealth has not only enabled the state to promote economic modernisation but has also created historical narratives that encourage a new kind of legitimacy. While the state dominates the material infrastructure and resources of the country, it has become increasingly important to extend this domination to the symbolic realm of ideas and visions of the past, present and future.

The economic awakening/renaissance (*al-nahḍa*) itself is a major departure from previous patterns and development. Official historical narratives account for the political, economic and social transformation experienced in the last hundred years under the Saʿudi ruling group. More importantly, narratives about the past create a framework within which Saudi Arabia, people and government, are situated. State narratives eliminate contentious facts and competing interpretations, to the extent that they create a vision of the past with its own images, rhetoric and symbols. This chapter investigates how state control over ideas generates compliance and extends the domination of the ruling group. It also shows that state control over public imagination cannot be completely successful. Narratives of the state produce alternative visions and counter-discourses that remain rooted in the historical imagination of people in Saudi Arabia.

OFFICIAL HISTORIOGRAPHY

The historical narratives of the Saʿudi state perpetuate particular representations of the past that aim to bind rulers and ruled. These narratives are not concerned with historical accuracy or facts, but with establishing obedience to the rulers. Official narratives portray the ruling group as a hegemonic force in the history of the country. State historiography has become the medium through which this is achieved. History textbooks, produced under the auspices of the Ministry of Education, contain statements about the past that shape the imagination of young Saʿudis and create a consciousness of their national identity. An analysis of the content of such textbooks shows that this national identity oscillates between a general Islamic context and a local dimension.[1]

As the teaching of early Islamic history forms a considerable part of the curriculum, pupils are taught about the golden age of Islamic civilisation. The rise of Islam marks the beginning of historical time for Saʿudi pupils. The local dimension starts with the teaching of Saʿudi–Wahhabi history. The local history of the country is closely linked with the development of the eighteenth-century Wahhabi reform movement and its adoption by the Al Saʿud.

The 1993 editions of the official school history textbooks illustrate this.[2] Under the sponsorship of the Ministry of Education (Wizarat al-Maʿarif), an eminent Saʿudi scholar, ʿAbdullah al-ʿUthaymin, a history professor at King Saʿud University, wrote several volumes that constitute the bulk of the history curriculum. The content of the school textbooks is an abridged version of his ideas on modern Saʿudi history published in more detail elsewhere (al-ʿUthaymin 1995; 1997). Although school textbooks tend to be simplistic, they nevertheless reiterate a historical narrative that has become hegemonic in Saudi Arabia.[3]

History instruction prepares a pupil to understand the rise of Islam, the life of the Prophet (*sirat rasul allah*), the establishment of the early Muslim state, the life of the Muslim caliphs, the period of the Crusades and the Ottoman Empire. Islamic history is projected as a succession of episodes, each leading to the strengthening of Islam and Muslims and the flourishing of Islamic civilisation in all its artistic, intellectual, scientific and military manifestations. A sense of nostalgia for the glorious past permeates these representations of Islamic history. They concentrate on the 'ideal' Muslim community as it existed at the time of the Prophet.

The celebration of Islamic history is interspersed with a discussion of a number of factors that led to weakness. First, historical texts emphasise that the issue of succession to the caliphate plagued Islamic history. According to the texts, the problem of succession resulted in the proliferation of religious sectarianism. The historical narrative highlights the negative and divisive nature of sects, called *firaq munḥarifa*. This includes Saba'iyya, Khawarij, Baṭniyya, and Isma'iliyya. The text remains silent on the first division, over the succession of the first caliph, Abu Bakr, at the expense of the Prophet's cousin, ʿAli. This schism is important as it resulted in the development of Shiʿa Islam, but the texts tend to ignore it. The omission of the Shiʿa from history is significant. No mention is made of the establishment of Shiʿism as a sect or of Shiʿa religious beliefs and practices. While the texts remind pupils of minor sects which do not have many followers in the modern world, they overlook one that has substantial living followers in Saudi Arabia and elsewhere. Saʿudi pupils remain ignorant of the origins and beliefs of some of their compatriots and neighbours.

Second, the texts affirm the divisive nature of tribal solidarity (*ʿaṣabiyya qabaliyya*). In these narratives, there is an unequivocal rejection of tribal identity, supported by evidence from the Qur'an and *aḥadith*. The texts allege that tribalism leads to *taʿaṣub* (fanaticism) on the basis of blood ties. Kinship loyalty should be replaced by loyalty to faith. The consequences of this discourse are paramount given the fact that Saʿudi society has been organised along tribal lines, with kinship solidarity being one of the most cherished axes of social organisation. This discourse advocates a shift from tribal consciousness to Islamic consciousness.

In addition to rejecting sectarianism and tribalism, the texts denounce secular ideas such as Arab nationalism. While Arabic language and poetry are celebrated in the Arabic language programme, history textbooks reiterate the opinion of the most respected religious authority in the country, Shaykh ʿAbd al-ʿAziz ibn Baz,[4] who described Arab nationalism as 'an atheist *jahiliyya*, a movement of ignorance whose main purpose is to fight Islam and destroy its teachings and rules. Many Arabs adopted it; they are the enemies of Islam. This is celebrated and encouraged by atheists. It is a wrong movement and a falsification' (al-Shaʿfi and Hilmi 1993: 89). History textbooks highlight that Arab nationalism is 'European in origin, Jewish in motivation. It leads to conflict, division, and chauvinism. It contradicts the spirit of Islam' (ibid.). Nationalism is represented as a conspiracy promoted by the West and Zionism to undermine the unity of Muslims. The use of the rhetoric of atheism undermines the legitimacy of a number of neighbouring Arab states. The texts declare that nationalism is an illegitimate movement. These judgements shape public opinion and encourage an aversion towards 'atheist' others.

Other secular movements with similar dangerous consequences include communism. It is described as a movement leading to the enslavement of the individual by materialism and the abandonment of spiritual and moral qualities. Similarly *al-taghrib* (Westernisation) leads to the loss of Islamic ideals and practices. Politically, Westernisation encourages 'the introduction of Western political systems, political parties, and parliaments to the detriment of social cohesion and consensus. Westernisation promotes misery and suffering among Muslims' (al-Shaʿfi and Hilmi 1993: 93). Socially, Westernisation is depicted as undermining Muslim conduct. It leads to 'mixing between the sexes, [the] opening of night-clubs, disappearance of the veil, the promotion of interest in banking, and the celebration of non-Islamic holidays such as Christmas, Mother's Day, and Labour Day. It also leads to speaking European languages to the detriment of native tongues, and the enrolment of students in missionary schools' (ibid.).

The texts consider the negative aspect of *al-ʿammiyya*, the movement that calls for the replacement of classical Arabic with spoken dialect. It is described as 'an internal force aiming to destroy the intellectual and linguistic heritage of the Muslim *umma*. It undermines people's ability to understand and appreciate the messages of the Qurʾan and classical Arabic literature' (al-Shaʿfi and Hilmi 1993: 91).

Islamic history in Saʿudi schools is taught with a strong sense of mystification. This history is constructed as inevitable. It unfolds the story of a civilisation marked by achievement and success, only to be undermined by the acts and ideas of those who abandoned the true spirit of Islam. Sectarianism, tribalism, nationalism, communism and Westernisation are described as responsible for social disintegration. According to history textbooks, stagnation became the fate of the Muslim *umma* under the influence of such forces: people abandoned their faith in the pursuit of alien concepts. The texts allude to the urgency of bringing the *umma* to the right path.

It is at this juncture that the Wahhabi movement and the foundation of the first Saʿudi–Wahhabi state (1744–1818) are introduced. Wahhabism and the Saʿudi state become corrective mechanisms bringing the *umma* to the right path. It is also at this juncture that Saʿudi pupils move from general Islamic history to the localised past of their own country.

In their final year at school Saʿudi pupils are taught a comprehensive history which deals with the rise of the Wahhabi movement and the three Saʿudi states. The narrative ends with a celebration of the achievement of the present realm. The starting point for Wahhabi and Saʿudi history is 'the state of chaos that loomed large among the Muslims of the Arabian Peninsula in the eighteenth century' (al-ʿUthaymin 1993: 9).

On the geography of the Arabian Peninsula, the texts present four regions: Hijaz, the south-west, the east and Najd. They confirm that the population in those regions experienced a general state of moral, intellectual, religious and political decay. After a brief introduction to the local regional leaders, the texts describe the political conditions as characterised by competition, rivalry and disintegration. According to the official narrative, peaceful coexistence between various local groups was absent and remained a condition to be aspired to. The economy is described as diversified, including the practice of nomadism, agriculture and trade. Pilgrimage revenues are also mentioned. Economic prosperity, however, was undermined by political instability and the predominance of strife, rivalry and competition between greedy local rulers. This was also the fate of education, described as virtually absent in a savage society. With the exception of the major towns of Hijaz and central Arabia, where local religious specialists taught the principles of Islam, the majority of the inhabitants, according to the texts, remained ignorant.

The most emphasised attribute of the Arabian population was its immersion in *bidaʿ* (innovations) and *khurafat* (myths), both considered outside the realm of true Islam. The texts paint a picture of this population as beset by injustice and superstition. The discussion of the pre-Saʿudi– Wahhabi era leads to the conclusion that 'all regions which later became part of Saudi Arabia were in need of religious reform, *iṣlaḥ dini*, to abolish elements which were against Islam, and political reform, *iṣlaḥ siyasi*, to unite the country and the tribes for peace and stability' (al-ʿUthaymin 1993: 12).

According to the texts, the region that was the most disposed to promote reform was Najd, because of its geographical position away from Ottoman control. The rise of the Wahhabi movement in Najd was a 'natural event' in an area predestined to play a leading role. Najd is described as not only the geographical centre of the Arabian Peninsula but also as its religious and political heart. As such its significance is paramount not only in the past but also the present and the future.

Saʿudi historical narratives create memories of a population riven by warfare, instability and rivalry as a prelude to the paramount role of the Wahhabi call adopted by the Saʿudis in the eighteenth century. The narratives assert the leading role of the Najdi religio-political leadership in delivering the rest of Arabia from its previous state of 'chaos and ignorance'. Such narratives remain superficial when dealing with the pre-Saʿudi–Wahhabi period. They are preoccupied with negative descriptions of local politics and society. These negative images are contrasted with the stability brought about by the Wahhabi call and its adoption by the Saʿudi leadership. The Wahhabi movement becomes hegemonic as an ideology at the heart of establishing order and stability. It is projected as an inevitable response to an urgent and encompassing crisis. The religious and political supremacy of Najd over other regions is given considerable treatment in the narrative. It follows that other regions should appreciate their delivery from ignorance, thanks to the effort of the Al Saʿud political elite who adopted Wahhabism and promoted its message.

Having established the inevitable ascendancy of the Wahhabi movement, the texts introduce the first attempt at unification under the banner of the Saʿudis in the mid-eighteenth century. The pact between Muhammad ibn ʿAbd al-Wahhab and Muhammad ibn Saʿud in 1744 is described as a crucial moment in the history of Arabia. Underlying the pact is a division of labour: the Al Saʿud are described as the military and political arm of the religious reformer. Without their effort, the second Arabian *jahiliyya* (age of ignorance) would have been prolonged to the detriment of faith and social cohesion.

A substantial part of the historical narrative is dedicated to the formation of the present state. This is described under the theme of unification. The unification process is projected as reclaiming the historical right of the Al Saʿud to rule over territories that had belonged to their ancestors since the eighteenth century. It is important to note that 'unification' rather than 'conquest' is used to describe the military campaigns in Arabia after the capture of Riyadh by Ibn Saʿud in 1902. The historical narrative emphasises Ibn Saʿud's capture of the town, a story of heroism orchestrated by Ibn Saʿud and forty men.[5] A textbook describes the legend:

> Ibn Saʿud and his men entered the governor's house and found his wife, who told them that the governor was in Qaṣr al-Masmak with his garrison. They waited until the morning. When the governor emerged, he was attacked by Ibn Saʿud and his men. The governor of Riyadh was killed. The inhabitants of Riyadh rushed to greet their new Saʿudi ruler. This is how ʿAbd al-ʿAziz was successful in his first attempt to unify the country. (al-ʿUthaymin 1993: 72–3)

The official historical narrative fails to explore the resistance of the various tribal confederations and regions. Ibn Saʿud's battles against his enemies are listed in a factual manner without offering an interpretation of their consequences and significance. After a pupil is introduced to a series of successful battles, his attention is drawn to the achievements of the new realm. The texts project the emergence of the state as an indigenous process without locating it in a wide international context, for example the First World War and the role of Britain.

Chapter after chapter outlines the process of 'modernisation' in the areas of education, health, technology, welfare and communication. This is labelled *al-nahḍa*, the awakening under the auspices of Saʿudi kings.

A final chapter illustrates the role of the kingdom in the contemporary Arab world. Saudi Arabia is projected as a champion of Arab causes in general and supporter of regional Gulf interests.[6] Attention is also drawn to Saudi Arabia's role in the Islamic world. The text emphasises that Saudi Arabia was behind the founding of several international Muslim organisations as an indicator of its commitment to the concerns of Muslims.[7]

The historical narrative of the textbook anchors Saʿudis in a wide Islamic context. The emphasis is put on Saudi Arabia as part of an Islamic *umma*. A global Muslim identity is promoted as a wide framework within which individual Saʿudis should be placed. This is followed by a strong emphasis on the role of the Saʿudi ruling group in bringing unity to fragmented regions and populations. In such narratives, pupils are denied knowledge of their local past and traditions. The past is constructed in negative terms. Neither local tradition nor folk culture is celebrated. Saʿudis emerge from the classroom with a vision of the pre-Saʿudi–Wahhabi past as a dark episode marked by fragmentation and disunity. The text emphasises that salvation came with the Wahhabi reform movement and its adoption by the Saʿudi rulers. The latter are projected as saviours, who in the process of restoring their ancestors' rights over the territories of the Arabian Peninsula managed to deliver the rest of the population from its state of ignorance. In this historical narrative, loyalty to the ruling group is celebrated. As local regional history is ignored, one cannot expect the development of loyalty to land or people (ʿAṭṭar 1988: 158).

The school has become the arena in which cultural discontinuity is experienced. Local character and culture are submerged. Saʿudi students are not encouraged to identify with their compatriots. History textbooks encourage a break from local identity in the pursuit of a universal ideal, the Muslim *umma*. The text also excludes any identification with a wider Arab entity, given its negative portrayal of Arab nationalism.[8]

Historical memory is concerned with promoting the legitimacy of the ruling group at the expense of creating a national identity. History textbooks overlook the achievements of the people in all its manifestations. While the early Muslim period is celebrated as an ideal episode of the past, Saʿudi pupils are reminded of the degeneration in the pre-Saʿudi–Wahhabi era. The golden Islamic age is contrasted with the darkness of the second Arabian *jahiliyya*, the age of ignorance before the rise of the Wahhabi movement.

The negative description of the past is echoed in other historical studies of specific aspects of the Arabian population. Consider for example the evaluation of nomadism and tribalism by a contemporary Saʿudi historian who is also a granddaughter of Ibn Saʿud. In the context of a historical study of the *ikhwan* settlements, the author stresses that 'there was a need to channel bedouin energy which had so far been directed towards raids, theft and enmity into more legitimate goals' (ʿAbd al-ʿAziz 1993: 53). The sedentarisation of the nomadic population that followed the establishment of the *ikhwan* settlements early in the twentieth century is described as a function of the genius of Ibn Saʿud, who

> was the first ruler in the Arabian Peninsula to have realised that the bedouin cannot be educated and changed unless he settles. He cannot have discipline unless he inhabits a house. The mobile bedouin without a house can suddenly become the enemy of stable government. The king introduced *tawṭin*, sedentarisation, to replace tribal custom and tradition with the holy *shariʿa*. (ibid.: 49)

The breaking of tribal allegiance is portrayed as an act dictated by Islam. It is carried out with a justification that overlooks political and economic considerations. In fact it becomes part of a religious duty – to enforce the rule of the *shariʿa*. While state narratives condemn the social and political dimensions of *badu* life, the state continues to glorify the folkloric aspects associated with tribalism and pastoral nomadism. In the Janadiriyya, an annual festival organised under the auspices of the National Guard, the state invests heavily in celebrating *badu turath*, bedouin heritage. The King, senior princes and others perform the Najdi *ʿarḍa* (sword dance). It is broadcast on television to a wider audience. The Janadiriyya is an occasion for the recitation of Nabati poetry in praise of the ruling group and also a platform for displaying *badu* material culture including the tent, the camel, the coffee pot and the sword. Every year the state renews its 'allegiance' to the tribal heritage and shows its commitment to preserving it. Most Saʿudis remain sceptical. Saʿudi writer Fawziyya Abu-Khalid succinctly expressed this scepticism in her article 'A Heritage and a Heritage' (Arebi 1994: 57), quoted at the beginning of this chapter. In state representations of tribalism, only folklore is retained.

Just as tribalism is depicted as the antithesis of the Muslim moral order, regional identities are also dismissed in this historiography. There is a deliberate attempt to dilute the character of the various regions, with the exception of that of Najd. Saʿudi historiography emphasises the central role of Najd in the unification of the country. Not only was Najd the homeland of the Wahhabi reform movement, but also the traditional homeland of the Al Saʿud. In historical memory, Najd is projected as the region responsible for the delivery of salvation.

State narratives do not dwell on the period of King Saʿud (1953–64). This is not surprising given the power struggle that was associated with this turbulent episode of contemporary history. Pupils are denied this knowledge in the pursuit of a grand narrative that celebrates 'stability' and 'modernisation'. Moreover, state narratives treat oil as *niʿma*, a Godsent gift with the underlying assumption that it was a reward for efforts sanctioned by a divine authority and administered by a pious leadership. The oil concession of 1933 is treated as a function of Ibn Saʿud's political wisdom and foresight. Neither the lives of the early Saʿudi workers nor the involvement of an American oil company feature in this narrative. The 'Saʿudisation' of ARAMCO in the 1980s is depicted as a natural process following the training of Saʿudis and the availability of local expertise. While the process of this transfer is glossed as an evolutionary development, pupils remain ignorant of how and why it took place. The rhetoric of 'nationalisation' is avoided as it would invoke images of politicisation and struggle against a foreign company. The fact that the 'Saʿudisation' of ARAMCO was not completed until very recently would also become problematic. State narratives eliminate contentious facts that cast doubt on the political agenda of the ruling group.

POLITICAL SPEECH

Political speech tends to reiterate the themes embedded in historical studies, but also contradicts some aspects of this historiography. Consider the speech that King Fahd delivered after the Gulf War when he introduced a series of reforms.[9] The King opened his speech with the traditional Islamic formulae of greetings, and then proceeded to remind his audience of a 'historical reality', rooted, in his words, in 'historical facts'. The main focus was on how Saudi Arabia, as a society and as a political system, was born in modern times:

> In modern history, the first Saʿudi state was established on the basis of Islam more than two and a half centuries ago, when two pious reformists – Imam Muhammad ibn Saʿud and Shaykh Muhammad ibn ʿAbd al-Wahhab, may God

have mercy on their souls – agreed on that. This state was established on a clear programme of politics, rule, and sociology: this programme is Islam-belief and *shariʿa*. (Bulloch 1992: 30)

The King then proceeded with a general narrative that evoked shared historical memories of the way the kingdom was formed. The speech specified the main historical actors. It is assumed here that the incidents of official history were not selected at random from the great variety of events, but were chosen carefully so as to establish the official view of the political system. The King's version of history selected the pact between the Al Saʿud and the Wahhabi reformist movement as the turning point that marked the emergence of modern Saudi Arabia. The speech described the time preceding the 1744 Saʿudi–Wahhabi pact as one of fear and disunity, implying a general Hobbesian state of nature, characterised by moral and social disorder. The pact was then portrayed as delivering people from social, political, religious and moral degeneration, and leading to an era in which security, consensus, brotherhood and solidarity prevailed. The King then moved to the events of more recent history, the unification of Saudi Arabia by Ibn Saʿud: 'We remained faithful to Islam, belief and *shariʿa*, during the reign of King ʿAbd al-ʿAziz, who built and unified Saudi Arabia on the basis of this programme, although he faced difficult historical conditions. In spite of these difficulties, he insisted on applying the Islamic programme in government and society' (ibid.).

In this speech the King commented on *waṭan wa muwaṭinuun* (nation and citizens). While the rhetoric portrayed the two within a general Islamic and Arab framework, the main emphasis was on the specific and unique features of Saʿudi society and government. This specificity was projected as a function of Saudi Arabia's separate historical development, which gave the country its present character. While the country remained part of the Islamic and Arab *umma*, the King's discourse invoked the 'difference', 'separateness' and 'uniqueness' of the Saʿudi nation. He continuously reminded his audience of *waḍʿal-mamlaka al-mumayyaz*, the kingdom's unique position. This difference was projected as a product of the superiority of Saʿudi 'unique custom, tradition, society, culture and civilisation'. This discourse tried to achieve two goals: first to establish that Saudi Arabia was part of a larger entity, namely the Arab and Muslim world, which implied that it espoused their causes and shared their concerns. Once this was established, it prepared the audience to accept the second principle, of separate development within that larger entity. The implications centred on the issue of government. Cultural specificity seems to require separateness at the level of government and politics.

The role of the individual was given superficial attention in the speech. This was done in the context of the King's discourse on the country's modernisation and future development. He stated: 'The Saʿudi citizen is the basic pivot for the advancement and development of his homeland and we shall not spare any effort in doing all that will ensure his happiness and reassurance' (Bulloch 1992: 30). The role of the individual became important only towards the end of the speech, when the King made projections for the future. No mention of Saʿudi citizens was made earlier. In fact, the earlier parts of the speech focused solely on Islam and the role of the Al Saʿud. The responsibility for the future, however, was laid on the individual who then became the agent of 'progress and advancement' (Al-Rasheed 1996b: 370–1).

Both political speech and historiography highlighted the darkness of the pre-Saʿudi–Wahhabi era. Saʿudis were constantly reminded of a historical episode from which they were delivered thanks to two major historical actors, the Wahhabi reformer and the Al Saʿud. This interpretation of the past seemed to incorporate two claims. It satisfied the religious establishment, as Wahhabism was given credit for a message that transformed society and brought it back to the true path, and it highlighted the role of the Al Saʿud in the process of modernisation. Political speech, however, alluded to the Arab character of Saudi Arabia, an issue that was overshadowed in state history textbooks. We have seen how history textbooks described Arab nationalism as an 'atheist *jahiliyya*'. The oscillation between an Islamic identity and an Arab heritage remained a contradiction that has not yet been resolved. King Fahd delivered his speech at a time when an indigenous Islamist opposition was beginning to gather momentum after the Gulf War of 1991. Highlighting the Arab character of Saudi Arabia was perhaps a political weapon against the rising tide of Islamist discontent. While King Fahd could not undermine the role of the Wahhabi movement in consolidating the first Saʿudi state of 1744, his 'Arab' rhetoric was an attempt to carve a space in public imagination for alternative sources of identity. The marginalisation of the Islamic foundation of the state came to a climax with the centennial celebrations, discussed later in this chapter.

THE HISTORICAL NARRATIVE CHALLENGED

Recently, the neglect of regional history in the official historical narrative has encouraged the production of counter-narratives written by Saʿudi intellectuals from the regions (Al-Rasheed 1998). Their work celebrates local tradition and culture. Al-Ḥasan's two volumes on the history of the Shiʿa of Hasa mark the beginning of the process of writing history from a position of marginality. The official historical narrative is undermined by such writings. As official narratives deny the Saʿudi Shiʿa a position in the country's historical memory, represented by their omission from textbooks, al-Ḥasan reintroduces his community in historical time as active agents.[10] He declares that his objectives are to 'first, introduce the authentic history, culture, and identity of the Saʿudi Shiʿa community, which are omitted from the Saʿudi narrative as if they do not exist. Second, highlight the discrimination of the Shiʿa under Saʿudi rule' (al-Ḥasan 1993: vol. 1, 7).

Al-Ḥasan's work presents the origins of the Shiʿa community as dating back to the times of the Prophet Muhammad. He lists the major Shiʿa tribal groups in Hasa, Qatif and Hijaz, and acknowledges that Shiʿa tribal origins cannot be easily traced because the community had been settled in the oases and towns longer than the rest of the population. According to al-Ḥasan sedentarisation led to the weakening of tribal allegiance and the loss of the memory of genealogies. He dismisses the claim that because the Shiʿa dialect resembles Iraqi dialect, one should immediately conclude that the community originated in Iraq. Linguistic resemblance is interpreted as a function of the theological and religious links that the Saʿudi Shiʿa had maintained with the Shiʿa centres of religious learning in Iraq. He concludes that the Shiʿa are an indigenous group rooted in Saudi Arabia, a counter-claim to Saʿudi official discourse, which claims that the Shiʿa have their origins in Iraq and Iran.

Al-Ḥasan's work summarises Shiʿa history in the nineteenth century and highlights Saʿudi attempts to subjugate them. He celebrates the intellectual development of the community in the area of literature and Islamic knowledge.

Al-Ḥasan's history offers an interpretation of the incorporation of Hasa into the Saʿudi realm around 1913. While history textbooks, referred to earlier, describe the process as 'unification', al-Ḥasan labels it *iḥtilal*, occupation. He challenges the accuracy of Ibn Saʿud's claim that he was merely 'restoring his ancestor's historical rights over this territory'. Hasa was an Ottoman province in the sixteenth, nineteenth and twentieth centuries. Al-Ḥasan shows that in the nineteenth century Saʿudi rule in Hasa lasted for only thirty-one years and was disrupted by local revolts. He also dismisses the Saʿudi narrative, which argues that the local inhabitants of Hasa 'invited' the Saʿudis to rescue them from Turkish rule.[11]

Al-Ḥasan's work is an attempt to rewrite a regional history inspired by a political agenda. His themes are reiterated in other Shiʿa publications, including *al-Jazira al-ʿArabiyya*.[12] This magazine provided a forum for highlighting the theme of regional identity, not only of the Shiʿa but also of other groups such as the Hijazis. The magazine argues that regional identity has been undermined by *siyasat al-tanjid* (Najdisation), a reference to the supremacy assumed by Najd in both the official narrative and in politics. One author questions official representations of this supremacy in which this is described as delivering the rest of the Arabian Peninsula from political and moral degeneration. His interpretation deconstructs this hegemonic myth by emphasising that the present unity of the regions is based on two pillars: *ʿaṣabiyya najdiyya* (Najdi solidarity) and *ʿaṣabiyya madhhabiyya* (sectarian solidarity). The so-called unification process replaced the traditional economic and social interdependence of the various regions by total dependence on Najd and its ruling group. Najdis, according to the author, dominate at the expense of other regions. The rhetoric of the author centres on political inequality between Najd and other parts of Saudi Arabia (*al-Jazira al-ʿArabiyya* 1992: vol. 6, 12–18).

In an attempt to emphasise regional specificity a Hijazi anthropologist highlights the importance of regional dress, which has been a marker of Hijazi identity (Yamani 1997). But the consolidation of the state has been accompanied by a homogenisation of dress, to the detriment of local identity. It has become general practice for Saʿudi men to wear the long white shirt and head-cover, while all women wear black veils. The religious police enforce the dress code, as it is considered part of creating and enforcing an Islamic moral order that dictates the principle of modesty. This uniformity in the public sphere masks regional diversity, as expressed in a variety of clothing styles. According to Yamani:

> Some have argued that depriving the people of their ethnic dress identity amounts to a transformation to be compared to the changes dictated during the colonial era. In other words some people feel that such radical change underlines the political dominance of the ruling elite. At the time of the unification of the Kingdom in 1932, one way the ruling elite endeavoured to control the vast country was through eliminating ethnic differences. Thus the founder of the Saudi Arabian Kingdom, Abdul Aziz al-Saud, decreed that all men serving in government position must wear the Najdi Bedouin dress, the clothing seen widely in Saudi Arabia today. (Yamani 1997: 57–8)

The political and social domination of Najd, mentioned in the writings of the Saʿudi Shiʿa, is echoed here. The imposition of the Najdi dress style on all regions is interpreted as an aspect of the homogenisation imposed by the ruling group on Hijaz. Yamani assumes that historically there has been a distinct 'Hijazi ethnic identity', which has been manifested in local custom and tradition. While in public such an identity is denied expression, it remains confined to the private sphere and centred on marriage practices and cuisine during the month of Ramaḍan (Yamani 1997).

In a similar tone, an anthropological study of local socio-economic developments in ʿUnayzah, one of the major towns of Qasim, highlights the importance of trade and agriculture. The study challenges the dominant historical narrative about the warring tribes of the Arabian Peninsula by examining the presence of organised political and economic infrastructures. The focus of the study is not the 'tribes' but the urban settlement of a town and the processes of political and economic production.[13] One of the authors, who is from ʿUnayzah, states that 'the indigenous process of state formation in Najd predates the present Saudi Arabian state by several centuries . . . In addition to the well known roles played by ʿAbd al-ʿAziz and the Al Saʿud, this study calls attention to the roles of the merchants and urban groups from Najd in the process of state formation' (al-Torki and Cole 1989: 233–4).

This shift in focus undermines most of state rhetoric about the historical role of the Saʿudi state in bringing about, or even creating, peace and order. In their evaluation of the role of local amirs, the authors stress that they 'provided a number of functions such as defence, mediation, and adjudication that are usually associated with states. In this regard, the amirs acted not as tribal elders or shaykhs but as the heads of de facto political formations' (al-Torki and Cole 1989: 233). This is contrasted with official historical images of local leadership in the pre-Saʿudi–Wahhabi era, where local amirs are described as greedy manipulators who were constantly engaged in war against each other to maximise their own fortunes at the expense of stability. This study is partly a reaction to so-called 'Orientalist' negative stereotypes about the Arabian population where the image of the mighty bedouin is dominant. This image happens to be also dominant in the official historical narrative of the state: descriptions of the bedouins as ignorant savages are reproduced in official historiography without a serious evaluation of their validity. In ʿUnayzah, the authors claim, 'raids and warfare figure prominently in the local folklore, mainly in the form of poetry. Conflict and violence are the things that capture the popular imagination' (ibid.: 29). These negative images of the past have actually been integrated into official historiography.

This kind of intellectual activity, represented by reinterpretations of social and political life, may well mark the beginning of a process in which the official historical narrative is challenged. This literature undermines the official narrative by highlighting regional specificity, culture and tradition. In Hasa, Hijaz and Qasim the official narrative has produced counter-claims about authenticity that resist homogenisation. A Saʿudi national identity within the context of a universal Muslim *umma* may continue to be celebrated in official historiography and political speech, but alternative narratives are being produced to anchor Saʿudis in the context of lived experience. While these alternative narratives draw on Islam, they add an aspect often obscured in official representations, that is, the celebration of local tradition within the general Islamic framework. Unlike official historiography, these alternative narratives do not condemn the past nor do they highlight the alleged moral and social degeneration of previous generations. They try to highlight regional character based on a more plausible reading of the past.[14]

In addition to this scholarly work on Saʿudi society produced by highly qualified Saʿudi social scientists and historians, another kind of counter popular literature has been in circulation since the 1970s. This literature is produced by Saʿudi dissidents abroad and other Arab writers sponsored by governments opposed to Saʿudi policies – for example, Iran in the 1980s and Iraq and Libya in the 1990s. It was previously published in Lebanon and Egypt, but more recently most of it has been printed in the West, mainly in London. While by nature scholarly literature has a limited circulation, popular leaflets, regular magazines and booklets reach a wider circle of Saʿudis who are eager to purchase it during their regular holidays abroad. It is easily accessible and can be purchased at newsagents and even supermarkets in areas where there is a high concentration of Arab immigrant communities in London, Paris and other major European cities. Most of these publications are banned in Saudi Arabia, but Saʿudis find ways of taking them back to the country. It is difficult to estimate the circulation of a particular publication, but anecdotal evidence suggests that it is common for Saʿudis to acquire several copies of the same booklet and pass them on to friends at home. Arab shop assistants in some neighbourhoods in London are eager to publicise this literature and draw the attention of potential purchasers to the latest publications.

This literature does not represent serious evaluations of Saʿudi history or present development, but it responds to current political and economic affairs. It challenges the official versions of events and exposes the contradictions and inconsistencies of their interpretations by the state. For example, the murder of King Faysal in 1975 and the siege of the Mecca mosque in 1979 generated several commentaries and counter-interpretations. Among the titles that appeared at the time are *Faysal: Murderer and Murdered* (al-Shamrani 1988b), *The Earthquake of Juhayman in Mecca* (al-Qaḥṭani 1987) and *Revolution in Mecca* (Abu Dhar 1980). Some of these publications highlight incidents of corruption among the royal family, their scandals in the country and abroad, and undermine the credibility of important political figures (al-Shamrani 1988a). The appropriation of oil wealth for personal gain by members of the Al Saʿud and their functionaries constitutes a popular theme in counter-literature (ʿAbdullah 1990; al-Qaḥṭani 1988b). Speculation about internal rivalries and factionalism among members of the ruling group is also abundant (al-Qaḥṭani 1988a; al-Shaykh 1988). In the majority of cases authors use pseudonyms. Some of their publishing houses can be identified, whereas many others remain obscure or imaginary.

Such publications capitalise on an urgent desire among Saʿudis to seek alternative sources of interpretation of current affairs. The fact that this literature is forbidden in Saudi Arabia adds to its allure. Its wide availability abroad, its trashy stories, daring images and even cartoons add to its appeal. Writers who offer alternative visions, no matter how incoherent or unconvincing, tend to be popular in a society where censorship by the state has produced equally implausible slogans and rhetoric. This literature subverts official propaganda and resists its power to manipulate public imagination. The manipulation of this public imagination reached its climax with the 1999 centennial celebrations.

THE CENTENNIAL CELEBRATIONS: THE CAPTURE OF RIYADH REVISITED

Although the Kingdom of Saudi Arabia was founded in September 1932, the government surprised its citizens and outside observers by deciding to celebrate the centenary of the rule of the Al Saʿud on 22 January 1999 (in the year 1419 AH), when the kingdom was only sixty-seven years old. The confusion stemmed from the fact that the capture of Riyadh by Ibn Saʿud (in the Muslim calendar this took place on 5 Shawal 1319) was chosen to mark the beginning of the process of unification that culminated in the formation of the kingdom in 1932. In January 1999 the capture of Riyadh was a hundred years old. This event became the legend around which the government mobilised its resources to mark one hundred years of Saʿudi rule.

While the capture of Riyadh has always been dominant as a narrative in the historiography, it has never been celebrated as a national event. In 1950 jubilee celebrations of the capture of Riyadh were announced, but these were cancelled one week before they were due to commence.

6 Invitation to the centennial celebrations, 1999.

The deputy minister of foreign affairs at the time explained to the invited foreign embassies that cancellation was due to objections from the King's religious advisers, who declared that in Islam only *ʿid al-fiṭr*, marking the end of Ramaḍan, and *ʿid al-aḍḥa*, marking the pilgrimage season, could be celebrated. Other explanations related to the fact that the King was greatly distressed by the death of his sister and did not wish to indulge in festivities (al-Rashid 1985: 18).

While pressure from religious advisers resulted in the cancellation of the celebration in 1950, the same pressure failed to produce a similar result in 1999. Just before the festivities were to begin, it was reported that Shaykh ʿAbd al-ʿAziz ibn Baz had issued a *fatwa* in which he declared that the festivities were an 'imitation of non-believers'. Such celebrations were considered a kind of innovation in the Islamic tradition. One week before the celebrations, copies of the *fatwa* were stuck on walls and at the entrances to mosques in Riyadh. While the government proceeded with its plans, it was reported that coloured lights and elaborate decorations had vanished from shop windows (*al-Quds al-Arabi*, 4 January 1999).

The spirit of the centennial celebrations was conveyed in a poem that appeared not only in local publications sponsored by the Ministry of Information but also in international newspapers, for example the *Financial Times* (23 September 1998). The poem was meant to embody the thoughts and emotions of Ibn Saʿud as he was preparing for his legendary capture of 'his ancestors' capital' with his most loyal companions. The poem documents the slaughter of Ibn Rashid's governor, ʿAjlan, in Qaṣr al-Masmak, a mud-brick fortress turned now into a national museum in the old quarter of Riyadh. The poem begins with Ibn Saʿud lamenting his exile in Kuwait:

> Banished was I from the heart of Arabia,
> Riyadh, my home, had been stolen by others.
> Banished was I, and my father and mother,
> brothers and sisters, deprived of our birthright.
> Sadness we felt for the years that denied us
> the feel of the sand of the Najd in our hand.

After describing the kindness and hospitality encountered during the family's exile in Kuwait, Ibn Saʿud is believed to have asked

> 'Who will ride at my side on this perilous venture?'

The raiding party arrived at night in Riyadh and waited for ʿAjlan to appear after the early morning prayers:

> The fate of the amir of Riyadh was sealed.
> He must die for who will risk life and limb to expel ibn Rashid?
> Sixty answered my call, young and brave, one and all.
> With all our strength, we will give what you need
> We will stand by your side when the battle is joined
> until each of us falls – or Riyadh is freed.
>
> When ʿAjlan, the amir, appeared in the open,
> We struck as the lion descends on its prey.
> Ibn Juluwi forced open the gate of the fortress,
> the rest of our brothers then joined in the fray.
> The garrison knew that resistance was futile,
> Al Saʿud had returned to their home on that day.

The act of capturing Riyadh was completed, and Ibn Saʿud reflects on the event:

> Looking back through the decades, the taking of Riyadh
> was merely one step on a path, hard and long.
> After many a battle, I put my heart into
> building a nation, devout, proud and strong,
> with justice its sword and faith as its shield,
> in the land where the message of God was revealed.

With this focus on the capture of Riyadh, the centennial celebrations were obviously not meant to mobilise the country along broader national

7 Advertising Ibn Saʿud's biography on CD-ROM.

themes. The spectacle was designed to mark one hundred years of Al Saʿud's dynastic rule. More specifically, the celebrations were a glorification of the era of Ibn Saʿud. Above all, they were homage to the achievements of a single man rather than to the achievements of the 'people' or the 'nation', who are defined in general and vague Islamic terms. The people were projected as recipients of *niʿma*, and were expected to renew their allegiance to its sources.

The state mobilised vast resources to mark the event. Its control over the print, visual and electronic media enabled an unprecedented coverage of the celebrations, both in Saudi Arabia and abroad. Saʿudis followed the celebrations on local television broadcasts, while the rest of the world watched them on satellite television. The Ministry of Information published hundreds of leaflets, booklets and publicity literature documenting phases of *al-nahḍa* during the last hundred years. The slogan of the festivities was 'a hundred years of unification and construction'. Special glossy photographic books containing pictures taken of Ibn Saʿud during various phases of his life were distributed among Saʿudi and foreign guests. This was accompanied by the production of a historical synopsis of his life on CD-ROMs and videos. Saʿudi embassies distributed this vast literature abroad.

Saʿudi financial companies, banks, hospitals, universities, schools and various state institutions placed congratulatory statements to the royal family in Saʿudi newspapers. Saʿudi readers are familiar with advertisements of this kind, which often appear during the two Muslim festivals. The centennial advertisements addressed the King, the Crown Prince and other senior members of the royal family with words of 'gratitude for a hundred years of *amn*, peace, and *istiqrar*, stability'. Advertisements included poetic and Qurʾanic verses superimposed on portraits of Ibn Saʿud occupying the central part and surrounded by photographs of King Fahd, Crown Prince ʿAbdullah, and Interior Minister Prince Nayef. One advertisement included seven photographs of senior members of the royal family in addition to the central one of Ibn Saʿud, printed on the background of a map of the whole of the Arabian Peninsula *(al-Sharq al-Awṣat*, 25 January 1999: 6). Sometimes the background consisted of a photograph of Ibn Saʿud riding on a horse or camel. The centennial celebrations were an occasion for the renewal of allegiance to present members of the royal family, who capitalised on the heritage and memory of their father.

Newspapers were also full of heroic poetry in Nabati and classical style. Saʿudi poets celebrated the life of Ibn Saʿud and his conquests. The above quoted poem was one among several compositions. It was, however, unusual in the way it captured the spirit of the festivities: it was published not only in the Saʿudi press, but also in international newspapers with wide circulation and prestige. In the historical literature and in poetry, the language invokes images of chivalry, piety, military skills, heroism, generosity, bravery, justice, scholarship and other qualities attributed to the founder, *al-muʾassis*. The images of Ibn Saʿud as *asad al-jazira* (Lion of the Peninsula) and *ṣaqr al-jazira* (Falcon of the Peninsula) establish him in historical memory as an extraordinary figure to be remembered for his legendary qualities. Other qualities emerge from the usage of labels such as *imam* and king, thus anchoring royal power in an Islamic framework.

A special theatrical performance, *Malḥamat al-tawḥid* (the Epic of Unification), written by Badr ibn ʿAbd al-Moḥsin, a grandson of Ibn Saʿud, was performed on stage in Riyadh to mark the event. The epic's title draws on the double meaning of *tawḥid*, both the unification of the country and the oneness of God. It tells the story of a man and woman and their reflections on the political, social and economic situation in Riyadh prior to its capture by Ibn Saʿud. The epic culminates with the dramatic capture of Riyadh, bringing a new era of prosperity. Several popular Saʿudi singers took part in the event, together with over a thousand participants in minor roles. The performance was produced by a British producer and recorded on cassettes, videos and CD-ROMs.

The centennial celebrations sealed the development of an 'ancestor cult' around Ibn Saʿud, which so far has been embedded in state-sponsored historiography. While in other Arab countries, states have been preoccupied with consolidating personality cults around living presidents, in Saudi Arabia the cult venerates a dead ancestor. Ibn Saʿud has become a totem, a symbol around which national unity is expected to revolve. He is a symbolic figure invested with a whole range of meanings; his name invokes the beginning of historical time. The name is also associated with the present *al-nahḍa* and the transformation of the country.

The ancestor cult that has been developed around Ibn Saʿud is consolidated by the restoration of his artefacts, each capturing an aspect of his eminence. His first car, aeroplane, sword, Qur'an, royal seal, and other objects have been restored. These were displayed for the public to see and appreciate his grandeur. Artefacts known to have belonged to Ibn Saʿud have become icons, representing his many attributes. His Qur'an represents his piety and commitment to Islam, his sword stands for his bravery and vitality, his car and aeroplane symbolise his technological innovations. In this iconography, the pious Ibn Saʿud is also a moderniser; the man of the sword is also a scholar.

8 Publicity literature from the centennial celebrations, 1999.

The Pictorial Book of King ʿAbd al-ʿAziz, published by the Ministry of Information (1996c), captures all these attributes in pictures and portraits of the King. Individual portraits of the 'young warrior' are followed by those of the 'wise statesman' seated on elaborate chairs in his palaces and surrounded by his advisers and retainers. A special collection of portraits of the King with his sons, brothers and other members of the royal family conjure images of the benevolent father and family man (*al-Majala*, December 1999: 12–18). One photograph of Ibn Saʿud shows him participating in the famous tribal sword dance, *ʿarḍa*, in Riyadh among his 'sons and people'. Other photographs show him hosting lavish feasts for foreign guests. Early meetings with British officers and envoys are documented in pictures followed by later portraits of the King with world leaders, including Roosevelt, Churchill, King Faruq of Egypt and King ʿAbdullah of Jordan. Images of Ibn Saʿud in various local and international contexts encourage a sense of his immortality as a symbolic figure in the public imagination.

Ibn Saʿud's words were remembered and documented in several volumes. One publication lists his sayings as they were cited in foreign sources, thus casting an aura of international recognition of his wisdom. Here is a sample of Ibn Saʿud's words as listed in one of the publications of the Ministry of Information:

> I have conquered my Kingdom with my sword and by my own efforts; let my sons exert their own efforts after me. (Saudi Arabia 1998a: 68)
>
> Go into battle sure of victory from God. Have no doubt of his sustenance and support. (ibid.)

And his final words on his deathbed:

> Faysal, Saʿud is your brother.
> Saʿud, Faysal is your brother.
> There is no power and no strength save in God. (ibid.)

In a society where 'sayings' are usually attributed to the Prophet Muhammad in the Ḥadith tradition, the documentation of Ibn Saʿud's words bestows on him a sense of sacredness, celebrated at the time of the centennial festivities. His advice to his sons before his death is remembered for its underlying wisdom and insight; it is relevant to the present, when succession to the throne is subject to speculation given the deterioration of King's Fahd's health in the 1990s. Ibn Saʿud's words recall a unity expressed by the ageing father. As such it should be respected by the present generation, hence the highlighting of this special saying in published material.

Had it not been for possible objections from the religious authorities against representations of the human form, it would have been possible to erect a monument in one of Riyadh's central squares as homage to the founder. Instead, Qaṣr al-Masmak, the site where the murder of the governor of Riyadh took place in 1902, has become the 'historical site', the monument which has acquired a sacred significance. In a country where so far the only sacred shrine has been the holy mosque in Mecca, Qaṣr al-Masmak, a profane site associated with the act of murder, has been elevated to the status of sanctity. While most Saʿudis are familiar with the official story of the capture of Riyadh, it is now possible to visualise it. The door leading to the interior courtyard of the palace is marked with special reference in publicity literature: 'This door has witnessed the fighting between the ruler of Riyadh ʿAjlan and the late king ʿAbd al-ʿAziz when the main fight occurred at this gate. The spearhead of the lancer of king ʿAbd al-ʿAziz can still be seen pierced in the door' (Ministry of Education 1997).

Although ʿAjlan was in fact killed by Ibn Saʿud's cousin Ibn Juluwi, the founder's participation in the so-called battle of Riyadh is marked by the trace of his lancer's spearhead. The interpretation of the event centres on projecting it as a heroic act, against a background of fear and apprehension. While Ibn Saʿud remains invisible as a figure at Qaṣr al-Masmak gate, attention of visitors to the site is drawn to the trace of his spearhead. The mystification of Ibn Saʿud's legacy continues. He emerges as a venerated totem; his immortality is ensured by the constant references to his images, words, deeds and historical sites.

Qaṣr al-Masmak was one site among several buildings that form the King ʿAbd al-ʿAziz Historical Centre, a series of restored buildings in Riyadh inaugurated by King Fahd during the celebrations. The cost of the restoration was estimated at $166 million (Firman Fund: 1999: 5). The centre includes Ibn Saʿud's mosque, Murabaʿ palace, al-Darah, a public research library hosting among other things Ibn Saʿud's private book collection, and the King ʿAbd al-ʿAziz conference hall. These have become national monuments, a constant reminder that Ibn Saʿud's memory can be anchored in several shrines, each with its own sanctity.

In addition to paying homage to the central totemic figure, the centennial spectacle celebrated the life and achievements of his descendants. The ancestor cult of Ibn Saʿud includes other revered personalities. His descendants are recognised as important perpetuators of the founder's legacy. In printed material, photographs of previous kings accompanied that of their father, though smaller in size. Where images of previous kings were occasionally included, the main focus tended to be concentrated on King Fahd and the present most senior members of the royal family. Although no images of female relatives of Ibn Saʿud appeared in the centennial literature, his sister Nura was considered deserving of an article, published in a Saʿudi newspaper *(al-Sharq al-Awṣat*, 11 February 1999). In a society in which the feminine voice is silenced in the public sphere, it was surprising that the celebrations included a biography of this early female companion of Ibn Saʿud. The article highlighted her contribution and described her as a 'constant support and a source of inspiration for her brother' (ibid.).

Foreign and Arab testimonies enhance the credibility of the narrative. The totem is venerated not only by contemporary Saʿudi poets and scholars, but also by outside observers and commentators. The credibility of the ancestor cult is anchored in a wider international context. Citations from well-known foreign sources in praise of Ibn Saʿud are assembled and printed as slogans celebrating his achievement, wisdom and political genius. Citations from the works of Philby, Rihani, van der Meulen, Bell and de Gaury among others permeate the historical narrative as a testimony to his extraordinary life and efforts.

Contemporary Arab and foreign scholars were drawn into the celebrations as participants in the 'Conference of Saudi Arabia in 100 Years', organised as part of the celebrations. The opening statement of this unprecedented scholarly meeting described the event:

> The conference will inform the whole world of the most successful experiment in progress and civilisation. The secret behind it is the attachment of this nation and its leadership and people to Islam. The foundation was laid by kind ʿAbd al-ʿAziz, may God rest him in peace, and it was maintained by his grateful sons up to the reign of the Servant of the two Holy Mosques, King Fahd, may God protect him and bestow on him health. (Saudi Arabia 1999b: 8–9)

The conference had eight stated objectives, which fall within three broad themes: first, highlighting the importance of the Islamic foundation of the kingdom; second, highlighting aspects of *al-nahḍa* during the reign of Ibn Saʿud and his sons; and third, highlighting the role of the kingdom in the Gulf, Islamic, Arab and international contexts (ibid.: 16). These objectives are not new; they are a reiteration of the main focus of official historical narratives. They are a restatement of the well-rehearsed rhetoric in official historiography. Saʿudi and foreign academics were mobilised. Participants presented 200 papers in more than sixty panels over a period of three days. The scholarly spectacle was interspersed with visits to the national museum, poetry recitals, lavish feasts and the display of national heritage.

The conference was organised along the lines of major international academic meetings, but the content was different. In the Saʿudi version of a centennial conference, a monolithic historical narrative was on display. This was an occasion for establishing a historical truth rather than one for debate or reinterpretation. Both Saʿudi citizens and foreign guests were participants in the consolidation of the ancestor's cult, in which the official historical narrative is internalised and reproduced in a consistent manner. The state defines the parameters of speech, images and symbols, which are in turn converted into the language of academic and scientific research. The process conveys an 'objective' dimension on state propaganda. Official rhetoric is then endowed with a power of its own.

The ancestor cult of Ibn Saʿud is dominant in Saudi Arabia. It is founded on the belief in an epical ancestor whose name is generalised to the whole population. The state shares with the people a preoccupation with genealogy. Without a genealogy, the state would be outside the comprehension of its citizens who, in spite of decades of *nahḍa* and official rhetoric in favour of a universal Muslim *umma*, still cherish descent. The official narrative is contradictory in the way it condemns people's identifications with genealogies while it fixes its own as a historical truth in social memory. It demands from its citizens a kind of historical amnesia *vis-à-vis* their own genealogies, while subjecting them to a celebration of its own line of descent, a journey which always begins with Ibn Saʿud, the founder. The centennial celebrations can be read as a text whose main objective was to delineate the genealogy of the state at a time when this seemed to be doubtful and could even be subjected to competing interpretations. As the majority of Saʿudis have access to sources of information beyond state control, it has become imperative for the state to formulate its own narrative about its origins and invite Saʿudis themselves to participate in its construction and maintenance. Their participation as poets, academics and artists is a testimony to the fact that the official text has been successfully internalised by some (but not all) Saʿudis to the extent that it can be reproduced without variation or betrayal. The internalisation of the rhetoric of the state by some Saʿudi citizens after decades of being subjected to it indicates that in a society where language has always been power, a contentious vocabulary and set of utterances has become hegemonic.

The ancestor cult of Ibn Saʿud is central for the consolidation of national unity. It is the symbol for mobilising a society divided by regional diversity and tribal allegiances. The ancestor cult plays a role similar to that played by the rhetoric of Islam. It is meant to mask localised identities and alternative sources of loyalty. Official narratives capitalise on the transformation of society under the auspices of Ibn Saʿud. The narratives invite people to abandon their own ancestors in favour of an omnipotent symbolic ancestor, who has been projected as 'the ancestor' of the nation.

The centennial celebrations not only marked a hundred years of Saʿudi modern history, but also initiated Saʿudis into the ancestor cult. They unfolded the story of a mystified past, the pre-Ibn Saʿud era where chaos and instability reigned among a fragmented and backward population. Separation from that dark past followed the capture of Riyadh in 1902. Between 1902 and 1932, a period of liminality and apprehension was juxtaposed on Ibn Saʿud's various battles of unification. This rite of passage was depicted as a journey from 'darkness', 'poverty', 'moral, social and political decay' to 'affluence', 'prosperity', 'peace' and 'civilisation'. The contrasted images were documented in words, pictures and sounds. Crucial for this rite is the role of the ancestor, who was prematurely venerated and revered in 1999 even before his realm reached its hundredth anniversary. In a society that is not known for elaborate rituals and festivities, the centennial spectacle was outstanding.[15] Given Wahhabi condemnation of saint worship and ancestor cults common in other parts of the Arab and Islamic world, the staging of the spectacle represented the triumph of the Saʿudi royal family over its *ʿulama* and their doctrine. The celebrations confirmed the state as master of the symbolic world and historical interpretation.

THE CENTENNIAL CELEBRATIONS CHALLENGED

Like the official historical narratives, the centennial celebrations generated alternative discourses that undermine their hegemonic images, slogans and rhetoric. Above all, this alternative discourse questions the eminence of Ibn Saʿud and members of the royal family. It casts doubt on their leading role in the historical process. While alternative narratives could not be manifested in public, they have been expressed in private domains and abroad. State control prevents any public debate on the validity of the celebrations and their timing and content. But it cannot silence people in the privacy of their homes.

Reactions to the centennial celebrations ranged from apathy to expressions of disgust. Some Saʿudis refused to become participants in the festivities, and did not place congratulatory statements or poetic praise of the capture of Riyadh in local newspapers. Others preferred to see them as mere ceremonial, corresponding to what is described as 'snow, an insubstantial pageant, soon melted into thin air' (Cannadine and Price 1987: 1).

In Islamist circles, objections to the celebrations were centred on the view that such festivities represent a form of *bidaʿ*, thus reiterating the *fatwa* against them mentioned earlier. An opinion was expressed that the capture of Riyadh was a minor incident in the unification process. As such it did not deserve an ostentatious spectacle. Instead, the state should have celebrated 250 years of reformist Islam, which had a greater impact on the modern history of Saudi Arabia. Some Islamists expressed doubt as to whether the unification would have been at all possible without the message of Muhammad ibn ʿAbd al-Wahhab. In their views, the centennial celebration shifted the focus to a later incident in modern history, whose significance remains minor compared with the impetus of Wahhabism.

The Movement for Islamic Reform in Arabia (MIRA) criticised the glorification of Ibn Saʿud that accompanied the celebrations. In one publication, Ibn Saʿud is described as having become *maʿṣum* (infallible), evoking images of the infallible *imam* in the Shiʿa tradition. Objections were voiced as to how the ancestor cult turned him into a 'sacred figure': 'ʿAbd al-ʿAziz is scholar, generous, brave, pious, clever, warrior, honest, forgiving, and just. These are qualities often associated with prophets. Some Saʿudis see him as a king among other kings whereas others consider him a criminal and a traitor made by the British' (MIRA n.d.: Communiqué 147).

While such criticism is impossible in Saudi Arabia, it finds expression electronically and through the medium of the facsimile machine. The messages of the Islamist opposition have been transmitted from abroad. They touch upon sentiments that remain dormant under censorship. While Islamists may refer to the celebrations as *bidaʿ*, the heart of the matter lies in the fact that celebrating the last hundred years is bound to marginalise an important date in Islamists' historical imagination: the rise of the Wahhabi reform movement of 1744. Islamists consider this as the historical date suitable for national celebrations. The debate about whether such celebrations constitute an un-Islamic *bidʿa* masks a deeper cleavage in Saʿudi society and a struggle between the state and people over historical consciousness. State narratives are no longer dominant, as they are challenged by people who are products of state modernisation. Islamists are now capable of producing their own historical narratives, thanks to formal education and training in state universities and abroad. They also produce their own poetry (CDLR 1995) and video tapes to counter state-sponsored artistic work.

While Islamist criticism remained grounded in religious principles, others criticised the celebration on the basis of their 'vulgarity' and ostentatious display of empty slogans during times of economic hardship. The fall in oil prices throughout the 1990s and successive budget deficits could not have produced a worse moment for extra spending, according to some Saʿudi bankers and merchants. These views were expressed privately: they were exchanged among a close circle of intimate and trusted friends. Several Saʿudis have pointed out the contradiction involved in the display of portraits of senior princes after decades of banning statues, images, and even paintings of human figures, by the government.

People exchanged jokes to undermine the slogans of the celebrations. One popular joke of the time states that the Saʿudi government changed the number of the companions of Ibn Saʿud who helped him capture Riyadh from forty to sixty men: this was done in order to avoid Ibn Saʿud being described as 'Abu ʿAli and the forty thieves', a story well known in both Arabic and Western popular culture. This humour exposes the ability of the state to alter history for its own purposes. Many Saʿudis are aware of the manipulation of historical facts by the state. With the exception of those who participated in the celebrations in various capacities, the majority of Saʿudis remained spectators. Their constant search for alternative sources of information about their past and different interpretations of their current affairs is a testimony to the fact that state control over the imagination is neither complete nor successful. So far this control has generated compliance, accompanied by minor resistance of the kind discussed above. The voices of dissent remain scattered and lacking in any form of organisation. While this is the case, the state strives to dominate the public imagination and draw Saʿudis into its construction according to well-defined rhetoric, images and symbols.

CHAPTER 8

The challenges of a new era

The festivities of the centennial celebrations marked a century of unity, prosperity and modernisation, according to official narratives; but they also concealed a fermenting internal crisis that erupted as the third Saʿudi state entered the second millennium. The twenty-first century started with three major challenges: first, a fragmented state, headed by an ailing King; second, a strained economy, under the pressure of low oil prices, unemployment and national debt; and third, terrorism.

Added to the internal challenges was the troubled relationship with the USA that followed 9/11, and tense relations with other regional players – mainly Qatar, Iran and Syria. Saudi Arabia found itself criticised by the US administration and media, while Qatar, a neighbouring Gulf country, used its newly founded al-Jazeera television channel to put pressure on Saudi Arabia in order to gain some economic concessions relating to territorial disputes, and its oil and gas expansion. Saʿudi relations with Syria and Iran deteriorated following the assassination of pro-Saʿudi Lebanese prime minister Rafiq al-Hariri, the occupation of Iraq in 2003 and the Israeli invasion of Lebanon in 2006.

Some of Saudi Arabia's internal challenges subsided after the oil boom of 2003. By 2008 royal politics had stabilised, the stagnating economy was energised and the threat of terrorism had been contained. The relationship with the USA had improved by the time Crown Prince ʿAbdullah became King in August 2005. Common strategic interests with the USA allowed the Saʿudi leadership to re-emerge triumphant. A reconciliation with Qatar in 2008 silenced al-Jazeera's criticism of Saudi Arabia, but relations with Syria and Iran remained tense. This chapter traces the challenges that Saudi Arabia faced, both internal and external.

INTERNAL CHALLENGES

The fragmentation of the state

In 2000 the ailing King Fahd (1982–2005), who had suffered a stroke in the mid-1990s, was still on the throne, but his half-brother, Crown Prince ʿAbdullah, was acting King, a position he held for almost a decade (1996–2005). Although it was clear that King Fahd could not function given his deteriorating health, he occasionally appeared to preside over the Council of Ministers and greet foreign visitors. The King delegated many responsibilities to his sons, especially the young and inexperienced ʿAbd al-ʿAziz. King Fahd's powerful full brothers – Prince Sultan, minister of defence; Nayef, minister of the interior; Salman, governor of Riyadh (three of the so-called Sudayri Seven); and half-brother ʿAbdullah, Crown Prince and commander of the Saʿudi National Guard – maintained the semblance of unity. Foreign minister Prince Saʿud al-Faysal seemed to lose monopoly over foreign policy to his cousin, the powerful Saʿudi ambassador to the USA, Prince Bandar ibn Sultan, the architect of Saʿudi–US relations for two decades.

During Fahd's prolonged illness, his brothers consolidated their power and control over important government ministries and emerged as independent power holders to be reckoned with. At this juncture the Saʿudi state began to appear as if it consisted of multiple actors, each carving out for himself a space and a network of followers in the absence of a strong central leadership. During the decade of Fahd's illness, multiple clans within the Al Saʿud family ruled Saudi Arabia. Each son of the founder, Ibn Saʿud, and their sons usually headed a clan, whose power was contained in a ministry or important government position. The centralised state whose foundation had been laid down by King Faysal in the 1970s (see chapter 4) gave way to fragmentation as each powerful Saʿudi prince began to carve out resources and influence, encouraged by the lack of a strong central head of state. While he was acting King, Crown Prince ʿAbdullah, in effect merely one political actor among many, struggled both to establish his credentials among the competing princes and to introduce new policies. He could do little more than await formal confirmation of his role upon the death of King Fahd.

Observers of Saʿudi politics speculated on whether ʿAbdullah would be sidelined by his half-brothers when King Fahd died. Although later developments proved such speculations inaccurate, they resulted from the increased influence of a group of princes who had amassed wealth and power during the reign of King Fahd. Observers pointed to the growing influence of a royal bloc, consisting of the so-called Sudayri Seven, at the expense of other princes in the royal household (Scott Doran 2004). However, in the twenty-first century it is more accurate to describe Saʿudi royal politics as consisting of circles of power, whereby each of the powerful key princes presides over a network of influence and government offices, rather than forming definite blocs. These circles of power preferred to keep King Fahd in office as long as possible, without any faction being able to impose its will and replace the leadership with a younger and more energetic king. They preferred to rule Saudi Arabia as a headless tribe, whose strength lies in its segments rather than in strong leadership. The segments corresponded to the strong clans that developed within the royal household (Al-Rasheed 2005).

The emergence of royal circles of power ended the highly centralised state that King Faysal established and consolidated in the late 1960s and early 1970s. King Fahd continued the tradition of the one-man state, but allowed his full brothers to consolidate their mini-fiefdoms within that state. By the 1990s his brothers had grown older, more powerful and wealthier. Their children, now more educated and ruthless in pursuing their own careers within the state, appeared on the scene. Having presided over important key ministries such as Defence and the Interior, as well as the intelligence services and paramilitary institutions, senior princes developed their own states within the state, while junior ones operated in their fathers' shadows. It was obvious that King Fahd could not rule without taking into account the individual interests of the new emerging power holders, each now embedded in the state institutionally, administratively and financially. While keeping his half-brother Prince ʿAbdullah as Crown Prince and commander of the National Guard for several decades, and his full brothers as heads of Ministries of Defence and the Interior, he made sure that his own sons and his other brothers developed powerful centres of patronage, wealth, influence and military might.

During King Fahd's reign, members of the ruling house thus remained contained, gradually building their own resources and circles of influence but without posing any threat to the absolute monarch. When King Fahd suffered a stroke, all princes had a vested interest in keeping his image and role intact. None was strong or daring enough to call for the abdication of an ailing King or to challenge the de facto circles of power within the state. Saʿudi internal politics stagnated, its resources dwindled, the population began to be agitated, and violence erupted in many cities. During this period politics consisted of doing nothing; the main objective was to keep King Fahd alive as long as possible (ibid.: 211).

Crown Prince ʿAbdullah became one player in a circle of powerful princes. Despite his early promises to curb royal extravagance and tighten royal belts following Fahd's overspending, an oil crisis loomed and an overwhelming national debt accumulated as a result of the Iran–Iraq war of the 1980s and the liberation of Kuwait in 1991. ʿAbdullah proved incapable of controlling the proliferation of princely powers across state institutions. The circle consisted of the minister of defence, Prince Sultan; the minister of the interior, Prince Nayef; the governor of Riyadh, Prince Salman; and the Al Faysal, the descendants of deceased King Faysal, who controlled foreign policy (Saʿud al-Faysal), intelligence services (Turki al-Faysal until he became ambassador in London and later Washington) and the governor of first ʿAsir and later Mecca (Khalid al-Faysal). Added to the already existing circles, there emerged the descendants of King Fahd himself, who had carved an institutional and financial niche for themselves during their father's reign. Each prince was embedded in a state or quasi-state institution. These institutions included the traditional and powerful ones, such as the interior, national security, defence and foreign affairs, and institutions of soft power, for example pilgrimage, religion, sport, art, charity, media, local government, tourism and non-governmental organisations.

During the last years of King Fahd's reign, the Saʿudi state became a government of 'big men', who assumed titles and amassed wealth while leaving the daily running of their fiefdoms to their sons and technocrats. Each prince made sure that one of his sons succeeded in the running of the institution he had presided over for several decades.

The national purse suffered throughout the late 1990s, while the royal one continued to grow, and by 2000 Saudi Arabia was on the verge of an economic, political and social crisis. Younger second-generation princes, entrepreneurs from Saʿudi collateral branches and in-laws had already emerged as powerful actors. Many pursued their own narrow interests; others promoted the interests of large corporations, within whose parameters they operated freely. Second-generation princes such as al-Walid ibn Ṭalal, Bandar ibn Sultan, Muhammad ibn Nayef, Mutib ibn ʿAbdullah and Khalid al-Faysal operated in this milieu. Official princes combined power and wealth while non-official ones pursued projects at home and abroad to further their wealth and influence (Al-Rasheed 2008a).

Today the Saʿudi state is better described as consisting of multiple actors. Some have consolidated their influence abroad. Saʿud al-Faysal, Turki al-Faysal, Khalid ibn Sultan and Bandar ibn Sultan have reached out to international audiences. Prince Turki al-Faysal, ex-ambassador in London and Washington and ex-director of intelligence services, conducted diplomacy at Whitehall and the State Department, but spent a lot of time touring British and American universities, mosques, churches and think tanks. He sponsored academic conferences, invited guests and gave annual lectures. Senior princes such as Prince Nayef, Prince Sultan and Prince Salman concentrate their efforts on the home front, although they occasionally engaged in overseas overtures by patronising religion, culture, media and security. Against this background, Crown Prince ʿAbdullah and his advisers turned their attention to the strained economy.

Reforming a failing economy

In 2000 Saudi Arabia faced low oil prices, a mounting national debt and rising unemployment. The economic wealth of the first Saʿudi oil boom of the 1970s (discussed in chapter 5) had been plundered in the 1980s and 1990s. Saʿudi sponsorship of three wars (the Iran–Iraq war, the Afghan war and the liberation of Kuwait), coupled with mismanagement of the economy and several chaotic five-year development plans, resulted in serious debt and rising unemployment. As a result of low oil prices during the 1980s and 1990s, the first oil boom dwindled to a lingering memory from the past. The economic slowdown was only reversed with the dramatic increase in oil prices from 2003.

The acting King, Crown Prince ʿAbdullah, hinted in various speeches at the necessity to tighten belts and limit expectations. He occasionally mentioned the retreat of the welfare state and the dependency it had generated among the population, who should no longer expect to live off handouts given by the state. He visited poor and marginalised neighbourhoods in Saʿudi cities and promised to alleviate hardship. It was the first time that poverty in the land of oil wealth was mentioned or publicised in the Saʿudi media. The plight of several peripheral regions in Saudi Arabia was highlighted. The south-western region of ʿAsir and the northern provinces, as well as poor neighbourhoods in Riyadh and Jeddah, became the focus of media and academic studies. Saʿudi researchers highlighted the problem of uneven development, which had resulted in peripheral regions and zones lacking basic services, health facilities, schools, universities and job opportunities.

Urban poverty became the focus of attention in a country whose centennial celebrations had recently glorified development and prosperity. Al-Batha, a poor neighbourhood in Riyadh, represented in a shocking manner the level of urban degeneration, poverty, illiteracy, crime and deprivation among immigrants from Jazan province in the south-west, who had flooded into this neighbourhood in the 1980s and 1990s. Many had fled their home region in search of job opportunities, access to fundamental education and health services, as well as the opportunity to draw on the resources of charities, donations and begging that exist in the capital around mosques, street corners, shopping centres and royal palaces. Although the majority of residents in al-Batha regarded their situation as having improved in the capital, their neighbourhood remains one of the poorest urban centres, plagued by low educational achievement, unemployment and other social ills. Behind the veneer of ultra-modern building complexes, museums, monuments, palaces, airports and industrial cities, substantial sections of Saʿudi society remained backward. Both villagers and bedouin who migrated to the big cities found themselves in poverty with few prospects for social mobility. They occupied dilapidated buildings and mud-brick houses, long abandoned by their original owners, who had moved to the newly emerging residential neighbourhoods of Riyadh and Jeddah. They shared the decaying urban spaces with poor and illegal foreign immigrants, who found occasional employment in the unskilled menial labour market, selling vegetables and second-hand clothes, and mending cars (al-Naim 2004).

The northern town of Sakakah in al-Jawf province seems to have been bypassed by the early development plans of the 1980s and 1990s. Frontier towns on the edge of the desert and far away from the administrative, political and economic hubs of Saudi Arabia remained underdeveloped. Sakakah, in particular, suffered from the problem of uneven development in Saudi Arabia whereby the big cities in the Hijaz, central province and the eastern region attracted most of the investment and services. It seems that the first oil boom of the 1970s had passed without these frontier towns achieving access to basic services. The poor in the peripheral regions migrated to the big cities and in the process created pockets of serious urban poverty and deprivation (al-Falih 2000).

Between 2000 and 2003 Saudi Arabia was not in a position to do much about the failing economy that produced seriously marginalised populations in the distant provinces and the big cities. Government services and subsidies shrank under the pressure of the increasing population. The celebrated achievements, the construction boom and the early spending on prestigious projects failed to provide for basic needs in health, education and employment. At the same time, the wealth of the 1970s had produced rich princes as well as entrepreneurs and business contractors, who belonged to old commercial families or newly emerging ones, benefiting from close relationships with government and power circles.

The national debt of the public sector to private banks increased from $20.4 billion in 1995 to $35 billion in 2001. The budget deficit for 2002 was estimated at $12 billion. Between 2000 and 2003 Saʿudi economic growth slowed down. The overall government budget deficit increased to 6 per cent of GDP as oil revenues fell and non-oil revenues showed only a small increase. Government domestic debt rose to 97 per cent of GDP by the end of 2002.[1]

Reforming the economy centred on reducing cost and increasing revenues. Three general steps were taken to achieve this goal: liberalisation of the Saʿudi economy, with the objective of reducing the role of the state; privatisation of government corporations, starting with telecommunications and electricity; and the speeding up of an application, placed in 1993, to join the World Trade Organisation (Niblock 2006: 122). Economic reforms were formally introduced with the establishment of the Supreme Economic Council in 1999. The council was responsible for evaluating economic, industrial, agricultural and labour policies, in addition to attracting foreign investment and opening Saʿudi markets (ibid.: 125). According to the International Monetary Fund, economic measures remained modest and limited until 2000. It seems that no serious progress on the three fronts took place at a time when the Saʿudi economy and population would have benefited from such reforms. It was only after the second oil boom of 2003 that economic reforms really began to materialise.

From 2000, oil prices began to increase. The previous stagnation of the Saʿudi economy was suddenly reversed. In 2000 Saudi Arabia produced 8,310 million barrels per day, reaching 9,225 million in 2008. While there was no substantial increase in production, oil prices reached unprecedented levels. From a low of $27 per barrel in 2000, Saʿudi oil fetched over $140 in the summer of 2008, almost five times more expensive than it had been at the beginning of 2002 (*The Economist*, 5 January 2008).

This dramatic increase in oil prices was reflected in greater budgets, which allowed the Saʿudi government to announce a programme of spending on new development projects, industrial cities and infrastructure. The promise to limit spending on the welfare state was reversed, or slowed down, thanks to new revenues. Table 6 illustrates how Saʿudi budgets more than doubled over a period of eight years. From a figure of SAR235,322,00 in 2000, the government announced a budget of SAR528,924,50 in 2008.

In December 2007 the Saʿudi Council of Ministers announced the biggest budget in its history. ʿAbdullah, now King, unveiled the figures,

Table 4. *Saʿudi oil production*

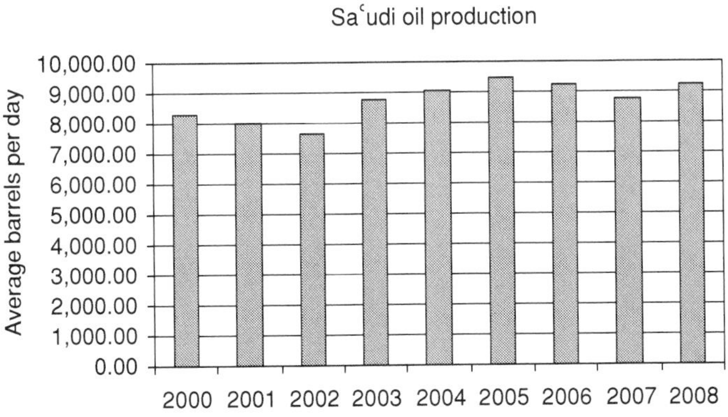

Source: International Energy Agency.

Table 5. *Oil prices 2000–2008*

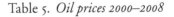

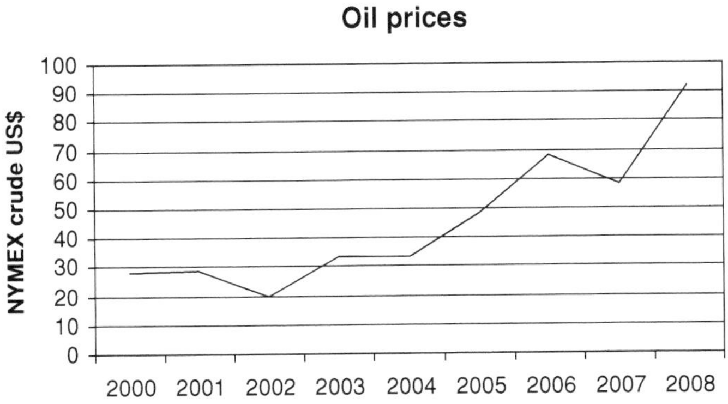

Source: NYMEX Crude–Reuters, January 2008.

emphasising that the first aim was to reduce public debt: 'By the grace of God, we have been able to pay back a part of the debt to bring it down to SAR366 billion by the end of the current fiscal year' (*Arab News*, 10 December 2007). The national debt, which had plagued Saudi Arabia in the 1990s and stood at almost 100 per cent of the GDP, was reduced to 26 per cent, standing at around SAR366 billion in 2007 (ibid.).

Table 6. *The Saʿudi budget*

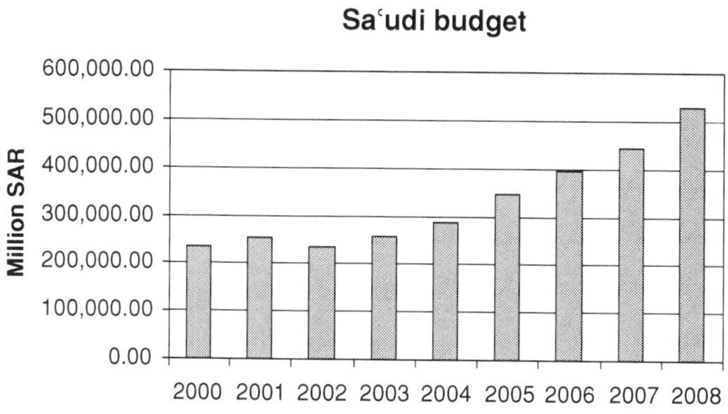

Source: Saudi Arabian Monetary Agency.

The second objective was to allocate greater resources to education and manpower development. Almost SAR105 billion was devoted to education, with plans to open a new university, forty-one colleges and more than two thousand schools. The government emphasised its commitment to science and technology to equip Saʿudi job seekers with skills more appropriate to the private sector. Other substantial spending was dedicated to health and social affairs (SAR44.4 billion), with plans to open 8 new hospitals and 250 primary care centres. Municipal services (SAR15.5 billion), transport and telecommunication (SAR16.4 billion), water and agriculture (SAR28.5 billion), loans to real estate and industrial development funds, and credit and agricultural banks (SAR216 billion) all received substantial increases in budget allocation.[2]

The budget data announced in 2007 do not disclose information on military spending. Other sources indicate that the Saʿudi defence budget in 2005 was nearly SAR25.4 billion, which covered defence and security affairs. Arms imports to the kingdom during 2001–5 totalled SAR1.728 billion (*Gulf Yearbook 2006–2007* 2007: 249–50), thus making Saudi Arabia one of the top spenders on defence not only in the Gulf region but also the world. The current oil boom meant that more is spent on defence contracts, the purchase of equipment and the development of manpower. From 2000, Saudi Arabia diversified its sources. In addition to arms purchases from Britain and the USA, it drew on military supplies from France, Canada, Italy, Germany and elsewhere. The development of the Saʿudi Air

Table 7. *Unemployment (% active population)*

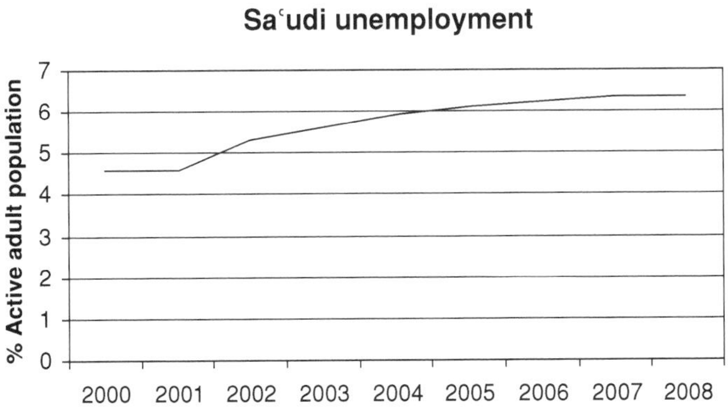

Source: ILO/Euromonitor.

Force took priority with the finalisation of a $13 billion deal in 2005 to buy seventy-two super-modern Eurofighter Typhoon planes, together with spare parts, and technical and training support. By the end of 2005 Saudi Arabia had increased its spending on defence and security by 21 per cent, amounting to $91 billion.

The new oil boom and the budget figures announced by the government masked real and serious unemployment, made worse by a dramatic increase in the population and in the number of those entering the labour market every year. Saudi Arabia has one of the highest population growth rates in the world, standing at 3.9 per cent per annum, resulting in a population of 16.53 million, according to the 2004 census (Winckler 2008). The over-representation of young Saʿudis in the population – almost 56.4 per cent are under the age of twenty – means that new pressures on services such as health, education and the labour market are not easily absorbed despite greater budget spending (*The Gulf in a Year 2003* 2004: 71).

In 2002 the government announced employment and labour-force data for the first time. Male unemployment stood at over 6 per cent and female unemployment at 15.8 per cent. These figures increased in 2004 to an overall unemployment rate of 9.6 per cent (Niblock 2006: 115). In general, it was estimated that only 19 per cent of the Saʿudi working-age population forms part of the labour force (ibid.: 116). Official statistics are often disputed, and, according to some sources, real unemployment rates are possibly around 30 per cent.

Despite several Saʿudisation programmes, announced and implemented throughout the last two decades of the twentieth century, Saudi Arabia had over 7 million foreign workers, almost 30 per cent of its population. The government's Saʿudisation schemes may have achieved some success in the public sector, but the private sector strongly resisted their imposition. As a result, many young and educated Saʿudis found themselves without employment. Graduates of the various universities, especially those who attended religious education institutes, had limited skills in a competitive labour market, after the privatisation and liberalisation policies. Women's unemployment emerged as yet another problem to deal with, given the increasing number of female graduates who were looking for jobs outside the traditional sector of education that in the past absorbed a substantial section of the female labour force. In 2006 and 2007 the Ministry of Labour tried to make it compulsory for businesses trading in female products to employ women, and encouraged Saʿudis to set up job centres for Saʿudi female housekeepers and household staff. Both initiatives were strongly resisted by Saʿudis in general and conservatives in society. Elite women running their own businesses benefited from the opening up of the Saʿudi economy and the new opportunities created with the oil boom of 2003. Women were elected to chambers of commerce, and participated in international economic forums against a background that restricted their full participation in the economy. The women who depended on salaried jobs struggled to find such jobs in a market that maintained strict segregation in all economic and business sectors. Private companies refrained from employing women on the basis of the high cost of providing separate facilities for female staff and the extra benefits for childcare and transport that usually accompany having female employees. Already-existing women's banks and companies struggled to contain the rising demand for female employment. Unemployment in general remained problematic despite the dramatic increase in state revenues in the first decade of the twenty-first century.

The new economic boom coincided with the US dollar losing more than 30 per cent of its value. New Saʿudi wealth was partially consumed by the dramatic increase in the cost of ongoing and future development projects, leading to high inflation, estimated in 2008 at 4.1 per cent (*Elaph*, 30 January 2008). By the summer of 2008, inflation was above 10 per cent. While Saudi Arabia has benefited from the dramatic increase in oil prices, it suffered from an increase in global commodity prices, especially basic food products, believed to have increased by 13 per cent in 2007–8, despite government subsidies (SAMBA 2008b). As the population began to feel the pressure of rising prices for food and consumer goods, the government was forced to announce salary increases from 2005 onward.

While in general the Saʿudi economy looked much better in 2008, there remained some important gaps, especially in terms of meeting the needs of the population and generating the jobs demanded by the new generation of young Saʿudis seeking employment. Within the first eight years of the twenty-first century the Saʿudi economy moved from being on the verge of a serious crisis to a second oil boom. It remains to be seen whether the government's new economic policies and budgets will deliver longer-lasting prosperity than that of the early 1970s. The euphoria of the second economic boom paved the way for a real transfer of power from the ailing King Fahd to Crown Prince ʿAbdullah. The new oil boom strengthened the position of the Crown Prince when he finally became King in 2005.

The years of terror, 2001–2006

The Grand Mosque siege of 1979 and two major terrorist attacks in the 1990s (in Riyadh and al-Khobar) seemed to belong to the past, but they were both indicators of a fermenting social, political and religious crisis, which began to unfold violently in the twenty-first century. Having beheaded Juhayman ibn Muhammad al-ʿUtaybi, the leader of the mosque siege, and captured the perpetrators of the 1995–6 attacks, Saudi Arabia came to realise under the pressure of militant violence that it had a serious and more fundamental problem on its doorstep.

As the Saʿudi leadership was struggling to turn the tide of economic stagnation and the failure of previous development plans, it came face to face with the global terrorism that started in New York and moved rapidly to Saʿudi cities. When it transpired that fifteen of the nineteen hijackers who flew three planes into the World Trade Center and the Pentagon were Saʿudis, Saudi Arabia and its leadership initially went into a state of denial. The Saʿudi hijackers, who had organised and carried out the plot under the leadership of an Egyptian, Muhammad Atta, and Usama Bin Laden's sponsorship, came from the peripheral and marginalised south-western province of ʿAsir. While the Bush administration was careful not to implicate Saudi Arabia, the American press spared no opportunity to link the attacks on America to Saʿudi Wahhabi preaching, finance, charities and pan-Islamic education centres. For the first time Saudi Arabia was on the receiving end of American media accusations.

While awaiting the publication of the various American commissions and reports on 9/11, Saudi Arabia had no choice but to open its borders to inquisitive journalists, reporters and more serious investigators. Some went to provincial towns and villages to interrogate the hijackers' parents and relatives. Although the famous US 9/11 Commission[3] stated clearly that it found no evidence to support accusations against Saudi Arabia, the image of the country was tarnished – some would say beyond repair – at least in the USA. Saʿudi–US relations went through a cooling-off period, with the latter imposing strict visa restrictions on Saʿudi nationals. American journalists, congressmen and think-tank consultants debated the merits of the hitherto close US–Saʿudi relationship and cooperation. Saʿudi students and businessmen in the USA recounted unpleasant stories about interrogation, detention and other inconveniences encountered during their visits to or stays in the USA. Many cancelled trips and suspended their studies or business during the months after 9/11. The Saʿudi leadership fought to clear its name. It hired public-relations consultants, sponsored conferences and lectures, and engaged Americans in debates. The Saʿudi ambassador in Washington, Prince Bandar ibn Sultan, appeared on American television to defend his country and distance it from the terrorism that had hit America. It was not long before Saudi Arabia itself was hit by the terrorism of al-Qaʿidah.

Throughout the 1990s, Saudi Arabia had struggled to contain the Islamist opposition, commonly referred to as al-Sahwa. The government imprisoned its most outspoken figures, personalities such as Shaykh Salman al-ʿAwdah and Ṣafar al-Ḥawali, but released them in 1999, together with hundreds of supporters and sympathisers. Other Islamists fled to Afghanistan, where Usama Bin Laden had established training camps in 1996, or took refuge in London, from where they continued their media campaign against the Saʿudi government. However, by 2001 a different kind of violent Islamist radicalism, closely linked to the operations of Usama Bin Laden and al-Qaʿidah in Afghanistan appeared on the Saʿudi scene.

The USA's response to the 9/11 attacks was to launch a specific military campaign against the Taliban who hosted Bin Laden in Afghanistan and announce the beginning of what it called a global 'War on Terror'. Within weeks, and before it encountered terrorism on its own soil, Saudi Arabia severed diplomatic relations with the Taliban and enlisted in America's global war. It allowed US planes and troops stationed in Saudi Arabia to participate in military action against Bin Laden and the Taliban. King Sultan Air Base and its command and control centre became important for a speedy military campaign in Afghanistan (Cordesman and Obaid 2005: 12).

Senior Taliban leaders, together with Bin Laden and his close aides, went into hiding, but their followers were killed, captured or dispersed to other countries. Al-Qaʿidah training camps were destroyed. The USA sent hundreds of captured Arabs and Muslims to Guantánamo Bay detention camp; Saʿudis constituted the largest number, an indication of the reception of al-Qaʿidah's message and ideology within Saudi Arabia. Many Saʿudis commended Bin Laden for hitting at the heart of America's military (the Pentagon) and financial centres (New York). There is no doubt that 9/11 allowed Bin Laden an unprecedented – although momentary – popularity, especially in Saudi Arabia.

It did not take long for Bin Laden's global Salafi jihadi movement to become a local feature of Saʿudi Islamism, threatening both state and society. After 9/11 and the demise of the Taliban in 2001 and 2002, it was evident that some well-trained al-Qaʿidah operatives had found their way back to Saudi Arabia. They proved to be the core element of the newly formed al-Qaʿidah in the Arabian Peninsula, a sub-branch of Usama Bin Laden's original al-Qaʿidah organisation in Afghanistan. They regrouped, reached out for support among religious scholars, and collected funds for future operations. Both Usama Bin Laden, who had been stripped of his Saʿudi nationality in 1994, and al-Qaʿidah in the Arabian Peninsula came to the public's attention. They became linked to the worst terror campaign in Saʿudi history. A jihadi Salafi trend had already been fermenting in Saudi Arabia, but the return from Afghanistan of Saʿudi jihadis after being ousted by the Americans in 2001 proved to be a catalyst for the consolidation of a new generation of militants, who had trained in Afghanistan throughout the 1990s (Al-Rasheed 2007: 134–74). These jihadis had developed and nourished a discourse very different from that of the Sahwis in the 1990s. The latter recognised the legitimacy of the Al Saʿud leadership but demanded the Islamisation of the state's policies in economic, social, political, media and military spheres. Their famous Memorandum of Advice, discussed earlier in this book, did not challenge the Al Saʿud or demand the overthrow of the regime.

Al-Qaʿidah in the Arabian Peninsula was totally different from this Islamist opposition of the 1990s. It was inspired by a theology that excommunicated the Saʿudi regime, dubbing it un-Islamic, mainly for its association with the so-called infidels. While the 1990s Sahwis had objected to King Fahd calling upon infidels to assist the Saʿudi state during the liberation of Kuwait, al-Qaʿidah denounced the Saʿudi leadership for assisting infidels in their war on a Muslim state – the Afghan Taliban, which had given shelter to Usama Bin Laden and his followers, both Arab and Saʿudi. This ideological difference between the early Sahwis and al-Qaʿidah proved to be important in justifying al-Qaʿidah's level of violence inside Saudi Arabia in 2003.

Justification for al-Qaʿidah's violence in the streets of Riyadh and elsewhere revolved around two central themes: the un-Islamic illegitimate third Saʿudi state; and the expulsion of infidel American troops from the country. These justifications appeared in pamphlets, booklets and *fatawa* that circulated on the internet; some had been written in the 1990s, while others were an immediate response to the American invasion of Afghanistan in 2001. Many young Saʿudi religious scholars were infuriated by the demise of the Taliban, long considered an ideal Islamic state, that had no subservient relations with infidels, applied a literal interpretation of the *shariʿa* close to that dominant among the Saʿudi Wahhabi scholars, and offered shelter to Usama Bin Laden and his followers, despite international pressure to expel him and close his training camps.

Although the USA announced the transfer of its military personnel from Saudi Arabia to Qatar in 2003, the campaign of terror inside Saudi Arabia was about to begin. In May 2003, less than two years after 9/11, suicide bombers struck an expatriate residential compound in the heart of the capital, killing thirty-five people and injuring hundreds, both Saʿudis and foreigners. This was followed by another similar attack in November, which left seventeen dead. By 2004, terrorist attacks had targeted petrochemical sites in Yanbuʿ, the American consulate in Jeddah, expatriate residential compounds in al-Khobar, and headquarters of the security forces and the Ministry of the Interior in Riyadh. Foreign nationals, journalists, expatriate workers and military consultants and contractors from the USA and European countries were kidnapped and killed in the capital and other cities across Saudi Arabia.[4] Horrifying images of beheaded Westerners, wounded Saʿudis and bombed buildings flooded the internet, contributing to a campaign of fear that shattered the myth of Saudi Arabia as a safe haven amidst a turbulent Arab sea. Not a month passed between 2003 and 2005 without the security services announcing the death or capture of terrorists or the discovery of hidden funds and weapons in villas and apartments, or buried in remote sites.

Al-Qaʿidah succeeded in killing more that 200 people in Saudi Arabia, but above all it undermined the state of tranquillity, prosperity and security that the country had enjoyed for decades. Al-Qaʿidah felt confident and secure enough to establish an internet media empire, release regular electronic magazines (*Ṣawt al-Jihad*) and communiqués, produce films about would-be martyrs preparing for their attacks, and publish obituaries, military manuals and sermons preaching the obligation of *jihad* and justifying violence in the Land of the Two Holy Mosques, long considered a controversial strategy whose theological justification was not straightforward.[5]

Tight internal security measures such as concrete protection barricades, checkpoints and armed security personnel and vehicles appeared in the major cities and on roads linking various regions. Funerals of deceased Saʿudi security personnel, victims of confrontation with al-Qaʿidah operatives, created a sombre image of a country held hostage by a relatively small number of terrorists.

The regularity of attacks inside Saudi Arabia, coupled with international pressure after 9/11, forced the Saʿudi government to act swiftly to deal with the menace. Military and intelligence solutions were the immediate response. These were aimed at increasing security measures around possible targets, such as government, military, industrial and oil complexes, in addition to foreign embassies and residential compounds. The second step was to arrest suspects before they could commit more terrorist attacks. Saudi Arabia issued a series of lists that included the names and photographs of wanted al-Qaʿidah operatives in the kingdom; the majority were Saʿudi nationals with a few Arab suspects. By 2005 the government had arrested more than 600 individuals and questioned 2,000 others. In military confrontations between al-Qaʿidah and government internal security agencies, there was only one option: surrender or be killed. Many al-Qaʿidah operatives chose the second option. For example, Yusuf al-Aiyri[6] and ʿAbd al-ʿAziz al-Muqrin, leaders of al-Qaʿidah in the Arabian Peninsula, and their successors died in violent confrontations with the Saʿudi security forces; the latter suffered considerable losses, attributed to lack of expertise, training and coordination (Cordesman and Obaid 2005: 124).

The sheer number of attacks between 2003 and 2005 forced the Saʿudi government to admit that military and intelligence measures might not be sufficient to deter future al-Qaʿidah sympathisers or prevent their cooperation with existing cells. Saudi Arabia entered a period of soul searching to identify the causes of terrorism, and devise a cure. The previous perception had been that the only threats to the country were external, from Iran in the 1980s and Iraq in the 1990s. In the twenty-first century, however, internal security overrode all other concerns, real or imagined. The major question for most Saʿudis was who to blame for the eruption of jihadi violence on such a grand scale, in a country that had enjoyed relative internal security, with only a fading memory of street violence and bloody confrontations.

Immediately after 9/11, the government went into a state of denial, sheltering behind the fact that Usama Bin Laden was no longer a Saʿudi citizen, and that his ideological orientation had nothing to do with Saʿudi – i.e. Wahhabi – religious interpretations. Outspoken princes went as far as to deny the existence of Wahhabiyya. The minister of the interior, Prince Nayef, announced that the 9/11 atrocities were a product of Egyptian Muslim Brotherhood radicalism and the discourse of Sayyid Qutb and Ayman al-Zawahiri, both alien to Saudi Arabia. The Saʿudi religious establishment supported the leadership, denouncing this allegedly alien ideology, which it claimed had found its way into Saʿudi society through acts of charity and hospitality, referring to the fact that Saudi Arabia had welcomed the exiled Muslim Brotherhood cadres who had fled Egypt in the 1960s and Syria in the 1980s and settled in Saudi Arabia, teaching at Saʿudi schools and universities.[7] Explanations of this sort subsided – or rather, became redundant – as violence moved to Saʿudi cities in 2003, when it transpired that al-Qaʿidah was a home-grown phenomenon that drew on a theology at the heart of Saʿudi–Wahhabi religious interpretations. Its pamphlets and magazines cited the work of both the founding fathers of Wahhabiyya and later interpreters who were at the heart of Saʿudi religious texts and interpretations. The government and its media spokesmen described Saʿudi terrorists as contemporary Khawarij, thus invoking the rejectionist group of early Islamic historical periods. Al-Qaʿidah activists, their ideologues and supporters were believed to have gone astray, precipitating murder and chaos, undermining economic prosperity and threatening the lives of innocent Muslims in the sacred territory of Saudi Arabia, the land where Islam emerged and where a pious Muslim leadership reigned to ensure the unity of Islam and Muslims.

When violence hit Saʿudi cities, liberally inclined Saʿudi authors, academics, intellectuals and journalists, who had grown intolerant of the social and religious restrictions that had been enforced following the Mecca mosque siege in 1979, jumped at the opportunity and situated the violence in its Saʿudi context. They blamed government policies that indulged the religious establishment and allowed it to propagate what they called the discourse of intolerance and hatred towards other Muslims and Westerners. Through expansion in religious education, Islamic charitable foundations and religious summer camps, the government had allowed radical preachers to develop their infrastructure and infiltrate government institutions, boosting the control of radicals over society, especially young and impressionable Saʿudis.[8] The policy of supporting the Afghan *jihad* in the 1980s was believed to have backfired. Many argued that the state survived the ramifications of the mosque siege, only to adopt the demands of the perpetrators as it endeavoured to increase the grip of radical preachers on the public sphere. Some writers distinguished between the loyal official *ʿulama* and the dissidents of the 1990s, who were held responsible for radicalising the youth of the country through their inflammatory speeches and anti-American sermons. Their anti-American preaching resonated with the unemployed, dispossessed and marginalised youth, who found refuge and solace in *jihad* and martyrdom. Saʿudi social and religious conservatism was regarded as an anachronism leading to radicalisation and confrontation. The religious narrative that had justified the establishment of the Saʿudi state, its religious teachings and educational material came under scrutiny not only in the USA but also inside Saudi Arabia.[9] Wahhabiyya became a contested religious discourse, defended by official *ʿulama* and denounced by those who aspired towards weakening the hold of its institutions and preachers on the population. By the twenty-first century, however, there were various strands within Wahhabiyya, which had already been fragmented and diversified into a broader spectrum of interpretation and belief. At one end was the loyal quietist tradition of the official *ʿulama*, who held important positions as councillors to the royal household, and *qadi*s, who guarded the security of the regime against any attempt to destabilise it. At the other end was a group of young preachers and activists, who claimed to remain loyal to the old message of Muhammad ibn ʿAbd al-Wahhab. The latter launched scathing attacks on those whom they dubbed the '*ʿulama* of the sultans', who issued *fatawa* in support of political decisions on the basis of pragmatism and expediency. The battle between the two camps intensified as violence erupted on the ground. The government responded by imprisoning preachers who disseminated anti-government propaganda and called for a renewal of the *jihad* obligation against infidels and the Saʿudi security services, who were seen as agents of a *kafir* (blasphemous) leadership.

Both 9/11 and terrorism on Saʿudi soil contributed to the fragmentation of the Saʿudi Islamist field. Active *ʿulama* associated with the so-called Islamic awakening (Sahwis) who had been released from prison in the late 1990s began to distance themselves from jihadi radicalism. When accused of inciting Saʿudi youth, the Sahwis asserted their loyalty to the state and denounced terrorism. In an attempt to absolve themselves of any responsibility, they appeared on television, wrote articles, publicised sermons and offered to cooperate with government agencies to de-radicalise sympathisers and even persuade wanted activists to give themselves up to government security agencies. The Sahwi shaykhs Salman al-ʿAwdah and Ṣafar al-Ḥawali were enlisted in this de-radicalisation project. While both lacked sympathy for the USA, they disputed the theological justification for attacking civilians, especially inside Saudi Arabia. They denounced al-Qaʿidah in the Arabian Peninsula, but fell short of openly denouncing Bin Laden or describing him as a Kharijite. They favoured dialogue and rehabilitation programmes to reform those who had gone astray by following Bin Laden's call to expel infidels from Saudi Arabia using a violent terror campaign that killed Muslims and infidels alike. They called for fair trials in order to encourage those involved in terrorism or supportive of jihadi theology to give themselves up.[10]

As the government campaign to bring jihadi violence under control gathered momentum, the occupation of Iraq by the USA in April 2003, accompanied by images of the fall of Baghdad to coalition forces and the toppling of Saddam's regime, added a new dimension that increasingly and rapidly began to have an impact in Saudi Arabia. While the invitation of foreign troops to Saudi Arabia in the early 1990s had helped crystallise the Islamist Sahwa opposition, the occupation of Iraq gave a new impetus to radical and violent jihadism in Saudi Arabia. Together with the 2001 Afghan war, this new military occupation ensured that Saudi Arabia, along with its alliance with the USA and enrolment in the 'War on Terror', would become yet another axis along which violence was justified in the publications of al-Qaʿidah and its ideologues inside Saudi Arabia. It is certain that as the government tightened its security measures, and arrested or killed a substantial number of jihadis, some Saʿudi activists fled to neighbouring Iraq and joined the al-Qaʿidah forces there. Others preferred to stay behind and launch a campaign against the Saʿudi government itself. The occupation of Iraq contributed to a fragmentation of the jihadi movement in Saudi Arabia: one group of jihadis called upon Saʿudis to travel to Iraq to defend 'Sunni brothers' who had been marginalised by American occupation, Shiʿa empowerment and Iranian backing. Other jihadis called upon Saʿudis to remain in Saudi Arabia and join the ranks of al-Qaʿidah in the Arabian Peninsula.[11]

The occupation of Iraq was yet another challenge facing the Saʿudi government during the early years of the twenty-first century. It was clear that the government wished to see Saddam Husayn overthrown and his army defeated; yet it was aware of the Saʿudi public mood, especially within Islamist circles, that would denounce any foreign military campaign against a neighbouring Muslim and Arab state and would, above all, object to any direct Saʿudi involvement in such an attack. The strongest objections to the war originated among Saʿudi religious scholars. A Saʿudi shaykh, Naṣir al-ʿOmar, described the attack as a new crusade, and warned Arabs of the consequences. He stated that America would use all its means to dominate the Muslim world and that Muslims should therefore resist, applying all resources, including education, military confrontation, economic pressure, and social and psychological force (Al-Rasheed 2006: 158).

On 13 March 2003, Saʿudi writers, intellectuals and professionals with nationalist, leftist and liberal orientations signed a letter addressed to American President, George Bush. They welcomed democratic change in Iraq, and most definitely in their own country, now held hostage to terrorism, but insisted that such change should not be brought about by an unjust war. Others welcomed the demise of the Baʿthist regime in Iraq, and applauded American efforts to establish democratic government, starting with Iraq but with the hope that democratic reforms would follow in other Arab countries, including Saudi Arabia.

The government opted for an indecisive position, hiding behind a confused rhetoric of open objections to the occupation in international and Arab forums alternating with implicit approval, and even secret cooperation. In 2002 Saudi Arabia had declared that it would allow US use of Saʿudi military facilities to attack Iraq only if there was UN approval for it. Later that year, in November, Crown Prince ʿAbdullah insisted that the Saʿudi armed forces would under no circumstances set foot in Iraq. By March 2003 it became clear that 'Saudi Arabia will not play a pivotal role in case the US attacks Iraq. It will play a secondary role.' The government pressurised the USA not to reveal to the outside world that it was using Saudi Arabia as a take-off point for its attack on Iraq (ibid.: 156).

While the 2001 occupation of Afghanistan and the 2003 occupation of Iraq are relevant regional events that dramatically influenced the outbreak of terrorism in Saudi Arabia, they are not the main causes. Saʿudi jihadism had strong indigenous roots, and could not simply be explained as a reaction to a turbulent historical moment that affected two Muslim countries with which Saudi Arabia had in the past been involved. Saudi Arabia had contributed to the liberation of Afghanistan from Soviet occupation in the 1980s, and supported Saddam Husayn against Iranian revolutionary expansion after 1979. Afghanistan slipped away from Saʿudi influence with the rise of the Taliban and the arrival of Usama Bin Laden in Qandahar in 1996. Similarly, Saddam Husayn turned against his early Gulf sponsors, including Saudi Arabia, when he invaded Kuwait in 1991. Both Saʿudi adventures therefore proved to be short-term strategic successes, that came to haunt the leadership and precipitate a violent terror campaign inside the country. Afghanistan and Iraq became catalysts for an old and well-embedded set of problems, pertinent to Saudi Arabia.

Many explanations have been put forward to identify the causes of jihadism in Saudi Arabia. Among these we find references to authoritarian rule and torture chambers; the absence of democracy, civil society and political participation; misguided Western foreign policy that antagonises Saʿudi youth; socio-economic deprivation, marginalisation and alienation of troubled Saʿudis; unemployment and increasing economic inequality; bigoted Saʿudi–Wahhabi religious educational material; Muslim Brotherhood extremist ideology; the emergence of nationalist–Islamic solidarity; al-Jazeera's anti-Western broadcasting; the failure of Islamists to topple their near enemies; the fragmentation of religious authority in the Muslim world; and the quest for a mystical activist globalised piety. The list of hypothesised causes is very long indeed. Regardless of whether there is consensus over the main cause, we assume that the destruction of the World Trade Center in New York, the al-Muhayya compound in Riyadh and many other spectacular acts of terrorism emanate from the same causes, simply because the professed and publicised ideology, strategy and outcome are the same. Here we tend to confuse context with causes.

Another problematic, yet equally constructed, concept is the term jihadism itself. Everywhere we find references to the medieval theologian Taqi al-Din Aḥmad ibn Taymiyya (1268–1328) and the eighteenth-century founder of Wahhabism, Muhammad ibn ʿAbd al-Wahhab (1703–92); we conclude that jihadism draws on these sources, which have in turn become part of the ideology of terror. Others come across references to the Egyptian Sayyid Qutb (1906–66) and the Palestinian ʿAbdullah ʿAzzam (1941–89), and conclude that the ideology of the Egyptian Muslim Brotherhood as it developed in the twentieth century, rather than Wahhabiyya, is the source of inspiration. In an attempt to implicate, accuse or prove innocent, we are left with simplistic statements misguided by preconceived ideological and political positions. Yet if there is a Saʿudi jihadi inspirational discourse, it must be seen as a hybrid construction deeply rooted in the last three decades of the twentieth century that is desperate to anchor itself in an authentic Islamic tradition, yet reflecting serious borrowing from the discourse of Western modernity. The outcome is a cross-fertilisation of sources that is both transnational and local. Today the ideology of jihadis is a postmodern hybridity, whose sources, if we can accurately identify them, are found in both the past and present, and in both the Muslim and Western worlds. The result is a devastating ideology that inspires novices, glorifies reinvented ancestors, and could potentially induce a future cataclysmic war between two binary oppositions, defined politically, morally, economically, socially and culturally as poles that will never meet or overlap. The ideology is one of difference, against a background of incredible similarity and a desire to be like the despised other, who nevertheless must be eliminated (Al-Rasheed 2009).

Contemporary Salafi jihadis are products of modernity. They are modern but not modernists. Contemporary Saʿudi jihadis die for faith, not land; and despite their professed rejection of it, they share the modernity of the West. Like Western post-industrial consumer capitalist societies, they call for a global world order, in which Muslim solidarity overrides ethnic and national boundaries. In this respect, they share the rationale of the free capitalism of the late twentieth century and the post-national free global market, prominent in neo-liberal political theologies. More specifically, jihadis incorporate the Western ethos of changing the world by action. While reason and profit are central in the Western neo-liberal modernity project, faith is crucial in the jihadi narrative. Making Islam hegemonic in the world, rather than on an equal footing with other narratives, in a manner similar to the way in which Western neo-liberalism struggles to become hegemonic as a world-view, is the common thread. Today, this can only be achieved through a process of privatisation that empowers individual Muslims in the face of real or imagined adversaries. Similarly, Western neo-liberalism insists on both a subjective experience of the world and a privatisation of pleasure and pain, loss and gain, and wealth and poverty, to improve life, spread prosperity and dominate as a world system. Without these two processes, both jihadism and late Western modernity would fail in the contemporary world.

Saʿudis have been receptive to the messages of al-Qaʿidah because, although their regime glorifies its commitment to Islam and Muslim causes, many jihadis feel that it in fact 'assists' Western powers to control the Muslim world. They are indoctrinated in a theology that calls upon them to obey their leaders, while it denounces other Muslims and their states as un-Islamic. The government has a strong alliance with the USA, which guarantees Saʿudi security, yet many preachers insist that pious Muslims should dissociate themselves from infidels – and even nourish hatred towards them in their hearts. While the religious establishment remains loyal to the Saʿudi leadership, it is no longer the sole voice of Islam. Modernity and information technology have led to a fragmentation of the religious field in Saudi Arabia. Al-Qaʿidah and its ideologues have exploited the information revolution to contribute to this fragmentation, and propagate the discourse of defiance, resistance and terrorism. Its Saʿudi ideologues draw on the early texts of Wahhabiyya, which happen to be the same sources of official Islam in the country, but offer alternative interpretations.

Political activism in Saudi Arabia has not developed alternative political ideas, but remains immersed in religion, from which al-Qaʿidah draws its inspiration and justification. The government destroyed all other contemporary sources for imagining an alternative political system and failed to provide venues for real political participation or civil society. Saʿudis therefore turned to religion not only to articulate political and social change but also to justify terror. The al-Qaʿidah operatives are undoubtedly a small minority in Saudi Arabia, yet their ideas and the theological sources they draw on resonate with and are familiar to large sections of Saʿudi society. The government launched a rehabilitation campaign to re-educate the captured al-Qaʿidah members, yet it seems that the main problem is that it is engaged in a religious battle with its own sources of legitimacy, the set of Wahhabi principles upon which the state was founded. By 2008 terrorist attacks had declined, which allowed the state to claim that it has succeeded in containing the menace, yet it is likely that the trend of violence will reappear and claim many lives for a simple reason: the al-Qaʿidah ideology is not alien to Saudi Arabia, but stands at the heart of the foundation myth of the state.

EXTERNAL PRESSURES

Saudi Arabia and the USA: friend or foe?

After 9/11, relations with the USA, which had guaranteed the security of Saudi Arabia during two previous regional wars (the Iran–Iraq war in the 1980s and Saddam's occupation of Kuwait in 1990), became strained. In Washington, think-tank consultants, policy makers, administrators and academics identified Wahhabiyya as the ideological source that inspired terrorism. Consequently, the American administration started putting pressure on the Saʿudi leadership to control, reform and even uproot radical preachers and interpretations within Saudi Arabia. The early Wahhabi discourse that had inspired Saʿudis and other Muslims to fight in Afghanistan when it was under Soviet occupation had become a dangerous tool for radicalisation, intolerance and terrorism. Steps such as reforming the Saʿudi educational curriculum, sacking radical preachers and controlling Friday sermons were seen as important measures in the global 'War on Terror'. It was thought that these steps should be accompanied by a more open social policy, similar to that adopted in the economic sphere. Social liberalisation should be manifested in allowing debates about diversity, coexistence and tolerance, which would benefit Saʿudi society as a whole, but especially women, minorities and liberals. There were also calls to improve the Saʿudi record on human rights and religious freedom. Religious and social reforms were seen as important steps towards lessening the controls of Wahhabiyya on Saʿudi society, giving rise to diversity and tolerance. The American administration of George Bush had faith in the Saʿudi leadership to curb the zealots in Saʿudi society and eliminate radicals, in a manner similar to that applied when the first Wahhabi rebellion challenged the Saʿudi leadership in 1929, and later in 1979. So while the USA offered security and intelligence cooperation to deal with violence, it expected the Saʿudi leadership to deal with the more complex issue of reforming society and religion, but in a cautious and circumspect manner. While the rhetoric of democratisation was occasionally adopted in Washington, it was believed that any serious political participation, for example national elections, would bring undesirable elements to power at this specific historical moment. The Saʿudi leadership knew that mending fences with the USA after 9/11 would require adopting some of the recommended social and religious reform measures.

After the occupation of Iraq in 2003 and the beginning of the Sunni insurgency, which included al-Qaʿidah militants, among other groups, Saʿudi jihadis appeared on the Iraqi scene and took part in suicide bombings against US troops, the Iraqi army and Shiʿa.

In 2006 a Saʿudi Ministry of Interior spokesman, Mansour al-Turki, finally acknowledged the participation of many Saʿudis in the insurgency in Iraq. However, he stated that 'there isn't any organised terror finance and we will not permit any such unorganised acts' (Al-Rasheed 2008c). While officials stress that the government is doing all it can to prevent the flow of Saʿudis to Iraq, they admit that they cannot control it. Saudi Arabia endeavoured to secure its borders with Iraq by building a wall, in the hope of deterring jihadis travelling to and from Iraq. Moreover, the government claims to have tightened its control over charitable donations aimed at financing the Iraqi Sunni insurgency.

The confirmation of Saʿudi participation in the Iraqi insurgency came from Prince Nayef, the interior minister, in June 2007. In a speech addressing senior religious scholars, he suggested that the clerics are not doing enough in the fight against militants. After reports claiming that the sons of prominent religious scholars tried to get into Iraq, he told them: 'Do you know that your sons who go to Iraq are used only for blowing themselves up? Iraqi officials told me that themselves . . . Are you happy for your children to become instruments of murder?' (ibid.).

In 2007, according to American military sources, 45 per cent of those who participated in violence in Iraq were Saʿudis, most of them engaged in suicide bombings. Israeli sources, which seem to have a vested interest in exaggerating the figures, claim that within six months in 2004, almost 61 per cent of insurgents killed in Iraq were Saʿudis. In discussions of alleged Saʿudi support of the insurgency, it is claimed that 'the Saudi government either looked the other way or gave tacit approval to Saudi jihadis who flocked to Iraq, choosing to kill two birds with one stone: the "martyring" of home-grown Wahhabi extremists while supporting Sunni co-religionists against Shiʿite domination' (ibid.). Furthermore, the US ambassador to the United Nations, Zalmay Khalilzad, stated that 'Saudi Arabia and a number of other countries are not doing all they can to help us in Iraq. At times, some of them are not only not helping . . . they are doing things that [are] undermining the effort to make progress' (ibid.). Jihadi sources, which also have a vested interest in portraying the jihadi insurgency as a global Islamic project, tend to exaggerate the participation of Saʿudis, perhaps to boost future recruitment and encourage others to either join or donate money in support of the insurgency.

Other reports, mainly those drawing on Saʿudi intelligence sources, dispute the number of Saʿudis in the Iraq insurgency. It is claimed that inflated figures are often given to perpetuate the myth of foreign insurgents in Iraq, in an attempt to absolve the USA and the Iraqi government from any responsibility vis-à-vis the deteriorating security situation. Cordesman and Obaid (2005) have estimated that Saʿudis constitute only 12 per cent of foreign insurgents, amounting to 350 recruits. Iraqi sources of the Association of Muslim Scholars dispute the claims of the number of foreigners in the Iraqi insurgency. Its spokesman, Harith al-Dhari, declared that 90 per cent of the insurgents are Iraqi (Al-Rasheed 2008c).

Although the Saʿudi government claims to have arrested many young men on their way to Iraq, both US officials and Iraqis continue to accuse the Saʿudi government of complacency. The Iraqi foreign minister, Hoshyar Zibari, expressed his concern over the role played by neighbouring Arab countries. He told the US press: 'We hope that Saudi Arabia will keep the same distance from each and all Iraqi parties'(ibid.). Iraqi government television channels broadcast interviews with Saʿudi insurgents detained in Iraq and discuss the dangers of their Wahhabi *takfiri* ideology (the labelling of non-Wahhabi Muslims as unbelievers). They are accused of precipitating sectarian civil war in Iraq, first under the banner of Abu Musab al-Zarqawi and later under the leadership of his successors. Counter-insurgency experts working with General Petraeus in Iraq claim that the insurgents' leaders tend to be foreign, including Saʿudi veterans, while grass-roots insurgents are Iraqis.

Despite the early silence of officials in the USA and Saudi Arabia, Iraqi accusations and the disputed figures, many young Saʿudis have died or are imprisoned in Iraq. Their exact numbers will probably never be known. Their corpses are counted on the internet and their 'martyrdom' and obituaries are celebrated and glorified by supporters at home. Saʿudi journalists continue to debate their participation in the local press while the government insists that it is difficult to control its own borders with Iraq to prevent the travel of jihadis, who take other routes in their search for martyrdom. While *jihad* inside Saudi Arabia has subsided, after an initial outbreak after 9/11, the occupation of Iraq has given some Saʿudi would-be jihadis a new destination, to which they travel to defend Sunnis against what they claim is a Shiʿa–Iranian takeover of Iraq that was made possible with American support.

For obvious reasons, official political and religious discourse does not endorse *jihad* in Iraq. The state does not openly facilitate the travel of jihadis or subsidise their journeys in a manner reminiscent of the Afghan experience. There have been no public sermons glorifying *jihad* in Iraq or official jihadi festivals sanctioned by the state or the *ʿulama*. The government admitted that some Saʿudi activists in the Hijaz and Qasim were involved in clandestine recruitment and collection of donations. In February 2007, about a dozen activists were arrested and accused of inciting the youth to travel to Iraq. Later, in Qasim, religious scholars and businessmen were also arrested on the same charge. It is difficult to assess the veracity of government accusations, as the cases of those detained are not brought to court.

While the American administration put pressure on the Saʿudi leadership to launch an internal religious and social reform programme and control the departure of its jihadis to Iraq, Saudi Arabia in the twenty-first century lost control over not only the religious sphere but also the destiny and orientations of its own citizens. Transnationalism, globalisation and information technology have made it difficult for the state to control its own citizens or limit the proliferation of radical religious discourse, most of which has retreated to alternative media channels such as the internet.

After a period of doubt and tension, the Saʿudi–US strategic alliance was revived under the pressure of mutual interest. Crown Prince ʿAbdullah tried hard to mend fences with the USA after 9/11 and posed for photographs holding hands with President Bush in Crawford, Texas, in April

2005. He promised to reform Islam, and promote love for the 'infidel other' in the kingdom's educational curriculum. The relationship with the USA remained based on a deadly triangle: Saʿudi oil; geo-strategic location; and, ironically, the disputed Saʿudi religion (Bronson 2006). ʿAbdullah promised to increase oil production to stabilise prices. He also continued to allow the USA to employ Saudi Arabia's strategic location to launch the war on Afghanistan in 2001 and Iraq in 2003. Throughout the 1980s the USA had enjoyed the support of the Saʿudi Wahhabi religious establishment, during the Cold War and the liberation of Afghanistan from Soviet occupation. After 9/11, however, the same religious establishment came under suspicion. The USA wanted ʿAbdullah to 'tame' religion in Saudi Arabia. ʿAbdullah sacked preachers and pledged to reform the Saʿudi educational curriculum. The Americans wanted to retain the Al Saʿud, but without the ideology that brought them to power and on the basis of which they derived their legitimacy. ʿAbdullah had to move cautiously because the religious establishment enjoyed the patronage of other princes. More importantly, abolishing Wahhabiyya would deprive the Al Saʿud of their *raison d'être*.

Both Crown Prince ʿAbdullah and the Americans knew that they were locked in an eternal marriage, cemented since the 1980s by King Fahd and ex-Saʿudi ambassador in Washington, the King's nephew, Bandar ibn Sultan. After 9/11, the question was how to continue the 'special relationship' without antagonising the in-laws on both sides. The American administration occasionally espoused the rhetoric of democratisation to silence an American constituency increasingly critical of the kingdom, its radical interpretation of Islam and its record on human rights. On the Saʿudi side, the departure of American troops stationed in the country to neighbouring Qatar was meant to pre-empt jihadi pledges to 'remove infidels from the Arabian Peninsula'. Neither measure silenced critical voices or prevented bombings. Terrorist attacks continued in Saudi Arabia; in fact, they increased in frequency and magnitude, before tailing off by 2005, while many Americans continued to ask whether Saudi Arabia was friend or foe.

New and old regional competitors

Saudi Arabia continued to work with other Gulf states under the auspices of the Gulf Cooperation Council. Because of its size, resources and importance to Islam, Saudi Arabia assumed greater weight than the other small Gulf states. It was the 'big brother' under whose cloak the smaller states operated while striving to maintain their individual economic, political and military autonomy. The advent of terrorism that reached places such as Kuwait and Qatar ensured that emphasis was placed on security and intelligence cooperation between the various Gulf countries. Some in the region expressed concern over Saʿudi religious preaching that reached their mosques, charities and religious education centres. Nevertheless, harmonious relations were maintained, only to be disturbed by a newly emerging actor, Qatar, which became more assertive and active in both regional and international politics under its relatively young, energetic leadership. Shaykh Hamad ibn Khalifa al-Thani overthrew his father in a bloodless coup in 1995 and endeavoured to challenge his country's marginality, assisted by its oil and gas resources. He rescued the BBC television Arabic service, a joint venture with Saudi Arabia, after the latter withdrew its support when this channel aired interviews with Saʿudi Islamists critical of the regime. Qatar adopted the project that became al-Jazeera in 1996. Qatar had old unresolved border disputes with Saudi Arabia, in addition to new ones following the coup of 1995, when Saudi Arabia sided with the overthrown Qatari amir against his son. Some Qatari officials accused Saudi Arabia of supporting dissident members of the al-Thani family to regain power after the 1995 coup (Blanchard 2008).

Between 2000 and 2007, Saʿudi relations with Qatar deteriorated, and almost reached the point of no return, with Qatar launching a media campaign against Saudi Arabia via its powerful and influential al-Jazeera channel. Qatari pressure on Saudi Arabia to resolve border disputes and facilitate new gas installations passing through Saʿudi territorial waters found an outlet in the media. Al-Jazeera, denied access to Saudi Arabia, managed to become the sole Arab television channel to allow strong criticism of Saʿudi policies, leadership, corruption and repression. It was the first time that media criticism of Saudi Arabia was initiated in the Gulf, rather than from Cairo or Baghdad, the traditional early platforms. The Saʿudi media retaliated and scrutinised Qatar's policies, especially when it expelled members of the al-Murra tribe to Saudi Arabia and withdrew their nationality. A Saʿudi-sponsored Arab newspaper in London published scathing personal attacks on the Qatari amir's wife, Shaykha Moza. In 2002 Saudi Arabia withdrew its ambassador from Qatar, while al-Jazeera continued its critical reporting on Saudi Arabia. Serious economic disputes arose in 2006 when Saudi Arabia objected to the UAE–Qatari Dolphin Undersea Natural Gas Pipeline project, on the grounds that the pipeline would pass through Saʿudi territorial waters without its approval. Saudi Arabia established al-Arabiyya television channel, based in Dubai, to counter the attacks of Qatar's al-Jazeera.

Relations with Qatar improved only in 2007 when Amir Hamad al-Thani visited Riyadh, initiating a rapprochement. This was followed in 2008 by a visit to Qatar by Prince Sultan, the Saʿudi minister of defence, who had been the subject of a damning al-Jazeera documentary on his alleged corruption in the al-Yamama arms deal with Britain.[12] Saudi Arabia announced its intention to return its ambassador to Qatar, perhaps on condition that the latter silence al-Jazeera's criticism of Saudi Arabia. In fact, from June 2008 al-Jazeera refrained from reporting on controversial Saʿudi issues.

The tension between Saudi Arabia and Qatar was part of a larger pattern. Within the Arab world, Saudi Arabia fell out with Syria over Lebanon and Hizbollah. The assassination of the pro-Saʿudi Lebanese prime minister, Rafiq al-Hariri, in 2005 and the Israeli war on Lebanon in 2006 opened a new chapter of antagonism between Syria and Saudi Arabia that replaced the cooperation of the 1990s, when Syria had offered troops to assist in the liberation of Kuwait. Saudi Arabia was critical of Hizbollah, blaming it for provoking Israel by kidnapping Israeli soldiers in the summer of 2006. Hizbollah's Syrian backers, together with Iran, became arch-enemies of Saudi Arabia. Syria's uncompromising position and reluctance to join the so-called moderate Arab axis, together with Iran's policies in Iraq and its nuclear weapon programme, created new politics in the region that have threatened to precipitate new military confrontations in both the Gulf and Lebanon. Saudi Arabia headed the axis of the so-called moderates, a coalition that included Egypt, Jordan and other Gulf states, while Iran supported the so-called radicals, among whom Syria, Hizbollah and Hamas were prominent.

At the beginning of the twenty-first century the Arab world looks divided and infested with small wars being fought along sectarian, tribal and ideological lines. The USA expects Saudi Arabia to play an important role in any future confrontation with Iran. At the heart of this situation lies the emergence of Iran as a regional hegemonic power, striving to penetrate the Arab world through the sponsorship of groups such as Hamas and Hizbollah, thus undermining the leadership role of Saudi Arabia, long awaited after Egypt removed itself from the Israeli–Palestinian crisis when it signed a peace treaty with Israel in 1979.

During Crown Prince ʿAbdullah's time as acting King, he revived the Arab peace initiative proposed in the Beirut Arab League summit in 2002. Neither the Palestinians nor the Israelis were enthusiastic about the initiative, as it failed to resolve the problems around the status of Jerusalem and the right of return for Palestinian refugees, as well as other details relating to Jewish settlements in the occupied territories and the 1967 borders. The Saʿudi-backed initiative failed to generate a consensus. Other problems emerged when the Islamist movement Hamas won an election and challenged the Palestinian Authority of Mahmoud Abbas. Palestinians fell into internal conflict and violence, which eventually led to Hamas establishing sole control over Gaza, leaving the Palestinian Authority confined to the West Bank. Saudi Arabia offered to mediate between the warring Palestinian factions, bringing them to Mecca in 2006 in an attempt to reach an agreement, end internal fighting and form a conciliatory national government.

In a similar vein, Saudi Arabia tried to mediate between Iraqi Sunnis and Shiʿa, who had been fighting a deadly sectarian war since 2003. Delegates representing Iraqi religious scholars, officials and factions met in Mecca under Saʿudi sponsorship, but failed to curb the violence or put an end to the sectarian and political conflict in Iraq. By 2008 it was clear that Saudi Arabia was not in a position to influence the situation in Iraq or facilitate a reconciliation between its various factions.

Saudi Arabia under ʿAbdullah aspired to a leading role in the Arab region, but its efforts collided with the new realities of the Arab world. Saudi Arabia is no longer a neutral player, able to appeal to Arab unity and Muslim solidarity. In Palestine and Lebanon it became entangled in a web of relations with certain factions, which compromised its mediation efforts. It sided with the official governments of both countries, losing the neutrality that would have allowed it to play a more constructive role in mediating conflict and diffusing tension. In Iraq, it confronted Iran head on. Its jihadis killed Iraqi Shiʿa, who turned violently against their Sunni compatriots. Iraq is no longer a place where Saudi Arabia can exert an influence. In the words of Saʿudi foreign minister Saʿud al-Faysal, the USA handed Iraq to the Iranians. Similarly, Syria moved closer to Iran and, under the pressure of ongoing media wars between the two countries, reconciliation with the Syrian regime became dependent on the latter withholding its cooperation with Iran and limiting Iran's influence among groups such as the Palestinian Jihad and Hamas and the Lebanese Hizbollah, all of which have close relations with both Syria and Iran.

In the twenty-first century, Saudi Arabia managed to rise above its own internal problems and remain relatively stable compared to the turbulent situation in other Arab countries. The performance of the economy improved, although unemployment and uneven development continued to affect the majority of Saʿudis. While terrorism subsided in 2007 and 2008, the government announced that it would take a long time for the battle against radicalism to be won. Both Saʿudi royalty and society, the subject of the next chapter, are gradually stretching the boundaries, the former experimenting with limited religious and social reforms, hoping to modernise authoritarian rule, while the latter is engaging with new forms of mobilisation and defiance.

CHAPTER 9

Modernising authoritarian rule

In the post 9/11 period, the Saʿudi state faced mounting pressure to appropriate the rhetoric of reform and introduce a series of reformist measures and promises, although none posed a serious challenge to the rule of the Al Saʿud. This involved the opening up of the public sphere to quasi-independent civil society associations, limited municipal elections and a relatively free press. Reform of the royal house, aimed at dealing with possible future problematic succession to the throne, was also part of a general trend. The first part of this chapter deals with state-initiated reforms whose objective was to modernise authoritarian rule without risking the loss of too much power to the constituency.[1]

Equally, Saʿudi society showed unprecedented social mobilisation and activism, triggered by increasing globalisation, the proliferation of the discourse on democratisation, human and minority rights, and demands for political participation. Locally, the shock of terrorist violence brought Saʿudi intellectuals face to face with the shortcomings of their religious, political and economic conditions, which were labelled breeding-grounds for the violence that erupted in the twenty-first century. Academics, religious scholars, lawyers, writers, journalists, women and minorities all demanded new forms of governance to replace the traditional authoritarian practices of coercion, surveillance, exclusion and patronage. The second part of this chapter discusses the mobilisation of Saʿudi society, which centred on new demands and aspirations different from those promoted by the Islamist contestation of the 1990s.

THE STATE REFORMIST AGENDA

The National Dialogue Forum 2003

Faced with violent terrorist attacks, the government realised that its security and intelligence agencies could only deal with some aspects of the problem;

it needed to enlist society itself to fight the menace and defend the realm. It reached out to official *ʿulama*, established religious institutions, academics, writers and journalists, hoping to enlist them in a newly founded forum, the King ʿAbd al-ʿAziz Centre for National Dialogue. In August 2003 the government announced the formation of a new platform that would assemble carefully selected intellectuals and professionals to engage in open debate about pressing social, religious and cultural issues, according to a predetermined agenda. The government issued a declaration regarding the first meeting, which

> attracted the elite of the country and in the spirit of fraternity and Islam, they held discussions on national matters and reached constructive recommendations that enhance adherence to the Islamic faith and confirm national unity . . . The main objective is to combat extremism and foster a pure atmosphere that give[s] rise to wise positions and illuminating ideas that reject terrorism and terrorist thought . . . the dialogue will not accept turning freedom into obscene abuse, name calling or attacking the national and good ulama.[2]

This statement set the parameters for future dialogue sessions, while excluding any reference to political reforms that might challenge the rule of the house of Saʿud.

The National Dialogue Forum became an annual event, held in various cities. Meetings have taken place in Riyadh, Madina, Mecca, Jeddah and Buraydah. Each year, the government-appointed organising committee announces a new topic for discussion and recruits speakers, who prepare presentations relevant to the chosen subject. Topics have included terrorism and extremism, religious excess and moderation, religious tolerance and difference, youth problems, education, labour and women's rights. After discussions lasting several days, the meetings end with a series of recommendations, which remain non-binding and without an executive body to implement them. The recommendations are usually listed in a letter addressed to the King. According to the National Dialogue general secretary, Faysal ibn Muamar, the recommendations are advisory and not legislative, but 'there are ideas that are currently under study to take into more serious actionable consideration . . . everyone is calling for implementation of the recommendations according to a timetable'.[3] It is understood that these recommendations will inform the relevant government agencies and policy makers.

The National Dialogue Forums were initially closed to the general public, but after a few years they were broadcast on television. This carefully staged forum has become a public event attracting commentators, supporters and critics. With the proliferation of internet discussion boards and other new communication technology, such as text messaging and Youtube, it has become possible for Saʿudis outside the annual forums to debate and discuss the merits of these institutionalised new platforms.

The first National Dialogue session was held in Riyadh in June 2003, a month after the first major terrorist blast hit the capital and three months after the occupation of Iraq. The severity of the terrorist attack and the shadow of the occupation shaped the theme and agenda of the meeting. While no specific recommendations were formulated, calls for respect of the leadership and national unity emerged from the first preparatory event organised by the National Dialogue Committee.

The second National Dialogue meeting was held in Mecca in December 2003. Its theme was Extremism and Moderation, thus reflecting the government's agenda to combat terrorism and extract a public statement denouncing violence and rejecting its ideological discourse. Sixty academics and experts in various fields, ranging from *shariʿa* specialists to sociologists, psychologists, media specialists and educationists, took part in the meeting. The participating *ʿulama* emphasised the middle path of Islam (*al-waṣatiyya*); psychologists theorised the personality disorder of the terrorist; sociologists highlighted the contributing environmental, social and educational factors; economists stressed the relevance of marginalisation and economic deprivation; political scientists highlighted the importance of participation and human rights; and media specialists debated the role of the media, freedom of expression and the reporting of religious sermons. After several sessions of discussion, eighteen recommendations were announced, stressing above all the need for national unity and tolerance of difference. Some recommendations addressed the need to agree on definitions of Islamic concepts that mark the boundaries between Muslims and non-Muslims. The proliferation of unsolicited *fatawa* and religious opinions should be limited and subjected to control and scrutiny, according to one recommendation. Other recommendations called for widening political participation through elections and civil society institutions. On terrorism, a recommendation to rehabilitate and re-educate those who repent was endorsed. In general, the meeting backed government measures to enlist institutions and people who contribute to the public sphere through sermons, publications, lectures, education and social work to support the state in its efforts to end the wave of violence that had erupted in Saudi Arabia.[4]

Successive National Dialogue Forums dealt with women's issues, their role in society and contribution to it (June 2004). Women participated in the meeting and presented their views on matters related to their current situation and future economic prospects in a country where they form the majority of university graduates but remain marginalised in the labour force. Clashes between those who support more traditional roles for women and those who aspire towards greater participation and visibility erupted during the meeting. The latter were accused of promoting a Western agenda, the purpose of which was to destabilise society and threaten its Islamic piety and authenticity. The debate ended without serious consideration of the major challenge of absorbing the increasing number of educated women into the Saʿudi economy. Some female participants thought that conservatives and traditionalists had hijacked the meeting. This prompted them to send a separate list of recommendations to Crown Prince ʿAbdullah, who met privately with a small number of female delegates.

Dialogue meetings on the youth, their radicalisation, current unemployment and future development were less heated. Participants called for an acknowledgement of the role young Saʿudis, who constitute the majority in the demographic profile of the country, can play in the future, and how this needs to be encouraged and supported through youth programmes, training and employment. These measures are considered a shield against apathy and boredom, both of which may lead to extremism and destructive, anti-social behaviour.

The government had two objectives behind the institutionalisation of the Dialogue Forums. First, it was responding to the international media scrutiny of Saudi Arabia that followed 9/11. The image of Saudi Arabia as a closed, secretive society, with limited public debate, needed to be corrected – and even reversed. While the government allowed international and global media to carry out investigative journalism on its soil for the first time, it endeavoured to create an atmosphere of openness and transparency through staged dialogue and consultation.

Second, the government was desperate to enlist civil society in taking responsibility for curbing the extremism and violence of the first years of the twenty-first century. One recurrent theme in all National Dialogue sessions was terrorism. This has confirmed the National Dialogue in its role as a platform whereby participants from various intellectual and professional backgrounds denounce violence, reconsider their previous ideological orientations, and assert their allegiance to the state and commitment to national unity.

The National Dialogue Forum is a state-run association, created under both internal and international pressure, to diffuse tension, alter perceptions, involve society in dialogue with the leadership and deliver loyalty. As such, the meetings are far from being an independent initiative, organised and run by autonomous civil society associations, although the government and the civil servants in charge of organisation have endeavoured to fix them in the public imagination as free platforms for consultation. The early enthusiasm surrounding the first meetings gave way to apathy, prompting one journalist to comment on the body language of participants in a later Jeddah session, some of whom looked as if they were enjoying a siesta during a hot afternoon in a five-star hotel. The euphoria surrounding this new initiative faded away with routinisation and regularity.[5]

Many Saʿudis welcomed the initiative at first, as it gave intellectuals and professionals with different orientations an opportunity to present ideas, research findings and hope to influence policy; yet many realised that this dialogue would not produce serious political change.[6] Political reform was simply not on the agenda, as later events, discussed in this chapter, proved. Serious political change remains elusive. The government proved resistant to calls for constitutional change that would bring an elected national *shura* council to replace the 120-member appointed consultative body, the *majlis al-shura*. Allegiance to the leadership and consensus over its reform agenda was sought after each meeting. Social, security, religious and economic themes dominated the forums, with no prospect of a serious political reform agenda finding its way to the top of the list of themes to be discussed. Bluntly put, the National Dialogue is a step towards modernisation of authoritarian rule, without any serious impact on the course political reform takes in Saudi Arabia. It embodies a strong patronising and paternalistic approach towards Saʿudi society and its public intellectual and professional figures, who were meant to learn the alphabet of debate rather than push their own reform agenda on the government. Instead of critically assessing the merits of the National Dialogue, the Saʿudi official press highlighted the absence of public dialogue (*thaqafat al-ḥiwar*), which only confirmed the state narrative about the infantile and backward condition of Saʿudi society. Many applauded the state for educating its citizens in how to debate public issues within the limited confines of a government-sponsored national dialogue. The Saʿudi state invited its citizens to identify their culpability for the violence on the street, but ensured that the discussion would never allude to the direct role of the state and its religious institutions in creating the conditions that gave rise to the jihadi terrorism, both globally and locally. No discussant dared to link the violence to the wider political context or to previous foreign policy measures, such as involvement in the Afghan *jihad* in the 1980s, when the government appeased Islamists by succumbing to their agenda and increasing its sponsorship of Islamic education and charities, to boost its own Islamic credentials. Instead, participants scrutinised society, its conservatism and intolerance of difference, all believed to have contributed to the terrorist crisis in the country. Intellectuals and religious scholars were invited to engage in self-criticism and profess loyalty to the leadership.

Nevertheless, the National Dialogue Forums should not simply be dismissed as window dressing. The fact that Saʿudis were brought from all sectors and intellectual backgrounds to debate important topics long considered taboo, and only discussed behind closed doors, is an achievement in itself, in a country where top-down policy has been a feature of governance for many decades. Whether the forums will directly influence policy is yet to be seen. So far the government's social, religious and educational reforms have incorporated aspects of the forums' recommendations. In the area of religious education and youth development programmes, one may find traces of uncontroversial ideas discussed during the forums' sessions. For example, the government declared its intention to reform the religious curriculum in schools, and sacked preachers known for 'extremist' ideas. It also announced that 2,000 mosque *imams* who had violated prohibitions against the preaching of intolerance had been suspended from their positions, and 1,500 were sent for re-education (Royal Embassy of Saudi Arabia 2004). It also announced programmes to modernise education in general and improve foreign language skills, in response to improving the educational profile of young people and their competitiveness in an open labour market. But the government still resists formally opening the public sphere to women, although it is gradually giving them limited space in public events and in the media. Female journalists appear at official public events and report on them for newly founded satellite television channels such as al-Ikhbariyya. Businesswomen have also participated in economic forums held in Jeddah, and some accompanied Crown Prince ʿAbdullah on foreign trips to the USA, China and India. These symbolic acts were directed towards an international audience, eager to report on the new wave of social *infitaḥ* (openness), clarifying the Saʿudi enigma and lifting the veil on its most hidden secrets. The leadership capitalised on this opportunity to project an image of a country undergoing gradual social and economic modernisation that nevertheless remains grounded in its Islamic traditions and faithful to its authentic culture. Critical voices, especially those of the marginalised traditional ʿ*ulama*, were raised to condemn the increased visibility of women in the public sphere, but the leadership simply felt confident enough to ignore them.

So far the government has ignored calls to establish a separate ministry for women and social affairs, and has resisted removing women from the guardianship of their male relatives, or even allowing them to drive cars. Women were totally absent from local municipal elections, both as voters and as candidates. The exclusion of Saʿudi women from public life and the restrictions they face with respect to labour and movement have remained high on the agenda of international human rights organisations, without the Saʿudi leadership taking any notice of their critical opinions. The government often uses the pretext of *khuṣuṣiya*, the uniqueness of the Islamic tradition of Saudi Arabia, to opt out of implementing international treaties on the elimination of gender discrimination and religious freedoms.

Municipal elections 2005

The same external pressures that prompted the Saʿudi leadership to stage the National Dialogue Forums, coupled with internal demands for reform, led to an announcement of the intention to modernise local municipal councils that deal with the delivery of services in the thirteen provincial regions of Saudi Arabia. In October 2003 the Council of Ministers announced the broadening of citizen participation in the municipalities: half of their members were to be elected, and the remaining half appointed. This announcement led to the organisation of municipal elections in February 2005.

Major administrative cities began to prepare voting stations. Eligible male voters were invited to register and receive voting cards. In Riyadh, the number of registered voters did not exceed 18 per cent of those eligible to vote, representing only 2 per cent of the population of the city (Menoret 2005: 2). A great level of interest, reflected in the high proportion of registration and participation, was evident in the eastern province, the home of a substantial Shiʿa minority. In the small Shiʿa city of Qatif, 46,000 registered voters were counted, almost half the number of those in the capital.

In all cities, candidates were mainly local businessmen, activists and professionals, who came from different backgrounds. Most of the candidates (60 per cent) held university degrees. Some had Islamist orientations, while others were identified as leaning towards a liberal agenda, or simply drawing on their tribal capital. The Islamists were supported by endorsements from known public figures and religious scholars, who praised the candidates' piety and commitment to public good. Drawing on both modern campaigning strategies, through SMS messaging and the internet, and on traditional hospitality, the Islamist candidates secured most of the seats in big Saʿudi cities such as Riyadh and Jeddah and smaller ones such as Madina, Tabuq and Taʾif (Menoret 2005).

The election results reflected the changing composition of the population of cities that now host a large proportion of the Saʿudi middle class. This class has been growing steadily since the 1970s. Most of its members are employed in the public sector, but many have recently found opportunities in the growing private sector. The liberalisation of the economy promises to increase their numbers and lessen their dependence on employment in the government bureaucracy. They have expertise in administration and employment, and display entrepreneurial spirit. Election candidates sought the prestige of being elected rather than simply appointed to public office. Some of them were wealthy enough to sponsor their own election campaigns, which involved entertaining hundreds of potential voters, and offering hospitality prior to election dates.

The success of the so-called moderate Islamists in the municipal elections reflected the weakness of those with a more liberal orientation. The latter had relatively limited popularity and engagement with Saʿudi society. Commentators on the elections pointed to their marginalisation; they had no access to public forums, unlike the Islamists, who capitalised on the support of important religious scholars in key institutions of education, mosques, charities and administration.

The elections were significant but limited. They generated unprecedented euphoria, and reflected the readiness of Saʿudi society to engage with modern democratic procedures, despite its lack of democratic institutions and a vibrant civil society. In some respects, the elections brought the trappings of democracy without posing a serious challenge to authoritarian rule. There were some reports that the elected councillors did not meet even months after being elected to office. Some elected members resigned two years after being elected to municipal councils as a result of frustration and inability to reach decisions on the delivery of services.

Despite government's efforts to launch what was dubbed a historic opportunity to engage citizens in the functioning and administration of their regional municipal councils, it seems that 'Saudi citizens took a sceptical or apathetic view of these elections' (Menoret 2005). This is attributed to the fact that municipalities are seen as having limited authority, as they are mainly concerned with delivering basic services, and have no power to influence budget allocation or land development. Two years after the elections, a Saʿudi commentator stressed that 'the municipal councils proved to be powerless . . . more than half the decisions have not been carried out. Most of the others have been in support of central government' (*New York Times*, 26 April 2007).

The elections remain, nevertheless, an important step towards modernising an authoritarian government that has been put under both international and local pressure to institute reform. Saudi Arabia was seen as catching up with other Arab authoritarian regimes: the euphoria of local and national elections in some Arab countries in 2005 reflected widespread hope for a broader reformist agenda, starting with economic and social change, but which fell short of altering the structure of authoritarian rule, limiting the abuse of human rights, or restricting the coercive security measures of the regimes. The elections in Saudi Arabia were the result of a top-down decision implemented in a society with limited independent institutions and little freedom of assembly. Saʿudi society remains weak vis-à-vis the state, which prohibits communal action, with the exception of that which takes place under government sponsorship and authorisation. From literary salons to sports clubs, camel pageants, poetry recitations and elections to journalists' and commerce associations, the state controls the seeds of potential civil society and independent mobilisation. Through paternalism and patronage, it co-opts groups and creates the semblance of liberalisation. Nothing exemplifies these strategies like the move to establish a human rights watchdog.

Co-opting human rights

Saudi Arabia has acceded to four United Nations conventions: the International Convention on the Elimination of All Forms of Racial Discrimination (1997); the Convention on the Elimination of All Forms of Discrimination Against Women (2000); the Convention Against Torture and Other Cruel, Inhuman or Degrading Treatment or Punishment (1997); and the Convention on the Rights of the Child (1996).[7] However, in 2004 Saudi Arabia was one of the few countries in the world that did not have local independent organisations promoting, monitoring and defending human rights.

With mounting global pressure and a greater opening of communication and media channels, the discourse on human rights and reports on Saʿudi violation of human rights circulated in the global public sphere, and reached the public in Saudi Arabia itself. The United Nations' human rights forums, Amnesty International, Human Rights Watch and Arab human rights organisations continued to monitor and publicise abuses in Saudi Arabia. These centred on the plight of immigrant workers, political prisoners, human trafficking and women, as well as children's and minority rights.

In 2004 a group of Saʿudi activists and reformers held meetings with a view to establishing the first independent human rights organisation, which they called al-Lajna al-Ahliyya li Ḥuquq al-Insan (Human Rights Social Committee). The group included journalists, writers, academics and lawyers from all regions of the country. In a pre-emptive strike, the government announced the establishment of a new body, the Human Rights Commission (HRC), following a royal decree signed by the head of the Council of Ministers. According to the royal decree, the HRC is linked directly to the Council of Ministers; its objective is to protect human rights, according to international treaties and charters. The head of the HRC is appointed directly by the head of the Council of Ministers. Membership in the HRC consisted of eighteen appointed full-time members and six part-timers, headed by Turki al-Sudayri.[8] It did not begin its work until 2007.

While the HRC was obviously a government watchdog rather than an independent civil society association, another organisation emerged that struggled to maintain the semblance of independence. The National Society for Human Rights (NSHR) was established to implement international human rights charters signed by Saudi Arabia, according to government publicity (Royal Embassy of Saudi Arabia 2004). The NSHR had forty-one members, most of them occupying government positions. Like the HRC, this new body assumed the status of a government-approved rather than an independent non-governmental organisation (International Crisis Group 2004: 20). It established a website,[9] issued newsletters, published annual reports and received complaints. It became a link with representatives from independent international human rights organisations such as Amnesty International and Human Rights Watch. It received researchers from international organisations and facilitated their research and visits to Saudi Arabia, becoming a gatekeeper, a point of entry to those who explored the human rights situation in Saudi Arabia.

The NSHR opened a complaints section on its website. This currently includes a plethora of serious grievances regarding violations of labour rights, the abuse of women and other personal security violations. Aggrieved individuals are invited to post summaries of their cases, with the promise that the NSHR will take them up with the relevant authorities or government departments.

In 2008 the activity section of the NSHR's website was, however, empty – perhaps reflecting the organisation's limited scope for action and lobbying. Nevertheless, the NSHR has taken the cases of Saʿudi prisoners in Guantánamo Bay on board, and occasionally posts an update on their plight. Similarly, the case of a Saʿudi prisoner in an Israeli prison is regularly highlighted. The NSHR also publicises the cases of Saʿudi prisoners in Lebanon and Iraq, where many are detained on suspicion of engaging in terrorist activities.

So far, however, the NSHR has not publicised the plight of prisoners of opinion, political activists or dissidents held in Saʿudi prisons without trial for several years. It has refrained from mentioning any violation of human rights by Saʿudi security agencies, the Ministry of the Interior, or the Committee for the Propagation of Virtue and Prohibition of Vice. Independent lawyers, for example ʿAbd al-Raḥman al-Laḥim, have worked on cases involving women who have been raped and deaths resulting from confrontation with the religious police. Most of the complaints published on the NSHR's website are related to domestic violence against women, child abuse and other non-political cases. The society does not concern itself with general rights such as freedom of opinion and assembly or the right to hold national elections or demonstrations in the country. The fact that its members are government employees raises doubts about its neutrality and independence. In May 2008 a Saʿudi academic, Matruk al-Faleh, was dragged from his office by security agents; one of his colleagues in the political science department of King Saʿud University, a member of the NSHR, has been unable to publicise his case. Al-Faleh's arrest followed a letter he circulated on the internet about the terrible state of Saʿudi prisons, where one of his colleagues, ʿAbdullah al-Ḥamid, had been serving a six-month prison sentence for inciting female relatives of prisoners to assemble in front of a prison in Buraydah where their husbands, fathers and brothers had been detained without trial for several years. Such cases highlight the limitations of the NSHR, exposing it as yet another cosmetic move towards modernising authoritarian rule without posing a serious challenge to old practices.

Despite the establishment of a government body (the HRC) and a government-approved organisation (the NSHR) with a mandate to protect and monitor human rights, conditions remain poor, according to international sources.[10]

In paying lip service to human rights, Crown Prince ʿAbdullah capitalised on his newly constructed image as champion of reform, while many Saʿudis continued to experience the excesses and abuses of authoritarian rule in their daily lives. Small measures such as the municipal elections, the HRC and the NSHR are important symbolic acts that diffuse tension, respond to international pressure and confirm the leading role of the King. The leadership does not, however, respond favourably to reform initiatives if they originate in Saʿudi civil society. Any successful step towards greater political participation must have the patronage of royalty. Equally, the protection and monitoring of human rights are better served by top-down organisations that are closely linked to the highest level of leadership. Reform from above remains the acceptable path towards small gains by the constituency. The state reform agenda became the key to preparing the constituency for a new era – that of the new King.

A NEW KING

When King Fahd finally died in August 2005, the royal family respected the line of succession and installed ʿAbdullah as King, while each powerful senior prince remained secure in his position as head of a key government office.

It was hoped that ʿAbdullah's birth in 1924, a result of King ʿAbd al-ʿAziz ibn Saʿud's strategy of marrying the daughters and widows of defeated historical enemies, would end the enmity between the ousted northern Haʾil emirate (see chapter 2) and the newly emerging Saʿudi kingdom. ʿAbdullah's Shammari mother, Fahda bint ʿAsi al-Shraym, was the widow of Saʿud ibn Rashid, who ruled over the Rashidi emirate before its collapse at the hands of the Saʿudi–Wahhabi forces in 1921. ʿAbdullah continued the tradition of his father, and included among his many wives daughters of the al-Shaʿlan of ʿAniza, al-Fayz of Bani Ṣakhr and al-Jarba of the Iraqi branch of the Shammar tribe.

On the basis of his mother's background, a plethora of images were cultivated around ʿAbdullah. Images of the King as the repository of the tribal Arab–bedouin heritage flourished as Saudi Arabia drifted into globalisation and consumer culture. Having had a traditional upbringing in the royal court and with no formal modern instruction, ʿAbdullah capitalised on this heritage. His maternal connections and limited education, together with an early speech impediment, had delayed his rise to stardom among the many sons of the founder of the kingdom, Ibn Saʿud.

It was only in 1962, thirty years after its foundation, that ʿAbdullah secured a permanent position in the Saʿudi kingdom. He became commander of the Saʿudi National Guard, a military force consisting of the early tribal warriors who had conquered vast territories for the Al Saud in the name of *jihad* against Arabian blasphemy. In 1929, once the conquests were achieved, this tribal force was regularised and rebellious groups were rooted out, with the help of the British Royal Air Force. The loyalists were assembled in small units forming a paramilitary force whose task was to protect the royal house. Under ʿAbdullah's leadership this force developed into a modern tribal militia, on a par with the Saʿudi army, which was led by Prince Sultan. In 1985 ʿAbdullah made the National Guard the sponsor of tribal heritage, folk dances, camel races and tribal poetry through the institutionalisation of the Janadiriyya festival. ʿAbdullah became second deputy prime minister in 1975, and first deputy prime minister in 1982.

As Crown Prince, ʿAbdullah became de facto ruler in 1995, following the prolonged illness of King Fahd (1982–2005), and King in August 2005. His main challenge was to retain power amidst an ageing group of powerful princes, each desperate to become King.

ʿAbdullah inherited a kingdom torn by ideologically opposed groups, unemployment, corruption, insecurity and terrorism, yet enjoying a second oil boom. In 1995 his National Guard in Riyadh was forced to confront terrorism, when an important building housing Americans providing military training support was blown up. The trend was repeated in the oil-rich eastern province when al-Khobar Towers were bombed in 1996.

ʿAbdullah tried to deal with urgent domestic concerns. The restructuring of the Saʿudi economy, along with joining the World Trade Organisation and speedy privatisation, failed to absorb young, unemployed Saʿudis. Women's employment became an issue in need of urgent remedies. Ethnic, sectarian and regional tensions erupted with the occupation of Iraq and the increasing polarisation between Sunnis and Shiʿa in the region. The education system was called into question for its failure to produce skilled workers, and was criticised for inspiring radicalism. State religion itself became problematic, and was questioned not only by the USA but also by Saʿudis.

Many Saʿudis urged ʿAbdullah to act on pressing social, educational, youth and economic issues when he was Crown Prince during the long illness of King Fahd. A minority considered these problems a reflection of the political marginalisation of society and the limited opportunities for political participation. Some began to call for a radical transformation of the political system from absolute to constitutional monarchy.

Unable to engage in serious internal political reforms, ʿAbdullah invested in his reputation abroad. Regional Arab politics is always fertile ground for boosting Arab leaders' credibility and for diverting attention from shortcomings at home. Following the footsteps of previous Arab rulers, he concentrated on Palestine. His Arab peace initiative, initially presented to *New York Times* journalist Thomas Friedman, and re-launched during the Beirut Arab League summit in 2002, failed to bring peace in return for land. ʿAbdullah proposed peace in return for an Israeli withdrawal to the 1967 borders, pressed for the right of return for Palestinian refugees, and called for a Palestinian state with Jerusalem as its capital. Israel did not accept.

The initiative's revival in March 2007 did not bring tangible results among the warring Palestinians and Israelis. With the accession of Hamas to power in Gaza, internal Palestinian conflict erupted between this organisation and Fatah. Drawing on Mecca's symbolic significance in the imagination of Muslims, ʿAbdullah endeavoured to hold meetings there to reconcile the warring Palestinian factions. Fighting continued, and claimed many lives.

In April 2003 the USA's occupation of Iraq removed a regional competitor. ʿAbdullah, together with other Gulf rulers, breathed a short-lived sigh of relief over the demise of Saddam's regime. Little did they know that the occupation would unleash one of the most deadly and bloody wars in the history of the Arab world close to their borders. Nobody expected that the promised model democracy in Iraq would pose any threat to other dictators in the region. However, thoughts as to how to contain the ongoing Iraqi sectarian war and the newly established al-Qaʿidah in Iraq became urgent issues for ʿAbdullah. More importantly, Iran with its nuclear programme emerged as the new regional power, dictating not only the outcome of the Iraq war but also interfering in the very fabric of Arab society and politics, through its patronage of Shiʿa communities and Sunni political groups. With a substantial Shiʿa minority in the oil-rich Saʿudi eastern province, ʿAbdullah became nervous over the emerging Shiʿa power.

ʿAbdullah, together with Mubarak of Egypt and King ʿAbdullah of Jordan, expressed alarm over the emerging so-called 'Shiʿa crescent'. Protecting the interests of Iraqi Sunni co-religionists was problematic given the complexity of the Iraqi scene and the presence of al-Qaʿidah, which also presented itself as a defender of the Sunnis. ʿAbdullah denounced sectarian killings and insisted on the unity of the Iraqi state. Once again Mecca, where the warring Iraqi Sunni and Shiʿa leaders and religious scholars pledged to outlaw the shedding of Muslim blood, proved to be a good place to hold a meeting under Saʿudi patronage. However, neither this meeting nor an increased US military presence stopped suicide bombers targeting civilians in Iraqi cities.

Iran's growing influence in the region needed a counter-force to balance it. The USA looked to Saudi Arabia, but failed to recognise that, although he was sitting on vast oil revenues, ʿAbdullah's credentials were very thin even among Sunni Muslims in the region. Above all, ʿAbdullah was not able to use the wisdom of old age, traditional authority or charisma to his advantage to claim a special place among Arab rulers. Saudi Arabia had striven to replace Egypt after the latter's ascendancy in 1979, but ʿAbdullah could not, nearly three decades later, fill the vacuum as his brother King Faysal had done.

The thirty-three-day Israeli–Hizbollah war in the summer of 2006 and the Saʿudi failure to push for an immediate ceasefire further eroded ʿAbdullah's credibility. As the Israeli press ran several articles praising ʿAbdullah, and the Saʿudi-owned media, echoing official Saʿudi statements, referred to Hizbollah's war with Israel as an 'adventure', the King's reputation, both inside Saudi Arabia and in the wider Arab world, was questioned. During that summer, ʿAbdullah fell out with Bashar al-Asad of Syria, who referred to defeated Arab rulers as 'half-men'. After that war, the polarisation of Arab politics between the so-called moderates, under the leadership of Saudi Arabia, and the radicals, under Iran's patronage, became more acute, and ʿAbdullah's ability to reconcile the two camps disappeared.

In addition to the rift with Syria over Lebanon and previous tension with Libya over an alleged attempt to assassinate him, ʿAbdullah could not contain the animosity of other partners within the Gulf Cooperation Council (GCC). The deterioration of relations with Qatar over territorial disputes and the blunt media approach of al-Jazeera created an uneasy relationship with this small but wealthy emerging state. The old Egyptian–Saʿudi rivalry occasionally surfaced as Egypt was not enthusiastic over building a bridge joining Sharm al-Shaykh and Saudi Arabia. Both still compete over the leadership of the Arab world, and are equally desperate to claim credit for cooling off Arab hot spots.

As the new King, ʿAbdullah needed a powerful media campaign to inscribe in the imagination of his people and the international community the beginning of a new era. The funeral of King Fahd was broadcast on Saʿudi-owned satellite television channels, followed by images of the new King receiving the oath of allegiance from a wide range of constituencies representing different sections of Saʿudi society. Members of the royal family promoted the semblance of unity and accepted ʿAbdullah as King. Key princes knew that his rule would not undermine their position or threaten their well-established control over policy, financial allocations or influence in the state. ʿAbdullah appointed Sultan Crown Prince and confirmed the other princes in their ministerial positions. The position of a second deputy, a long-established role, remained vacant.

ʿAbdullah immediately set about dismantling the old image of the monarchy and replacing it with a new set of constructions. The old façade of a prince close to conservatism, tradition and tribal values was replaced with that of a modern monarch, a champion of reform and the eradicator of poverty. He toured the various Saʿudi provinces, danced with his subjects and promised the alleviation of hardship and deprivation. His royal tours had one aim: to tie the constituency to the new realm and enforce his role as the leader. Yet the King knew that his ability to push for serious political reform was curtailed by other powerful senior princes, especially those who controlled the regime's internal and external security, namely the ministers of the interior and defence. The internal confrontation between the state and al-Qaʿidah from 2003 only highlighted the central role these ministries played in Saudi Arabia. Although ʿAbdullah himself was in command of the Saʿudi National Guard, he was only able to balance the influence of the other princes rather than determine the general evolution of the political affairs of the kingdom. He had to accept the fragmentation of Saʿudi politics and the proliferation of decision-making centres within the state. ʿAbdullah became the champion of the modernisation of authoritarian rule in Saudi Arabia.[11]

Reforming the royal house: the Committee of Allegiance

In October 2007, in the face of the fragmentation of royal politics and the consolidation of powerful contestants to the throne, ʿAbdullah started the first initiative to reform the internal affairs of the royal house. He announced by royal decree the establishment of the so-called Committee of Allegiance, whose main function is to ensure a smooth succession to the throne after the deaths of King ʿAbdullah and Crown Prince Sultan. The committee came into existence in December 2007, when King ʿAbdullah received its members and urged them to 'stand united, settling any differences by transparent dialogue and without allowing external forces to interfere in their private affairs' (*Arab News*, 11 December 2007). The committee consisted of thirty-five members: the surviving sons of the kingdom's founder, Ibn Saʿud, and the sons of those who had already died. Old and ill princes were represented by their sons. Prince Mishal, former deputy defence minister and governor of Mecca, was appointed its chairman. The only commoner on the committee is Khalid al-Towayjri, the head of the royal court (*diwan*), who was appointed as clerk (*amin sir*).

The committee's constitution states that it will become active only after the deaths of King ʿAbdullah and his successor, Sultan. Given the age of the surviving sons of Ibn Saʿud, the committee is meant to 'elect' a king by consensus from among them or their sons. Under its regulations, once a king dies the committee holds a meeting in order to officially name the new king. Within ten days, the new king must name his crown prince, or he may ask the committee to nominate one. In anticipation of old age and illness, the committee statute includes the setting up of a medical committee to report on the health of the king and crown prince. It will submit its report in a sealed envelope and in secrecy to the chairman of the committee, who can make it available to other members in the context of the committee's meeting.

The Committee of Allegiance is an institutionalised mechanism whose main purpose is to regulate the transfer of office from one King to another should the succession be unclear in the event of the deaths of King ʿAbdullah and Crown Prince Sultan.[12] The previous principle of succession, which determined the transfer of kingship horizontally among the sons of Ibn Saʿud, may not be possible in the future; thus the committee introduces the possibility of either skipping a senior prince or princes, and even moving vertically to a grandson of the founder of Saudi Arabia. Old age and ill health, both of which already affect the existing potential heirs to the throne, may pose future challenges to the succession. The existing sons of Ibn Saʿud are all in their late seventies and eighties, and are likely to suffer prolonged illness, as King Fahd did. To safeguard against the accession of an aged, incapacitated king to the throne, just because the horizontal seniority principle needs to be respected as it had been in the past, the committee allows the election of a king by bypassing unfit ones or even choosing one from among members of the second generation. In theory, the committee would ensure consensus among contestants by electing a future king and crown prince. Yet it remains to be seen whether this process will deliver a smooth succession in the future, especially when members of the second generation enter the contest for leadership at the highest level, following the deaths of King ʿAbdullah and Crown Prince Sultan.

While awaiting this eventuality, each key senior prince has placed one or more of his sons as deputies and aides. The sons of current king, crown prince, minister of the interior, minister of defence and other junior princes are in key government positions, well placed to push for leadership roles in the future. It is likely that sons of the current senior princes will inherit their fathers' ministries in case of sudden death, yet it may prove to be more complicated if members of the second generation enter competition for the kingship. The prospect of Muhammad ibn Nayef, Mutib ibn ʿAbdullah, Bandar ibn Sultan, Khalid ibn Sultan or even al-Walid ibn Ṭalal competing for kingship may prove to be a real challenge for the Committee of Allegiance. Currently neither King ʿAbdullah nor other senior princes can adopt a vertical succession principle that would exclude the surviving sons of Ibn Saʿud and their descendants in favour of placing kingship within the confines of one line of descent. For the time being, the committee may be the best option available to the royal house to tidy its internal affairs, in the absence of real and possible intervention from Saʿudi society or competition within the royal household.

The Committee of Allegiance is proof that politics and leadership are the domain of royalty, outside the influence of any other body in the kingdom. The absolute monarchy persists regardless of any pressure, internal or external, for greater political inclusion and participation. The royal family excluded Saʿudi society, or what is often called 'the people who tie and loose' (*ahl al-ḥal wa al-ʿaqd*), from dealing with an issue seen as a strictly royal prerogative. The committee is meant to deliver the candidate for kingship to the Saʿudi people, who would later offer their oath of allegiance. Saudi Arabia does not have institutions or pressure groups that would push for the appointment of one man as King at the expense of another contestant. Even the religious establishment is not represented or consulted by the committee. There is no elected representative body that may influence the committee's decision. The battle for the future King will be fought and resolved among royalty in secret meetings. This new arrangement ensures the continuity of the monarchy against the hazards of demography, internal competition and conflict, and in isolation from society or pressure groups outside the royal house.

Development as alternative to political reform

Having secured the bureaucratisation of royal succession, the King, senior princes and royal entrepreneurs turned to the constituency in an attempt to win its acquiescence. The old mechanism of distributing largesse was revived with the new wealth of 2003. In a manner reminiscent of the 1970s, royalty entered a race to distribute surplus, increase dependency and win loyalty. The revenues are now not only more substantial but are also the sources of largesse. Each prince and his sons became centres for the distribution of handouts, job opportunities in their own private financial and business institutions, and other benefits to which citizens could not gain access through the usual state welfare bureaucracies.

Educational scholarships were reinstated after a period of disruption and slowdown in the 1980s and 1990s. Both men and women were sent abroad on government scholarships, while others enrolled in newly established local institutes and training colleges. Yet none were guaranteed employment upon completing their studies. Rising inflation and basic food prices were dealt with by regular increases in salaries. The government reversed its policy and promised to subsidise rice, grains and other basic food products.

In a manner similar to that of the 1970s, the King announced a development programme, involving the establishment of six new industrial cities. Work began on King ʿAbdullah's Economic City, north of Jeddah, promising employment in industrial plants – mainly petrochemicals, aluminium, steel and fertilisers – banking services and shipment. The city is meant to provide new job opportunities and residence units for workers (Mouawad 2008). The plan includes building houses, schools and mosques for the future workforce. So far the government has relied on thousands of foreign construction workers, mainly from China and the Far East, to build this city. The rising prices of construction material such as cement and steel have added to the cost of the project, thus absorbing millions of dollars in oil revenues.

The state reformist agenda involved reaching out to the international community to shed the bad publicity associated with 9/11. King ʿAbdullah visited the USA, and many European and Asian capitals. He met with Pope Benedict in the Vatican and called for greater dialogue between the Abrahamic faiths. In 2008 he sponsored a conference in Mecca where more than 400 Islamic scholars met to discuss the possibility and future of interfaith dialogue. While Muslim scholars from all over the world debated the prospects and limitations of such dialogue, some Saʿudi religious scholars condemned it, embarrassing the leadership and undermining its efforts to bring Christian, Jewish and other non-Muslim scholars face to face on Saʿudi soil. Shaykh ʿAbd al-Raḥman al-Barak issued a statement declaring interfaith dialogue un-Islamic. Some religious scholars feared that the government would succumb to international pressure demanding recognition of and freedom for other religions and the building of churches in Saudi Arabia, as in the Gulf, where Christian churches and Hindu temples have already been established to cater for the rising number of non-Muslim expatriate workers. While the King was reaching out to other faiths, Saʿudi scholars issued petitions against the Shiʿa, accusing them of heresy and blasphemy, and warning against their influence in Saʿudi society itself.

SOCIETY'S REFORMIST AGENDA

While the Islamist contestation of the 1990s demanded the Islamisation of the state, Saʿudi intellectuals and activists in the twenty-first century, including Islamists, moved away from this objective to call for constitutional monarchy and greater political participation, respect for human rights, transparency, and limiting the powers and excesses of the Ministry of the Interior. Activists in Saʿudi society hoped that King ʿAbdullah would be able to curb the surveillance and harsh security measures of the ministry, whose grip on the population increased under the pretext of the War on Terror.

Saʿudis calling for political reform

In the post-9/11 period, a new trend crystallised within Saudi Arabia, consisting mainly of liberals, Islamists and others. This trend came to be known as advocates of constitutional reform, *duʿat al-iṣlaḥ al-dusturi*.[13] Most of them were academics, professionals, writers and businessmen, and were an amalgamation of people with different past ideological orientations. Some had strong connections with the 1990 Islamist movement, others were ex-nationalists (Nasserites and Baʿthists) and communists. Many had served prison sentences in the past. They came together, overlooking their ideological differences, to pursue an encompassing reform agenda that unites people with different – and even opposing – political views. They called for reform that was situated in the Islamic tradition and would not undermine the role of the Saʿudi leadership. They were encouraged by the leadership's willingness to adopt the vocabulary of reform, and reach out to the constituency in an attempt to contain and fight terrorism.

Constitutional reformers petitioned ʿAbdullah to establish an elected consultative assembly, to replace the 120-member appointed Consultative Council he had inherited from King Fahd. They also called for the separation of powers, the independence of the judiciary and respect for human rights. Between 2003 and 2005, more than six petitions were sent to ʿAbdullah asking for basic freedoms and political participation. Many observers dubbed this wave of petitions the 'Riyadh Spring', leading Saudi Arabia into the twenty-first century as a state of institutions rather than princes. One of the most important petitions, in January 2003, clearly demanded constitutional rule in Saudi Arabia. Personalities such as ʿAbdullah al-Hamid, Matruk al-Faleh, ʿAli al-Dumayni Muḥammad, Saʿid al-Tayyib, and more than one hundred signatories articulated a new reformist agenda centred on several points: the priority of political reform; the grounding of constitutionalism in Islamic jurisprudence; the promotion of national unity; the centrality of the Saʿudi leadership; and equality and social justice.

In later petitions, the same signatories highlighted the dangers of ignoring calls for political reform and of marginalising society in future consultations and the policy-making process. While they continued to address the leadership with great deference, pledging loyalty and obedience, the language of later petitions reflected their frustration and disappointment over the leadership's unwillingness to heed their demands. The group of activists involved in this mobilisation were given mixed messages. They received encouragement from one section of the leadership, only to be reprimanded by another prince. Many petitioners were summoned to the Ministry of the Interior for questioning and warnings, after having met with the King, who expressed his willingness to listen to their calls. The local press remained silent on the wave of mobilisation, unable to publish any of the petitions that circulated freely on the internet and were later published in booklets outside Saudi Arabia.

The reformers' dream was shattered when the powerful minister of the interior, Prince Nayef, arrested many petition signatories in 2004; they later received prison sentences ranging between seven and nine years.[14] Reformers had been under the illusion that ʿAbdullah would initiate reforms on becoming King. All he was able to do, however, was to release the prisoners by royal decree in 2005 and drop charges against other dissidents and activists; many have had their passports confiscated, and are barred from travel abroad and from communicating with the international media (MacFarquhar 2005; Fattah 2007). King ʿAbdullah thus failed to stop the wave of oppression that his powerful brother Prince Nayef spread across the country. Arrests continued, with ʿAbdullah unable to control the excesses of his brother, all carried out under the pretext of the War on Terror (Middle East Economic Survey 2004). In February 2007 a new wave of arrests led to the imprisonment of more than fifteen people, whose crimes are still unknown. They were joined by bloggers and internet writers who expressed sympathy with political prisoners or exposed the excesses of the security services in prisons.

By 2008 the wave of petitions ended, as many reformers were silenced after being released from prison – in some cases their freedom was conditional on refraining from any future activism. Those who remained committed to the project and continued to issue petitions or publish critical opinions were returned to prison, to serve sentences related to their activities. ʿAbdullah al-Ḥamid, who was released from prison in 2005, returned to it in 2007, with his brother ʿIsa, following their mobilisation of a small demonstration by Saʿudi women at the gates of a famous prison in Buraydah. Other reformers announced their withdrawal from the constitutional reform group and wrote articles criticising their former comrades. It is difficult to ascertain whether this was triggered by pressure or personal decision. It was clear, however, that the state was able to contain the constitutional reform movement and precipitate internal schisms among people whose previous ideological orientations differed so much. The coming together of the reformers under one overarching umbrella with a common set of demands was a short-lived experience, which gathered momentum under the specific pressures Saudi Arabia was facing. The state remains strong in fragmenting emerging political trends, having at its disposal a massive coercive power and other groups who are willing to condemn any signs of politicisation. It continues to use official religious scholars, together with appointed judges, to condemn political opponents and activists. Calls for constitutionalism were met with a statement condemning the un-Islamic nature of man-made constitutions and a reminder that the constitution of Saudi Arabia is the holy book. The reformers remained an elite group, who failed to reach a wide section of Saʿudi society. Their supporters among the youth publicised their plight, sent messages to international and Arab human rights organisations, and disseminated their reform message via the internet. They remained, however, unorganised and incapable of mobilising people on the ground.

Minorities: the quest for recognition

At the same time as constitutional reformers were putting forward their demands, minorities such as the Shiʿa in the eastern province and the Ismaʿiliyya in the south-west were equally engaged in mobilisation that centred on demands pertaining to their status as religious minorities in Saudi Arabia. The Saʿudi Shiʿa, who had ended their confrontation with the regime in 1993 and returned to Saudi Arabia, found a window of opportunity in the constitutional reform movement a decade later. Some Shiʿa activists joined the constitutional reformers and signed their various petitions. They became active supporters of the constitutional reform movement, abandoning the narrow focus of their previous activity, which had centred on issues limited to the amelioration of the plight of the Shiʿa community. Shiʿa activists were keen to be seen as part of the nation rather than a separate community, in a region where Shiʿa ascendance in Iraq, following the overthrow of Saddam in 2003, was beginning to worry not only Saudi Arabia but other Arab regimes.[15]

Well-known Shiʿa activists and religious scholars such as Ḥasan al-Saffar, Tawfiq al-Sayf, Jaʿfar al-Shayeb and Najib al-Khunayzi were given the green light to enter the public sphere. The Shiʿa scholar Ḥasan al-Saffar was invited to participate in one of the National Dialogue Forums and share a platform with hardline Saʿudi Salafis. Shiʿa writers published articles in the local press calling for religious tolerance and an end to discrimination against the 'other'. Jaʿfar al-Shayeb, a well-known activist, was elected to the Qatif municipal council in 2005. Shiʿa public figures emphasised themes such as religious tolerance and national unity. Their criticisms of Wahhabi extremism and radicalisation were welcomed by the local official press under the pressure of terrorist attacks. Like other Saʿudi religious scholars, writers and journalists, the Shiʿa were enlisted in the War on Terror by a regime prepared to exploit their serious concerns over radical Sunni groups achieving more influence in Saudi Arabia. The Shiʿa had been the first group to be targeted in previous Wahhabi *fatawa*, which had condemned them as *rafiḍa*, rejectionists who had distorted Islam. The rising influence of Shiʿa in Iraq did little to disperse sectarian tension in Saudi Arabia, as *fatawa* excommunicating the Shiʿa in general continued to be issued by well-known Saʿudi scholars such as Naṣir al-ʿOmar, Ṣafar al-Ḥawali, ʿAbd al-Raḥman al-Barak and others. Some Sahwi scholars such as Salman al-ʿAwdah avoided mentioning the Shiʿa in sermons and media programmes.

Shiʿa activists who in the 1980s, inspired by the 1979 Iranian revolution, had called for revolutionary change, now emphasised the importance of all-encompassing notions of citizenship, regardless of sectarian affiliation. In 2003, more than 400 Shiʿa religious scholars, academics, professionals and writers signed a petition entitled *Partners in the Nation*, in which they called for recognition of their sect and representation in government, the Consultative Council, the Council of Higher Ulama and Saʿudi-sponsored international Islamic organisations, and sent it to ʿAbdullah, Crown Prince at the time. The petition highlighted continuous religious and economic discrimination against the Shiʿa, despite the formal reconciliation and government promises of 1993. The signatories pledged allegiance to the leadership and emphasised the centrality of national unity, which they said could only be achieved through equality, the ending of discrimination in education and employment, the criminalising of religious intolerance and hatred, a ban on *fatawa* against their sect and respect for Shiʿa religious courts and rituals.

While the government has done nothing to prohibit *fatawa* against the Shiʿa, its religious establishment, represented by the Grand Mufti, ʿAbd al-ʿAziz al-Sheikh, avoided discussion of the Shiʿa question, while other *ʿulama* occasionally issued *fatawa* excommunicating the Shiʿa and warning Muslims that they were dangerous conspirators. The sectarian war in Iraq that followed the occupation, and the rising influence of Hizbollah in Lebanon, brought a wave of *fatawa* condemning the Shiʿa, who were depicted as blasphemous agents of Iran. An old, influential Wahhabi scholar, Naṣir al-ʿOmar, issued a booklet entitled *al-Rafiḍa in the Land of Monotheism*. The pamphlet clearly stated that the Shiʿa are a sect outside true Islam. He listed their privileges, schools, mosques and mourning houses (*husayniyat*) in the eastern province, which he considered a dangerous sign, reflecting their pre-eminence (al-ʿOmar, n.d.). He then surveyed their control over economic and educational sectors in the same region and their missionary work during the pilgrimage season. He concluded that the Shiʿa are clearly guilty of *shirk* (associationist practices), and that they should be stopped before they spread their misguided rituals and beliefs. Another Sahwi shaykh, Ṣafar al-Ḥawali, issued a strong statement, refuting Shiʿa claims that they are discriminated against in Saudi Arabia, and warning the government against adopting a conciliatory stance. He contrasted the development of the eastern province with his own region, ʿAsir, and concluded that the Shiʿa had benefited from oil wealth while his home region lagged behind. He claimed that the Shiʿa's sense of suffering discrimination is the fault of their religious scholars, who impose high taxes on them, which they willingly pay (Al-Rasheed 2007: 90). Finally, he warned the government that if it were to address the alleged Shiʿa grievances, other groups and regions in Saudi Arabia would demand equal treatment, thus offering an opportunity for civil disobedience, dissent, chaos and division of the country along regional and sectarian lines. This contrasts with what Shiʿa activists have demanded, namely an end to discrimination and inequality, which they feared would promote feelings of exclusion and separatist tendencies.

In June 2008, while King ʿAbdullah was chairing an international conference in Mecca for the promotion of interfaith dialogue at which many Iranian Shiʿa representatives were present, a group of twenty-two Saʿudi scholars signed a letter condemning the Shiʿa.[16] The conference was attended by Ayatollah Hashemi Rafsanjani, chairman of the Iranian

Assembly of Experts and former president, who was taken on a tour around Saʿudi cities. Using the platform of the Friday sermon, Tawfiq al-Amer, a Shiʿa scholar in the eastern province, denounced the Sunni *fatwa* and defended the Shiʿa against the disparaging opinion of *al-nawaṣib*, a pejorative Shiʿa name for those Sunnis who hate *ahl al-bayt* (the Prophet's household). He was arrested after his sermon, but was later released from prison. The government remained silent on the hate *fatwa* of the twenty-two Wahhabi scholars, who continue to hold special seminars and lectures in their Riyadh mosques. It nevertheless sent Sunni shaykh Muḥammad al-Nojaymi to meet Shiʿa cleric Ḥasan al-Ṣaffar in an attempt to defuse sectarian tension and explain that the official *ʿulama* did not endorse the *fatwa*.

In general, Shiʿa mobilisation throughout this period led to greater visibility in the public sphere, manifested in permission to stage their annual mourning rituals in specially designated places. They remained, however, caught between government promises and the *fatawa* of radical *ʿulama*. They opted to engage with the former and await a gradual improvement of their situation. The state has succeeded in fragmenting the Shiʿa opposition, much as it was able to diffuse the constitutional reform movement by appropriating the rhetoric of reform. Some Shiʿa activists remain outside Saudi Arabia, perhaps as a move to maximise their options in the future. There are, however, loud, critical Shiʿa voices in Washington and London. Many of their grievances are posted on their internet news sites and discussion forums. The new Shiʿa media platforms may prove to be important mobilising forces in the future.

Other minorities have also come forward, such as the Ismaʿiliyya of Najran and other peripheral cities in the south-west, who went public for the first time in 2003. Ismaʿili activists sent a petition to the Saʿudi leadership entitled *The Homeland is for All, and All are for the Homeland.* Like the Shiʿa, the Ismaʿiliyya asserted that they belong to Saudi Arabia, and pledged allegiance to the leadership. They complained about economic deprivation and religious discrimination. They highlighted the plight of Ismaʿili prisoners of opinion, abuses in prisons and communal punishment. They specifically objected to the so-called *takfiri fatawa*, religious opinions that label them outside Islam, and demanded that the leadership put a stop to them and punish those Wahhabi scholars who issue them. The Ismaʿili petition drew attention to the government policy of settling non-Ismaʿilis in their region in order to alter the sectarian composition of these areas. This involved the confiscation of Ismaʿili land and the settlement of outsiders in their midst. They also considered the lack of development projects and advanced education centres to be impediments to integration and national unity.

Other religious groups, for example Sufis in the Hijaz, became more visible. Various initiatives to highlight the cultural specificity of this cosmopolitan region, protect its Islamic heritage and architecture, stress its historical religious pluralism and document the diversity of its Islamic past allowed Hijazi intellectuals, religious scholars and public figures to give interviews to the international media; some were very critical of what was dubbed Wahhabi domination, extremism and rejection of other Islamic schools of thought and jurisprudence. As long as they pledged allegiance to the Saʿudi leadership and reiterated its role in protecting and respecting the diversity of Saudi Arabia, including the Hijaz, they were allowed to articulate their reservations regarding the Wahhabi movement and its scholars. This was acceptable at a time when the leadership wanted to enlist all regions to fight radicalisation and terrorism. Hijazis, like the constitutional reformers, the Shiʿa and the Ismaʿiliyya, found an opportunity to denounce the Wahhabi tradition, whose pioneers had excommunicated them for their Sufi practices such as visiting saints' tombs, celebrating the Prophet's birthday and other ritualistic practices defined by Wahhabis as forms of heresy. One of their main religious figures, Shaykh al-Maliki, known for his Sufi orientation, had been denounced in a *fatwa*, which led to his exclusion from official religious forums. When he died in 2004, top Saʿudi leaders attended his funeral, in an attempt to reflect the government's new policy of recognising the religious diversity of the country and reach out to his followers.

The religious rights of minorities became the axis along which many groups mobilised. The Shiʿa abandoned their revolutionary rhetoric and opted for engagement with the state, when the latter wanted to demonstrate its new policy of inclusion. All minority groups developed alternative media channels to mobilise their followers and expose injustices. While the Ismaʿiliyya are latecomers, the Shiʿa have had a long history of confrontation with the regime, outlined in previous chapters. Today the Saʿudi government cannot simply ignore their demands, given the new regional context of the occupation of Iraq. While the state can act swiftly to suppress Shiʿa mobilisation, as it did the radical Salafi trend, it knows that any future confrontation with Iran may leave Saudi Arabia exposed to unrest in the Shiʿa cities of the eastern province. So far the leadership has tried to build bridges with Iran, calling for dialogue and diplomacy. Yet sections of Saʿudi society remain receptive to radical *fatawa*, which condemn the Shiʿa and other non-mainstream religious groups.[17]

Women's quest for equality

For a very long time women have been a silent minority in Saudi Arabia, although numerically they may outnumber men. They are excluded from public office and barred from voting in municipal elections. Their movement and employment are restricted. Exclusion of and discrimination against women have been attributed to many factors, including strict Wahhabi Islamic interpretations, tribal tradition and general conservatism. While such factors are also present in neighbouring Gulf countries, it is only in Saudi Arabia that one finds extreme forms of sexual segregation, uncontrolled polygamy,[18] limited employment opportunities and general invisibility in the public sphere. While women have failed to be elected in national and local elections in all Gulf states, some have been appointed to public ministerial office, for example in Kuwait.

In the past the Saʿudi state used restrictions on women to boost its Islamic credentials and demonstrate its respect for *shariʿa*. Women became symbols for the piety of the leadership, signs to be read by the constituency to affirm the commitment of the state to Islam. Women were the visible sign of the wave of Islamisation that the government adopted in the 1980s in response to internal challenges from Islamism, for example Juhayman's seizure of the Mecca mosque in 1979, and the Islamist contestation of the 1990s. However, in the twenty-first century, and under the rhetoric of reform, the state has adopted a more open approach to the issue. This has encouraged Saʿudi women to see the leadership as a guardian of women's rights and a promoter of gradual emancipation that does not pose a serious departure from the general parameters of Islamic tradition. The leadership, and especially King ʿAbdullah, have allowed women a greater presence, for example in economic, educational and social domains. Foreign Minister Saʿud al-Faysal and his brother Turki, ex-ambassador in Washington, have expressed support for the emancipation of women but also emphasised that the conservative Saʿudi society is still not ready to make serious changes that would antagonise and alienate a large section. They both expect women to be allowed to drive in the future, when all are ready for this revolutionary step. At the same time, the minister of the interior, Prince Nayef, emphasised his rejection of any drastic change that would lead to Saʿudi women becoming like Western women. He stressed that Saʿudi women enjoy their full rights as defined by Islam. Such speeches occasionally emerge in the context of addressing religious scholars and representatives of the Committee for the Propagation of Virtue and Prohibition of Vice. Many women praise King ʿAbdullah for his receptiveness to their aspirations.

However, they would like to see him curb the influence of extremist Wahhabi scholars, who resist any opening up of the public sphere to women and continue to issue *fatawa* calling for women to be confined to traditional roles revolving around the house and the upbringing and education of children.

Saʿudi women are given mixed signals regarding the prospect of state-led social change. Furthermore, not all of them support greater emancipation, and some have joined the hardline Islamists who envisage a traditional role for women, although a moderate emancipation agenda is formulated by some outspoken Islamist figures. For example, judge ʿAbd al-ʿAziz al-Qasim and Sahwi shaykh Salman al-ʿAwdah argue that in Saudi Arabia female exclusion is a social rather than an Islamic tradition. Tribal heritage and practices have been confused with the Islamic tradition, leading to misguided interpretations of Islamic texts. They have urged scholars to try and isolate the social from the religious in order to reach a better understanding of the status of women in Islam. They agree that there are no clear Islamic texts supporting the ban on women driving. Other hardline Islamists, such as Ṣafar al-Ḥawali, have remained faithful to strict interpretations that contribute to the confinement of women and their continuous exclusion.

Academics and businesswomen became more visible and assertive in demanding greater participation in the economy, employment and contribution to social and educational affairs. The women activists who drove their cars in Riyadh in 1990, defying the ban on women driving, were rehabilitated and returned to their jobs. Since 2003 they have taken the opportunity to voice their support for the leadership in fighting religious extremism, which they hold responsible for their subordination. Many argued that the exclusion of women represents the other side of radicalisation that produced terrorism and suicide bombers. Many female academics and writers have highlighted the interconnection between violence and the sexual segregation that is still enforced in Saudi Arabia. They appeared in the National Dialogue Forums, especially the one that dealt with women's issues, to highlight the need to terminate the restrictions on women's employment. Several women continued to demand the right to move freely and the termination of male guardianship over them. They exposed injustices in courts over divorce and custody of children. A Saʿudi television presenter, Rania al-Baz, was badly beaten up by her husband. Images of her disfigured face flooded the international media and Saʿudi internet web pages. Her case was publicised after she documented her ordeal in a book, published in French with the help of a French organisation. A woman, who came to be known as Fatat al-Qatif (the girl from Qatif), was gang raped by seven men. She was accused of being found in a situation of *khilwa*, intimate encounter with a man unaccompanied by a chaperon, for which she received a prison sentence and 200 lashes, while her rapists received lenient short prison sentences. Her case was also publicised outside the country. Under pressure from the USA and international human rights organisations, the King issued a statement pardoning the girl. Another woman was divorced from her husband, against the wishes of both partners, by a Saʿudi court on the pretext that they were genealogically incompatible (her husband belonged to a tribal group that did not match hers), a condition that allows a judge to annul the marriage according to some Islamic interpretations of the conditions of legitimate marriage. A small group of women activists expressed their wish to form an independent organisation defending the rights of women and calling on the leadership to lift the ban on driving. So far no such women's organisation exists, yet there are several charities, under the directorship of famous princesses, helping women.

Other women objected to the idea, considering any change the product of a Western conspiracy to undermine the authentic tradition and heritage of the country, in addition to breaking the cohesion of family life in Saudi Arabia. They signed all-female petitions urging the leadership not to respond to external criticism or internal pressure from Saʿudi women whom they described as 'Westernised' and 'lacking moral integrity'. They affirmed that Saʿudi women enjoy the privilege of not being responsible for the economic welfare of the household, free from the burden of driving cars, and are in fact happy with their current situation, which is dictated by the *shariʿa*. Some upper-class women share these views, which they express in the context of interviews with Western media.

While debate on women remains heated and divisive within Saudi Arabia, international human rights organisations highlight their plight. According to a recent report, gender discrimination remains common practice. Male guardianship over adult women is held to be the source of gender discrimination. Guardianship means that women must seek permission from male relatives to travel, work, study or marry. This also limits women's ability to report abuse and violence to the relevant authorities or make decisions regarding their health, children, career and future. Such decisions are the prerogative of their male relatives. Supported by religious scholars, the state claims that it is simply applying Islamic law, but without recognising the multiple interpretations that other Islamic scholars have developed in the past. It continues to defend just one interpretation, which happens to be one of the strictest in the Muslim world.

New literary expressions: the sexualisation of politics and violence

By 2000 a new generation of young Saʿudi novelists began to emerge on the Saʿudi and Arab literary scene.[19] They published their novels outside Saudi Arabia, mainly in Beirut and Cairo. These novels have found a place on the shelves of book fairs in various Saʿudi cities, despite some sexually explicit and daring descriptions. Some novels have been translated into English and included in Western reviews of Arabic literature in prestigious English newspapers and literary journals.[20]

One recurrent theme dominates the new wave of literature: terrorism. Some novelists have chosen to delve into the psyche of young terrorists, situate them in the social milieu of impoverished neighbourhoods, expose their alleged sexual frustration and troubled relationship with the opposite sex, describe their fantasies about the seventy virgins awaiting them in heaven, and denounce the religious scholars who subjected them to prolonged brainwashing (al-Hamad 2005; al-Huthlul 2004). Disoriented young men, who go through troubling experiences as a result of the rapid changes that have swept society, followed by guilt and shame, leading to redemption through martyrdom, were themes that dominated many novels. It must be noted that it is easy to draw a caricature of a terrorist, despite serious scholarly research on those who have committed acts of terrorism inside Saudi Arabia and globally. This literature has a strong but obvious political message, clothed in sensational sexuality. Some authors produced superficial literary statements on a complex security and political crisis. They found the solution to terrorism in employment opportunities and jobs, to lure the youth away from boredom, adventure and violence. Others sought a way out in limiting the role of religion in the public sphere and replacing it with modern mass culture and entertainment, such as football, theatre, music and cinema.

Several Saʿudi novelists, including Turki al-Ḥamad, Hani Naqshabandi and a Saʿudi female journalist, ʿAlla al-Huthlul, delved into a process whereby the sexualisation of politics became a means to an end, mainly to denounce the strict religious tradition of the country that is blamed for all ills. They fell easily into the category of liberal Saʿudi writers for their daring criticism of the religious sphere, without necessarily questioning the intimate relationship between the state and its religious tradition, both of which were contributing factors to the terrorism that erupted in the twenty-first century. The new generation of Saʿudi novelists hid behind fiction to deliver strong critical messages that denounced the conservatism and radicalisation of Saʿudi religion and society.

Other novelists, especially women, surprised the literary milieu with their daring novels about their own sexual adventures, both real and virtual. Titles such as the *Girls of Riyadh* and *Women of Vice*,[21] by Raja al-Sani and Samar al-Moqrin respectively, attracted a lot of attention that oscillated between praise and condemnation. Long invisible in the public sphere, young female writers described in great detail the illicit sexual experiences and fantasies of their heroines, thus unveiling the most cherished intimate secrets of private lives. As expected, liberal Saʿudi literary critics regarded these novels as the beginning of sexual liberation and the emancipation of women, while Islamists and conservatives condemned the novelists and called for the banning of their books. This literature, very similar to that enjoyed by adolescents in other parts of the world, became a symbol of Saʿudi female emancipation in the eyes of both Western and Saʿudi commentators. Hiding behind fictional characters, Saʿudi female novelists delivered a strong message to their society, simply and bluntly shedding the traditional image of the pious mother, obedient sister and submissive daughter and replacing it with that of a daring woman, who engages with her body and indulges her lust and desires. They followed a generation of male novelists who were equally concerned with the expression of sexuality in a conservative society, for example Turki al-Ḥamad's trilogy about growing up in Riyadh in the 1970s and Ghazi al-Goṣaybi's work on similar themes. Now women contribute to this genre of literature and risk the wrath of their society, though they are acclaimed outside it.

Novels dealing with terrorism and sexuality are expressions of the privatisation of politics and its sexualisation in a country where political activities are curtailed and freedom of expression limited. While not many Saʿudis are capable of freely and directly engaging in politics without the risk of arrest, many have found solace in fictionalised and sexualised political selves. Saʿudis used to say that three taboos are fixed in the country: politics, religion and sex. Today only politics remains prohibited. The 'political' has retreated from the traditional domain of activism and mobilisation to that of the self and its intrigues. Under the government policy of social and economic *infitaḥ*, sexual fantasies and criticism of religious conservatism are on the agenda of both the leadership and liberal constituencies in Saʿudi society.

This genre of so-called liberal novels has provoked a response from other writers with an Islamic agenda. Islamist novelists have written short stories to denounce liberal accusations relating to terrorism and to demonstrate the noble message of *jihad* in places such as Afghanistan in the 1980s or Bosnia in the 1990s. They have created a counter-image of committed young

Muslims (*multazim*), fighting for the supremacy of their faith and the defence of Muslims (al-Hodayf 2006). No novelist, however, has dared to glorify those suicide bombers who engage in violence inside Saudi Arabia. Their lives and obituaries remain hidden in the virtual world of the internet. On sexuality, Islamist novelists celebrate a platonic love that leads to marriage, family, security and legitimate intimacy between men and women. They condemn illicit sexuality, adopting a moralising and preaching tone that makes their literature limited in both its literary style and theme. Saudi Arabia is yet to produce novelists who match the great names of other Arab countries. The advent of new communication technology may have cut short the development of a Saʿudi literary genre of outstanding international significance. Perhaps the work of ʿAbd al-Raḥman Munif, author of *Cities of Salt*, was a unique development associated with the early shock of oil.

Virtual forums: anonymity of politics

New communication technologies offer an alternative public sphere for all Saʿudis to express opinions, post short films and photos and express views on almost all aspects of life. Internet discussion boards became popular from 2003, followed by Paltalk chat rooms, blog sites, Youtube, Facebook and other print, visual and oral electronic communication tools. Many young Saʿudis use these novel means to flirt with the opposite or same sex, publicise scandals, communicate with friends and like-minded people, and create virtual communities who seek to link up with others. Both young men and women access the internet to express themselves, rather than simply consume what this new technology offers. They are no longer spectators, but are avid participants in global communication forums.

Some frustrated politically minded people write commentaries on the political, social and economic conditions in their blog pages.[22] Others join discussion boards, using pseudonyms to criticise officials, condemn injustice and publicise abuses of human rights. Hundreds of discussion boards have emerged, each with a specific political orientation. Liberal, nationalist, jihadi, Islamist and pro-government discussion forums have mushroomed on the internet, drawing thousands of members and commentators to their pages. Other popular discussion boards deal with entertainment, sexuality, sport and music. Support for jihadi violence, radical *fatawa*, obituaries and images of so-called martyrs retreated to the internet. New jihadi discussion boards appeared throughout 2003–8; some were able to stay on the internet for a long time, while others disappeared or were hacked into by opponents and security services.

The government has joined the race to censor the internet through a special science and technology institution. Under the pretext of protecting Islam, morality and virtue, a plethora of websites are regularly blocked. The government regularly censors political and human rights sites. It also uses the World Wide Web to catch potential terrorists and those who post radical messages and sermons. It launched a virtual electronic rehabilitation programme, al-Sakina, to foster dialogue with those who have gone astray and succumbed to *thaqafat al-irhab* (the ideology of terrorism). This virtual forum supplemented its general *munasaha* programme, an advice initiative implemented in special detention centres where potential believers in this ideology are detained until they declare their repentance and denounce their former wrong beliefs. At this stage, they are released back into the community.

Whether new communication technology will foster serious political change remains doubtful. So far it has allowed Saʿudis to express themselves without incurring the wrath of a political system that remains closed to serious and real democratisation. So far virtual communication has contributed to the increased polarisation of Saʿudi society along ideological, regional, tribal and sectarian lines. Radical messages that are often prohibited in the real public sphere find a place on the internet. Boasting about tribal origins, glorifying jihadi violence, denouncing the Shiʿa, undermining the authority of religious scholars, promoting atheism, celebrating sexuality and other themes are expressed freely by a young generation of computer-literate Saʿudis.

Critical voices using their real names on the internet are often arrested. Bloggers have had their pages blocked, and one or two have ended up in prison after posting critical opinions. The internet has facilitated the transformation of Saʿudi society from secrecy to transparency. Its individual and social crises, its shortcomings and serious dilemmas are no longer hidden secrets, guarded against intruders. Today, Saʿudis scrutinise themselves through these novel means of transmission and communication, and expose their secrets to the outside world. The veil has truly been dropped. It is difficult, almost impossible, to go back to the *status quo ante*. The dropping of the veil may not, however, lead to the dismantling of the practices of authoritarian rule in the short term, although in the long term it may be an unavoidable and inevitable consequence. Only then can we ascertain whether modernising authoritarian rule was a successful measure, in lieu of serious political change to move Saudi Arabia beyond cosmetic reforms.

Conclusion

Saudi Arabia entered the twenty-first century with real problems. Its ageing leadership, growing national debt, economic slowdown, rising unemployment and shrinking welfare services combined to pose a serious challenge. One of the wealthiest states in the region – and the world – failed to contain the rapid increase in population and resulting preponderance of a cohort of young men and women, all frustrated at the limited prospect of finding employment. The festivities of the late twentieth century masked the gaps in uneven regional development programmes and the fermenting Islamist dissent.

This dissent culminated, not in Saudi Arabia, but in New York, on the morning of Tuesday 11 September 2001. Among those who attacked the World Trade Center were fifteen young Saʿudi men, who had been drawn to the global jihadi movement under the leadership of another Saʿudi, Usama Bin Laden, and an Egyptian, Ayman al-Zawahiri. Two years later, *jihad* came home to haunt the Saʿudi leadership and kill hundreds of Saʿudis in the streets of Riyadh, Jeddah, Mecca and Dammam.

The world was stunned, not by Bin Laden's involvement, as he had previously announced his intentions to launch a war against Christians and Jews, dubbed the 'new crusades', but by the participation of young Saʿudi men, long known for their acquiescence, respect of authority and deference to their leadership and religious scholars. More than any other historical event, 9/11 announced the beginning of a new era for Saudi Arabia. Two new chapters (chapters 8 and 9) in this updated edition trace the challenges, both internal and external, facing the country in the twenty-first century.

Was Saudi Arabia prepared to deal with the challenge of the new global terrorism? Were the Saʿudi leadership, religious tradition, wealth, overseas charity and educational programmes responsible for the global and local Islamic militancy? These were questions that began to be asked not only by the international community but by Saʿudis themselves. After a short period of denial, Saudi Arabia came to recognise that it has a serious problem, home grown and in need of urgent action. The government mobilised its security agencies, increased its military budget, developed the capacity of its internal emergency security forces and launched a campaign to arrest suspects and kill terrorists before they could unleash their human bombs. Between 2001 and 2008, many suicide bombers died with their victims, who included Saʿudis, Westerners, Asians and Arabs. Saudi jihadis proved to be capable of inflicting serious damage and launching a media campaign glorifying their mission, under the rhetoric of removing infidels from the Arabian Peninsula. Their leaders, ideologue religious scholars, and followers combined their efforts to terrorise the population, draw new recruits into the movement, and celebrate the noble duty of *jihad* in the Land of the Two Holy Mosques.

While Saudi Arabia was engaged in an internal battle with its own jihadis, two wars, one in Afghanistan and one in Iraq, complicated the scene and fuelled more violence in the country. Saudi Arabia was heavily involved in both Iraq and Afghanistan. It had supported Saddam's war against Iran in the 1980s, and had contributed money and young men to liberate Afghanistan from Soviet occupation. In the twenty-first century, it began to pay a high price for its foreign policy. Saʿudi jihadis who had trained and fought in Qandahar and Kabul returned to Saudi Arabia in 2001, after the demise of the Taliban regime and the dispersal of al-Qaʿidah activists, determined to ignite the flames of *jihad* in their own homeland. The Wahhabi religious tradition that called upon Saʿudis to obey their pious leadership was reinterpreted and reformulated to justify the branding of the Saʿudi regime as a *kafir* (blasphemous) state. Saudi Arabia preferred to blame the Egyptian Muslim Brotherhood for global terrorism. However, it was clear that those who engaged in terrorism in Saudi Arabia drew on the teachings of Muhammad ibn ʿAbd al-Wahhab rather than Sayyid Qutb, an Egyptian, although they may have benefited from the organisational skills of other Arab Islamist movements.

While the Saʿudi local war on terror was just beginning, the leadership recognised that security measures were not enough; it enlisted society to fight the menace. In return, it promised reform. This opened a Pandora's box in Saudi Arabia, and lifted the veil from one of the world's most secretive and opaque societies. The leadership had a limited vision of the reform it was prepared to implement. It announced a series of measures, all helping to modernise authoritarian rule without posing any real challenges to the leadership. King ʿAbdullah became the champion of reform, but the Saʿudi state was showing signs of fragmentation and pluralism. It was no longer a one-man state; it was a state with multiple actors, each competing to carve out a position for himself. This affected the state's reform agenda and contributed to its incoherence.

In the twenty-first century, Saʿudi society became more vocal and articulate in expressing its wishes and vision. Deprived of real avenues for political participation, mobilisation and activism, Saʿudi intellectuals grouped to produce petitions presented to the leadership, calling for a constitutional monarchy. Reform and repression progressed hand in hand. While the government resisted the idea of constitutional monarchy, it favoured limited local municipal elections, establishing a National Dialogue Forum and paying lip service to human rights through new government-sponsored organisations. The dramatic increase in oil revenues, development projects and the promise of prosperity were substitutes for structural political change that would lead to limitations on the power of the royal family and its hold over major decision-making bodies. Saudi Arabia is still an absolute monarchy, but with multiple heads.

The evolving third Saʿudi state is now at a crossroads. Either it implements serious political changes to governance and increases political participation or it risks losing the ability to contain future dissent. So far black gold has saved the house of Saʿud from both terrorist violence and social discontent. It remains to be seen whether the current second oil boom will have a lasting impact that spares Saudi Arabia future contestation, civil unrest and violence. But it is certainly premature to conclude that Saudi Arabia will shortly inaugurate a fourth state in which the country is ruled by elected institutions rather than a number of princes.

Appendix I

AL SAᶜUD RULERS IN DIRᶜIYYAH (1744–1818)

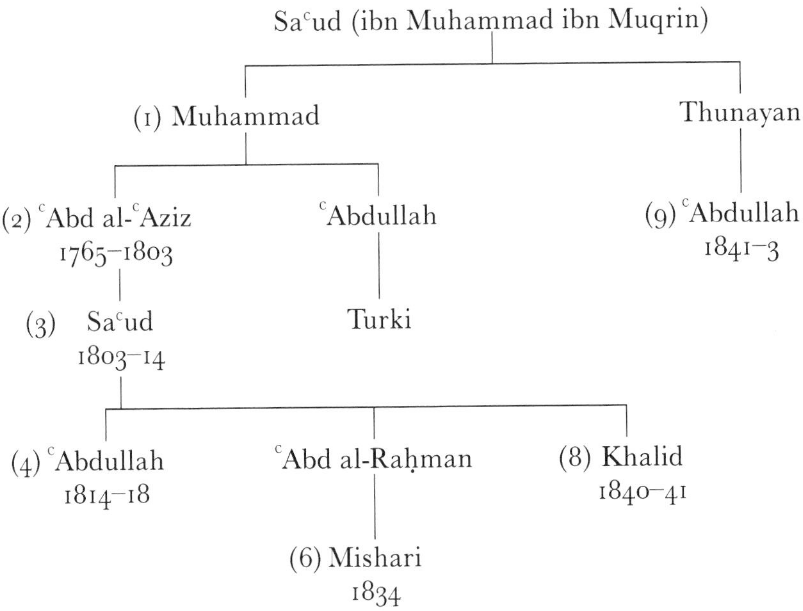

For rulers 5 and 7 see appendix II.

Appendix II

AL SAʿUD RULERS IN RIYADH (1824–1891)

(5) Turki (Ibn ʿAbdullah)
1824–34

(7) Faysal
(1834–8)

(10) (1843–65)

(11) ʿAbdullah
1865–71

(14) ʿAbdullah
(1875–89)

(12) Saʿud
(1871–70)

Muhammad

(13) ʿAbd al-Raḥman
1875

(15) ʿAbd al-Raḥman
1889–91

ʿAbd al-ʿAziz (Ibn Saʿud)
1902–53

ʿAbd al Moḥsin

Musaʿid

Saʿd

Turki

ʿAbdullah

Muhammad

For rulers 6, 7 and 8 see appendix I.

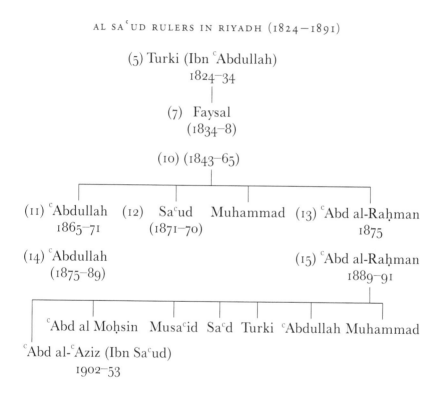

Appendix III

IBN SAʿUD'S SONS (1900–1953)

Turki (b. 1900)
Saʿud (b. 1902)
Faysal (b. 1904)
Muhammad (b. 1910)
Khalid (b. 1912)
Naṣir (b. 1920)
Saʿd (b. 1920)
Fahd (b. 1921)
Manṣur (b. 1922)
Musaʿid (b. 1923)
ʿAbdullah (b. 1923)
Bandar (b. 1923)
Sultan (b. 1924)
ʿAbd al-Moḥsin (b. 1925)
Mishʿal (b. 1926)
Mitʿab (b. 1928)
ʿAbd al-Raḥman (b. 1931)
Ṭalal (b. 1931)
Mishari (b. 1932)
Nayef (b. 1933)
Nawwaf (b. 1933)
Badr (b. 1933)
Turki (b. 1934)
Fawwaz (b. 1934)
ʿAbd al-Illah (b. 1935)
Salman (b. 1936)
Aḥmad (b. 1940)
ʿAbd al-Majid (b. 1940)
Mamduḥ (b. 1940)
Hithlul (b. 1941)
Mashhur (b. 1942)
Ṣaṭṭam (b. 1943)
Miqrin (b. 1943)
Ḥumud (b. 1947)

Notes

1 SOCIETY AND POLITICS, 1744–1818 and 1824–1891

1 On the architecture of Dirʿiyyah, see Facey 1997.
2 See ibn Bishr 1930; ibn Ghanam 1970; ibn ʿIssa 1966; Vassiliev 1998.
3 See al-ʿUthaymin 1995.
4 See ʿAbd al-Rahim 1976; Abu Ḥakima 1967; Cook 1988.
5 See Abu ʿAliya 1969; Winder 1965.
6 See ibn Rashid 1966; al-Dakhil 1966; al-ʿUthaymin 1981; Al-Rasheed 1991; al-Zaʿarir 1997.
7 On Hijazi society and politics, see Mortel 1991; 1994. On the nineteenth century see Ochsenwald 1984, on the twentieth century see Teitelbaum 2001.
8 See Anscombe 1997 and Fattah 1997.

2 THE EMERGING STATE, 1902–1932

1 Official Saʿudi historical accounts consider the capture of Riyadh from its Rashidi governor in 1902 as the date marking the beginning of the third Saʿudi state. This, however, is inaccurate. The Kingdom of Saudi Arabia was declared in 1932. Chapter 7 discusses the significance of this event in Saʿudi historiography.
2 See Anscombe 1997. On the Shiʿa of Hasa in the twentieth century see Steinberg 2001.
3 For full details of the capture of Haʾil and the fate of the Rashidi amirs see Al-Rasheed 1991.
4 The incorporation of ʿAsir in the Saʿudi realm is described in Bang 1996 and al-Zulfa 1995.
5 For more details on the collapse of Sharifian rule in Hijaz see Troeller 1976 and Kostiner 1993.
6 Three religious titles were current in Arabia in 1900: *muṭawwaʿ* (a volunteer who guards public conduct), *imam* (leader of prayer, but can also refer to the leader of the Muslim community), and *qaḍi* (judge). It was common for one person to perform several functions. The proliferation of religious titles in Saudi Arabia is a recent phenomenon, dating to the time of King Faysal (1964–75).

7 Ibn Saʿud's new title as *imam* should not be confused with the leader of prayer (see note 6). When he became *imam*, he was meant to be not only leader of prayer but also leader of the Muslim community.
8 A Saʿudi commentator on the role of the *muṭawwaʿa* considers them a fleet of spies who were dispatched by Ibn Saʿud under the guise of educating the tribes in religious matters to gather information on tribal relations and alliances. See ʿAbdullah 1995. The *muṭawwaʿa* may have performed 'spying' functions, but their contribution to state building goes beyond this limited role.
9 Helms mentions that Ibn Saʿud tried to restrain the *muṭawwaʿa* as early as 1914 when he sent them letters indicating that they should exercise moderation among the tribal confederations whom they were meant to bring back to the true path of Islam. See Helms 1981: 132. Ibn Saʿud's letters, however, failed to curb the zeal of the *muṭawwaʿa* and their followers among the *ikhwan* tribal force that they helped to create.
10 See al-Ḥasan 1994.
11 The *ikhwan* rebellion of 1927–30 is described in Kishk 1981; Kostiner 1993; Dickson 1949; 1956; Habib 1978; Leatherdale 1983; Troeller 1976; and Glubb 1960.
12 The first Saʿudi–Yemeni war is discussed in chapter 3.
13 The non-tribal foundation of the twentieth-century Saʿudi state is explored in al-Fahad 2001, where he argues against Kostiner's (1993) interpretation of the Saʿudi state as a tribal chieftaincy.
14 According to Leatherdale:

> George Rendel, head of the Foreign Office's Eastern Department, felt that the new name was something for which he personally could take some credit. Rendel was informed that Ibn Saʿud wished to call his state after his own name (Sauʿudiya). Rendel advised that this name would not be fully understood by the international community and came up with 'Saudi Arabia', a suggestion which was adopted. (Leatherdale 1983: 147)

3 CONTROL AND LOYALTY, 1932–1953

1 "Ara'if' is a Najdi term often used to refer to the retrieval of wandering or stolen camels. Ibn Saʿud's cousins are referred to by this name to indicate that they were 'retrieved' or returned to the domain of Ibn Saʿud. See al-Dakhil 1982: 103–4.
2 Other less prominent collateral branches of the Al Saʿud are the Al Thunayan and Al Farḥan. See Peterson 1993: 142–3.
3 For further details see Kostiner 1993.
4 No confirmation of this information is available to the author.
5 This argument is popular in Saʿudi opposition literature. See al-Saʿid 1981.
6 Several authors reiterate the argument that Ibn Saʿud's marriages were political strategies enhancing his alliance with important families in Arabia. See al-Zirkili 1972 and Philby 1952.
7 Among other sons of Ibn Saʿud, Ṭalal ibn ʿAbd al-ʿAziz, famous for his launching of the Free Princes' opposition group in the 1960s, was born to

an Armenian concubine, Munayyir. See Samore 1983: 49–50. Ṭalal's political career is discussed in the next chapter.

8 Descriptions of the *majlis* in nineteenth-century Arabian emirates are found in European travel literature, for example Blunt 1968 and Doughty 1979.

9 *Majlis al-dars* was different from the formal weekly meeting that Ibn Saʿud held with the *ʿulama.*

10 For example, in Jeddah the King used the residence of the Saqqaf merchant family.

11 Before his death, Ibn Saʿud was disturbed by a series of scandals involving several of his sons. Their royal palaces and their regular travel abroad drained his resources to the extent that his treasurer, Ibn Sulayman, sometimes refused to pay. This made Ibn Sulayman unpopular with, for example, Saʿud. For further details see Almana 1980: 196–7 and Howarth 1964: 212–17.

12 For more details on the organisation of taxation during the early years of the Saʿudi state, see Chaudhry 1997: 58–65. However, one must be careful not to exaggerate 'Saʿudi fiscal policies' in the 1930s and 1940s.

13 On Saʿudi–Russian relations, see Vassiliev 1998: 296.

14 In 1923, Ibn Saʿud negotiated an oil concession with Major Frank Holmes, an entrepreneur from New Zealand. The Lebanese American Amin Rihani travelled to Arabia as an intermediary and interpreter. In 1928, the concession lapsed, as Holmes could not find an oil company interested in buying it. See Long 1997: 61; Vassiliev 1998: 312–13; al-Shaykh 1988: 63.

15 For full details of the oil concession, see al-Shaykh 1988.

16 After the First World War Britain established the Iraq Petroleum Company, the sister of Anglo-Persian which explored for oil in Iran. Both companies took over the Turkish Petroleum Company. In doing so British-owned companies controlled oil production in Iraq and Iran, the two main producers in the Middle East in the interwar period. For further details, see Brown 1999: 9–34.

17 Philby's company, Sharqiyyah, was a trading company that acted as agent for Ford and Marconi in Saudi Arabia. According to one source, Philby sold 1,450 cars to Ibn Saʿud in the late 1930s, which increased Ibn Saʿud's debt to £140,000. See Brown 1999: 55.

18 See chapter 4 for details of the rupture in Saʿudi–British relations after the Second World War.

19 For photographs of the Murabaʿ palace by de Gaury and van der Meulen, see Facey 1992: 312, 313, 314, 315 and 316. The Murabaʿ palace is now part of a complex of buildings and museums that were restored for the 1999 centennial celebrations.

20 During the Second World War, ARAMCO experienced labour shortages. The company used Italian prisoners of war captured in East Africa to train Saʿudi and Arab workers. See Brown 1999 and Holden and Johns 1981.

21 During the Second World War, Ibn Saʿud maintained his neutrality, but sent envoys to Germany. One such envoy was a Libyan who had fled his country

and placed himself in the service of the Saʿudi King. See Holden and Johns 1981: 128.

22 In the 1940s, Ibn Saʿud was tormented by the behaviour of some of his sons. Drinking parties in royal palaces became embarrassing and he had to respond to criticism by the *ʿulama*. For further details, see McLoughlin 1993: 178.

23 The famous Hijaz railway between Damascus and Madina was disrupted during the First World War. It was Arabia's first experience of a railway. See al-ʿAmr 1974.

24 It seems that Ibn Saʿud was not impressed by Churchill's present. He offered the Rolls Royce to his brother ʿAbdullah.

25 It was common knowledge that Ibn Saʿud favoured sons born from marriages with non-Saʿudi women. These women and their children received special treatment and lavish gifts. In memory of the King, Ṭalal ibn ʿAbd al-ʿAziz wrote a book in homage to his father. See Al-Saʿud 1999.

4 THE POLITICS OF DISSENT, 1953–1973

1 Ibn Saʿud's finance minister, Ibn Sulayman, occasionally delayed payment to princes even after the King had given his permission. Ibn Sulayman often quarrelled with Saʿud when the latter demanded more cash from the treasury.

2 Only scattered information on the 1953 and 1956 strikes among ARAMCO workers is found in the literature on Saudi Arabia. See Abir 1988 and Buchan 1982.

3 The later development and modernisation of the National Guard is discussed in Cordesman 1997.

4 In 1950s and early 1960s, both Faysal and Saʿud travelled abroad for medical treatment. Their absence coincided with the turbulent political climate in the country.

5 ARAMCO's role in drawing Washington's attention to Saudi Arabia is discussed in Anderson 1981.

6 The Berlin blockade of 1948–9, the Soviet explosion of the atomic bomb in 1949 and the fall of China to communism in the same year were behind Washington's fears. See Anderson 1981.

7 Photographs of Faysal praying became symbols of his piety and Islamic politics. His participation in the oil embargo in 1973 and his desire to pray in the al-Aqsa mosque in Jerusalem granted him unprecedented popularity in the Arab and Muslim world.

8 On the role of merchants in state formation in Arabia during the eighteenth and nineteenth centuries, see Fattah 1997. For the twentieth century, see Chaudhry 1997. Both authors, however, exaggerate the role of 'mercantile classes' in Arabia in pre-modern and modern times.

9 Faysal's reign was also associated with the commercialisation of land and its redistribution. Land redistribution was accompanied by the sedentarisation of bedouins as a result of development projects targeting this population. For further details, see Fabietti 1984 and Fernea 1987.

10 During the 1970s Saʿudi princes did not use their names for commercial and business enterprises. This tradition has been maintained until the present day. Faysal's sons and other princes disguised their ownership of companies. In this respect, they differed from ordinary merchant families whose names were associated with their own trading companies, for example the Jaffalis, Rajḥis, Bin Ladens and others.

11 Among other princes, Ṭalal ibn ʿAbd al-ʿAziz and Musaʿid ibn ʿAbd al-ʿAziz married into the Lebanese elite families of al-Solḥ and al-Kaʿki respectively.

12 A series of events troubled the Arab world in 1969. Regimes in Libya, Sudan and Somalia were overthrown by the military. The British, so far the guardians of the small Gulf states, started evacuating their forces. Saudi Arabia feared the intensification of the activities of Marxist and Baʿthist groups, especially in south Yemen. Its fears were not unjustified. For further details see Abir 1988: 114.

5 FROM AFFLUENCE TO AUSTERITY, 1973–1990

1 In the 1970s American scholarly literature on Saudi Arabia was very limited. According to one survey, only 6 out of 120 books and 19 out of 5,500 articles mentioned the kingdom. For further details see Long 1985: 1.

2 A previous conflict with the United States centred on Yemen in the early 1960s. For a brief history of Saʿudi–US differences see Halliday 1982: 128.

3 The F-15 aircraft sold to Saudi Arabia lacked important equipment and avionics, making future upgrading for attack missions impossible. See Long 1985: 60 and Cordesman 1984: 205–7.

4 In 1927 Ibn Saʿud was criticised by the *ʿulama* for his serial marriages. See chapter 2.

5 The mosque siege was terminated with the assistance of Jordanian troops and American and French advisers. For further details, see Abu Dhar 1980: 161–5.

6 On discrimination against the Shiʿa see al-Ḥasan 1993.

7 Interview with Hamza al-Ḥasan, January 1993.

8 Since the 1980s, Saudi Arabia has tried to lessen its dependence on Arab workers and replace them with South Asians. However, in some sectors (for example education) this strategy was not possible. On the Yemeni workers in Saudi Arabia and the Gulf crisis in the 1990s see Okruhlik and Conge 1997.

9 See al-Torki 1986 on Jeddah elite women in the 1980s.

10 On Saʿudi civil servants, see Heller and Safran 1985.

11 On Yamani and Al Saʿud, see al-Qaḥṭani 1988b.

12 On the global impact of the Iranian revolution see Esposito 1990.

13 On pilgrimage matters see Leverrier 1996.

14 After the Camp David agreement and the marginalisation of Egypt, Saddam Husayn began to entertain the idea of playing a leadership role in the Arab world.

15 Throughout the 1980s, Iranian pilgrims continued to chant anti-American slogans during the pilgrimage season. Saudi Arabia was targeted during these events.

16 GCC states excluded Iraq and Yemen from the council for obvious reasons. For more details on membership matters see Peterson 1988.

17 With the exception of Oman and Bahrain, none of the GCC states had special military agreements that would have provided the United States with air-base facilities. Kuwait in the 1980s opposed any concessions that would bring American military forces into the Gulf. For further details see MacDonald 1984: 105.

18 The American Rapid Deployment Force initially consisted of three marine brigades of 5,500 each, to be ready by 1983. This force was associated with 'over the horizon' American support, but it still needed access to air and port facilities. For further details see MacDonald 1984.

19 Reagan's new policy was known as seeking 'strategic consensus', which emphasised partnership with friendly governments. See MacDonald 1984: 102.

6 THE GULF WAR AND ITS AFTERMATH, 1990–2000

1 See Cordesman 1997.

2 On Saʿudi defence and security during the 1980s see Safran 1985.

3 During the Gulf crisis, the Saʿudi government encouraged this openness in a desperate attempt to dilute Western media criticism of its political system and government.

4 On the Gulf War and the liberation of Kuwait see Friedman 1991.

5 Copies of the Memorandum of Advice were distributed in Saudi Arabia and abroad, especially in London after the establishment of the CDLR in the British capital.

6 On the concept of advice and criticism in Islam see Asad 1993: 200–36.

7 For an abridged version of the reforms see Bulloch 1992.

8 For an evaluation of the reforms see Ishow 1997 and Agate 1997.

9 Amnesty International Reports in the 1990s highlighted the increase in cases of torture and imprisonment in Saudi Arabia immediately after the Gulf War. The latest of these reports was published in 2000.

10 Episodes of this opposition are discussed in chapters 4 and 5. The opposition magazine *Ṣawt al-Taliʿa* documented the development of the opposition of this era. See *Ṣawt al-Taliʿa* 1973–6.

11 Al-Masʿari fought a battle in British courts against the British government's decision to deport him to the Dominican Republic. He won the case to remain in Britain after incurring exorbitant legal fees that came out of CDLR's funds.

12 On the aspirations of Saʿudi youth see Yamani 2000.

7 NARRATIVES OF THE STATE, NARRATIVES OF THE PEOPLE

1 The project of writing Saʿudi history had always been part of Ibn Saʿud's policy to consolidate the state. Several of his Arab functionaries produced memoirs and monographs describing his conquests in Arabia. Fuʾad Ḥamza

(1936), Ḥafiẓ Wahba (1964) and Khayr al-Din al-Zirkili (1972), among others, fall into this category of state-sanctioned historiography. In the 1950s, intellectual ARAMCO officials contributed to this historiography, which was also approved of by the state. The work of the Arabist Rentz (1948) and the geologist Twitchell (1958) were among the first attempts to write a kind of Saʿudi history that glorified the role of the state. From the 1970s a new generation of state-sponsored Saʿudi historians began to emerge, thanks to oil wealth that allowed the training of indigenous scholars inside the country and abroad.

2 The main volumes consulted in this study are *al-Sira al-nabawiyya wa tarikh al-dawla al-islamiyya* (The Prophet's Biography and the History of the Islamic State, Shaʿfi and Hilmi 1993), *Tarikh al-ḥaḍara al-islamiyya* (The History of the Islamic Civilisation, al-Shaʿfi and Hilmi 1992) and *Tarikh al-mamlaka al-ʿarabiyya al-saʿudiyya* (The History of the Kingdom of Saudi Arabia, al-ʿUthaymin 1993). These volumes are taught during the last three years of secondary education.

3 For a full analysis of the history curriculum see Al-Rasheed 1999b.

4 Shaykh ibn Baz's views on Arab nationalism have been expressed in various *fatwas* and treatises on the subject.

5 Al-ʿUthaymin, among other historians, lists sixty names. See al-ʿUthaymin 1995: 359–61.

6 Examples include Saudi Arabia's role in establishing the Arab League and the Gulf Co-operation Council.

7 Examples include the Muslim World League in Mecca, mentioned earlier in this book.

8 The negative representation of Arab nationalism in the 1990s is contrasted with a more positive evaluation of the movement in the 1960s. For further details see Athopaiti 1987 and ʿAṭṭar 1988.

9 The reforms introduced in this speech were discussed in the previous chapter.

10 Western sources on the Shiʿa of Saudi Arabia include Quandt 1981, Buchan 1982, Goldberg 1986, Ende 1997 and Kostiner 1987.

11 Al-Ḥasan shows that under Ottoman rule the Shiʿa enjoyed greater freedom than they experienced under Saʿudi rule.

12 The Saʿudi Shiʿa opposition in London published the monthly magazine *al-Jazira al-ʿArabiyya*. The magazine was discontinued in 1993. For further details see Al-Rasheed 1998 and Fandy 1999. Since 1993, a new Saʿudi Shiʿa academic journal has appeared in Lebanon under the title *al-Waḥa*. The theme of Shiʿa identity is explored in *al-Waḥa* 1999: vol. 15, 157–62.

13 On other urban settlements in Najd, see Al-Rasheed 1991.

14 It is not surprising that several Saʿudi social scientists write in English and are based abroad. Social scientists share this experience with several other Saʿudi writers and literary figures, whose literature is published abroad. On Saʿudi women writers see Arebi 1994. For alternative literature produced in exile see ʿAbdullah 1997.

15 With the exception of weddings, Saʿudi society does not indulge itself in elaborate celebrations. Occasions marked with festivities in other Muslim

countries, for example the birth of the Prophet and the Muslim New Year, tend to pass without a celebration.

8 THE CHALLENGES OF A NEW ERA

1 International Monetary Fund, Public Information Notice 03/143, December 2003.
2 SAMBA 2008a and *Arab News*, 10 December 2007.
3 See 9/11 Commission 2004: 171.
4 BBC security correspondent Frank Gardner suffered a serious attack while in the al-Suwaydi neighbourhood in Riyadh. His cameraman died but he survived the attack. See Gardner 2006.
5 Jihadis entered into debate among themselves regarding the justification for targeting Saudi Arabia. The full details of this debate are in Al-Rasheed 2007.
6 Yusuf al-Aiyri was declared the leader of al-Qaʿidah in the Arabian Peninsula. He was believed to have been behind several terrorist attacks in Riyadh and other cities before Saʿudi security forces killed him in 2004. For further details on his biography and ideology see Meijer 2005 and 2008 and Al-Rasheed 2007.
7 The role of the Egyptian and Syrian Muslim Brotherhood cadres in Saudi Arabia has not been fully investigated. There are references to their activities in Kepel 2003. I have argued elsewhere that the Muslim Brotherhood cadres were themselves influenced by Saʿudi religious discourse, and it is simplistic to contribute the rise of the Saʿudi jihadi trend to their activities. See Al-Rasheed 2007: 59–101.
8 Since 9/11, Saʿudi academics and journalists have published articles in which radicalism was attributed to either the Sahwi trend or the religious establishment's interpretations, which dominate the Saʿudi religious studies curriculum. Outspoken figures include Mansour al-Noqaidan, Khalid al-Ghanami, ʿAli al-Musa and Turki al-Hamad.
9 Freedom House published a damning report on the Saʿudi educational curriculum. See Freedom House 2006.
10 The Sahwi shaykhs Ṣafar al-Ḥawali and Muḥsin al-Awaji offered to act as mediators between the government and the jihadis.
11 Jihadi debate about whether Saʿudis should go to Iraq to participate in the resistance flooded the internet after 2003. For full details, see Al-Rasheed 2007.
12 *Sawda al-Yamama* was an al-Jazeera documentary film about the alleged corruption of both Prince Sultan and his son Bandar during the weapons-purchase deal with the British firm BAE. The British government halted the investigation into the matter by the Serious Fraud Office in 2006–7. The Saʿudi leadership was infuriated by the film but was unable to prevent it being broadcast.

9 MODERNISING AUTHORITARIAN RULE

1 Modernising authoritarian rule is sometimes dubbed 'upgrading', a phenomenon that emerged in many Arab countries in the post-9/11 period.

Heydemann (2007) specifies four developments that, in his opinion, reflect the process of upgrading. These are: appropriating and containing civil society; managing political contestation; capturing the benefits of economic reform; and diversifying international linkages.

2 See www.saudiembassy.net, 2 August 2003.

3 See Qusti 2007.

4 Many articles appeared in the Saʿudi press on the need to accept the 'other' following the National Dialogue Forum. *Al-Waṭan* and *Arab News* took the lead in promoting tolerance through their opinion sections of the newspaper. See Qusti 2004.

5 Saʿudi officials stressed that no boundaries are imposed on the National Dialogue meetings. See Qusti 2007.

6 Those who bluntly called for political reform of the Saʿudi monarchy were operating outside the National Dialogue Forum. Their various petitions will be discussed later in this chapter.

7 The United Nations Development Programme monitors compliance with international human rights treaties: see UNDP 2008.

8 Human Rights Commission at www.haq.ksa.org.

9 See National Society for Human Rights at www.nshr.org.

10 See Human Rights Watch 2008a and 2008b.

11 The Saʿudi press glorified ʿAbdullah and remained silent on his inability to deal with urgent political demands. For a typical statement on the great role of ʿAbdullah in the Saʿudi press, see Saud 2008, in the Saʿudi electronic newspaper *Elaph*.

12 Awadh al-Badi publicised the merits of the Allegiance Committee as a step towards reforming the royal house. See al-Badi 2008.

13 The activism of this group, together with the various petitions they sent to the leadership, is documented in a single volume, published in Beirut. See Duat al-Islah al-Siyasi 2004.

14 As early as 2005, Simon Henderson noted the repression of the reformers' trend in Saudi Arabia. See Henderson 2005.

15 A new discourse on coexistence started to appear among Shiʿa activists. See Ibrahim 2007.

16 The statement of the twenty-two Wahhabi ʿ*ulama* was published on the internet. See Statement of 22 Wahhabi scholars on the Shiʿa 2008; al-Sadoun 2008.

17 The Shiʿa continue to express worries over the increasing number of *fatawa* against them, following the occupation of Iraq. For further details see Fattah and Abou al-Samh 2007.

18 Maha Yamani explains that polygamy is directly encouraged by state religious scholars. She studies the phenomenon from legal and social perspectives. See Yamani 2008.

19 Names include ʿAbduh Khal (1989 and 2003) and Hani Naqshabandi (2007); even princes began to publish social and historical novels, interwoven with autobiography. See, for example, al-Saʿud 2004. Al-Saʿud's novel was banned

as it delved into the life of his Baluchi slave mother, who lived in King Saʿud's harem.

20 Raja al-Sani's novel *Girls of Riyadh* was translated into several European languages. The novel captures the virtual lives of four Saʿudi women through their e-mail messages.

21 In addition to al-Sani, both journalist Samar al-Moqrin and writer Zaynab Hifni were condemned for their novels' explicit sexual messages. Their media appearances are transmitted on Youtube, with comments posted by viewers. In Western circles Hifni is hailed as a progressive author who talks and writes about sex and taboos. Her Saʿudi audience condemns her.

22 Saʿudi female bloggers were also active on the internet. See Sheikh 2007.

Bibliography

It has not been possible to provide date, place of publication and publisher for all Arabic items in this list. Arab authors are listed according to their last names, ignoring the definite article al-. Political pamphlets are listed under the names of political groups or organisations.

NEWSPAPERS AND MAGAZINES

The Economist
Financial Times
al-Ḥaras al-Waṭani
al-Ḥayat
al-Jazeera al-ʿArabiyya
al-Majala
Middle East International
al-Quds al-ʿArabi
al-Sharq al-Awṣat
Saudi Gazette
Ṣawt al-Ṭaliʿa
al-Waḥa
al-Yamama

SAUDI OFFICIAL PUBLICATIONS

Saudi Arabia 1996a *Le Royaume d'Arabie saoudite: guide pratique*, Ministry of Information

1996b *Architecture des mosquées: le modèle saoudien de construction des maisons de Dieux*

1996c *The Pictorial Book of King ʿAbd al-ʿAziz*, Ministry of Information, Foreign Information

1997 *al-Masmak Museum*, Ministry of Education

1998a *A Brief Account of the Life of King ʿAbd al-ʿAziz (Ibn Saʿud)*, Ministry of Information (centennial edition)

1998b *A Country and a Citizen for a Happy Decent Life*, Ministry of Information
1999a *Directorate of Centennial Celebrations*
1999b *Mu'tamar al-mamlaka al-ʿarabiyya al-Saʿudiyya fi mi'at ʿam* [Conference of the Kingdom of Saudi Arabia: 100 Years], Directorate of the Centennial Celebrations
n.d. *Darat al-malik ʿabd al-ʿaziz: kitab taʿrifi* [King ʿAbd al-ʿAziz Centre: an introductory book]

OTHER WORKS

9/11 Commission 2004 *The 9/11 Commission Report: Final Report of the National Commission on Terrorist Attacks Upon the United States*, New York: Norton & Company

Aba-Namay, R. 1993 'Constitutional Reforms: A Systemisation of Saudi Politics', *Journal of South Asian and Middle Eastern Studies*, 16/3: 43–88
ʿAbd al-ʿAziz, M. 1993 *al-Hujjar wa nata' ijuha fi ʿasr al-malik ʿabd al-ʿaziz* [al-Hujjar and their consequences during the era of King ʿAbd al-ʿAziz], London: Saqi Books
ʿAbd al-Rahim, A. 1976 *al-Dawla al-saʿudiyya al-'ula 1745–1818* [The first Saʿudi state, 1745–1818], Cairo
ʿAbdullah, A. 1990 *al-Bitrol wa al-akhlaq* [Oil and morality], Dar al-Ḍuha
1995 *al-ʿulama wa al-ʿarsh: thuna'iat al-ṣulṭa fi al-saʿudiyya* [The ʿ*ulama* and the throne: the duality of authority in Saudi Arabia], London: Dar al-Rafid
1997 *Wahhabi wa ṣarukh ṣini* [Wahhabi and a Chinese missile], Dar al-Qasim
Abir, M. 1988 *Saudi Arabia in the Oil Era. Regime and Elites: Conflict and Collaboration*, London: Croom Helm
1993 *Saudi Arabia: Government, Society and the Gulf Crisis*, London: Routledge
Abu ʿAliya, A. 1969 *Tarikh al-dawla al-saʿudiyya al-thaniya 1840–1891* [A history of the second Saʿudi state, 1840–1891], Riyadh
Abu Dhar 1980 *Thawra fi rihab mecca* [Revolution in Mecca], Dar Ṣawt al-Ṭaliʿa
1982 *Munaḍil min al-jazira* [Hero from the peninsula], Dar Ṣawt al-Ṭaliʿa
Abu Ḥakima, A. (ed.) 1967 *Lamʿ al-shihab fi sirat al-shaykh muhammad ibn ʿabd al-wahhab* [The brilliance of the meteor in the life of Muhammad ibn ʿAbd al-Wahhab], Beirut
Abu Ḥamad, A. 1992 *Empty Reforms: Saudi Arabia's New Basic Laws*, New York: Human Rights Watch
Admiralty 1916 *Handbook of Arabia*, London: HMSO (Naval Intelligence Division)
Agate, P. 1997 'L'Arabie Saoudite: quel état et quel(s) droit(s)', in A. Mahiou (ed.), *L'Etat et droit dans le monde arabe*, Paris: CNRS
Almana, M. 1980 *Arabia Unified: A Portrait of Ibn Saud*, London: Hutchinson Benham
al-Alusi, M. n.d. *Tarikh najd* [A history of Najd], Cairo
Amnesty International 2000 *Saudi Arabia: A Justice System without Justice*, London
al-ʿAmr, S. 1974 *The Hijaz under Ottoman Rule 1869–1914*, Saudi Arabia

Anderson, I. 1981 *Aramco, the United States and Saudi Arabia: A Study of the Dynamics of Foreign Oil Policy*, Princeton: Princeton University Press

al-ʿAngari, H. 1998 *The Struggle for Power in Arabia: Ibn Saud, Hussein and Great Britain 1914–1924*, Reading: Ithaca Press

Anscombe, F. 1997 *The Ottoman Gulf: The Creation of Kuwait, Saudi Arabia and Qatar*, New York: Columbia University Press

Anthony, J. 1984 'The Gulf Cooperation Council', in R. Darius, J. Amos and R. Magnus (eds.), *Gulf Security into the 1980s: Perceptual and Strategic Dimensions*, Stanford: Hoover Institution Press

Arebi, S. 1994 *Women and Words in Saudi Arabia: The Politics of Literary Discourse*, New York: Columbia University Press

Asad, T. 1993 *Genealogies of Religion: Discipline and Reasons of Power in Christianity and Islam*, Baltimore: Johns Hopkins University Press

Athopaiti, A. 1987 'Analysis of the Treatment of Arab and World History in Saudi Arabian and Egyptian High School Textbooks', Ph.D. thesis, University of Pittsburgh

ʿAṭṭar, M. 1988 'Quest for Identity: The Role of the Textbook in Forming the Saudi Arabian Identity', Ph.D. thesis, University of Oregon

Ayubi, N. 1991 *Political Islam: Religion and Politics in the Arab World*, London: Routledge

al-Azmeh, A. 1993 *Islam and Modernity*, London: Verso

al-Badi, A. 2008 'The Allegiance Committee', *Bulletin of the Arab Reform Initiative*, 14 February, available at www.arab-reform.net

al-Baghdadi, I. 1882 *ʿUnwan al-majd fi bayan aḥwal baghdad wa al-basra wa najd* [Glory in the history of Baghdad, Basra and Najd], London: Dar al-Ḥikma

Bahry, L. 1982 'The New Saudi Woman: Modernizing in an Islamic Framework', *Middle East Journal*, 36/4: 502–15

Bang, A. 1996 *The Idrisi State in ʿAsir 1906–1934: Political, Religious and Personal Prestige as State Building Factors in the Early Twentieth Century*, Bergen: Centre for Middle Eastern and Islamic Studies

al-Bassam, A. 1978 *ʿUlama najd khilal sitat qurun* [Najdi *ʿulama* during six centuries], Mecca: al-Nahḍa al-Haditha

Benoist-Mechin, J. 1957 *Arabian Destiny*, London: Elek Books

Birks, J., I. Seccombe and C. Sinclair 1988 'Labour Migration in the Arab Gulf States: Patterns, Trends, and Prospects', *International Migration*, 26/3: 267–86

Blanchard, C. 2008 *Qatar: Background and US Relations*, Washington: Congressional Research Service

Bligh, A. 1984 *From Prince to King: Royal Succession in the House of Saud in the Twentieth Century*, New York: New York University Press

1985 'The Saudi Religious Elite (ʿulama) as Participants in the Political System of the Kingdom', *International Journal of Middle East Studies*, 17/1: 37–50

Blunt, A. 1968 *A Pilgrimage to Nejd, the Cradle of the Arab Race: A Visit to the Court of the Arab Emir and our Persian Campaign*, 2 vols., London: John Murray

Braun, U. 1988 'The Gulf Cooperation Council's Security Role', in B. Pridham (ed.), *The Arab Gulf and the Arab World*, London: Croom Helm

Bronson, R. 2006 *Thicker than Oil: America's Uneasy Partnership with Saudi Arabia*, Oxford: Oxford University Press

Brown, A. 1999 *Oil, God, and Gold: The Story of Aramco and the Saudi Kings*, Boston: Houghton Mifflin

Buchan, J. 1982 'Secular and Religious Opposition in Saudi Arabia', in Niblock (ed.)

Bulloch, J. 1992 *Reforms of the Saudi Arabian Constitution*, London: Gulf Centre for Strategic Studies

Cannadine, D. and S. Price 1987 *Rituals of Royalty: Power and Ceremonial in Traditional Society*, Cambridge: Cambridge University Press

Carr, E. 1961 *What is History?* London: Penguin

Chaudhry, K. 1997 *The Price of Wealth: Economies and Institutions in the Middle East*, Ithaca: Cornell University Press

Committee for the Defence of Legitimate Rights in Saudi Arabia (CDLR) 1994 *Madha taqul lajnat al-difaʿ ʿan al-ḥuquq al-sharʿiyya fi al-jazira al-ʿarabiyya* [What does the Committee for Legitimate Rights in the Arabian Peninsula say?], London

1995 *Diwan al-iṣlaḥ* [An anthology of reform poetry], London

Cook, M. 1988 'The Expansion of the First Saudi State: The Case of Washm', in C. Bosworth, C. Issawi, R. Savory and A. Udovitch (eds.), *The Islamic World: From Classical to Modern Times*, Princeton: Darwin Press

Corancez, L. 1995 *The History of the Wahhabis from their Origin until the End of 1809*, trans. E. Tabet, Reading: Garnet

Cordesman, A. 1984 *The Gulf and the Search for Strategic Stability: Saudi Arabia, the Military Balance in the Gulf, and Trends in the Arab–Israeli Military Balance*, Boulder: Westview

1997 *Saudi Arabia: Guarding the Desert Kingdom*, Boulder: Westview

Cordesman, A. and N. Obaid 2005 *Saudi Militants in Iraq: An Assessment and Responses*, Washington: Centre for Strategic and International Studies, available at www.csis.org

Crawford, M. 1982 'Civil War, Foreign Intervention, and the Quest for Political Legitimacy: A Nineteenth-century Saudi Qadi's Dilemma', *International Journal of Middle East Studies*, 14: 227–48

Daḥlan, A. 1993 *Tarikh ashraf al-hijaz 1840–1883* [A History of the Hijaz Sharifs, 1840–1883], London: Saqi Books

al-Dakhil, S. 1966 'al-Qawl al-sadid fi akhbar imarat al-rashid' [Conclusive words in the history of the Rashidi emirate], in Ibn Rashid (ed.)

1982 *Sulayman ibn ṣaliḥ al-dakhil: ḥayatuh wa aʿmaluh* [Sulayman ibn Ṣaliḥ al-Dakhil: his life and work], collected by M. Ajil, Basra: Centre for Arab Gulf Studies

de Gaury, G. 1951 *Rulers of Mecca*, London: George Harrap & Co.

Dekmejian, H. 1994 'The Rise of Political Islam in Saudi Arabia', *Middle East Journal* 48/4: 627–43

1995 *Islam in Revolution: Fundamentalism in the Arab World*, New York: Syracuse University Press

Detalle, R. (ed.) 2000 *Tensions in Arabia: The Saudi–Yemeni Fault Line*, Baden Baden: Nomos Verlagsgesellschaft

Dickson, H. 1949 *The Arab of the Desert*, London: Allen & Unwin

1956 *Kuwait and her Neighbours*, London: Allen & Unwin

Doughty, C. 1979 *Travels in Arabia Deserta*, 2 vols., Cambridge: Cambridge University Press

Doumato, E. 1992 'Gender, Monarchy and National Identity in Saudi Arabia', *British Journal of Middle Eastern Studies*, 19/1: 31–47

2000 *Getting God's Ear: Women, Islam and Healing in Saudi Arabia and the Gulf*, New York: Columbia University Press

Dresch, P. 2000 *A History of Modern Yemen*, Cambridge: Cambridge University Press

Duat al-Islah al-Siyasi 2004 *Rabi al-saoudiyya wa mukhrajat al-qam*ʿ [The Saudi Arabian spring and the way out of repression], Beirut: Dar al-Kunuz

Duguid, S. 1970 'A Biographical Approach to the Study of Social Change in the Middle East: Abdullah Tariki as a New Man', *International Journal of Middle East Studies*, 1/1: 195–220

al-Dumayni, A. 2005 *Zaman al-sijn, azniat al-horiyya* [Prison time, times of freedom], Beirut: Dar al-Kunuz

Dunn, M. 1995 'Is the Sky Falling? Saudi Arabia's Economic Problems and Political Stability', *Middle East Policy*, 3/4: 29–39

Ende, W. 1997 'The Nakhawila: A Shiʿite Community in Medina, Past and Present', *Die Welt des Islams*, 37/3: 264–348

Esposito, J. 1990 *The Iranian Revolution: Its Global Impact*, Miami: Florida International University Press

Fabietti, U. 1984 *Il Popolo del Deserto: i Beduini Shammar del Gran Nafud Arabia Saudita*, Laterza: Roma-Bari

Facey, W. 1992 *Riyadh: The Old City*, London: IMMEL Publishing

1997 *Dirʿiyyah and the First Saudi State*, London: Stacey International

al-Fahad, A. 2001 'The ʿImama vs. the ʿIqal: Haḍari–Bedouin Conflict and the Formation of the Saʿudi State', paper presented at the Second Mediterranean Social and Political Research Meeting, March 2001, European University Institute, Florence

al-Falih, M. 2000 *Sikaka al-jawf fi nihayat al-qarn al-ishrin* [Sikaka al-Jawf at the end of the twentieth century], Beirut: Bissan

Fandy, M. 1998 'Safar al-Hawali: Saʿudi Islamist or Saʿudi Nationalist?', *Islam and Christian–Muslim Relations*, 9/1: 5–21

1999 *Saudi Arabia and the Politics of Dissent*, Basingstoke: Macmillan

al-Faqih, S. n.d.a *Kayfa ufakir al-saʿud: dirasa nafsiyya* [How the Al Saʿud think: a psychological study], London: Movement for Islamic Reform in Arabia

n.d.b *al-Niẓam al-saʿudi fi mizan al-islam* [The Saʿudi regime in Islam], London: Movement for Islamic Reform in Arabia

n.d.c *Zilzal al-sa'ud: qiṣat al-ṣaḥwa al-islamiyya fi bilad al-ḥaramayn* [The earthquake of Al Sa'ud: the story of the Islamic awakening in the Land of the Two Holy Mosques], London: Movement for Islamic Reform in Arabia
Fattah, H. 1997 *The Politics of Regional Trade in Iraq, Arabia and the Gulf 1745–1900*, Albany: State University of New York Press
2007 'After Saudis' First Steps, Efforts for Reform Stall', *New York Times*, 26 April
Fattah, H. and R. Abou al-Samh 2007 'Saudi Shiites Fear Gains Could be Lost', *New York Times*, 5 February
Fernea, R. 1987 'Technological Innovation and Class Development among the Bedouin of Hail', in B. Cannon (ed.), *Terroirs et sociétés au Maghreb et Moyen-Orient*, Paris: Maison de l'Orient
Field, M. 1984 *The Merchants: Big Business Families of Saudi Arabia and the Gulf States*, New York: Overlook Press
Firman Fund 1999 'Saudi Arabia Economic Trends and Outlook', http://tradeport.org/ts/countries/saudiarabia/trends.html
Fraser, C. 1997 'In Defense of Allah's Realm: Religion and Statecraft in Saudi Foreign Policy Strategy', in S. Rudolf and J. Piscatori (eds.), *Transnational Religion and Fading States*, Boulder: Westview
Freedom House 2006 *Saudi Arabia's Curriculum of Intolerance*, available at www.freedomhouse.org
Friedman, N. 1991 *Desert Victory: The War of Kuwait*, Annapolis: Naval Institute Press
Gardner, F. 2006 *Blood and Sand*, London: Bantam Press
Gause, F. G. III 1990 *Saudi–Yemeni Relations: Domestic Structures and Foreign Influence*, New York: Columbia University Press
1994 *Oil Monarchies: Domestic and Security Challenges in the Arab Gulf States*, New York: Council on Foreign Relations
2000a 'The Persistence of Monarchy in the Arabian Peninsula: A Comparative Analysis', in Kostiner (ed.)
2000b 'Saudi Arabia over a Barrel', *Foreign Affairs*, 79/3: 80–94
Glubb, J. 1960 *War in the Desert*, London: Hodder & Stoughton
Goldberg, J. 1986 'The Shi'i Minority in Saudi Arabia', in J. Cole and N. Keddie (eds.), *Shi'ism and Social Protest*, New York: Yale University Press
Golub, D. 1985 *When Oil and Politics Mix: Saudi Oil Policy, 1973–1985*, Harvard: Harvard Middle East Papers 4
al-Goṣaybi, G. 1991 *Ḥata la takun fitna* [To avoid dissent]
Grayson, B. 1982 *Saudi–American Relations*, Washington: University Press of America
The Gulf in a Year 2003 2004 Dubai: Gulf Research Centre
Gulf Year Book 2006–2007 2007 Dubai: Gulf Research Centre
Habib, J. 1978 *Ibn Saud's Warriors of Islam: The Ikhwan of Najd and their Role in the Creation of the Saudi Kingdom, 1910–1930*, Leiden: Brill
Halliday, F. 1982 'A Curious and Close Liaison: Saudi Arabia's Relations with the United States', in Niblock (ed.)

al-Hamad, T. 2005 *Rih al-jana* [The wind of heaven], Beirut: al-Saqi

Hameed, M. 1986 *Saudi Arabia, the West and the Security of the Gulf*, London: Croom Helm

Ḥamza, F. 1936 *Qalb al-jazira al-ʿarabiyya* [The heart of the Arabian Peninsula]

al-Ḥarbi, D. 1999 *Nisaʾshahirat min najd* [Famous women from Najd], Riyadh: al-Dara

al-Ḥasan, H. 1993 *al-Shiʿa fi al-mamlaka al-ʿarabiyya al-saʿudiyya* [The Shiʿa in the Kingdom of Saudi Arabia], Muʾasasat al-Baqiʿ li Iḥyaʾ al-Turath: vol. I, *al-ʿAhd al-turki (1871–1913)* [The Ottoman period (1871–1913)]; vol. II, *al-ʿAhd al-saʿudi (1913–1991)* [The Saʿudi period (1913–1991)]

al-Ḥawali, S. 1991 *Kashf al-ghamma ʿan ʿulama al-umma* [The lifting of the *ʿulama*'s distress], Dar al-Ḥikma

Heller, M. and N. Safran 1985 *The New Middle Class and Regime Stability in Saudi Arabia*, Harvard: Harvard Middle East Papers 3

Helms, C. 1981 *The Cohesion of Saudi Arabia*, London: Croom Helm

Henderson, S. 1994 *After King Fahd: Succession in Saudi Arabia*, Washington: Washington Institute for Near East Policy, Washington Institute Policy Papers 37

2005 'The Arrest of Saudi Reformers One Year On', Washington: Washington Institute for Near East Policy, Policy Watch 973, available at www.thewashingtoninstitute.org

Herb, M. 1999 *All in the Family: Absolutism, Revolution and Democracy in the Middle East Monarchies*, Albany: State University of New York Press

Heydemann, S. 2007 'Upgrading Authoritarianism in the Arab World', Washington: Saban Centre for Middle East Policy at the Brookings Institution, Analysis paper no. 13, October

al-Hodayf, M. 2006 *Nuqtat taftish* [Checkpoint], Riyadh: n.p.

Hogarth, D. 1904 *The Penetration of Arabia*, London: Lawrence & Bullen

1917 *Hejaz before World War I: A Handbook*, Cambridge: Oleander Press

1922 *Arabia*, Oxford: Clarendon Press

Holden, D. and P. Johns 1981 *The House of Saud*, London: Sidgwick

Howarth, D. 1964 *The Desert King: A Life of Ibn Saud*, Beirut: Librairie du Liban

Human Rights Watch 1999 *The Internet in the Middle East and North Africa: Free Expression and Censorship*, New York

2008a *Perpetual Minors: Human Rights Abuses Stemming from Male Guardianship and Sex Segregation in Saudi Arabia*, New York: Human Rights Watch

2008b *Precarious Justice: Arbitrary Detention and Unfair Trials in the Deficient Criminal Justice System of Saudi Arabia*, New York: Human Rights Watch

al-Huthlul, A. 2004 *al-Intihar al-majur* [Hired suicide], Beirut: al-Saqi

Ibn Bishr, O. 1930 *ʿUnwan al-majd fi tarikh najd* [Glory in the history of Najd], 2 vols., Mecca

Ibn Ghanam, H. 1970 *Tarikh najd* [The history of Najd], 2 vols., Cairo

Ibn ʿIssa, I. 1966 *Tarikh baʿḍ al-ḥawadith al-waqiʿa fi najd* [A history of some events in Najd], Riyadh

Ibn Rashid, D. 1966 *Nabtha tarikhiyya ʿan najd* [A short history of Najd], Beirut
Ibrahim, F. 2007 *al-Shiʿa fi al-saoudiyya* [The Shiʿa in Saudi Arabia], Beirut: al-Saqi
International Crisis Group 2004 *Can Saudi Arabia Reform Itself?* ICG Middle East Report no. 28, Cairo/Brussels: International Crisis Group
International Monetary Fund (IMF) 1999 *International Statistics Yearbook*, Washington
Ishow, H. 1997 'L'Arabie Saoudite: Les institutions politiques de 1992. Les droits de l'homme et l' état de droit', in A. Mahiou (ed.), *L'Etat de droit dans le monde arabe*, Paris: CNRS
al-Juhany, M. 1983 'The History of Najd prior to the Wahhabis: A Study of Social, Political, Economic and Religious Conditions in Najd during Three Centuries preceding the Wahhabi Reform Movement', Ph.D. thesis, University of Washington
Kechichian, J. 1986 'The Role of the ʿUlama in the Politics of an Islamic State: The Case of Saudi Arabia', *International Journal of Middle East Studies*, 18: 53–71
1993 *Political Dynamics and Security in the Arabian Peninsula through the 1990s*, Santa Monica: Rand
2001 *Succession in Saudi Arabia*, New York: Palgrave
Kepel, G. 2003 *Jihad: The Trail of Political Islam*, London: I. B. Tauris
Khal, A. 1989 *Mudun takul al-ushub* [Cities eat grass], Beirut: al-Saqi
2003 *al-Ṭin* [Mud], Beirut: al-Saqi
Kishk, M. 1981 *al-Saʿudiyyun wa al-ḥal al-islami* [The Saʿudis and the Islamic solution], Massachusetts
Kostiner, J. 1985 'On Instruments and their Designers: The Ikhwan of Najd and the Emergence of the Saudi State', *Middle Eastern Studies*, 21: 298–323
1987 'Shiʿi Unrest in the Gulf', in M. Kramer (ed.), *Shiʿism, Resistance and Revolution*, Colorado: Westview
1991 'Transforming Dualities: Tribe and State Formation in Saudi Arabia', in P. Khoury and J. Kostiner (eds.), *Tribes and State Formation in the Middle East*, London: I. B. Tauris
1993 *The Making of Saudi Arabia 1916–1936*, Oxford: Oxford University Press
(ed.) 2000 *Middle East Monarchies: The Challenge of Modernity*, Boulder: Lynne Rienner
Lacey, R. 1981 *The Kingdom*, London: Hutchinson & Co.
Lackner, H. 1978 *A House Built on Sand: A Political Economy of Saudi Arabia*, London: Ithaca Press
Leatherdale, C. 1983 *Britain and Saudi Arabia 1925–1939: The Imperial Oasis*, London: Frank Cass
Lees, B. 1978 *Who is who in Saudi Arabia*, London: Europa
1980 *A Handbook of the Al-Saud*, London: Royal Genealogies
Leverrier, I. 1996 'L'Arabie Saoudite, le pèlerinage et l'Iran', *Cahiers d'études sur la Méditerranée orientale et le monde turco-iranien*, 22: 111–47

Long, D. 1985 *The United States and Saudi Arabia: Ambivalent Allies*, Boulder: Westview

1997 *The Kingdom of Saudi Arabia*, Gainesville: University of Florida Press

Lorimer, J. G. 1908 *Gazetteer of the Persian Gulf, Oman and Central Arabia*, 2 vols., Calcutta: Government Print House

MacDonald, C. 1984 'Saudi Policy and the Gulf Security', in R. Darius, J. Amos and R. Magnus (eds.), *Gulf Security into the 1980s: Perceptual and Strategic Dimensions*, Stanford: Hoover Institution Press

MacFarquhar, N. 2005 'Saudi Reformers: Seeking Rights, Paying a Price', *New York Times*, 9 June

al-Masʿari, M. 1995 *al-Adilla al-shariʿyya ʿala ʿadam shariʿyyat al-dawla al-saʿudiyya* [*Shariʿa* evidence on the illegitimacy of the Saʿudi state], London: Dar al-Sharʿiyya

1997a *Muḥasabat al-ḥukkam* [The accountability of rulers], London: Dar al-Rafid

1997b *ʿAsl al-islam wa haqiqat al-tawḥid* [The origins of Islam and the truth of the doctrine of the oneness of God], London: Dar al-Rafid

McLoughlin, L. 1993 *Ibn Saud: Founder of a Kingdom*, Basingstoke: Macmillan

Meijer, R. 2005 'The "Cycle of Contention" and the Limits of Terrorism in Saudi Arabia', in Paul Aarts and G. Nonneman (eds.), *Saudi Arabia in the Balance: Political Economy, Society, Foreign Affairs*, London: Hurst & Co.

2008 'Yusuf al-Uyairi and the Transnationalisation of Saudi Jihadism', in M. Al-Rasheed (ed.), *Kingdom without Borders: Saudi Political, Religious and Media Frontiers*, London: Hurst & Co.

Meijer, R. (ed.) 2009 *Global Salafism: Islam's New Religious Movements*, London: Hurst & Co.

Menoret, P. 2005 'The Municipal Elections in Saudi Arabia 2005: First Steps on Democratic Path', *Bulletin of the Arab Reform Initiative*, available at www.arab-reform.net

Middle East Economic Survey 2004 'Saudi Reform' vol. XLVII, no. 2, 12 January

Miller, A. 1980 *Search for Security: Saudi Arabian Oil and American Foreign Policy 1939–1949*, Chapel Hill: University of North Carolina Press

Monroe, E. 1974 *Philby of Arabia*, London: Faber & Faber

al-Moqrin, S. 2005 *Nisa al-munkar* [Women of vice] Beirut: al-Saqi

Mortel, R. 1991 'The Origins and Early History of the Husaynid Amirate of Madina to the End of the Ayyubid Period', *Studia Islamica*, 74: 63–77

1994 'The Husaynid Amirate of Madina during the Mamluk Period', *Studia Islamica*, 80: 97–119

Mosa, A. 2000 'Pressures in Saudi Arabia', *International Higher Education*, 20: 23–5

Mouawad, J. 2008 'The Construction Site Called Saudi Arabia', *New York Times*, 20 January

Movement for Islamic Reform in Arabia (MIRA) n.d.a *al-Birnamij al-siyasi* [The political programme], London n.d.b *al-Qaḍiyya al-saʿudiyya bayn al-saʾil wa al-mujib* [The Saʿudi problem between question and answer], London

n.d.c *Communiqués* 1–47

n.d.d *Fi muwajahat al-saʿud* [Confrontation with Al Saʿud], London

n.d.e Bin Laden pamphlet, London

Mudhakarat al-naṣiḥa li ḥukkam al-saʿudiyya al-ʿumalaʾ [Memorandum of advice] n.d.

Munif, A. 1993 *The Trench*, trans. P. Theroux, New York: Vintage

Musil, A. 1928 *Northern Negd*, New York: American Geographical Society

al-Naim, A. 1425 AH [2004] 'al-Faqr al-hadari wa irtibatuhu bi al-hijra al-dakhiliyya' [Urban poverty and its links to internal migration], Ph.D. thesis, King Saud University

Naqshabandi, H. 2007 *Ikhtilas* [Fraud], Beirut: al-Saqi

Niblock, T. 1982a (ed.) *State, Society and Economy in Saudi Arabia*, London: Croom Helm

1982b 'Social Structure and the Development of the Saudi Arabian Political System', in Niblock (ed.)

2006 *Saudi Arabia: Power, Legitimacy and Survival*, London: Routledge

Ochsenwald, W. 1984 *Religion, Society and the State in Arabia: The Hijaz under Ottoman Control 1840–1908*, Columbus: Ohio State University Press

Okruhlik, G. and P. Conge 1997 'National Autonomy, Labor Migration and Political Crisis: Yemen and Saudi Arabia', *Middle East Journal*, 51/4: 554–65

al-ʿOmar, N. n.d. *al-Rafiḍa fi bilad al-tawhid* [Rejectionists in the land of monotheism] pamphlet, no publisher

Peck, M. 1980 'The Saudi–American Relationship and King Faisal', in W. Beling (ed.), *King Faisal and the Modernisation of Saudi Arabia*, London: Croom Helm

Pershit, A. 1979 'Tribute Relations', in S. Seaton and H. Claessen (eds.), *Political Anthropology: The State of Art*, The Hague: Mouton

Peters, F. 1994 *Mecca: A Literary History of the Muslim Holy Land*, Princeton: Princeton University Press

Peterson, E. 1988 *The Gulf Cooperation Council: Search for Unity in a Dynamic Region*, Boulder: Westview

Peterson, J. 1976 'Britain and "the Oman War": An Arabian Entanglement', *Asian Affairs*, 63/3: 285–98

1993 *Historical Dictionary of Saudi Arabia*, Metuchen: Scarecrow Press

Philby, H. St J. B. 1952 *Arabian Jubilee*, London: Hale

1955 *Saudi Arabia*, London: Benn

Piscatori, J. 1983 'Islamic Values and National Interest: The Foreign Policy of Saudi Arabia', in A. Daweesha (ed.), *Islam in Foreign Policy*, Cambridge: Cambridge University Press

al-Qaḥṭani, F. 1987 *Zilzal juhayman fi mecca* [The earthquake of Juhayman in Mecca], London: Safa

1988a *Ṣiraʿ al-ajniha fi al-ʿaʾila al-saʿudiyya* [A struggle of wings within the Saʿudi family], London: Safa

1988b *al-Yamani wa al-saʿud* [Yamani and Al Saʿud], London: Safa

Quandt, W. 1981 *Saudi Arabia in the 1980s: Foreign Policy, Security, and Oil*, Washington: Brookings Institution

Qusti, R. 2004 'Accepting Others in Saudi Arabia', *Arab News*, 29 December

2007 'National Dialogue Chief Says No Boundaries in Forums', *Arab News*, 20 April

Raḍwan, M. n.d. *Qiraʾa ṣariḥa fi mudhakarat al-naṣiḥa* [An explicit reading of the Memorandum of Advice], London: Dar-al-Ḥikma

Al-Rasheed, M. 1991 *Politics in an Arabian Oasis: The Rashidi Tribal Dynasty*, London: I. B. Tauris

1996a 'Saudi Arabia's Islamic Opposition', *Current History*, 95/597: 16–22

1996b 'God the King and the Nation: Political Rhetoric in Saudi Arabia in the 1990s', *Middle East Journal*, 50/3: 359–71

1997 'La Couronne et le turban: l'état saoudien à la recherche d'une nouvelle légitimité', in B. Kudmani-Darwish and M. Chartouni-Dubarry (eds.), *Les Etats arabes face à la contestation islamiste*, Paris: Armand Colin

1998 'The Shiʿa of Saudi Arabia: A Minority in Search of Cultural Authenticity', *British Journal of Middle Eastern Studies*, 25/1: 121–38

1999a 'Evading State Control: Political Protest and Technology in Saudi Arabia', in A. Cheater (ed.), *The Anthropology of Power*, London: Routledge

1999b 'Political Legitimacy and the Production of History: The Case of Saudi Arabia', in L. Martin (ed.), *New Frontiers in Middle East Security*, New York: St Martin's Press

2005 'Circles of Power: Royals and Society in Saudi Arabia', in Paul Aarts and G. Nonneman (eds.), *Saudi Arabia in the Balance: Political Economy, Society, Foreign Affairs*, London: Hurst & Co.

2006 'Saudi Arabia: The Challenge of the American Invasion of Iraq', in R. Fawn and R. Hinnebusch (eds.), *The Iraq War: Causes and Consequences*, London: Lynne Rienner Press

2007 *Contesting the Saudi State: Islamic Voices from a New Generation*, Cambridge: Cambridge University Press

2008a 'Introduction: An Assessment of Saudi Political, Religious and Media Expansion', in M. Al-Rasheed (ed.), *Kingdom without Borders: Saudi Arabia's Political, Religious and Media Frontiers*, London: Hurst & Co.

2009 'The Local and the Global in Saudi Salafi Jihadi Discourse', in Meijer (ed.)

2008c 'The Minaret and the Palace: Obedience at Home and Rebellion Abroad', in M. Al-Rasheed (ed.), *Kingdom without Borders: Saudi Arabia's Political, Religious and Media Frontiers*, London: Hurst & Co.

Al-Rasheed, M. and L. Al-Rasheed 1996 'The Politics of Encapsulation: Saudi Policy towards Tribal and Religious Opposition', *Middle Eastern Studies*, 32/1: 96–119

al-Rashid, I. 1985 *The Struggle between the Two Princes: The Kingdom of Saudi Arabia in the Final Days of Ibn Saud*, Salisbury, NC: Documentary Publications
Rentz, G. 1948 'Muhammad ibn ʿAbd al-Wahhab (1703/04–1792) and the Beginning of the Unitarian Empire in Arabia', Ph.D. thesis, University of California, Berkeley
al-Rifaʿi, M. 1995 *al-Mashruʿ al-iṣlaḥi fi al-saʿudiyya: qiṣat al-ḥawali wa al-ʿawdah* [The reform programme in Saudi Arabia: the story of al-Ḥawali and al-ʿAwdah]
Rihani, A. 1928 *Ibn Saud of Arabia*, London: Constable & Co. Ltd
Rosenfeld, H. 1965 'The Social Composition of the Military in the Process of State Formation in the Arabian Desert', *Journal of the Royal Anthropological Institute*, 95: 75–86, 174–94
Royal Embassy of Saudi Arabia 2003 Address to the Nation by Crown Prince Abdullah at the Conclusion of National Dialogue, 3 August, available at www.saudiembassy.net
2004 'First Independent Human Rights Organisation in Saudi Arabia', 3 July, available at www.saudiembassy.net
al-Sadoun, S. 2008 'Shuyukh al-bayanat' [The petitions Shaykhs], *Elaph*, 5 June
al-Ṣafadi, A. n.d. *Qanun al-fasad fi al-mamlaka al-ʿarabiyya al-saʿudiyya* [The law of corruption in Saudi Arabia], Manshurat Iqra
Safran, N. 1985 *Saudi Arabia: The Ceaseless Quest for Security*, Cambridge, MA: Harvard University Press
al-Saʿid, N. 1981 *Tarikh al-saʿud* [The history of Al Saʿud], Dar Mecca
Salame, G. 1993 'Political Power and the Saudi State', in A. Hourani, P. Khoury and M. Wilson (eds.), *The Middle East: A Reader*, London: I. B. Tauris
al-Salloum, H. 1995 *Education in Saudi Arabia*, Beltsville: Amana Publications
SAMBA 2004 *Saudi Arabia's 2005 Budget, 2004 Performance*, December, available at www.samba.com
2008a *Saudi Arabia's 2008 Budget: 2007 Performance*, January, available at www.samba.com
2008b *The Saudi Economy: Recent Performance and Prospects for 2008–2009*, April, available at www.samba.com
Samore, G. 1983 'Royal Family Politics in Saudi Arabia 1953–1982', Ph.D. thesis, Harvard University
Saud, F. 2008 'al-Malik Abdullah', *Elaph*, 20 June
al-Saʿud, S. 2004 *Qalb min banqalan* [A heart from Banqalan], Beirut: al-Farabi
Al-Saʿud, Ṭalal ibn ʿAbd al-ʿAziz 1999 *Ṣuwar min hayat ʿabd al-ʿaziz* [Portraits from the life of ʿAbd al-ʿAziz], 4th edn, Riyadh: Dar al-Shuf
Scott Doran, M. 2004 'The Saudi Paradox', *Foreign Affairs*, 83/1: 35–51
Seccombe, I. and R. Lawless 1986 'Foreign Worker Dependence in the Gulf, and the International Oil Companies: 1910–50', *International Migration Review*, 20/3: 548–74
al-Shaʿfi, M. and H. Ḥilmi 1992 *Tarikh al-haḍara al-islamiyya* [A history of the Islamic civilisation], Riyadh: Wizarat al-Maʿarif

1993 *al-Sira al-nabawiyya wa tarikh al-dawla al-islamiyya* [The Prophet's biography and the history of the Islamic state], Riyadh: Wizarat al-Maʿarif

Shamiyyah, J. 1986 *al-Saʿud: maḍihum wa ḥaḍiruhum* [Al Saʿud: their past and present], London

al-Shamrani 1988a *Mamlakat al-faḍaʾiḥ: asrar al-quṣur al-malakiyya al-saʿudiyya* [The kingdom of scandals: the secrets of royal palaces in Saudi Arabia], Beirut: Dar al-Insan

1988b *Faysal: al-qatil wa al-qatil* [Faysal: murderer and murdered], Beirut: Dar al-Insan

Sharara, W. 1981 *al-Ahl wa al-ghanima* [Kin and booty], Beirut

al-Shaykh, A., S. al-Dakhil and A. al-Zayir 1981 *Intifaḍat al-minṭaqa al-sharqiyya* [The uprising of the eastern province], Munathamat al-Thawra al-Islamiyya

al-Shaykh, T. 1988 *al-Bitrol wa al-siyasa fi al-mamlaka al-ʿarabiyya al-saʿudiyya* [Oil and politics in the Kingdom of Saudi Arabia], London: Safa

Sheikh, H. 2007 'Blogs Fast Becoming Place of Refuge for Women', *Khaleej Times*, 23 February

al-Sibaʿi, A. 1984 *Tarikh mecca* [A history of Mecca]

Sindi, A. 1980 'King Faisal and Pan-Islamism', in W. Beling (ed.), *King Faisal and the Modernisation of Saudi Arabia*, London: Croom Helm

Sluglett, P. and M. Sluglett 1982 'The Precarious Monarchy: Britain, Abd al-Aziz ibn Saud and the Establishment of the Kingdom of Hijaz, Najd and its Dependencies, 1925–1932', in Niblock (ed.)

Al-Sowayyegh, A. 1980 'Saudi Oil Policy during King Faisal's Era', in W. Beling (ed.), *King Faisal and the Modernisation of Saudi Arabia*, London: Croom Helm

Statement of 22 Wahhabi scholars on the Shia 2008 'Irifuhum wa ihtharuhum' [Know them and beware of them]

Steinberg, G. 2001 'The Shiites in the Eastern Province of Saudi Arabia (al-Aḥasaʾ), 1913–1953', in R. Brunner and W. Ende (eds.), *The Twelver Shia in Modern Times: Religious Culture and Political History*, Leiden: Brill

Taqi, S. 1988 *al-Wajh al-akhar li aḥdath mecca* [The other face of the events in Mecca], Tehran: Kayhan

Teitelbaum, J. 1998 'Sharif Husayn ibn ʿAli and the Hashemite Vision of the Post-Ottoman Order: From Chieftaincy to Suzerainty', *Middle Eastern Studies*, 34/1: 103–22

2001 *The Rise and Fall of the Hashemite Kingdom of Arabia*, London: C. Hurst & Co.

al-Torki, S. 1986 *Women in Saudi Arabia: Ideology and Behavior among Elite Women*, New York: Columbia University Press

al-Torki, S. and D. Cole 1989 *Arabian Oasis City: The Transformation of ʿUnayzah*, Austin: University of Texas Press

Tripp, C. 2000 *A History of Iraq*, Cambridge: Cambridge University Press

Troeller, G. 1976 *The Birth of Saudi Arabia: Britain and the Rise of the House of Saʿud*, London: Frank Cass

Twitchell, K. 1958 *Saudi Arabia*, 3rd edn, Princeton: Princeton University Press

United Nations Development Programme (UNDP) 2008 Human Rights Profiles: Saudi Arabia, available at www.arabhumanrights.org

al-ʿUthaymin, A. 1981 *Nashʾat imarat al-rashid* [The rise of the Rashidi emirate], Riyadh: Riyadh University

1993 *Tarikh al-mamlaka al-ʿarabiyya al-saʿudiyya* [A history of the Kingdom of Saudi Arabia], Riyadh: Wizarat al-Maʿarif

1995 *Tarikh al-mamlaka al-ʿarabiyya al-saʿudiyya* [A history of the Kingdom of Saudi Arabia], Riyadh: al-ʿUbaykan

1997 *Tarikh al-mamlaka al-ʿarabiyya al-saʿudiyya* [A history of the Kingdom of Saudi Arabia], Riyadh: Maktabat al-Malik Fahd al-Waṭaniyya

van der Meulen, D. 1957 *The Wells of Ibn Saud*, London: John Murray

Vassiliev, A. 1998 *The History of Saudi Arabia*, London: Saqi Books

Vitalis, R. 1997 'The Closing of the Arabian Oil Frontier and the Future of Saudi–American Relations', *Middle East Report*, 204: 15–21

1998 'Aramco World: Business and Culture on the Arabian Oil Frontier', in K. Merrill (ed.), *The Modern Worlds of Business and Industry*, Princeton: Princeton University Press

1999 review of Chaudhry, *The Price of Wealth*, in the *International Journal of Middle East Studies*, 31/4: 659–61

Wahba, Ḥ. 1964 *Arabian Days*, London: Arthur Barker Ltd

Wallin, G. 1854 'Narrative of a Journey from Cairo, to Medina and Mecca, by Suez, Araba, Tawila, al-Jauf, Jublae, Hail and Negd in 1845', *Journal of the Royal Geographical Society*, 24: 115–201

Wilkinson, J. 1987 *The Imamate Tradition of Oman*, Cambridge: Cambridge University Press

Wilson, P. and D. Graham 1994 *Saudi Arabia: The Coming Storm*, New York: M. E. Sharpe

Winckler, O. 2008 'The Surprising Results of the Saudi Arabian Demographic Census', *International Journal of Middle East Studies*, 40: 12–15

Winder, R. 1965 *Saudi Arabia in the Nineteenth Century*, New York: St Martin's Press

Yamani, M. 1997 'Evading the Habits of a Life Time: The Adaptation of Hejazi Dress to the New Social Order', in N. Lindisfarne-Tapper and B. Ingham (eds.), *Languages of Dress in the Middle East*, London: Curzon

1998 'Cross-Cultural Marriages within Islam: Ideals and Realities', in R. Berger and R. Hill (eds.), *Cross-Cultural Marriage*, Oxford: Berg

2000 *Changed Identities: The Challenge of the New Generation in Saudi Arabia*, London: Royal Institute of International Affairs

Yamani, Maha 2008 *Polygamy and Law in Contemporary Saudi Arabia*, Reading: Ithaca

al-Yassini, A. 1985 *Religion and State in the Kingdom of Saudi Arabia*, Boulder: Westview

1987 *al-Din wa al-dawla fi al-mamlaka al-ʿarabiyya al-saʿudiyya* [Religion and state in the Kingdom of Saudi Arabia], London: Saqi Books

Yizraeli, S. 1997 *The Remaking of Saudi Arabia*, Tel Aviv: Moshe Dayan Centre for Middle East and African Studies

al-Zaʿarir, M. 1997 *Imarat al-rashid fi haʾil* [The Rashidi emirate in Ha'il], Amman: Bisan

al-Zirkili, K. 1970 *Shibh al-jazira fi ʿahd al-malik ʿabd al-ʿaziz* [The Arabian Peninsula during the period of King ʿAbd al-ʿAziz], 1st edn, 4 vols., Beirut: Dar al-Qalam

1972 *al-Wajiz fi sirat al-malik ʿabd al-ʿaziz* [A short account of the life of King ʿAbd al-ʿAziz], Beirut: Dar al-ʿIlm

al-Zulfa, M. 1995 *ʿAsir fi ʿahd al-malik ʿabd al-ʿaziz* [ʿAsir during the reign of King ʿAbd al-ʿAziz], Riyadh: Maṭabiʿ al-Farazdaq

1997 *Imarat abi ʿarish wa ʿalaqatha bi al-dawla al-ʿuthmaniyya 1838–1849* [The emirate of Abu ʿArish and its relations with the Ottoman Empire], Riyadh: Maṭabiʿ al-Farazdaq

Index

9/11, 211, 222–4, 226, 227, 228, 275
Commission, 223

Abbas, Mahmoud, 240
ʿAbd al-ʿAziz (1765–1803), 20, 21, 191
ʿAbd al-ʿAziz (son of King Fahd), 212
ʿAbd al-ʿAziz al-Muqrin, 226
ʿAbd al-ʿAziz al-Qasim, 269
ʿAbd al-ʿAziz al-Sheikh, Grand Mufti, 265
ʿAbd al-ʿAziz ibn ʿAbd al-Raḥman Al Saʿud *see* Ibn Saʿud
ʿAbd al-ʿAziz ibn Mutʿib ibn Rashid, 37–8
ʿAbd al-Ḥamid al-Sarraj, 112
ʿAbd al-Muṭṭalib ibn Ghalib, Sharif of Mecca, 20, 32
ʿAbd al-Raḥman, 23–4, 37–8, 54, 143, 181
ʿAbd al-Raḥman al-Barak, Shaykh, 260, 264
ʿAbd al-Raḥman al-Laḥim (lawyer), 252
ʿAbd al-Raḥman al-Shamrawi, 112
ʿAbdul ʿAziz Pasha, 39
ʿAbdullah (1814–18), 22
ʿAbdullah (1865–71), 23, 69
ʿAbdullah (died 1889), 24
ʿAbdullah (half-brother of Ibn Saʿud), 71, 80
ʿAbdullah, Hashemite, 100
ʿAbdullah, King (2005–), 211, 217, 253–61, 276
development programme, 259–60
foreign visits, 260
royal tours, 257
ʿAbdullah, King (2005–), as Crown Prince, 136, 143, 144, 175, 181, 201
modernisation and, 245, 247, 253
new era challenges and, 211, 212–15, 222, 230, 236–7, 239–40
ʿAbdullah, King of Jordan, 255
ʿAbdullah, King of Trans-Jordan, 67, 204
ʿAbdullah, Sharif, 32
ʿAbdullah ʿAzzam, 231
ʿAbdullah ibn ʿAbd al-Laṭif Al Shaykh, 48, 52, 58, 59, 60, 75
ʿAbdullah ibn ʿAbd al-Raḥman, 105
ʿAbdullah ibn Juluwi, 39, 70, 82, 205
ʿAbdullah ba al-Khayr, 105
Abu Bakr, 184
Abu Dhabi, 111
Abu-Khalid, Fawziyya, 182, 189
activists, 236, 263–4, 266–7
Advice and Reform Committee (ARC), 178
Afghanistan
American invasion of, 225, 230, 237, 276
Bin Laden and, 178, 179
Saʿudi Islamists in, 223
Saʿudi jihadis and, 224
Saʿudi support in, 215, 227
Soviet invasion of (1979), 130, 138, 150, 154, 155, 230, 237, 276
see also Taliban
Aḥmad, amir of Kuwait, 63
Aḥmad, Prince, 143
Air Force, 219–20
al-Aiyri, Yusuf, 226
ʿAjlan, amir of Riyadh, 24, 38, 198, 205
ʿAjman tribe, 69, 74
ʿAli, Sharif, 43–4
Almana (interpreter), 86
Almana, M., 50
al-Amer, Tawfiq, 266
amirs
in historical texts, 195
majlis and, 79
Amnesty International, 251
al-ʿAngari, ʿAbdullah, 58
Anglo–Kuwaiti Agreement, 38
Anglo-Persian Oil Company, 88
Anglo–Saʿudi Treaty (1915), 40
Anglo–Turkish Convention (1913), 39
ʿAniza, 14, 74, 253
Arab League, 153
Beirut summit (2002), 239, 255

Arab nationalism, 102, 106, 108, 111, 115, 119, 277
Faysal's Islamic politics and, 129
rejection of by historical texts, 184–5, 188
see also Baʿthism; al-Naṣir, Gamal ʿAbd
Arab Petroleum Congress, 107
Arab revolt (1916), 3
Arab world in the 1950s, 110–13
Arab–Israeli conflict, 135, 150
1967 war, 102, 124–5, 134
oil embargo and, 130, 131, 132, 134
Arab–Jewish war (1947), 99
Arabian American Oil Company *see* ARAMCO (Arabian American Oil Company)
Arabian Peninsula, infidels in, 237
Arabic language, *al-ʿammiyya* movement and, 185
ʿAraʾif rebellion (1907–8), 56, 69–70
ARAMCO (Arabian American Oil Company), 10, 91, 92–6, 97, 101, 141
building of infrastructure and, 92
Dhahran 'American Camp', 92–3
in historical texts, 190
King Faysal and, 116
King Saʿud and, 103
managers, 92–3, 95–6
oil concession (1933) and, 89, 90, 100
Palestinian employees, 99–100
Saʿudi dissidents and, 95–6, 110, 126
Saʿudi workforce, 93–6, 108, 110
Saʿudi–American relations and, 100–1, 113
Saʿud's foreign policy and, 111
al-Ṭariqi and, 107, 108
ARC (Advice and Reform Committee), 178
armed forces, Saʿudi, 87, 108
al-Asad, President Bashar, 256
Ashraf, 29, 36
ʿAsi al-Shraym, Fahda bint, 253
ʿAsir, 265
Al Saʿud rule in, 20
capture of, 1, 3, 4, 43, 44–5, 67, 97
Idrisi rebellion in, 98
Ottoman occupation of, 1
Sharifian emirate and, 32
Association of Muslim Scholars, 235
Atta, Muhammad, 222
al-ʿAwdah, Salman, 161, 164, 170, 174, 223, 228, 264, 269

Badiʿa palace, 90
Badr ibn ʿAbd al-Moḥsin, 202
Baghdad Pact, 110, 111
Bahra Agreement (1925), 45, 64
Bahrain
Al Saʿud rule in, 20
Anglo–Saʿudi Treaty (1915) and, 40
Gulf Cooperation Council and, 152
Iran and, 151, 152
Bakri, ʿOmar, 175
Bandar ibn Sultan, 212, 214, 223, 237, 259
Bani Ṣakhr, 253
Banu Khalid tribe, 74
rebellion (1670), 13
rulers of Hasa, 14, 15, 16, 20, 34, 35
Banu Tamim tribe, 15
al-Banyan, Salih Salem, 52
Barakat, Sharif, 13
Basic Law of Government, 167–8
al-Batha, 215–16
Baʿthism, 102, 119, 129, 261
in Iraq, 102, 112, 119, 126, 151, 152, 230
al-Baz, Rania, 269
bedouins, 85
ARAMCO workforce and, 93
emerging Saʿudi state and, 8
in historical texts, 195
royal feasts and, 82
sedentarisation of, 133, 149, 189
Beirut, 271
Bell, Gertrude, 42, 206
Benedict, Pope, 260
Bin Laden, Usama, 178–9, 222, 223–6, 229–30, 275
birth rates, 145–6
Britain
al-Yamama arms deal and, 239
Anglo–Saʿudi Treaty (1915) and, 40–1
arms purchases from, 219
Baghdad Pact and, 111
Hadda and Bahra Agreements with (1925), 45, 64
Hasa and, 35
Ibn Saʿud's relationship with, 45–6, 91, 97–101
ikhwan rebellion and, 66, 68, 98
King Faysal's relations with, 115
Palestine and, 98
protectorates in Arabia, 37, 66
Rashidi emirate and, 28
Saʿudi state building and, 2–3, 4, 37, 40–1, 43, 44–5
Suez Crisis (1956) and, 111
Treaty of Jeddah (1927) and, 45–6
Zionism and, 98
budget (2000–8), 219
Buraymi border dispute, 111
Bush, President George W., 222, 230, 234, 236
businesswomen, 247

Cairo, 271
California Arab Standard Oil Company (CASOC), 89

Canada, military supplies from, 219
Carter Doctrine, 155
CASOC (California Arab Standard Oil Company), 89
CDLR (Committee for the Defence of Legitimate Rights in Saudi Arabia), 171–6, 178–9
centennial celebrations (1999), 11, 192
capture of Riyadh and, 197–208
challenges to, 208–10
Ibn Saʿud and, 197–208
Churchill, Winston, 91, 204
Cities of Salt (ʿAbd al-Raḥman Munif), 273
civil service, 83–6, 148
Committee of Allegiance, 257–9
Committee for the Defence of Legitimate Rights in Saudi Arabia (CDLR), 171–6, 178–9
Committee for the Propagation of Virtue and Prohibition of Vice, 252, 268
communication technology, 273–4
communism, 261
historical narratives on, 185
Saʿudi–American relations and, 114, 115, 138
Conference of Saudi Arabia in 100 years, 206–7
constitutional reform, advocates of, 261–3
construction, foreign workers, 260
Consultative Council, 118, 177, 180, 261, 264
Law of, 167, 168
consumerism, 124
Convention Against Torture and Other Cruel, Inhuman or Degrading Treatment or Punishment (UN), 250
Convention on the Elimination of All Forms of Discrimination Against Women (UN), 250
Convention on the Rights of the Child (UN), 250
Cordesman, A., 235
Council of Higher Ulama, 264
Council of Ministers, 91, 104, 118, 168, 217, 248, 251
customs duties, 85

Daḥlan, A., 31
debt, national, 217, 218
Defence, Ministry of, 86, 213
development programme, 259–60
al-Dhari, Harith, 235
Dirʿiyyah
Ottoman sacking of (1818), 22, 34, 53, 55
Saʿudi leadership in, 14–15
Wahhabism in, 16–17, 18
discrimination, 264–5, 268
dissident literature
oil industry and, 96
on Saʿudi history and development, 196–7
dissidents, 95–6, 110, 126, 196, 234–5, 262
see also activists
divorce, Ibn Saʿud and, 75–6
dress code, regional identity and, 194
driving, ban on women, 161–2, 269–70
al-Duwaysh, Faysal, 55, 58, 62–3, 65, 66, 141

economic crisis, 222
economic forums, businesswomen and, 247
economic recession, 144–5, 149
economic reform, 215–22
education, 106, 117–18, 120, 128, 139, 146, 218
historical narratives and, 183–90
scholarships, 260
of women, 117, 118, 120, 147, 260
Education, Ministry of (Wizarat al-Maʿarif), 183
Egypt, 239, 255
Arab nationalism and, 102, 106
Camp David Agreement and, 150
coup (1956), 108, 110
Faysal's relationship with, 128
Muslim Brotherhood, 112, 227, 231, 276
nineteenth-century invasion of Arabia, 22, 23, 26, 53
Ottoman occupation of, 13
peace treaty with Israel (1979), 239
rivalry with Saudi Arabia, 256
Saʿudi–American relations and, 115
Saʿud's alliance with, 112, 113, 114
Saʿud's exile in, 118
Suez Crisis (1956) and, 102, 108, 111, 112, 114
war with Israel, 125, 130, 131
Yemen and, 113, 115, 119, 124–5, 126
see also al-Naṣir, Gamal ʿAbd
Eisenhower Doctrine, 114
elections, candidates, 2005 municipal, 248–9
emirates, 6–8, 35–6
see also Rashidi emirate; Saʿudi–Wahhabi emirates; Sharifian emirate
employment, 260
Ende, W., 30
external pressures on Saudi Arabia, 233–41
extremism, 245
Extremism and Moderation (National Dialogue Forum), 244

Fahd, King, 10, 110, 143–50
centennial celebrations and, 203, 204, 205
as Crown Prince, 136, 138, 143
death of, 212–14, 253, 256
government reforms and, 167–8
Gulf War and, 159
liberation of Kuwait and, 224
Memorandum of Advice and, 164
speech, 190–2

succession and, 180–1, 254
transfer of power from, 222
United States and, 156, 237
al-Faleh, Matruk, 252, 262
al-Faqih, Saʿad, 172, 173, 175, 176, 177
Faruq, King of Egypt, 91, 204
Fatah, 255
Fatat al-Qatif, 270
fatawa, 225, 228, 265–7, 269
Al Faysal, 214
Faysal (Al Saʿud ruler, 1834–8), 23
Faysal, King (son of Ibn Saʿud), 10, 43, 72, 75, 83, 101, 116–24, 256
administrative and planning policies, 116–17
Arab world and, 124–9
assassination of, 120, 137–8
centralised state, 212–14
Council of Ministers and, 92, 104, 118
dissident literature on, 196
economic and social reforms, 118–19, 120, 129, 130, 133
education and, 117–18, 120, 128
Islam and, 102, 119–21, 127–8, 129, 133–4, 138–9, 191–2
Ministry of Foreign Affairs and, 86
oil embargo and, 131, 133–4, 136
oil revenues and, 116, 117, 118, 121–2
plot to overthrow (1969), 126
power struggle with Saʿud, 102, 103–5, 110
Saʿudi–American relations and, 115–16
al-Ṭariqi and, 107
visit to Washington, 100
Faysal, King of Iraq, 61, 67, 112
Faysal ibn Muamar, 243
Faysal ibn Musaʿid ibn ʿAbd al-ʿAziz, 137–8
Faysal ibn Turki, 34
al-Fayz family, 253
fertility rates, 145
finances, state revenues under Ibn Saʿud, 84–5, 89
fiqh, Wahhabism and, 20
First World War, 2, 4, 28, 37, 39–41, 43, 58
Firʿun, Rashad, 105
Foreign Affairs, Ministry of, 86
foreign workers, 146, 221, 260
France
military supplies from, 219
Suez Crisis (1956) and, 111
Free Officers, 108
Free Princes, 106, 108, 110, 118–19, 122
Friedman, Thomas, 255

Gaza, 255
GCC (Gulf Cooperation Council), 152–3, 237, 256
GDP (gross domestic product), 116, 133, 144
Germany, military supplies from, 219
Ghalib, Imam, 111
al-Ghamdi, Saʿid, 149
al-Ghargini, Khalid, 83
girls, education of, 117, 118, 120
Girls of Riyadh (Raja al-Sani), 272
Golub, D., 132
al-Gosaybi, Ghazi, 164, 272
Grand Mosque siege (1979), 10–11, 130, 139–42, 156, 196, 222, 227, 268
Guantánamo Bay detention camp, 224, 252
guardianship, over adult women, 270
Gulf Cooperation Council (GCC), 152–3, 237, 256
Gulf states, 239
Gulf War (1990), 11, 142, 156, 158–81
government reforms (1992) and, 180
Islamist opposition and, 158, 160–3, 164–6, 178–9, 192
MIRA and, 175
'secularist' demands for reform and, 163–4

Hadda Agreement (1925), 45, 64
Haʾil
capture of (1921), 41–2, 44
Juluwi governors in, 70
Rashidi emirate in (1836–1921), 25–9
rule of amirs in Riyadh, 23–4
al-Ḥakim, Khalid, 83
al-Ḥamad, Turki, 271, 272
Hamas, 239–40, 255
al-Ḥamid, ʿAbdullah, 252, 262, 263
al-Ḥamid, ʿIsa, 263
Hamilton, Lloyd, 88
Ḥamza, Fuʾad, 83, 86
al-Hariri, Rafiq, 211, 239
Hasa
Al Saʿud rule in, 20
Banu Khalid rulers of, 14, 15, 16, 20, 34, 35
customs duties, 85
ḥaḍar communities of, 86
historical narratives on, 193, 196
Ibn Saʿud visits as King, 82
Islam in, 33, 34–5, 62, 63, 85
Juluwi governors in, 70
nineteenth-century, 33–5
Ottoman occupation of, 1, 2, 13
Saʿudi state formation and, 1, 2, 3, 4, 9, 39, 60–1
Shiʿa tribal groups in, 193
al-Ḥasan, H., 193–4
al-Ḥawali, Dr Ṣafar, 160–1, 164, 170, 174, 223, 228, 264–5, 269
hijackers, 9/11, 222–3

Hijaz, 216
activists in, 236
Al Saʿud rulers in, 20
Arab revolt (1916) and, 3–4
army and police force, 86
capture of (1925), 42–6, 62, 67, 71, 81, 85
customs duties and taxes, 85
dress style and regional identity, 193–5
elite, 148
ḥadar communities, 86
Hasa and, 34
in historical texts, 186, 196
Ibn Saʿud as King in, 61, 62, 81
incorporation into Saʿudi state, 1, 2, 3, 4, 6, 9, 67
Islam in, 30, 62
Ottoman occupation of, 2, 13, 22
rural–urban divide, 30–1
Sharifian emirate, 7, 29–33, 36, 45
Sufis in, 267
tribal groups, 29–30, 32, 193
historical narratives *see* official historical narrative
Hizb al-Taḥrir, 175
Hizbollah, 239, 240, 265
Hogarth, D., 30
Homeland is for All, and All are for the Homeland (petition), 266
horse races, 81
human rights, 234, 250–3, 261
organisations, 270
Human Rights Commission (HRC), 251–3
Human Rights Social Committee (al-Lajna al-Ahliyya li Ḥuquq al-Insan), 251
Human Rights Watch, 251
Al Ḥumayyid, 34
Ḥusayn, King of Hijaz, 73
Ḥusayn, King of Jordan, 111, 124, 127
Ḥusayn, Sharif (1908–24), 2, 3, 30, 42, 43–4, 61
al-Huthlul, ʿAlla, 271

Ibn ʿAbd al-Wahhab, Muhammad, 15–17, 19, 25, 47, 48, 49, 51, 54, 65, 187, 209, 231, 276
Ibn Baz, ʿAbd al-ʿAziz, 139, 160, 163, 164, 166, 184, 198
ibn Bijad, Sultan, 66, 71
ibn Ḥithlayn, 66
ibn Khalaf, 55
ibn Khalifa al-Thani, Shaykh Hamad, 238
ibn Rashid, ʿAbd al-ʿAziz, amir of Haʾil, 37, 38, 39, 40, 41, 44
ibn Rashid, ʿAbdullah, amir of Haʾil, 23, 69
ibn Rashid, Muhammad, amir of Haʾil, 24, 26, 37
ibn Rashid, Muhammad, amir of Najd, 60
ibn Rashid, Saʿud, 253
Ibn Rifada, 97
Ibn Saʿud, 1, 12, 212
ancestor cult around, 202, 204–8
ʿAsir and, 97–8
brothers of, 69, 70–1
centennial celebrations and, 197–208, 208–10
consolidation of royal lineage, 9, 69–71, 71–7
cousins of, 69–70
death and succession, 10, 101
desert excursions, 80–1
dress, 78–9
establishment of Saʿudi state, 2–5, 8–10, 68, 69
First World War and, 2, 39–41
Hasa and, 35
historical narratives of, 191
horse races and, 81
ikhwan and, 55, 56–9, 59–66, 66–9, 84, 139
international politics and, 91
Islam and, 39, 87, 207, 208
majlis and, 77–83, 101
marriages and children, 9, 69, 71–7, 83, 253
meeting with Roosevelt, 100, 204
muṭawwaʿa of Najd and, 47–50, 52, 54–6, 59–66
oil wealth and, 10, 69, 87–9, 89–92
Palestine and, 98–100
royal court and, 9
royal feasts, 9, 82–3
state affairs and, 83–7, 104
ʿulama and, 87
Ibn Saʿud, military campaigns, 37, 77, 86–7
Haʾil (1921), 41–2
Hijaz (1925), 42–6, 61–2
Najd, 42, 44, 56, 60–1
Riyadh (1902), 4, 6, 25, 28, 37–9, 52, 54, 187, 197
ibn Saʿud, Muhammad, 16, 17, 187
ibn Sulayman, ʿAbdullah, 84–5, 86, 106
oil concession (1933) and, 88
Ibn Taymiyya, Taqi al-Din Aḥmad 231
ibn Taymur, Saʿid, Sultan of Muscat, 111
ibn Thunayan, ʿAbdullah, 23, 42
Ibrahim Pasha, 22, 53
al-Idrisi, Muhammad, 43
Idrisi emirate, 43, 97
ikhwan (Muslim tribal military force), 4, 37, 56–9
dress and manners, 55, 58–9
historical narratives of, 189
hujjar (village) settlements and, 57
Ibn Saʿud and, 55, 56–9, 59–66, 66–9, 84, 139
muṭawwaʿa of Najd and, 55, 56–9, 59–66, 67–8

National Guard and, 87
nomadic population and, 57
rebellion (1927–30), 63–6, 66–8, 71, 84
siege of mosque in Mecca and, 138–9
industrial plant, 260
information technology, 179, 232, 236
communication technology, 273–4
internet, 179–80, 225, 249, 262, 273–4
Institution of *Ifta'* and Scholarly Research, 139
interfaith dialogue, 260–1, 265
Interior, Ministry of, 169, 213, 225, 234, 252, 261, 262
International Convention on the Elimination of All Forms of Racial Discrimination (UN), 250
International Monetary Fund, 217
internet, 179–80, 225, 249, 273–4
petitions and, 262
investment, Sa'udi, in United States, 137
Iran
Baghdad Pact and, 110
Hizbollah and, 239
Iraq and, 240
King Faysal's foreign policy and, 127
nuclear programme, 255
regional influence, 255–6
relations with, 211
revolution (1979) and Islamic Republic of, 130, 138, 141, 150–2, 154, 156, 230, 264
Sa'udi dissidents in, 196
Shi'a influence of, 265
United States and, 135, 152, 154
war with Iraq (1980s), 130, 138, 150–2, 154, 156, 214, 215, 233, 276
Iranian Assembly of Experts, 265–6
Iraq, 3, 13, 21, 64, 67
Baghdad Pact and, 110
Bahra Agreement with, 45, 64
Ba'thist regime, 102, 112, 119, 126, 151, 152, 230
coup (1958), 112
Free Officers, 108, 112
Gulf War and, 152, 158, 159, 160–1, 163
Hashemites, 111–12
Ibn Sa'ud's foreign policy and, 100, 111
jihad in, 236
proposed model democracy, 255
Sa'udi dissidents in, 196, 234–5
Sa'udi–American relations (1970s), 135–6
Sa'ud's visit to, 112
Shi'a ascendance in, 264, 264–5
United States occupation of, 229–30, 237, 255, 267, 276
violence in, 234–6, 240
war with Iran (1980s), 130, 138, 150–2, 154, 156, 214–15, 233, 276
Islam
Basic Law of Government, 167, 168
in Hasa, 34, 35, 63–4, 85
in Hijaz, 30, 61–2
historical narratives of, 183–4, 185–6, 187, 188–9, 196
Ibn Sa'ud and, 39, 87, 207, 208
Islamist candidates, 2005 municipal elections, 248–9
Islamist movement (1990s), 261
King Fahd and, 191–2
King Faysal and, 102, 119–21, 127–8, 129, 133–4, 138, 139
King Khalid and, 138–43
majlis and, 80
modernity and, 5, 149–50, 161–2
in Najd, 4, 6, 8, 16–20, 36, 37, 46–56
oil concession and, 87–8
Sa'udi dress code and, 194
Sa'udi wealth and, 10
siege of mosque in Mecca, 10–11, 130, 139–42, 156, 196, 222, 227, 268
symbolic significance of Saudi Arabia for, 5
Syrian and Egyptian pilgrims and, 63
tribal heritage and, 269
umma (community), 11
see also ikhwan; Islamist opposition; *muṭawwa'a*; Shi'a community; Wahhabi movement
Islamic Development Bank, 128
Islamic Solidarity Fund, 128
Islamisation programme, al-Sahwa and, 224
Islamist novelists, 272–3
Islamist opposition, 11, 158, 160–2, 164–6, 171–80, 192
Advice and Reform Committee (ARC) and, 178
centennial celebrations, 209
Committee for the Defence of Legitimate Rights in Saudi Arabia (CDLR) and, 171–6, 178–9, 209
internet and, 179–80
media discrediting of, 170–1
MIRA and, 175–7, 178, 209
succession and, 180–1
terrorism and, 223–4, 229
Isma'ili activists, 263, 266–7
Israel
peace treaty with Egypt (1979), 239
Sa'udi–American relations (1970s), 135–6
war on Lebanon, 239
see also Arab–Israeli conflict
Israeli–Hizbollah war (2006), 256
Israeli–Palestinian crisis, 239

Italy
  military supplies from, 219
  Ottoman Empire and, 43

Jabal Shammar, 27, 28, 61
Janadiriyya festival, 189, 254
Japan, oil embargo and, 132
al-Jarba family, 253
al-Jawf province, 216
Jawhara bint al-Sudayri, 70
Jazan province, 216
al-Jazeera, 211, 238–9, 256
Jeddah
  capture of (1925), 44
  development in, 215–16
  economic forums and, 247
  National Dialogue Forum, 246
  Treaty of (1927), 45
Jerusalem, oil embargo and, 133
jihad
  Gulf War and, 163, 165
  ikhwan and, 64
  Wahhabism and, 17, 18
  warriors, 87, 232
jihadism
  causes, 231
  concept of, 231
Joint United States–Saʿudi Committee for Economic Cooperation, 137
Jordan, 239
  Arab–Israeli war (1967) and, 3, 67
  Baghdad Pact and, 111
  Hadda Agreement (1925) with, 45, 64
  Hashemites, 111
  Ibn Saʿud's foreign policy and, 100, 111
  King Faysal's foreign policy and, 127
Jubayl, conquest by Ibn Saʿud, 2
judiciary, Basic Law of Government and, 168
Juhayman ibn Muhammad al-ʿUtaybi, 139, 141, 142, 222, 268
Al Juluwi, 70

al-Kabir, Saʿud, 70
Kabul, 276
Karbalaʾ, Al Saʿud raid on, 21
Kennedy, John F., 115
Khalid (Al Saʿud ruler in Najd), 23
Khalid, King (1975–82), 10, 127, 138–43, 144
  as Crown Prince, 116, 118
Khalid (nephew of Ibn Saʿud), 71
Khalid (nephew of King Faysal), 137
Khalid al-Faysal, 214
Khalid ibn Sultan, 214, 259
Khalilzad, Zalmay, 235
Kharj, Al Saʿud rule in, 20
Khartoum, 126
al-Khobar Towers bombing, 254
Khomeini, Ayatollah, 142
al-Khunayzi, Najib, 264
khuwwa payments, Rashidi emirate and, 27, 28
King ʿAbd al-ʿAziz Centre, 243
King ʿAbdullah's Economic City, 260
King Saʿud University, 252
King Sultan Air Base, 223
Kuwait
  Al Sabah, 24, 37, 41
  Anglo–Kuwaiti Agreement, 38
  Anglo–Saʿudi Treaty (1915) and, 40
  British protectorate of, 67
  exile of Al Saʿud to, 24, 37, 48, 199
  Gulf Cooperation Council and, 152
  Gulf War and, 152, 158, 159, 160, 163, 230, 233
  Iran and, 151, 152
  jihad and, 64
  liberation of, 214, 215, 224, 239
  terrorism and, 238
  women in public ministerial office, 268

Labour, Ministry of, 221
labour force, 146–8, 220
al-Lajna al-Ahliyya li Ḥuquq al-Insan (Human Rights Social Committee), 251
largesse, sources of, 259–60
Law of the Consultative Council, 167, 168, 169
Law of the Provinces, 167, 169
Leatherdale, C., 66
Lebanon, 239, 240, 256, 265
liberal novels, 272
Libya
  Free Officers, 108
  relations with, 256
  Saʿudi dissidents in, 196
  Saʿudi–American relations (1970s) and, 135
literature
  expressions of change, 271–3
  terrorism and, 271
Longrigg, Stephen, 88

Madina
  Al Saʿud rule in, 20
  capture of (1925), 44, 63
  Sharifs and, 30
majlis, Ibn Saʿud and, 77–83, 101
Malḥamat al-tawḥid (theatrical performance), 202
al-Maliki, Shaykh, 267
manpower development, 218
marriages
  exogamous, 124
  of Ibn Saʿud, 9, 69, 71–7, 83

al-Mas'ari, Muhammad, 172, 173, 174–5, 177
Mashahida (Shi'a merchant community), 52
Mecca
  Al Sa'ud rule in, 20
  capture of (1924), 44, 63
  conference (1962), 127
  Iranian pilgrims and, 151
  National Dialogue Forum (2003), 244
  Ottoman occupation of, 13
  pilgrims in, 85–6, 89
  Sharifs of, 30, 31–2, 42–3
  siege of mosque (1979), 10–11, 130, 139–42, 156, 196, 222, 227, 268
  Wahhabism and, 20, 142
media
  centennial celebrations and, 198, 201–2
  international scrutiny, 245
  Islamist opposition and, 170–1
  Israeli and Sa'udi, 256
  Memorandum of Advice and, 165
  National Dialogue Forum and, 246
  political reform and, 262
  women and, 247
Memorandum of Advice, 164–6, 170, 173, 176, 224
merchants
  families in Hasa, 34
  Ministry of Foreign Affairs and, 86
Mesopotamia, Al Sa'ud raids on, 21
Midhat Pasha, governor of Baghdad, 34
military cooperation
  Gulf Cooperation Council (GCC) and, 153
  with United States, 137, 155–7
military spending, 218, 219
minorities, recognition for, 263–7
MIRA (Movement for Islamic Reform), 175–9, 209
Mishal, Prince (governor of Mecca), 258
Mishari, 23
modernity, 232
  authoritarian rule and, 242–74
  Islam and, 5, 149–50, 161–2
monarchy
  continuity of, 259
  succession in, 258–9
al-Moqrin, Samar, 272
Movement for Islamic Reform (MIRA), 175–9, 209
Moza, Shaykha, 238
Mubarak, President, 255
al-Muhajirun Organisation, 175
Muhammad (half-brother of Ibn Sa'ud), 70–1
Muhammad, Prophet, 29, 57, 62, 204
  historical narratives and, 183–4, 193
Muhammad 'Ali (Ottoman Sultan), 22, 31
Muhammad ibn 'Aiḍ, 32
Muhammad ibn 'Awn, Sharif (1856–8), 32
Muhammad ibn Ibrahim ibn Jubayr, Shaykh, 168
Muhammad ibn Nayef, 214, 259
al-Muhayya compound (Riyadh), 231
municipal councils, 249–50
municipal elections (2005), 248–50
Munif, 'Abd al-Raḥman, 96, 273
Munira (sister of Ibn Sa'ud), 70
Muraba' palace, 90
al-Murra tribe, 238
Musa'id ibn 'Abd al-Raḥman, 105
Muscat, 67, 111
Muslim Brotherhood, 227, 231, 276
Muslim League, 128
Muslim World League, 128, 168
muṭawwa'a, 4, 8, 37, 46–56
  Egyptian invasion of Arabia and, 53
  family connections, 51
  fiqh and, 47–8, 49
  Ibn Sa'ud and, 47–50, 53–5, 59–66, 67
  ikhwan and, 54, 55, 56–9, 63, 65, 67
  Mashahida and, 52
  new generation of, 150
  punishment and, 49–50, 54
  Sa'udi rulers and, 53
  settlements, 48
  tax collection and, 85
  trade and, 51
  tribal confederations and, 51–2, 55–6
  Wahhabism and, 48
  women and, 147–8
  zakat payments and, 49, 54, 85
Mutayr tribal confederation, 24
Mutib ibn 'Abdullah, 214, 259

Nada ibn Nuhayer, 55
Najd
  ḥaḍar communities of, 8, 86
  Hasa and, 33–4, 35
  in historical texts, 186–7, 190, 194
  Ibn Sa'ud as Sultan in, 61
  Ibn Sa'ud's military campaigns and, 42, 44, 56, 59
  Islam in, 4, 6, 8, 16–19, 36, 37, 46–56
  Ottoman Empire and, 13, 22
  population growth and employment opportunities, 148–9
  rural–urban continuum, 30
  Sa'udi expansion in, 14–15, 20, 21
  Sa'udi state formation and, 1, 2, 3, 4, 38, 39, 68, 194
Najran, 266
Naqshabandi, Hani, 271

Nasif, ʿAbdullah ʿOmar, 168
al-Naṣir, Gamal ʿAbd, 102, 106, 110–11, 112, 113, 119
  Arab–Israeli war (1967) and, 124
  Saʿudi–American relations and, 114, 115
  Yemen war and, 124–6
Nasserites, 261
nation building, 10–11
National Day celebrations, 12
national debt, 217, 218
National Dialogue Committee, 244
National Dialogue Forums, 242–8, 264, 269, 277
National Guard, 87, 109–10, 115, 123, 142, 189, 212–13, 254, 257
National Society for Human Rights (NSHR), 251–3
Nayef, Prince, 118, 143, 170, 201, 262, 268
  new era challenges and, 212, 214–15, 227, 234
al-Nojaymi, Shaykh Muhammad, 266
nuclear programme, Iran, 255
Nura (sister of Ibn Saʿud), 70, 206

Obaid, N., 235
official historical narratives, 11, 182, 183–90, 206–7
  centennial celebrations (1999) and, 11, 192, 197–208, 208–10
  challenges to, 192–7
  in political speech, 190–2
oil
  boom, 220, 221–2
  commercial production of, 89–92
  concession (1933), 69, 87–9, 100, 190
  crisis, 214
  embargo (1973), 10, 118, 130, 131–4, 135
  exports and GDP, 116, 144
  in historical texts, 190
  production, 90, 91, 218, 237
  revenues, 103, 116, 117, 118, 121–2, 133, 217
  society in 1940s and 1950s and, 92–6
  wealth, 6, 10, 106, 124, 129, 182, 197
oil prices
  2000–2008, 218
  decreases, 130, 144, 209–10
  increases, 130, 131, 132, 217, 221
Oman, 20, 40, 46, 111, 152
al-ʿOmar, Naṣir, 229, 264, 265
Onassis, Aristotle, 111
OPEC (Organisation of Petroleum Exporting Countries), 107, 131, 136
Organisation of the Islamic Conference, 128
Organisation of the Islamic Revolution, 142
Organisation of Petroleum Exporting Countries (OPEC), 107, 131, 136
Ottoman Empire, 1–2, 7, 13, 24, 121
  First World War and, 2, 4, 39–41, 43, 44
  Hasa and, 34–5, 39
  Hijaz and, 31–2, 33
  history of, 183
  Rashidi emirate and, 26, 28, 38
  Saʿudi–Wahhabi expansion and, 21, 22
Ottoman–Egyptian invasion of Arabia (1818), 1
Ottoman–Saʿudi Convention (1914), 39

Palestine, 113
  Ibn Saʿud's policy in, 98–100
  King ʿAbdullah and, 255
  oil embargo (1973) and, 134
  war (1948), 94–5, 108
Palestine Authority, 240
Palestine Liberation Organisation (PLO), 127, 132
Palestinians, 239–40
Partners in the Nation (petition), 264
peasantry in Hasa, 33
Peninsula Shield Force, 153
Pentagon, 222
Persian Gulf, Hasa and, 33, 34, 35
petitions, 261–2, 264, 266
Petraeus, General, 236
Philby, H. St John, 72, 73, 75, 78–9, 80, 83, 89, 206
pilgrimages, tax revenues from, 86, 89, 90, 121
PLO (Palestine Liberation Organisation), 127, 132
Political Committee of royal court, 85–6
political reform, 246, 257, 261–3
polygamy, 268
  Ibn Saʿud and, 71–6
population
  2004 census, 220
  growth, 145, 148, 216
poverty, urban, 215–16
power, royal circles of, 213–14
princes
  as 'businessmen', 122
  Free Princes, 106, 108, 110, 118–19, 122
  key, 213, 257
  patronage and, 122
  Sudayri Seven, 105, 143
Provinces, Law of, 167, 169
public sphere, women and, 247–8
punishment
  ikhwan and, 59
  muṭawwaʿa of Najd and, 49–50, 54

al-Qaḥṭani, Muhammad ibn ʿAbdullah, 139, 140
al-Qaʿidah, 178, 223–7, 229, 232–3, 234, 257
  in Arabian Peninsula, 229
  in Iraq, 255

Qandahar, 276
al-Qarni, Shaykh ʿAwad, 149
Qasim
  activists in, 236
  Al Saʿud rule in, 20, 24
  conquest by Ibn Saʿud, 4, 37, 38
  Juluwi governors in, 70
  Rashidi emirate and, 26
  ʿUnayzah, 195
Qaṣr al-Masmak, 205
Qatar, 225, 237
  1995 coup, 238
  Al Saʿud rule in, 20
  Anglo–Saʿudi Treaty (1915) and, 40
  Gulf Cooperation Council and, 152
  relations with, 211, 239, 256
  terrorism and, 238
Qatif, 270
  Al Saʿud rule in, 20
  conquest by Ibn Saʿud, 2
  municipal council, 264
  registered voters in, 248
  Shiʿa tribal groups in, 193
al-Quṣaybi, ʿAbdullah, 89
Qutb, Sayyid, 227, 231, 276

al-Rafida in the Land of Monotheism (al-ʿOmar), 265
Rafsanjani, Ayatollah Hashemi, 265
railways, 91, 92
rape, 270
Rashidi emirate, 2, 7, 8, 25–9, 36, 37–8, 109
  conquest by Ibn Saʿud, 2, 24, 28, 41–2
  Ibn Saʿud's marriages, 75
Rawḍat Muhanna, battle of (1906), 38
Reagan, Ronald, 155–6
reform, society and, 261–74
regional competitors, 237–41
regional identity, dress code and, 194
religion, state, 254
religious reform movement, 234, 236
revenues *see* state revenues
Riḍa, Muhammad ʿAli, 105
Riyadh
  Al Saʿud rule in, 20, 23–4, 25
  construction boom, 90–92
  ikhwan and, 58, 64–5, 67
  King ʿAbd al-ʿAziz Historical Centre, 205
  muṭawwaʿa of Najd and, 54, 59–60
  National Dialogue Forum (2003), 244
  oil wealth and, 90–1
  Qaṣr al-Masmak, 205
  registered voters in, 248
  street scene, 99
  uneven development in, 215–16
  violence in, 225, 254
  women's driving demonstration in, 161–2, 269
Riyadh, capture of, 4, 6, 26, 28, 37–9, 52, 54, 69, 70
  centennial celebrations and, 197–208, 209
  historical narratives of, 187
'Riyadh Spring', 261
Riyadh University, 117, 119
Roosevelt, Franklin D., 91, 100, 204
Royal Air Force (British), 254
Royal Guard, 87
al-Rumaiyḥi, Dawud, 126

Al Sabah (amirs of Kuwait), 24, 37, 41
al-Sadat, Anwar, 128
Saddam Husayn, 152, 154, 158–9, 161, 163, 229–30, 233, 255, 264, 276
al-Saffar, Ḥasan, 264, 266
al-Sahwa, 223, 224–5, 228, 229
  see also Islamist opposition
al-Saʿid, Naṣir, 95, 109
Sakakah, 216
al-Sakina, 274
Salafis, 264
  jihadi movement, 224
Salim I, Ottoman Sultan, 13
Salim al-Sibhan, 24
al-Sallal, ʿAbdullah, 112
Salman, Prince, 181, 212, 214–15
al-Sani, Raja, 272
al-Saqqaf, Khayriyyah, 147
satellite television, 247, 256
Saʿud (brother of Ibn Saʿud), 70
Saʿud (died 1875), 23
Saʿud, King (son of Ibn Saʿud), 10, 71, 72, 73, 75, 79, 83, 101, 102–10
  abdication and death, 110
  Council of Ministers and, 92, 104
  foreign policy, 111–13
  government finances and, 103
  historical texts and, 190
  King Faysal and, 118–19
  oil industry and, 96
  power struggle with Faysal, 102, 103–5, 110, 122
  visit to Washington, 100, 114
Al Saʿud rulers, 212
  centennial celebrations (1999) of, 11, 192, 197–208, 208–10
  criticisms of, 178–9
  fragile revival (1824–91), 22–4
  in historical narratives, 187–8
  origins of (1744–1818), 14–22
  al-Sahwa and, 224

Al Saʿud rulers (*cont.*)
state formation and, 1, 6
succession and, 180–1
Wahhabiyya and, 237
Saʿud al-Faysal, 155, 212, 214, 240, 268
Saʿud al-Kabir (Saʿud ibn ʿAbd al-ʿAziz), 70
Saʿud ibn ʿAbd al-ʿAziz (1803–14), 20, 22
Saʿudi–American relations, 212, 223, 232, 233–7, 256
1970s, 130, 133, 135–8
1980s, 154–8
Ibn Saʿud and, 100–1
see also United States of America
Saʿudi–Wahhabi emirates, 4, 7, 8, 14, 25, 31, 35–6
Hasa and, 34
in historical narratives, 185–6, 191
muṭawwaʿa of Najd and, 53
Rashidi emirate and, 26, 27
Saʿudisation programmes, 221
al-Sayf, Tawfiq, 264
Second World War
oil production and, 90, 91
Saʿudi–American relations and, 113
sectarianism, rejection of by historical texts, 184
security measures, 226
September 11 *see* 9/11
sexualisation of politics and violence, 271–3
Shakespear, Captain, 39–40
al-Shaʿlan family, 253
Shammar tribe
capture of Haʾil and, 41
Hasa and, 33
Ibn Saʿud's marriages, 75
Iraqi branch, 253
muṭawwaʿa of Najd and, 52, 55
National Guard and, 109
Rashidi emirate and, 25–6, 27, 36
Wahhabism and, 19
Sharifian emirate, 7, 8, 29–33, 36, 42–3, 44
Ottoman Empire and, 13
Sharm al-Shaykh, 256
al-Shayeb, Jaʿfar, 264
Shiʿa community, 63, 64, 85, 141, 141–2, 266
activists, 263–4, 267
discrimination against, 265
historical narratives and, 184, 193
Iran and, 255
riots (1979–80), 130, 141–3, 152
'Shiʿa crescent', 255
Sibila, battle of (1929), 66
SOCAL (Standard Oil of California), 88–9
social change, 269
social reform programme, 234, 236
socialism, Arab politics and, 102, 108, 115, 119, 126
South Yemen, Saʿudi–American relations (1970s) and, 136, 155
Soviet Union
Egypt and, 128–9
invasion of Afghanistan (1979), 130, 138, 150, 154, 155, 230, 276
Saʿudi–American relations and, 114
Saʿud's foreign policy and, 111
Standard Oil of California (SOCAL), 88–9
state affairs
fragmentation, 212–15
Ibn Saʿud and, 83–7, 104
legitimacy, 11
narratives, 182
reformist agenda, 242–53
religion, 254
state formation, 1–5, 37–68, 69
in historical narratives, 187–190
state revenues, 84–5
oil wealth and, 89, 90
as source of largesse, 260
Sudayri Seven, 105, 143, 212, 213
Suez Crisis (1956), 102, 108, 111, 112, 114
Sufi community, 267
suicide bombings, 234–5, 273
Sulayman the Magnificent, 13
Sultan, Prince, 110, 136, 143, 181, 212, 214–15, 239, 254
as Crown Prince, 257, 257–8, 259
Sunni groups, 264
fatwa against Shiʿas, 266
political, Iran and, 255
Supreme Economic Council, 217
Syria, 13
Al Saʿud raids on, 21
Arab–Israeli war (1967) and, 125
Baʿthism and, 102
relations with, 211, 239, 256
Saʿudi–American relations (1970s), 135

Taʾif, 20, 43, 63
Treaty of (1934), 97
Ṭalal ibn ʿAbd al-ʿAziz Al Saʿud, 101, 104–6, 108, 109, 110, 118
Taliban, 223–5, 230, 276
Tarfa (wife of Ibn Saʿud), 75
al-Ṭariqi, ʿAbdullah, 105, 106–7, 108, 116, 123
tawḥid, doctrine of, 19
taxes, 85–6, 121, 145, 265
revenues from pilgrims, 86, 89, 90, 121
see also zakat payments
al-Tayyib, Saʿid, 262
technology, 218
innovations, in reign of King Faysal, 120, 138
telegraph, Islam and, 65

terrorism, 267, 274
internal, 222–33, 241, 242, 244, 254, 261
al-Thani, Amir Hamad, 239
al-Thani, Shaykh Hamad ibn Khalifa, 238
al-Towayjri, Khalid, 258
trade, *muṭawwaʿa* of Najd and, 51
Trans-Jordan *see* Jordan
tribalism
emerging Saʿudi state and, 9
heritage, Islamic tradition and, 269, 270
historical narratives on, 184, 189–90, 193
in reign of King Faysal, 123
al-Turki, Mansour, 234
Turki, Prince 143
Turki al-Faysal, 214–15, 268
Turki al-Sudayri, 251
Turki ibn ʿAbdullah (Al Saʿud ruler, 1824–34), 22

unemployment, 220–1
National Dialogue Forum and, 245
United Arab Emirates
Gulf Cooperation Council and, 152
UAE–Qatari Dolphin Undersea Natural Gas Pipeline, 238
United Nations, 250–1
United States of America
arms purchases from, 219
Gulf War and, 158–60, 161
influence in rape case, 270
invasion of Afghanistan, 225
Iran and, 135, 152, 154
Islamist opposition and, 178, 180
Lend-Lease Program, 91, 101
Marshall Plan, 113
military cooperation with, 137, 155
occupation of Iraq, 229–30, 237, 255
oil concession (1933), 69, 87–9
oil embargo (1973) and, 10, 130, 131, 132, 133, 134
Saudi Arabia in 1950s and 1960s, 113–16
see also Saʿudi–American relations
universities, 117, 119
ʿUtayba tribe, 58
al-ʿUthaymin, ʿAbdullah, 183, 187
ʿUthman ibn Muʿammar, 16
ʿUyaynah, Wahhabi reform movement and, 16, 17

van der Meulen, D., 77, 101, 206
violence, 244–5, 247
voters, registered, 248

Wahba, Ḥafiẓ, 83, 86
Wahhabi movement/Wahhabiyya, 4, 5, 11, 15–22, 227, 228, 231, 232, 233–4, 237
centennial celebrations and, 209
extremism, 264
Hasa and, 34
in historical narratives, 188, 189, 190, 191–2
muṭawwaʿa of Najd, 48–9
Shiʿa Islam and, 39, 141–2
tradition, 267, 276
see also Saʿudi–Wahhabi emirates
al-Walid ibn Ṭalal, 214
'War on Terror', 223, 229, 233, 261, 262, 264
Westernisation, 245, 270
historical narratives on, 185
women, 234
demonstration (2007), 263
discrimination against, 268
driving demonstration in Riyadh, 161–2, 269
education of, 117, 118, 120, 147, 260
employment of, 147, 163, 268
media and, 247
National Dialogue Forum and, 245
novelists, 271–2
prohibition on exogamous marriages, 124
public sphere and, 247–8
quest for equality, 268–70
unemployment and, 221
Western agenda and, 245
Women of Vice (Samar al-Moqrin), 272
World Muslim Congress, 127
World Trade Center, 222, 231, 275
World Trade Organisation, 217, 254

Yaḥya, Imam of Yemen, 67, 73, 97–8
al-Yamama arms deal, 239
Yamani, M., 194
Yamani, Muhammad Zaki, 116, 118, 148
Yasin, Yusuf, 83, 86
Yemen, 7, 21, 43, 67
Arab workers from, 146
conflict in ʿAsir and, 97–8
Egypt and, 113, 115, 119, 124–5, 126
establishment of Arab Republic, 112, 115, 135
Free Officers, 108
Saʿudi–American relations and, 115
see also South Yemen
youth, National Dialogue Forum and, 245

zakat payments, 121
muṭawwaʿa of Najd and, 49, 54, 85
Rashidi emirate and, 27
Saʿudi–Wahhabi emirate and, 20, 21
Wahhabism and, 16, 17, 19
al-Zarqawi, Abu Musab, 235
al-Zawahiri, Ayman, 227, 275
Zibari, Hoshyar, 235
al-Zirkili, K., 79

65347733R00190

Made in the USA
Lexington, KY
09 July 2017